W9-ATH-522

Frederick Douglass

Engraved by J. C. Buttre.

Frederick Douglass

Frederick Douglass

FREEDOM'S VOICE, 1818-1845

Gregory P. Lampe

Michigan State University Press
East Lansing

All Michigan State University Press books are produced on paper which meets the requirements of American National Standard of Information Sciences—Permanence of paper for printed materials ANSI Z39.48-1984.

Michigan State University Press
East Lansing, Michigan 48823

Library of Congress Cataloging-in-Publication Data

Lampe, Gregory P.
　　　Frederick Douglass—freedom's voice, 1818–1845 / Gregory P. Lampe.
　　　　　p.　　　cm.

　　　Includes bibliographical references and index.
　　　ISBN 087013485x (alk. paper)/cloth
　　　ISBN 0870134809 (alk. paper)/paperback

　　　1. Douglass, Frederick, 1817?–1895—Oratory.
　　　E449.D75 L36 1998
　　　98000601

　　　04 03 02 01 00 99 98　　1 2 3 4 5 6 7 8

Rhetoric and Public Affair Series

Frederick Douglass photograph: Brown Brothers, Sterling, PA.

Senior Editor: Martin J. Medhurst

❧ Contents

Preface

ON 3 SEPTEMBER 1838 an unknown slave, Frederick Augustus Washington Bailey, escaped Maryland slavery. The twenty-year-old fugitive fled first to New York City and then to New Bedford, Massachusetts, where he changed his last name to Douglass. Three years later, he emerged on the public platform as a Garrisonian abolitionist with an electrifying speech at Nantucket, Massachusetts. For the next fifty-four years he devoted his life to the cause of his people—agitating for an end to slavery before the Civil War, working to define war aims and to enlist black soldiers during the conflict, and continuing the struggle for equal rights after the war was over. From 1841 until his death in 1895, this formerly unknown slave earned a reputation as the most distinguished and celebrated African American leader and orator of the nineteenth century.[1]

From the beginning of his career as an abolitionist lecturer, Douglass committed himself to using the power of oratory to destroy the institution of slavery. From 1841 through 1845, he campaigned tirelessly through Massachusetts, Rhode Island, Connecticut, New York, Pennsylvania, New Hampshire, Maine, Vermont, Ohio, and Indiana. He spoke nearly every day—often several times a day—to audiences large and small in public parks, town squares, churches, schoolhouses, abandoned buildings, and lecture halls. He endured all the day-to-day hardships, loneliness, and physical demands faced by an itinerant abolitionist lecturer. He traveled by foot, horseback, railroad, stagecoach, and steamboat in an effort to vitalize local and county antislavery societies. Often braving bricks, rotten eggs, verbal attacks, racist remarks, and threats of physical assault, he at times risked his life speaking against the peculiar institution. Day and night he told listeners about his slave experiences and addressed such issues as the injustice of racial prejudice, the proslavery character of the clergy, the superiority of moral suasion over political action, and the proslavery nature of the U. S. Constitution. Undaunted by hostile and apathetic audiences, he ventured into hamlets where the rhetoric of abolitionism had never been preached.

From the outset, Douglass overwhelmed white audiences with his oratorical brilliance and his intellectual capacity. As he spoke at one antislavery meeting after another, his fame spread rapidly among abolitionists throughout the North. His reputation rested chiefly upon the passionate streams of rhetoric by which he gave vent to an unyielding hostility toward slavery and racial prejudice. Accounts of his early speeches show that he elicited powerful, positive reactions from almost all white abolitionist audiences. Tall and physically imposing, he presented himself with dignity and self-assurance. Listeners consistently commented on his powerful physical presence, his captivating delivery, his rich and melodious voice, his clear and precise diction. His impassioned bursts of wit, satire, sarcasm, humor, invective, and anecdotes made powerful impressions upon his auditors. In addition, he often used time-honored rhetorical devices such as anaphora, metaphor, simile, allegory, alliteration, parallelism, mimicry, and antithesis. Those who heard him speak were astonished that such eloquence could come from a fugitive slave. Typical is the comment of a correspondent for the *Salem Register* who heard Douglass speak in November 1842:

> The most wonderful performance of the evening was the address of Frederick Douglass, himself a slave only four years ago! His remarks and his manner created the most indescribable sensations in the minds of those unaccustomed to hear *freemen* of his color speak in public, much more to regard a *slave* as capable of such an effort. He was a living, speaking, *startling* proof of the folly, absurdity and inconsistency . . . of slavery. Fluent, graceful, eloquent, shrewd, sarcastic, he was without making any allowances, a fine specimen of an orator. He seemed to move the audience at his will, and they at times would hang upon his lips with staring eyes and open mouths, as eager to catch every word, as any "sea of upturned faces" that ever rolled at the feet of Everett or Webster to revel in their classic eloquence.[2]

As with the people of Salem, Douglass' contemporaries were often at a loss to explain his rhetorical proficiency; they could not reconcile his genius with the nineteenth-century stereotype that blacks were genetically and culturally inferior. Indeed, African Americans were perceived as being inherently irrational, unalterable beings who were morally and intellectually inferior to whites.[3] As one auditor declared after hearing Douglass speak at Nantucket in August 1841, "It seemed almost miraculous, how he had been prepared to tell his story with so much power."[4] In fact, Douglass did nothing to discourage the view that his performance was miraculous. He declared in his second autobiography that he "had had no preparation" for his speech at Nantucket or for his succeeding work as a lecturer for the Massachusetts Anti-Slavery Society.[5] This view has become the standard lore of Douglass scholars, most of whom uncritically repeat what he said in his autobiography.[6]

When I began this study, I, too, was prepared to accept this view. As I examined Douglass' early life, however, I discovered that as a slave in Maryland he had gained valuable experiences that contributed powerfully to his understanding of rhetoric and to his development as an orator. When he addressed the meeting of abolitionists at Nantucket in August 1841, he did not come to the platform ignorant of the art of oratory and without knowledge of the antislavery movement. His interest in oratory and abolitionism began early in his life. As a slave, he experienced the power of the spoken word in a variety of ways, including secular storytelling, religious preaching, and slave songs and spirituals. At age twelve, he discovered Caleb Bingham's *Columbian Orator*, which had a profound impact on his life. This book formally introduced Douglass to the rules of oratory, supplied him with the words to meet proslavery arguments, and inspired him to master the art of oratory as a way to further the cause of liberty.[7] During the same period, Douglass learned of the abolitionists and immediately declared himself one. He also underwent a religious conversion to Christianity, a conversion that inspired him with hope and allowed him to pursue opportunities for oral expression such as conducting Sabbath schools and preaching to his fellow slaves. In addition, his religious conversion set him on a path to become a preacher.

As I examined the years Douglass spent in New Bedford from 1838 to 1841, I discovered that they, too, were of immeasurable importance to his growth as a speaker and to his development as an abolitionist. During this three-year period, Douglass moved primarily within New Bedford's large and thriving black community, where he found a wealth of opportunities to cultivate his understanding of oratory and abolitionism. Within weeks after his escape from slavery in 1838, he joined New Bedford's A. M. E. Zion Church, in which he advanced his public speaking skills as an exhorter, class leader, and licensed lay preacher. As a preacher, he received his first formal training as an orator and preached to the New Bedford A.M.E. Zion congregation on a regular basis. He also played a significant part in New Bedford's black abolitionist community. He attended and participated in many of their meetings and rapidly distinguished himself as one of their leaders. During this same period, Douglass was exposed to William Lloyd Garrison and his brand of abolitionism. These activities combined to prepare Douglass for the work he began as a lecturer for the Massachusetts Anti-Slavery Society in 1841.

In short, before Douglass' emergence at Nantucket, he had been attracted simultaneously to two platforms, one rooted in religion, the other in abolitionism. Both offered him numerous opportunities to address audiences and to develop his skills as an orator. Consequently, when he addressed the abolitionists gathered in Nantucket's Atheneum Hall in August 1841, he was far from unprepared. While it is true that he was ill equipped to address an audience composed chiefly of white people, "having been taught," in his words, "to regard white men as his superiors, and never for once thinking that he could receive from them the least countenance of approbation," he was well prepared to deliver a speech.[8] As a slave and as a fugitive, he had delivered many speeches to black audiences and had received formal and informal training as an orator.

These findings with regard to Douglass' early life and his years in New Bedford are presented in chapters one and two. In chapters three through nine, I examine Douglass' oratorical activities from the time of his emergence at Nantucket in August 1841 until his departure to England in August 1845, which brought to an end the first stage of his career as an abolitionist. As with Douglass' preparation for an oratorical career, his rhetorical activities from 1841 to 1845 are clouded with myths and misunderstandings. The standard view of Douglass during this time is that he limited his remarks to a simple narrative of his slave experiences, that he was very much under the influence of William Lloyd Garrison and the Massachusetts Anti-Slavery Society, and that he strictly followed the dictates of Garrisonian doctrine.[9] But as I began exploring Douglass' activities and charting his speeches on a daily basis, I discovered that these conceptions were not true. Even during his first few months as an abolitionist lecturer, Douglass did not confine his remarks to his slave experiences. Among the topics he discussed were the oppressive force of racial prejudice in the North, the superiority of moral suasion over political action in abolitionism, the dissolution of the Union as a means of fighting slavery, and the immorality of returning fugitive slaves to the South. Moreover, far from merely following Garrisonian doctrine, Douglass at times disagreed with Garrison and other white abolitionists in his speeches and, in general, was much more independent and outspoken than has been previously recognized.

Douglass also engaged in a wide range of rhetorical activities that have been overlooked or inadequately investigated by his biographers and by previous students of his oratory. During the first eight months of 1842, for example, he undertook his first solo speaking tour for the Massachusetts Anti-Slavery Society, participated in a series of antislavery lectures on Cape Cod with Garrison, Henry C. Wright, and George Bradburn, and traveled with Abby Kelley through western and central New York lecturing against slavery and racial prejudice. All of these activities were important for Douglass personally and for the growth of abolitionism, yet none has been adequately treated by previous scholars. The same is true of such pivotal events as Douglass' role in the 1844 Hundred Conventions tour of Massachusetts, his speeches in eastern Pennsylvania with Charles Lenox

Remond during the summer of 1844, and his varied oratorical activities from September 1844 to August 1845, activities that have been overshadowed in the scholarly literature by the attention paid to the publication in May 1845 of Douglass' *Narrative of the Life of Frederick Douglass, An American Slave, Written By Himself.* In all these activities, Douglass spoke with a power and eloquence that contributed mightily to the growth of the antislavery movement.

As I tracked Douglass through his oratorical activities from 1841 through August 1845, I found myself entering not just Douglass' world, but also that of the abolitionist lecturer in general. By following Douglass and his traveling companions on a daily basis from one place to the next, I found myself immersed in the full range of their rhetorical enterprise—how they procured meeting spots once they arrived in a town or city, how they publicized their meetings, what they said during the meetings and, in many cases, how they dealt with the opposition of anti-abolitionists who sought to disrupt their proceedings. Although we do not always have the texts of what Douglass and his compatriots said at these gatherings, we usually have newspaper and other accounts that provide insight into who spoke, the resolutions they debated, the impact of their speeches, and the outcome of the meetings. By piecing together the evidence from these sources—in combination with surviving speech texts—we can comprehend the complexity of the rhetorical environment in which Douglass and other abolitionist orators operated, the challenges and obstacles they faced, and the volatile nature of their campaign to bring an end to slavery.[10]

In addition, as I moved slowly and carefully through Douglass' speeches, I found an increasing number of errors and omissions in the itinerary of Douglass' oratorical activities prepared by John W. Blassingame and published in his edition of *The Frederick Douglass Papers.* Although Blassingame includes many of the places and dates of Douglass' speeches from 1839 through 1845, he often misdates meetings, misreports their locations and, at times, completely omits meetings. Douglass biographers Benjamin Quarles, Raymond Gerald Fulkerson, and William S. McFeely also commit errors and omissions when documenting Douglass' oratorical activities during this period. Altogether, more than 120 errors and omissions were discovered and corrected. These mistakes are documented in the endnotes that follow each chapter. I also discovered reviews of Douglass' oratory, speech excerpts, and even some complete speech texts overlooked by Blassingame and other previous scholars. As a corrective to the itinerary published by Blassingame in volume 1 of the *Douglass Papers,* I include a complete, corrected itinerary in appendix A. This itinerary lists every speech—complete with date and location—that Douglass can be documented as presenting from 1839 to 1845. Appendix B reprints a letter written by Douglass to William Lloyd Garrison on 8 November 1842. The second half of the letter includes a portion of a speech Douglass delivered in New Bedford, Massachusetts, defending George Latimer, a fugitive from slavery who had been arrested and jailed in Boston in October 1842. Although portions of this letter have been reprinted before, it has not heretofore been reprinted in full. Appendices C and D present two newly discovered complete texts of speeches by Douglass—one from a 28 May 1844 meeting of the New England Anti-Slavery Society in Boston, the other from a 12 August 1844 meeting of the Eastern Pennsylvania Anti-Slavery Society at Norristown. Neither speech is included in Blassingame's collection of Douglass' speeches and neither has been printed in any previous work on Douglass.

Notes

1. David W. Blight, *Frederick Douglass' Civil War* (Baton Rouge: Louisiana State University Press, 1989), xi. For similar assessments of Douglass' prominence as an orator, see Robert T. Oliver, *History of Public Speaking in America* (Westport, Conn.: Greenwood, 1978), 246; Waldo E. Martin Jr., *The Mind of Frederick Douglass* (Chapel Hill: University of North Carolina Press, 1984), ix; Henry Louis Gates, Jr., "Frederick Douglass and the Language of Self," in *Figures in Black: Words, Signs, and the "Racial" Self*, ed. Henry Louis Gates Jr. (New York: Oxford University Press, 1987), 103; Allison Davis, *Leadership, Love, and Aggression* (New York: Harcourt, Brace, Jovanovich, 1983), 17-26, 51-52, 60-61; Leon Litwack, *North of Slavery: The Negro in the Free States, 1790-1860* (Chicago: University of Chicago Press, 1961), ix-x; Robert Felgar, "The Rediscovery of Frederick Douglass," *Mississippi Quarterly* 35 (fall 1982): 427-31; Leslie Friedman Goldstein, "Morality and Prudence in the Statesmanship of Frederick Douglass: Radical as Reformer," *Polity* 16 (summer 1984): 606; Benjamin Quarles, *Black Abolitionists* (New York: Oxford University Press, 1969), 63; John Hope Franklin, *From Slavery to Freedom: A History of Negro Americans*, 3d ed. (New York: Knopf, 1967), 252-53; Ernest G. Bormann, "The Rhetoric of Abolition," in *Forerunners of Black Power: The Rhetoric of Abolition*, ed. Ernest G. Bormann (Englewood Cliffs, N.J.: Prentice-Hall, Inc., 1971), 14; John W. Blassingame, *Frederick Douglass: The Clarion Voice* (Washington, D.C.: National Park Service, 1976), 11; Louis Filler, *The Crusade Against Slavery, 1830-1860* (New York: Harper and Row, 1960), 161; Margaret Just Butcher, *The Negro in American Culture* (New York: Knopf, 1956), 145.

2. *Salem Register* in *The Liberator* (9 December 1842), 194.

3. Dickson J. Preston, *The Young Frederick Douglass: The Maryland Years* (Baltimore, Md.: Johns Hopkins University Press, 1980), xiii; Waldo E. Martin, Jr., "Frederick Douglass," in *American Orators Before 1900: Critical Studies and Sources*, ed. Bernard K. Duffy and Halford R. Ryan (New York: Greenwood, 1987), 137; George M. Fredrickson, *The Black Image in the White Mind: The Debate on Afro-American Character and Destiny, 1817-1914* (New York: Harper and Row, 1971), 1-24.

4. *National Anti-Slavery Standard*, 26 August 1841, 46.

5. Frederick Douglass, *My Bondage and My Freedom* (1855; reprint, New York: Dover, 1969), 358-59.

6. For instance, see Frederic May Holland, *Frederick Douglass: The Colored Orator* (New York: Funk and Wagnalls, 1891); James M. Gregory, *Frederick Douglass: The Orator* (1893; reprint, Chicago: Afro-Am Press, 1969), 288-89; Charles W. Chesnutt, *Frederick Douglass* (1899; reprint, New York: Johnson Reprint Corporation, 1970); Booker T. Washington, *Frederick Douglass* (Philadelphia: George W. Jacobs and Company, 1906); Nathan Irvin Huggins, *Slave and Citizen: The Life of Frederick Douglass* (Boston: Little, Brown, and Company, 1980).

7. *The Columbian Orator*, ed. Caleb Bingham (Boston: Manning and Loring, 1797).

8. "The Cambria Riot, My Slave Experience, and my Irish Mission: An Address Delivered in Belfast, Ireland, on 5 December 1845," in *The Frederick Douglass Papers, Series One: Speeches, Debates, and Interviews*, ed. John W. Blassingame (New Haven, Conn.: Yale University Press, 1979), 1:88.

9. For instance, see Gregory, *Frederick Douglass*, 28-30; Philip S. Foner, *Frederick Douglass* (New York: Citadel Press, 1964), 46-49; Huggins, *Slave and Citizen*, 2-3, 17-20; Benjamin Quarles, *Frederick Douglass* (1948; reprint, New York: Atheneum, 1968), 19-37; Ronald K. Burke, *Frederick Douglass: Crusading Orator for Human Rights* (New York: Garland Publishing, 1996), 14-15.

10. For a complementary approach to writing a rhetorical history, see Celeste Michelle Condit and John Louis Lucaites, *Crafting Equality: America's Anglo-African Word* (Chicago: University of Chicago Press, 1993).

Acknowledgments

THE RESEARCHING AND WRITING of this book has been a cooperative enterprise, and I hope all who have helped but are not named will know how deeply grateful I am. Archivists and librarians have been especially helpful in uncovering and gathering materials. The staff at the Wisconsin State Historical Society Library provided excellent assistance throughout the project. They handled my interlibrary loan requests with efficiency, as did the staff at the Memorial Library of the University of Wisconsin-Madison. Librarians across New York, Massachusetts, Rhode Island, and Pennsylvania offered significant help and advice. For access to their collections, I wish to thank the staffs of Boston Public Library, Harvard College Library, Brown University Library, the Frederick Douglass National Historic Site at Cedar Hill in Anacostia, Washington, D. C., Library of Congress, Nantucket Historical Association, Worcester Historical Museum Library, Columbia University Library, University Library of the University of Massachusetts at Amherst, American Antiquarian Society, Lynn Historical Society, Massachusetts State Historical Society, New Bedford Public Library, Old Dartmouth Historical Society, Rhode Island State Historical Society, Rochester Public Library, Rochester Historical Society, Syracuse University Library, Olin Library of Cornell University, University of Rochester Library, and the Pennsylvania Historical Society.

Rev. Willie L. Alldrich at Livingstone College in Salisbury, North Carolina, was of great assistance in helping me to understand the roles of class leader, exhorter, Sunday school superintendent, and lay preacher in the African Methodist Episcopal Zion Church. The faculty and staff at the University of Wisconsin-Rock County and the Communication Arts Department of the University of Wisconsin Colleges offered moral support and release time to work on the project. I especially wish to acknowledge Dean Jane Crisler, who offered valuable advice and support throughout the writing of the work. I am also grateful to the Communication Arts Department at the University of Wisconsin-Madison, which provided summer stipends in 1991 and 1993 to support my travel and research.

Throughout this project, many persons have encouraged and criticized my work. Professors Edwin Black, Lloyd Bitzer, Mark White, Hanns Hohmann, Fred Kauffeld, Michael C. Leff, Dilip Gaonkar, Richard Sewell, Sandra Adell, and William Van Deburg gave me encouragement and direction at various stages of the project. Susan Zaeske, Susan Zickmund, Robert Kraig, Jean Goodwin, and Karen Whedbee—all current or former graduate students in the rhetoric program—encouraged me throughout the writing of the book. Raymond Gerald Fulkerson, currently on the editorial staff of *The Frederick Douglass Papers* at Yale University, helped shape my understanding of Douglass as an orator, and I am very grateful for his advice and encouragement.

I am most grateful to my advisor, Stephen E. Lucas, who directed this work when it was a dissertation. His unfailing encouragement and support, his demand for clear thinking and precise writing, his high standards for scholarship, and his meticulous criticism of both my ideas and my prose, have improved this work immeasurably. I am deeply grateful for his patience, friendship, and wise counsel.

I owe my greatest debt of gratitude to my family. My mother and father, Evelyn and Harold Lampe, have encouraged me from the beginning. My sister, Valerie, has been there to offer understanding and support. My in-laws, Janice and Burton Lee, have supported my efforts throughout. I am most indebted to my wife, Jody, and our daughters, Thea and Tessa. For their patience, devotion, understanding, and love, I am eternally grateful, and to them I dedicate this work.

𝒞𝒽𝒶𝓅𝓉𝑒𝓇 𝒪𝓃𝑒

Frederick Douglass' Maryland Plantation Education: His Discovery of Oratory

ON 12 AUGUST 1841, after delivering his first speeches before a predominantly white abolitionist audience at Nantucket's Atheneum Hall, Frederick Douglass was invited to become a lecturer for the Massachusetts Anti-Slavery Society. Concerned with any publicity that could expose him to discovery and arrest by his master, he at first declined the invitation. But John A. Collins, general agent of the Massachusetts Anti-Slavery Society, refused to take no for an answer, and Douglass reluctantly accepted his request. "Here opened upon me a new life," he recalled in 1855, "a life for which I had had no preparation." As we shall see, however, Douglass was far from unprepared for a career in oratory. Uncritical acceptance of his claim that he was ill equipped to enter the antislavery campaign has clouded our view of his early life and preparation for his career as an abolitionist orator.[1] Douglass, in fact, was well prepared to enter the abolitionist crusade in August 1841 as a lecturer for the Massachusetts Anti-Slavery Society. His preparation began during his twenty-year enslavement, and by the time he escaped from slavery in 1838, he had gained valuable experiences that contributed to his understanding of rhetoric and his identity as an orator. It is possible to piece together these experiences from his autobiographies, from his later speeches, and from scholarly works on his life as a slave and on slave culture.[2]

This chapter provides a discussion of those forces and events in Douglass' life as a slave that contributed to his discovery of the power of the spoken word and prepared him for a career in oratory. Early on, he recognized the value and vitality of language. Certainly, his childhood experiences within the oral culture of the slave community exposed him to the importance of language: its content, tone, and rhythm. On the plantation, he was exposed to the African oral traditions of secular storytelling, religious preaching, and slave songs and spirituals. He had ample opportunities to observe his fellow slaves utilizing language and achieving impressive results.

During his enslavement in Baltimore, Douglass learned to read and write. By so doing, he realized the pathway to freedom was through literacy. Learning and mastering these skills were of incalculable importance to him, for everything else he did in his life was all but impossible without literacy. Equally important, during this same period, Douglass' religious awakening and conversion to Christianity helped prepare him for the public platform. His conversion gave him a religious perspective, which furnished him with hope and fueled his desire for freedom. It also gave him opportunities for oral expression in slavery through the medium of Sabbath schools and his role as a Methodist church class leader. In addition, by attending church services, in Baltimore before his escape, he was exposed to a wide range of preachers and rhetorical styles during his days. Most important, his religious conversion set him on a path to become a preacher, a vocation he pursued in New Bedford, Massachusetts, after his escape.

While a slave in Baltimore, Douglass read Caleb Bingham's *Columbian Orator*. Not only did this book offer him his first formal introduction to public speaking, it also deepened his hatred of the peculiar institution, gave him the words to meet proslavery arguments, and inspired him to master the art of oratory. In addition, during this time period, Douglass was exposed to the doctrines of abolitionism. Whenever possible, he would read newspaper accounts of the abolitionists' activities, and by age thirteen, he was a self-proclaimed abolitionist. He was also a member of the East Baltimore Mental Improvement Society. During their meetings, Douglass, the only slave member of the secret society, participated in debates and discussions with six free blacks on such issues as religion and the status of blacks in Maryland. Through his involvement in the society, he gained invaluable training and experience in public speaking. In light of all this, it is easy to see why James McCune Smith, a prominent black doctor and abolitionist, wrote in 1855 that Douglass' "plantation education" prepared him well for his "special mission" and "was better than any he could have acquired in any lettered school."[3]

I

"I was born in Tuckahoe," Douglass proclaimed in 1845, "near Hillsborough, and about twelve miles from Easton, in Talbot county, Maryland." Because his mother, Harriet Bailey, was a slave, he and his brothers and sisters were also slaves.[4] In fact, Douglass' black ancestors for a century or more before his birth had been slaves. They were a strong and closely knit group with deep roots in the Eastern Shore and a long tradition of determination and perseverance. These traditions were passed on to Douglass by his grandparents, Isaac and Betsy Bailey, with whom he spent the first six years of his life.[5]

Douglass' grandmother, Betsy Bailey, was the central figure in his early years. Having grown too old for field service, she was charged with the duty of raising and caring for the young children of the plantation. When she assumed the care of Douglass, most of the children in her charge were her grandchildren from her five daughters. His grandmother, Douglass recalled, "was held in high esteem, far higher than is the lot of most colored persons in the slave states." She was a recognized leader in the black community and a tower of strength in holding together her family. "Grandmama Betty," as she was called by those who knew her, was a good nurse, an expert in fishing and farming, and remarkably self-reliant—a trait she passed on to her children and grandchildren. From his grandmother Douglass also learned that he could trust women as confidants and sources of strength, a trust he carried with him during his enslavement and beyond.[6]

His grandmother, Douglass later wrote, "enjoyed the high privilege of living in a cabin, separate from the quarter, with no other burden than her own support, and the necessary care of the little children, imposed." Located on the outskirts of Colonel Lloyd's plantation, the cabin was close enough to the slave quarters to allow Douglass to absorb the oral traditions of the slave community—particularly the traditions of secular storytelling and religious preaching. These traditions provided Douglass with numerous opportunities for encountering the power of the spoken word and its ability to comfort, console, sustain, unify, inspire, motivate, and help his fellow slaves to cope in their times of distress. Douglass' African ancestors considered sound to be of importance, and they produced an oral tradition aimed at keeping the ears rather than the eyes sharpened. In the evenings, Douglass was entertained by tales that passed folk wisdom from one generation of slaves to the next. Some of the folk tales instructed him on how to act, live, and survive on the plantation. Others sounded the slaves' hopes and dreams, allowed slaves to express their hostility toward their masters, furnished a channel for relief, and provided a means of sharing the workings of the plantation system. Douglass listened as the storyteller artfully combined his narrative with song, striking imagery and metaphors, and an exhilarating oral style to bring a folk tale to light. While telling a tale, the storyteller produced sounds and noises to enhance the story. He chanted, mimicked, rhymed, and used his body to create sound and to suggest different characters. He produced the cries of birds and beasts, or strange noises springing from haunted places. He also expected Douglass and his fellow slaves to respond to his story with comments, laughter, and corrections. Indeed, the folk tale was as much a communal experience as the spiritual and the sermon.[7]

In addition to listening to folk tales, on Sundays and religious holidays Douglass listened to slave preachers using rich phrases, folk poetry, and vivid illustrations to excite the passions of their brethren in bonds. Slave preachers employed a vast range of rhetorical techniques in their sermons. Most sermons began with normal conversational speech, slowly built to a rhythmic cadence, and climaxed in a tonal chant with the congregation shouting, singing, dancing, and clapping their hands. The dynamic pattern of call and response between the preacher and his audience was vital to the progression of the sermon, for unless the spirit was roused and the congregation inspired to move, sing, shriek, and shout, the sermon was considered unsuccessful. The slave preacher also used dramatic hand gestures and strong vocal delivery to involve and engage his listeners. In addition, the sermon of the slave preacher contained lessons for Douglass on surviving the earthly trials of slavery and obtaining heavenly rewards. These lessons were rooted in the teachings of the Bible. Stories, characters, and images from both the Old and New Testaments permeated the preaching methods and prayer of the slaves. Preaching meant dramatizing the stories of the Bible and the way of God to his people. In this fashion, Douglass' informal education as a speaker began during his childhood days in bondage.[8]

II

After living with his grandparents for six years, Douglass was forced to move to the Lloyd plantation twelve miles from the secure surroundings of the cabin. Soon after reaching the plantation, Douglass experienced the power of the spoken word during a confrontation he witnessed between his mother and another slave woman who was mistreating him. The incident must have made a strong impression on Douglass, for he remembered it distinctly years later. The confrontation, he recalled, was "instructive as well as interesting." Soon after Douglass' arrival on the plantation, Lloyd's cook, Aunt Katy, whose duty it was to watch over the dozen slave children who were part of the household, had grown to dislike Douglass and, in addition to beating him, often starved him. The day of this incident, Douglass had offended Aunt Katy and, consequently, had not been given anything to eat since breakfast. Late in the evening, his mother came to visit. After Douglass explained what had happened that day, his mother angrily "read Aunt Katy a lecture which she never forgot." Harriet Bailey threatened the cook with "complaining to old master" on Douglass' behalf, for the master, "though harsh and cruel himself, at times, did not sanction the meanness, injustice, partiality and oppressions enacted by Aunt Katy in the kitchen." From this experience, Douglass witnessed the "bright gleam of a mother's love, and the earnestness of a mother's care." In addition, he experienced the power of the spoken word over his evil oppressor. "I was victorious," he recalled, "and well off for the moment; prouder, on my mother's knee, than a king upon his throne."[9]

Douglass' understanding of the power of the word in his daily life was further advanced by witnessing and participating in the secular songs and spirituals sung by slaves on the Lloyd plantation. Music was intimately connected with African custom and practice, and American slaves maintained this tradition. For the slaves, music was a central element in their daily expression and activities. Slaves sang as they planted and harvested crops, husked corn, sawed wood, rocked babies, and cooked meals. Indeed, they executed almost every imaginable task to the accompaniment of song. These songs often reflected the day-to-day experiences of the slaves—their troubles, their fears, and their hopes for release from bondage. The songs served to preserve communal values and solidarity among the slaves. Singing on the plantation also functioned as a time of refreshment and renewal amid the usual drudgery of slave life. In addition, slave songs and spirituals, like the songs of their African ancestors, often relied on metaphor, innuendo, and indirection. The songs reflected the slaves' efforts to express themselves to one another in the presence of whites. The slaveholder may have heard in the songs "unmeaning jargon," Douglass recalled, but for the slaves the songs were "full of meaning."[10]

No form of song contained more meaning for the slaves than the spiritual. Spirituals were at the heart of the worship experience and were often merged with prayers and sermons. Through the spirituals, slaves expressed their faith in God in moving, immediate, and dramatic terms. It was in the spirituals, moreover, that the characters, themes, and lessons of the Bible became dramatically real and took on special meaning for Douglass and his fellow slaves. Through the language of the spirituals, slaves could state the principal tenets of the Gospel. Biblical stories and lessons were committed to memory by means of song. In addition, spirituals sometimes expressed the slaves' desire for freedom in this world as well as in the next. Most important, they focused the consciousness of Douglass and his brethren in bonds upon the communal bond of faith.[11]

On the Lloyd plantation, slaves were generally expected to sing as well as to perform their work. Douglass was deeply affected by these songs. "I have sometimes thought," he reflected in later years, "that the mere hearing of those songs would do more to impress truly spiritual-minded men and women with the soul-crushing and death-dealing character of slavery, than the reading of whole volumes of its mere physical cruelty. They speak to the heart and to the soul of the thoughtful." Later in his life, Douglass traced his "first glimmering conception of the dehumanizing character of slavery" to these songs and recalled the power of the voice in "revealing at once the highest joy and deepest sadness" of the slaves. As an act of expression, the songs powerfully revealed the "horrible character of slavery." They "told a tale of woe . . . they were tones loud, long, and deep; they breathed the prayer and complaint of souls boiling over with the bitterest of anguish. Every tone was a testimony against slavery, and a prayer to God for deliverance from chains."[12]

The slave songs and spirituals Douglass heard and sang early in his life made a lasting impression on him. He recognized their value as a powerful mode of self-expression that allowed the slaves to transcend symbolically the severe restrictions of their environment by permitting them to voice deeply held feelings that ordinarily could not be expressed. "The songs of the slave," he wrote, "represent the sorrows of his heart; and he is relieved by them, only as an aching heart is relieved by its tears." Whenever Douglass recalled the slave songs, they served to deepen his hatred of slavery and to quicken his sympathies for his "brethren in bonds." Most important, as a youngster he began, through the medium of song, to realize the power of his own voice in giving expression to thoughts, deep feelings, and emotions.[13]

Although singing provided a safe means for self-expression in the presence of whites, expressing one's self openly by speech in their presence often carried severe penalties. While a slave on the Lloyd plantation, Douglass realized the price a slave could pay for speaking candidly to his or her master. One of the stories he heard about his master, Col. Edward Lloyd, made this point abundantly clear. He was told how Lloyd was traveling on horseback when he met a slave walking along the road. Lloyd, a man who owned many slaves, was not recognized by the slave as his master. When Lloyd asked the slave if he was treated well by his master, the slave answered, "No, sir." When asked if his master worked him too hard, the slave responded, "Yes, sir." According to the story, shortly afterward the slave was sold to a Georgia trader for finding fault with his master.[14]

Upon hearing this story, Douglass realized an important lesson about the language and rules of slavery. With the correct words, a slave could keep his life intact. Conversely, the wrong words could cause the slave to be, "without a moment's warning, . . . snatched away, and forever sundered, from his family and friends." For this reason, Douglass realized, "slaves, when inquired of as to their condition and the character of their masters, almost universally say they are contented, and that their masters are kind." The penalty for disclosing the truth was too severe. Instead, Douglass reasoned, slaves "suppress the truth rather than take the consequences of telling it." It was better to lie to the master, he learned, than to speak the truth, or simply to remain silent, for "a still tongue makes a wise head."[15]

During his two-year stay on the Lloyd plantation, Douglass witnessed the brutality and cruel treatment of the adult slaves on a daily basis. At an early age he saw what living in a world dominated by violence did to the human spirit, and what he saw supplied him with a passion against the inhumanity of slavery that remained with him until the day he died.[16] As an adult, he recalled vividly one of these instances of violence:

> I have often been awakened at the dawn of day by the most heart-rending shrieks of an own aunt of mine [Aunt Hester], whom he [my master, Captain Anthony] used to tie up to a joist, and whip upon her naked back till she was literally covered with blood. No words, no tears, no prayers, from his gory victim, seemed to move his iron heart from its bloody purpose. The louder she screamed, the harder he whipped; and where the blood ran fastest, there he whipped longest. He would whip her to make her scream, and whip her to make her hush; and not until overcome by fatigue, would he cease to swing the blood-clotted cowskin. I remember the first time I ever witnessed this horrible exhibition. I was quite a child, but I well remember it. I never shall forget it whilst I remember any thing. . . . It struck me with awful force.[17]

Indeed, the incident struck Douglass with such force that, as an abolitionist lecturer, he often recounted it to audiences as a signal instance of the horror and barbarity of the South's peculiar institution.

III

In 1826 Aaron Anthony sent Douglass to Baltimore to work for Hugh Auld. Auld had asked his brother-in-law for a young black slave to serve as a companion to his two-year-old son, Tommy. Douglass left the plantation with "inexpressible joy" and with the hope for a better life in Baltimore.[18]

When Douglass arrived in Baltimore, he found a noisy, bustling city—a city experiencing dramatic growth from a small port to a much larger industrial and commercial center linked to international markets. Douglass would soon discover that Baltimore had a sizable free black population, with 687 free black households making up 15 percent of the total households in the city. Altogether, there were 20,000 free blacks living in Baltimore in the 1830s, and they outnumbered slaves by a ratio of five to one. Through churches, schools, and voluntary associations, these free black Baltimoreans fostered an independent community within the larger city. While living in Baltimore as a slave, Douglass would make his way into the city's free black community, in which he became an active member of the black Methodist Episcopal Church, taught reading and writing in black night schools, and joined the East Baltimore Mental Improvement Society.[19]

The move to Baltimore was a major turning point in Douglass' life. The eight-year-old slave, "once treated as a *pig* on the plantation . . . was treated as a *child* now." He was placed under the supervision of Auld's wife, Sophia, and charged with the responsibility of taking care of and protecting Tommy. Mrs. Auld was a "kindhearted" woman, and her influence on Douglass was significant. She quickly became a mother figure for Douglass as she recognized his humanity and treated him more like a son than a slave. In her presence, Douglass later recalled, "I could talk and sing; I could laugh and weep; I could reason and remember; I could love and hate. I was human, and she, dear lady, knew and felt me to be so."[20]

Not only did Sophia Auld treat Douglass as a human being, she also stimulated in him an interest in language and in learning to read. "Mrs. Auld," Douglass recalled, "was not only a kind-hearted woman, but she was remarkably pious; frequent in her attendance of public worship, much given to reading the bible, and to chanting hymns when alone." Her habit of reading aloud from the Bible, he wrote, "awakened my curiosity in respect to this *mystery* of reading, and roused in me the desire to learn." One incident in particular appears to have had an especially powerful impact on Douglass in this regard. Later in his life, he recalled how he had fallen asleep one Sunday evening under the parlor table when he was awakened by the sound of Sophia Auld's voice, "mellow, loud, and sweet," reading Bible verses aloud from the book of Job. There was, for Douglass, enchantment in the way the words at once expressed beauty and despair. He was captivated by the manner in which Auld's voice made the words come alive from the printed page. "From that night," he recalled, "I date my thirst for knowledge." Moreover, Auld's tranquil voice empowered the young slave with the courage he needed to approach her to ask her to teach him to read. "Having no fear of my kind mistress," he recollected, "I frankly asked her to teach me to read; and without hesitation, the dear woman began the task."[21]

Within a very short time Douglass was reading, and Mrs. Auld "seemed almost as proud" of his progress as if he had been "her own child." When she told her husband, however, that she was teaching the slave to read, he became extremely angry. Hugh Auld "at once forbade" her to instruct Douglass further. Reprimanding his wife in front of her pupil, Auld said:

> If you give a nigger an inch he will take an ell. Learning will spoil the best nigger in the world. If he learns to read the Bible it will forever unfit him to be a slave. He should know nothing but the

will of his master, and learn to obey it. As to himself, learning will do him no good, but a great deal of harm, making him disconsolate and unhappy. If you teach him how to read, he'll want to know how to write, and this accomplished, he'll be running away with himself.[22]

The "very decided manner" of Auld's lecture to his wife convinced Douglass that his master "was deeply sensible of the truths he was uttering." Convinced by Auld that literacy and learning were the paths out of slavery, Douglass was more determined than ever to acquire both. "In learning to read," Douglass wrote later, "I owe almost as much to the bitter opposition of my master, as to the kindly aid of my mistress. I acknowledge the benefit of both." Equally important, by denying Douglass access to a formal education, Hugh Auld inadvertently forced him to pursue a program of self-education that he would continue for the remainder of his life.[23]

Of all Douglass' experiences in Baltimore, none had more impact than his discovery, at age twelve, of Caleb Bingham's *Columbian Orator*.[24] Douglass was inspired to purchase the book when he overheard "some little boys say that they were going to learn some pieces out of it for the Exhibition." With fifty cents earned from polishing boots, he bought a copy of the reader. It was one of the best investments of his life. The *Columbian Orator* was a collection of orations, poems, playlets, and dialogues celebrating patriotism, freedom, courage, democracy, education, and temperance. Designed to "inspire the pupil with the ardour of eloquence and the love of virtue," the selections in the book were intended "particularly for Dialogue and Declamation."[25]

"This volume was, indeed, a rich treasure," Douglass reflected in 1855, "and every opportunity afforded me, for a time, was spent in diligently perusing it." He found a number of pieces within the text particularly worthwhile. In his autobiographies, Douglass specifically mentioned Sheridan's "mighty speeches on the subject of Catholic Emancipation,"[26] Lord Chatham's speech "on the American War," and speeches by "the great William Pitt and by Fox" as addresses that he found particularly interesting. "These were all choice documents to me," Douglass recalled, "and I read them, over and over again, with an interest ever increasing because it was ever gaining in intelligence; for the more I read them, the better I understood them."[27]

The selection he found most fascinating, however, was a short piece entitled "Dialogue Between a Master and Slave," by John Aikin.[28] Douglass was so enamored of this dialogue that he "perused and reperused [it] with unflagging satisfaction." In *My Bondage and My Freedom*, Douglass explained the attraction of the dialogue, which began with the master rebuking the slave for attempting to escape. In response, the slave was "made to say some very smart as well as impressive things in reply to his master." Invited to defend his escape attempt, the slave accepted the challenge and made a "spirited defense of himself, and thereafter the whole argument, for and against slavery, was brought out." For every argument the master made in defense of slavery, the slave presented a convincing counterargument. "The master," Douglass mused, "was vanquished at every turn." In the end, the master was convinced to emancipate the slave, demonstrating to Douglass the "mighty power and heart-searching directness of truth, penetrating even the heart of a slaveholder, compelling him to yield up his earthly interests to the claims of eternal justice." "Powerfully affected" by the dialogue, Douglass dreamed of the day "when the well-directed answers made by the slave to the master . . . would find their counterpart" in him.[29]

Equally important, Douglass stated years later, through reading and rereading this dialogue, he was able to utter his own thoughts on bondage, and "to meet the arguments brought forward to sustain slavery." Clearly and systematically, the dialogue responded to many of the questions that troubled him about slavery and his personal condition. Should he be grateful for his master's kind treatment of him? The dialogue's message was strikingly clear on this point. Douglass should not be grateful for any kind treatment by his owners who, if they did treat him well, did so purely for their own advantage. Was it wrong to try to escape from slavery? Decidedly not, said the dialogue. The act of running away was justified because the slave was taking back the liberty that was legitimately his. Had Providence, in some way, ordained slavery? Again, the dialogue answered—human beings, not God, had created slavery. From the dialogue, Douglass learned "the secret of all slavery and oppression, and . . . ascertained their true foundation to be in the pride, the power and the avarice of man." Slaveholders, he saw, were no more than "a band of successful robbers, who left their homes and went into Africa for the purpose of stealing and reducing my people to slavery."[30]

Nor was this dialogue the only selection Douglass benefited from in the *Columbian Orator*. By reading Bingham's book "over and over again with unabated interest," he discovered the words to express his thoughts and feelings. The book, "gave tongue to interesting thoughts of my own soul," he recalled, thoughts "which had frequently flashed through my mind, and died away for want of utterance." He could now recite words that denounced slavery and injustice, that defended a slave's right to rebel and run away, and that celebrated human liberty and freedom.[31] At the same time, he learned that words—and especially words expressed in oratory—could be a powerful way to combat such an injustice as slavery. According to one of the speeches found in Bingham's collection, the most telling weapon for truth was the art of oratory:

> To instruct, to persuade, to please; these are its objects. To scat-
> ter the clouds of ignorance and error . . . to remove the film of
> prejudice from the mental eye; and thus to irradiate the benight-
> ed mind with the cheering beams of truth. . . . An Alexander and
> a Caesar could conquer a world; but to overcome the passions, to
> subdue the wills, and to command at pleasure the inclinations of
> men, can be effected only by the all-powerful charm of enraptur-
> ing eloquence.[32]

As Douglass read and reread the *Columbian Orator*, he recognized the possibilities of using oratory to "scatter the clouds of ignorance and error" that surrounded him in slave society.

Beyond showing Douglass the power of oratory and persuasive argu-ment, Bingham's book provided a twenty-nine-page essay entitled, "General Directions for Speaking; Extracted from Various Authors." Within these pages Douglass found detailed instructions on how to deliver an effective speech, instructions he followed to the letter in many of his early antislavery addresses.[33] Because it appears that Douglass' early rhetorical style and delivery were influenced profoundly by Bingham's essay, we need to look closely at its prescriptions.[34]

Bingham began his essay by declaring delivery the most important canon of rhetoric. Drawing upon the opinions of Cicero, Demosthenes, and Quintilian, he emphasized that the principal object of oratory was action, and that the primary trigger to action was the orator's manner of delivery. The most effective delivery, he advised, was natural and sincere. The ora-tor must adjust his voice so that "it rises, sinks, and has various inflections given it, according to the present state and disposition of the mind." He must also attend to "accent, emphasis, and cadence." The orator must dis-tinguish those words in a sentence which he believes are the "most impor-tant" and place "a greater stress of voice upon them than . . . upon the oth-ers." In addition, the speaker must speak loud enough to be heard. The voice, Bingham suggested, should be varied, "clear and distinct." Bingham also offered advice on the pacing of a speech. If the orator speaks too fast, he warned, he "destroys . . . the necessary distinction between sentence and sentence . . . by which mean, all the grace of speaking is lost, and in great measure, the advantage of hearing." Conversely, an orator who speaks too slowly "appears cool himself, [and] can never expect to warm his hearers, and excite their affections."[35]

Like the voice, Bingham advised, gestures should be varied and natural. The orator should not stand in the same position "like a statue," but should move naturally about the platform. Bingham believed that the ora-tor must use his face and eyes to show signs of sorrow, joy, anger, resentment, terror, and modesty. The eyes should always be "directed to some of the audience, and gradually turning from side to side with an air of respect and modesty, and looking at them decently in the face, as in common discourse." In addition, the speaker should stand erect and use "very moderate" hand and arm movements.[36] Bingham also offered advice about imitating others from the platform, advice Douglass took seriously in his frequent use of mimicry in his early abolitionist lectures. An orator may choose to impersonate another speaker, wrote Bingham, but "great care must be taken not to overact his part by running into any ludicrous or theatrical mimicry."[37]

Douglass learned from Bingham's book how to deliver each section of a speech. Upon arriving on the platform, the orator was directed to "first settle himself, compose his countenance, and take a respectful view of his audience." Once the audience was prepared to listen, the orator should begin his speech at a slow pace. Within the narration, "the voice ought to be raised to somewhat a higher pitch," though "matters of fact should be related in a very plain and distinct manner, with a proper stress and emphasis laid upon each circumstance." During the proposition, the "subject of the discourse should be delivered with a very clear and audible voice." Within the confirmation, speakers were instructed to use "a great variety both of the voice and gesture" so as to strengthen the orator's reasoning and heighten "the imagination of his hearers." During the confutation, "the arguments of the adverse party ought first to be repeated in a plain and distinct manner." If they appear "trifling and unworthy of a serious answer," instructed Bingham, the speaker should respond to them in a "facetious manner, both of expression and gesture," for "to attempt to answer, in a grave and serious manner, what is in itself empty and ludicrous, is apt to create a suspicion, of its having more in it than it really has." When coming to the conclusion, "both the voice and gesture should be brisk and sprightly. . . . If an enumeration of the principal arguments of the discourse be convenient . . . they ought to be expressed in the most clear and forcible manner." Bingham concluded his essay by stressing that "it is impossible to gain a just and decent pronunciation of voice and gesture merely from rules." The best way to become an orator, he recommended, was through "practice and imitation of the best examples." This may be one reason Douglass read the speeches, dialogues, playlets, and poems in the *Columbian Orator* "over and over again."[38]

The importance of the *Columbian Orator* in shaping Douglass' future cannot be overestimated. Bingham's book offered him a heroic perspective of oratory and a model for his own life that he appears to have found close to irresistible. Moreover, from all indications, Douglass' early oratory was influenced significantly by Bingham's meticulous instructions with respect to delivery, style, and arrangement. When speaking from the platform,

Douglass used a conversational, natural delivery style, logically arranged and carefully reasoned his speeches, and appealed with great effect to the emotions of his listeners. Following Bingham's advice and reading and rereading the selections included in the book enabled Douglass to merge two traditions—the oral tradition of the slave culture with the classical rhetorical tradition. Since his childhood, he had absorbed the exhilarating oral style of the storyteller and slave preacher. He had been exposed to their use of striking imagery, rich phrases, metaphor, repetition, parallelism, poetry, song, and rhythmic cadences. He had experienced the impact of dramatic gestures and stirring vocal delivery on his fellow slaves. He had listened to the storyteller enhance his tale by mimicking the sounds of nature and by creating the illusion of dialogue between characters. Certainly, Bingham's advice on the orator's use of voice and gesture, mimicry and imagery, complemented the knowledge Douglass had acquired within his slave experiences on the plantation, as did Bingham's instructions on the importance of appealing to the emotions and passions of the audience. Most important, Bingham's volume introduced Douglass to the rhetorical strategies of the orator and to a standard structure for organizing speeches. Now armed with a formal introduction to rhetoric and with the words of the great orators of the past, he could meld his experiences within the slave community with the classical art of oratory. It was a potent combination, one that would leave white listeners agog at his eloquence and power as a platform orator throughout his public career.

IV

A second development during Douglass' Baltimore years that had a profound impact on his life and vocation occurred shortly after he purchased the *Columbian Orator*. Reading Bingham's book stirred Douglass' feelings of depression and restlessness over being a slave—an emotional turmoil that ultimately led him to religion. His religious awakening inspired within him a sense of hope, mission, and purpose, and fixed him on a course toward becoming a preacher. Indeed, soon after his escape from slavery in 1838, he would become a licensed lay preacher in New Bedford's African Methodist Episcopal Zion Church.[39]

Although Douglass' religious nature may have been aroused initially during the time he spent with his grandmother and by the religious practices of the slave community, his formal conversion to Christianity was inspired by the sermons of Reverend Hanson, a white Methodist preacher residing in Baltimore. Reverend Hanson, Douglass later recalled, preached "that all men, great and small, bond and free, were sinners in the sight of God; that they were, by nature, rebels against His government; and that they must repent of their sins, and be reconciled to God, through Christ."[40]

Still, Douglass did not have a distinct idea of what was required of him or of how he could obtain God's gift of salvation. He consulted Charles Johnson, a black caulker and lay preacher, who advised him, "in tones of holy affection," to pray and even "what to pray for." For weeks Douglass suffered "through the darkness and misery of doubts and fears." In a revelation, he finally found peace "by having faith in Jesus Christ, as the Redeemer, Friend, and Savior of those who diligently seek Him." Now converted, Douglass "saw the world in a new light." He recalled how he "loved all mankind—slaveholders not excepted," and was determined to have the "world converted." Although he "abhorred slavery more than ever," he found new hope, and his desire for knowledge intensified—especially his desire to learn about the Bible. He picked up scattered pages of the Bible "from the filthy street gutters of Baltimore, and washed and dried them, that in the moments of my leisure, I might get a word or two of wisdom from them."[41]

During this period, Douglass became acquainted with a kindly old black man named Charles Lawson. "A more devout man than he," Douglass reminisced in later years, "I never saw." The young slave was totally enamored with Lawson, who became Douglass' "spiritual father" and "chief instructor, in matters of religion." Douglass never knew the identity of his natural father, and Lawson gave him a much-needed father figure and role model. Lawson was someone with whom Douglass could identify and look to for guidance. They shared many hours together, "high, refreshing times" spent "singing, praying and glorifying God." Attracted by Lawson's piety and simple, genuine goodness, Douglass spent much of his leisure time with him on Sundays, reading the Bible, praying, attending prayer meetings, and listening with great interest to Lawson's teachings and prophecies. "The good old man told me," Douglass recalled, "that the 'Lord had a great work for me to do'; and I must prepare to do it; and that he had been shown that I must preach the gospel." Lawson's words made a "deep impression" on the young slave's mind, and Douglass "felt that some such work" was before him. Lawson encouraged him "to go on reading and studying the scriptures" to prepare for his special mission and assured him that the "good Lord" would deliver him from bondage "in His own good time."[42]

Lawson had a profound impact on Douglass' character and destiny. By assuring him that he was to be "a useful man in the world," the old man fanned Douglass' "already intense love of knowledge into a flame." He also provided Douglass with a stronger sense of confidence and mission. "Thus assured, and cheered on, under the inspiration of hope," Douglass recalled, "I worked and prayed with a light heart, believing that my life was under the guidance of a wisdom higher than my own." Douglass now earnestly readied himself to preach the gospel.[43]

Not only did Lawson influence Douglass' spiritual beliefs and direction, he most likely influenced his decision to join the black Methodist Episcopal Church on Strawberry Alley in 1831. The small church with its congregation of free and slave blacks helped Douglass survive this period of his enslavement.[44] During a speech in 1891, he described the Strawberry Alley church and its impact on his life:

> I remember well the little, unpretentious house in which we used to gather. It was looked upon as a large church for us then, but would not be noticed now beside the many handsome edifices that have since been erected. Then we had no regular pastors. Ministers would be sent to us from the white conference, and if a colored preacher could be found sufficiently capable and intelligent to instruct us and preach to us, he was looked upon by the colored people as a marvel. Whatever honor I have attained, whatever successes have come to me in literature, in statesmanship, in learning, the light and inspiration was first gathered in the old church in Strawberry alley.[45]

Among the white preachers whose message and rhetorical techniques Douglass heard while a member of the Strawberry Alley church were Samuel Hanson and Beverly Waugh. Hanson was probably the same white minister that he credited with awakening his religious nature, while Waugh was the presiding elder at the Wilk Street Methodist Episcopal Church where Sophia Auld, Douglass' mistress, attended worship services. Reverend Waugh often visited Sophia Auld at home to "exhort and pray" whenever she felt her faith stumbling. Thus Douglass was exposed a good deal to Waugh's discourse, both at church and in the Auld household.[46]

During this period, Douglass also attended the Bethel African Methodist Episcopal Church, where he heard "the gentle voice" of a former Maryland slave, Rev. Edward Waters. Born into slavery at West River, Maryland, on 15 March 1780, Waters later purchased his freedom from his master. He was licensed as a local preacher of the African Methodist Episcopal Church in 1810 and was later ordained as a deacon in 1818. In 1820 he became an elder, and in 1836 he was elected the third bishop of the African Methodist Church. While attending Bethel, Douglass also listened to the Rev. Nathaniel Charles Peck, a freeborn Maryland black, "thunder the gospel into sinners' ears." Peck, a man of considerable power and influence within the Baltimore African Methodist Episcopal Church, became a popular leader at Bethel in the early 1840s. Like Waters, he preached often at Bethel and made a strong impression on Douglass.[47]

Occasionally, Douglass attended church at the Sharp Street Methodist Episcopal Church. Here he listened to a black preacher named Lewis G. Wells. During the outbreak of cholera in 1831, the black congregation from

Strawberry Alley was invited to attend Wells' church "to receive advice . . . as to how we should live during the epidemic." Wells, a local physician, lecturer, and minister, told Douglass and others attending "what to eat and what not to eat; how to cook it and how not to cook it; what to drink and what not to drink." In 1891 Douglass recalled that Wells was considered "great shakes" as a speaker and that his services were "always in demand." On another occasion, Douglass recalled that Wells was the first black man he had ever seen deliver a lecture from a written manuscript. Along with the other eminent black preachers to whom Douglass was exposed during this period, Wells inspired the teenage slave with his eloquence and provided a role model of what he, Douglass, would like to become.[48]

Feeling confident in Baltimore with his newly discovered sense of mission and personal worth, Douglass continued to pursue knowledge by reading the Bible, by absorbing the eloquence of white and black preachers, and by reciting the speeches in the *Columbian Orator*. He also shared his knowledge with other black people who were "anxious to learn and improve." Although his own reading and writing abilities were "limited," and he could carry his students only so far, he started "a night school on Wolfe street, and afterward one on . . . Fleet Street." Here he "freely imparted" his knowledge of reading and writing. Both schools, he recalled, "were well attended," and he found the work "profitable and pleasing." Increasingly, however, he viewed his slave status as a great obstacle to fulfilling his destiny. Too young to run away, he continued to hope and pray for freedom and resolved that one day he would be free.[49]

V

Douglass' future life was further shaped during his Baltimore years by his discovery in December 1831 that there were men and women working toward the abolition of slavery. "Every little while," he recalled years later, "I could overhear Master Hugh or some of his company, speaking with much warmth and excitement about 'abolitionists.'" Although he did not understand who or what abolitionists were, he observed that they were "hated and soundly abused by slaveholders." He also realized there was a connection between abolition and slavery, for "slavery was, in some sort, under consideration, whenever the abolitionists were alluded to." Abolitionists, moreover, were held accountable whenever a slave escaped from slavery, killed a master, struck down an overseer, set fire to a master's property, or committed a violent crime. "Hearing such charges often repeated," noted Douglass, "I, naturally enough, received the impression that abolition—whatever it might be—could not be unfriendly to the slave, nor very friendly to the slaveholder." He then set out to discover "*who* and *what* the abolitionists were, and *why* they were so obnoxious to the slaveholders."[50]

Douglass began his search by looking up the word "abolition" in the dictionary, but the dictionary provided little help—it defined abolition as "the act of abolishing." What was to be abolished remained a puzzle. A city newspaper, the *Baltimore American*, provided Douglass with the "incendiary information" denied him by the dictionary. Within its columns, he discovered a news article reporting that former president John Quincy Adams, who had recently returned to Washington as a Massachusetts congressman, had presented to Congress petitions demanding the abolition of slavery in the District of Columbia and the abolition of the slave trade between the states of the Union. The puzzle was solved. "The vindictive bitterness, the marked caution, the studied reserve, and the cumbrous ambiguity, practiced by our white folks, when alluding to this subject," Douglass recalled, "was now fully explained." For the first time, he realized that he and his fellow slaves who sought freedom were not alone. "There was great HOPE in those words," he wrote of his discovery of abolition. The thought "that the rascality of slaveholders was not concealed from the eyes of the world" and that he "was not alone in abhorring the cruelty and brutality of slavery" gave him "deep satisfaction."[51]

Before hearing of the abolitionist movement, Douglass recalled years later, he had "no hope of deliverance—no hope of any peace or happiness within this vale of tears." After learning of it, he wrote, "hope sprang up in my mind, and in the minds of many more. I knew, I felt, that truth was above error, that right was above wrong, that principle was superior to policy; and under the peaceful and beneficent operation of abolitionism, I felt that I should one day be free." From that point forward, whenever Douglass heard anyone discussing the abolition movement, he felt it a "matter of a personal concern" and drew near to listen. In addition, he avidly sought out articles copied into the local newspapers from abolition newspapers in the North. Whenever he met a slave with whom he believed "it safe to talk on the subject," he would share with him "the mystery" he "had been able to penetrate." Gradually, Douglass' knowledge and understanding of the abolition movement grew, and although "ignorant of the philosophy of the movement," he "believed in it from the first."[52]

VI

After Douglass had lived seven years in Baltimore, a dispute within the Auld family forced him to leave the city and return to rural Talbot County, Maryland. In March 1833, at age fifteen, he was removed from the Hugh Auld household and sent to live with Thomas Auld. The decision to return Douglass to St. Michaels was made after a quarrel between Hugh and Thomas Auld during which Thomas, Douglass' legal owner, demanded that the young slave be returned to him. Douglass deeply regretted having to move away from Baltimore. He was unhappy about leaving his pupils behind, as well as his "dear old father, the pious Lawson." He was also disappointed over departing because he had delayed plans of escaping to the North. Moving to the country would make any attempt to escape risky and difficult.[53]

Douglass quickly discovered that his new masters, Thomas and Rowena Auld, were cruel and selfish people. Although Thomas Auld was a prosperous merchant, he refused to provide his slaves—which included Douglass, his sister Eliza, his aunt Priscilla, and his cousin Henny—with enough food. For the first time in seven years, Douglass felt "the pinchings of hunger," and to survive, he resorted to stealing and begging for food. He also found it hard to adjust to Thomas Auld's personality and, after a brief time, their relations became strained. Douglass, who had little respect for his master, often boldly defended himself against Auld's "capricious complaints." Auld, Douglass charged, was a man "incapable of a noble action," a man wholly caught up in "the love of domination, the pride of mastery, and the swagger of authority." Auld could be cruel, but Douglass perceived his methods of discipline as cowardly and weak. Defiant from the start, Douglass revealed his low regard for his master by refusing to address him as "Master." Instead, he addressed him as "Captain" or addressed him without any title at all. This proved to be a source of constant irritation to Auld, who was anxious to be addressed properly and with respect but, according to Douglass, "lacked the firmness necessary to command us to do so." Auld tried to discipline the contemptuous Douglass, and even resorted to severely whipping him, but "without any visible improvement" in the slave's behavior.[54]

In August 1833 Thomas Auld attended a Methodist camp meeting where, much to Douglass' delight, "he came out with a profession of religion." As Douglass watched his master progress through the conversion process, he could not help thinking that Auld's discovery of religion would change his cruel and cowardly ways. Despite his hopes, however, Douglass was profoundly disappointed. Although Auld soon became a leading member of the local Methodist church and hosted traveling preachers, participated in revivals, and turned his home into a "house of prayer," his conversion did not change his harsh treatment of the slaves. "If religion had any effect on his character at all," Douglass asserted, "it made him more cruel and hateful in all his ways."[55]

In the weeks that followed Auld's conversion, Douglass continued to witness his master's cruel ways, particularly his beating of Douglass' lame cousin Henny. It was a scene he would later describe vividly on numerous occasions during his antislavery lectures to northern audiences. Later in his life, Douglass recalled how he had watched as Auld crossed and tied

Henny's wrists to a bolt in the joist and whipped "her with a heavy cowskin upon her naked shoulders, causing the warm red blood to drip," after which he would leave Henny "tied up in this horrid situation four or five hours at a time." Auld would justify the "bloody deed" by the quotation from the Bible, "He that knoweth his master's will, and doeth it not, shall be beaten with many stripes." This incident served as the inspiration for the "Slaveholder's Sermon" that would later become perhaps the most famous aspect of Douglass' rhetorical repertoire in his early abolitionist speeches.[56]

During his stay on Auld's plantation, Douglass was forbidden to continue the Sabbath school activities he had participated in while living in Baltimore. "I was neither allowed to teach, nor be taught," Douglass wrote later. "The whole community—with but a single exception, among the whites—frowned upon everything like imparting instruction either to slaves or to free colored persons." Thus when a young white man named Wilson asked Douglass to help him start a secret Sabbath school for the instruction of slaves who wanted to learn to read the New Testament, he seized the opportunity. Here was a chance to realize Lawson's prophecy that the "Lord had a great work" for him and that he must "preach the gospel." With a "dozen old spelling books, and a few testaments," Douglass and Wilson secretly began the task of teaching "some twenty young scholars" and "some old gray-headed men" to read the Bible. Their first meeting "passed delightfully," but their second meeting was "rushed by a mob." Armed "with sticks, stones, whips, and cowskins" and led by Thomas Auld and two other Methodist class leaders, the mob broke up the meeting and commanded the two instructors to "never meet for such a purpose again." Douglass later recalled that the incident "did not serve to strengthen my religious convictions." His joy over teaching and preaching was replaced by heightened feelings of frustration and anguish over being a slave.[57]

The remainder of Douglass' time in St. Michaels was short and bitter. Just nine months after he arrived, and after proving "unsuitable to his [master's] purpose," he was hired out to Edward Covey, a poor farmer and professional slavebreaker. Douglass' "impudence" and "spirit of insubordination" had made him unfit to be a field hand on Auld's plantation. Auld sent him to work on Covey's farm because he believed that Douglass' spirit needed to be brought under control. On 1 January 1834, Douglass walked the seven miles from St. Michaels to Covey's farm, where he would remain with his new master until Christmas.[58]

VII

During his first six months under "nigger-breaker" Covey's dominion, Douglass' spirit was indeed broken. Only three days after his arrival on the farm, he was brutally beaten with sticks for being unable to handle a team of oxen. For the next six months, Douglass was whipped every week. In addition to using the cowskin to break the spirit of slaves in his charge, Covey also relied upon "hard and continued labor" to teach his slaves obedience and humility. Douglass was forced to work in the fields in all weather, six days a week, from dawn until darkness, and in some seasons until midnight. Covey's harsh discipline took a heavy toll on Douglass. "I was broken in body, soul, and spirit," he recalled in his first autobiography. "My natural elasticity was crushed, my intellect languished, the disposition to read departed, the cheerful spark that lingered about my eye died; the dark night of slavery closed in upon me; and behold a man transformed into a brute!" Even on Sundays when he was not forced to work, Douglass passed the hours existing "in a sort of beast-like stupor," an unconscious mental state "between sleep and wake." At times, when he did awaken himself enough to think about running away, the thought would quickly vanish. His goal of one day becoming a preacher seemed impossibly out of reach. Douglass became so desperate that he even considered murdering Covey and then taking his own life.[59]

One Sunday he found himself standing on the banks of the Chesapeake watching the sailboats and reflecting on his fate. Tormented by the appearance of the boats moving freely about the bay, Douglass remembered pouring out his "soul's complaint . . . with an apostrophe to the moving multitude of ships":

> You are loosed from your moorings, and are free; I am fast in my chains, and am a slave! You move merrily before the gentle gale, and I sadly before the bloody whip! You are freedom's swift-winged angels, that fly round the world; I am confined in bands of iron! O that I were free! O, that I were on one of your gallant decks, and under your protecting wing! Alas, betwixt me and you, the turbid waters roll. Go on, go on. O that I could also go! Could I but swim! If I could fly! O, why was I born a man, of whom to make a brute! The glad ship is gone; she hides in the dim distance. I am left in the hottest hell of unending slavery. O God, save me! God, deliver me! Let me be free![60]

Douglass' prayerful lamentation was both emotional and lyrical. "Thus I used to think, and thus I used to speak to myself," he recalled, "goaded almost to madness at one moment, and at the next reconciling myself to my wretched lot." For Douglass, the speech act served as an intellectual and emotional release, and his misery, at least for the moment, was eased through oratory.[61]

Suffering grievously under Covey's cruel treatment and unable to tolerate any more, Douglass became increasingly determined to stand up to his master. In the middle of August 1834, he engaged Covey in a two-hour fight. "This battle with Mr. Covey," Douglass later noted, "was the turning point in my career as a slave." The incident began on a Friday afternoon, during one of the hottest days of the summer. Douglass, suffering under the effects of the heat, had fallen behind in his work. Upon discovering Douglass resting in the shade, Covey savagely kicked and beat him. Once Douglass recovered from his overseer's blows, he fled to Thomas Auld's home to complain of Covey's harsh treatment, but to no avail. The next day, Douglass returned to Covey's farm. Upon Douglass' arrival, Covey approached him with whip in hand, but before Covey could reach him, Douglass fled into the cornfield and hid. He remained hidden until Sunday, when he returned to Covey's farm. All was quiet until Monday morning, when Covey, carrying "a long rope," entered the stable where Douglass was working and tried to tie him up. Douglass resisted Covey and fought back. After nearly two hours, a bleeding and bruised Covey gave up and walked away. He never whipped Douglass again.[62]

The physical victory over Covey filled Douglass with hope and revived within him a sense of his own manhood. "It recalled to life my crushed self-respect and my self-confidence," Douglass later wrote, "and inspired me with a new determination to be A FREEMAN." It was "a glorious resurrection, from the tomb of slavery, to the heaven of freedom." Douglass resolved that "however long I might remain a slave in form, the day had passed forever when I could be a slave in fact."[63]

On Christmas Day 1834, Douglass, with his term of service fulfilled, left the Covey farm and returned to the Auld residence in St. Michaels. On 1 January 1835, he was hired out to William Freeland, a local farmer, who lived approximately three miles from St. Michaels. Douglass soon discovered that Freeland was a much different master than Covey. He had "some sense of justice, . . . some feelings of humanity, . . . [and] was free from the mean and selfish characteristics which distinguished the creature from which I had now, happily, escaped." Unlike Covey, Freeland "made no profession of religion." Freeland's lack of religion was a relief for Douglass. He had discovered by experience that religious slaveholders made the worst masters. "I have found them," he recalled, "almost invariably, the vilest, meanest and basest of their class. . . . Religious slaveholders, like religious persecutors, are ever extreme in their malice and violence."[64]

Although Freeland expected his slaves to work hard, he kept the work days at a reasonable length. He gave his slaves enough to eat and good farm tools with which to work the fields. Douglass now had a master who furnished him with adequate food, clothing, and shelter. His improved physical condition revived his dreams of being a preacher, and "shoots from the tree of liberty began to put forth tender buds, and dim hopes of the future began to dawn." As he later wrote, give a slave "a *bad* master, and he aspires to a *good* master; give him a good master, and he wishes to become his *own* master."[65]

Douglass' restlessness led him to start another Sabbath school. His "school" began informally in the spring as he taught the slaves with whom he worked on Freeland's farm their letters from his Webster's spelling book and read to them from his copy of the *Columbian Orator*. As the summer approached, "and the long Sabbath days stretched themselves over our idleness," Douglass "became increasingly uneasy, and wanted to establish a more formal Sabbath school." Each Sunday, "in the woods, behind the barn, and in the shade of trees" on Freeland's farm, he secretly taught thirty young slaves how to read the Bible. He remembered the violent end of his first attempt to teach a Sabbath school in St. Michaels and was careful to keep the latest meetings secret. With the coming of winter, Douglass induced a free black man who lived several miles from Freeland's farm to permit the group to meet in his home. There he read the Bible three nights a week and on Sundays and taught his students to write their letters. Every Sunday he preached to his fellow slaves from the New Testament. It was also during this period that he delivered, to his fellow slaves, his first formal abolitionist speeches and informally debated with them the subjects of slavery and liberty. "I have met several slaves from Maryland, who were once my scholars," he later wrote, "and who obtained their freedom, I doubt not, partly in consequence of the ideas imparted to them in that school." The school, which at times numbered forty students, continued until the end of the year and constituted one of the most satisfying experiences in Douglass' life.[66]

As 1835 drew to a close, Freeland contracted with Thomas Auld to purchase the services of Douglass for 1836. During January of that year, Douglass began to devise a plan to escape. His desire for freedom had been "benumbed" under the "brutalizing dominion of Covey" and postponed by his "truly pleasant Sunday school engagements" with his friends, but it had "never entirely subsided." With the coming of the new year, Douglass vowed to escape to the North before the year ended. In February, he finalized his escape plans and cautiously disclosed them to five of his closest friends, whom he tried to persuade to join him. "Thoroughly awakened, now, with a definite vow upon me," he recalled, "all my little reading, which had any bearing on the subject of human rights, was rendered available in my communications with my friends." To convince his fellow slaves of the immorality of slavery and their right to freedom, he drew from the *Columbian Orator* "with its eloquent orations and spicy dialogues, denouncing oppression and slavery—telling of what had been dared, done and suffered by men, to obtain the inestimable boon of liberty." In his efforts to gain their support, Douglass vigorously campaigned against slavery "and dashed against it the condemning brand of God's eternal justice, which it every hour violates." Later in his life, Douglass recalled that it was during these days of working to persuade his friends to join him in his escape plot that his career in public speaking began.[67]

Having convinced the five men to join him, Douglass and his coconspirators met throughout February and March, often at night and every Sunday, to discuss their escape plot. Each was aware of the severe penalties for trying to escape, and they knew that if they were caught, they would be subjected to "cruel torture" and "sold away to the far south." Douglass decided that the Easter holidays would provide the best opportunity for an escape attempt because it was a time when restrictions would be relaxed and many slaves would be traveling from one farm to another to visit relatives and friends. Consequently, their absence from the Freeland farm would go undetected and their movements would go virtually unnoticed. On the night before Easter Sunday, they planned to steal a large canoe, paddle to the head of the Chesapeake Bay, land, and then, following the north star, walk to freedom.[68]

During the week before Easter, food was prepared and stored, clothes were packed, and Douglass wrote a pass for each of the conspirators, "giving them permission to visit Baltimore for the Easter holidays." With each day, their anxiety increased. The morning of their planned escape, the one thing happened that Douglass most feared—someone informed the authorities of the plot. Only hours before the escape was to be executed, five constables came to the Freeland farm and arrested Douglass and his coconspirators. As he was being arrested in the kitchen of the Freeland home, Douglass slipped his forged pass, "unobserved," into the fire. On their three-mile walk to St. Michaels, he passed word among his fellow prisoners to swallow the passes which he had written. "Had these passes been found," Douglass later recalled, "they would have been point blank proof against us, and would have confirmed all the statements of our betrayer." Sensing that some doubt existed over their guilt and certain that they had destroyed the only concrete evidence against them, the five slaves, upon reaching St. Michaels and being questioned by Thomas Auld, denied any plot to escape to the North. Despite their denials, the five prisoners "were literally dragged . . . behind horses, a distance of fifteen miles, and placed in the Easton jail."[69]

Now in jail, Douglass and his friends were visited by slave traders. The five young men were certain they would be sold deeper South. Soon after the Easter holidays, William Freeland arrived at the county jail and arranged for the release of all the prisoners except Douglass, who was left alone to contemplate his future. As the instigator of the escape plot, he feared the worst. After remaining alone in jail for about a week, however, Douglass was released into the custody of Thomas Auld, who took him to St. Michaels. A few days later, much to Douglass' delight, Auld informed him of plans to return him to the household of Hugh Auld in Baltimore and promised that if he behaved himself properly, he would receive his freedom at age twenty-five.[70]

Soon after Douglass' return to Baltimore, Hugh Auld, apparently following the directions of his brother, hired Douglass to William Gardiner, "an extensive shipbuilder on Fell's Point." Here, Douglass was to apprentice as a caulker, a trade he had begun to learn years earlier while in Auld's shipyard in Baltimore when his master was a master shipbuilder. Gardiner's shipyard, however, "proved to be a very unfavorable place." Shortly before Douglass arrived, the white carpenters at the shipyard had threatened to strike if the free black carpenters were not discharged. The spirit of their feelings extended beyond free blacks to slaves. Hence, when Douglass began his job as an apprentice caulker, racial tensions were extremely high.[71]

Encouraged by the "cowardly workmen," the white apprentices "did their utmost" to make it impossible for Douglass to stay. At first, they coupled their calls to him with name-calling and curses, then they made murderous threats against him, and finally they resorted to violent attacks. He could handle any of the workers singly, but he was nearly killed late in 1836 when four apprentices attacked him at once. They assailed Douglass "suddenly and simultaneously" with bricks and a hand-spike. After knocking him nearly unconscious with the hand-spike, his attackers beat him with their fists and kicked him in the head when he tried to rise.[72]

The attack ended Douglass' apprenticeship at Gardiner's shipyard. After Sophia Auld nursed him back to health and he was able to work again, Hugh Auld arranged for him to be hired out as an apprentice to Price's Shipyard in Fells Point. During his time at Price's, he rapidly became expert at his trade and within a year was earning the highest wages paid to a journeyman caulker.[73] By the end of 1837, Auld allowed Douglass to seek his own employment, make his own contracts, and collect his own earnings. Yet he still had to turn over all his earnings to his master at the end of each week—a practice that infuriated Douglass.[74]

By the spring of 1838, Douglass had grown increasingly discontented with the arrangement of surrendering all his earnings to his master and with slavery in general. Realizing he needed to find a way to save money for another escape attempt, he applied to Hugh Auld for the "privilege of hiring" his time. In return, Douglass would pay his master three dollars a week, board and clothe himself, and purchase his own caulking tools. Whatever money he earned beyond three dollars was his to keep. From May through August, Douglass was as free of his master as slaves were allowed to become. He could live the life of a freeman as long as he paid his master three dollars every week.[75]

During this period of relative independence, Douglass seized the opportunity to pursue various intellectual and religious activities. Some of the young free black caulkers with whom he worked in the shipyards could read and write and had "high notions about mental improvement." To that end, they formed a secret organization called the East Baltimore Mental Improvement Society. Douglass was the only slave to be admitted into the group. Although it was unlawful for free blacks to associate with slaves, Douglass' friends disregarded this "unnatural law" and treated him "with all respect." Before this group, he delivered speeches and was "assigned a prominent part" in formal debates. The members argued passionately over topics ranging from the status of blacks in Maryland to classical theology.[76]

From 1836 to 1838 Douglass attended the Sharp Street African Methodist Episcopal Church in Baltimore. Although the church maintained an affiliation with the white-controlled Methodist Episcopal Church, the preaching and supervision of worship were generally left in the hands of local black preachers. Douglass quickly became a class leader at the Sharp Street Church. Each Sunday after worship services he directed class meetings by inquiring into the spiritual condition of each of the dozen members assigned to his care. He also was responsible for visiting the sick and delinquent members. Being a class leader was a position of authority that carried with it a degree of respectability and prestige. That Douglass attained this position as a slave is evidence of his growing stature within the black church community. In addition to being a class leader, he was a member of the church choir, and he probably participated in numerous church sponsored community activities. After his escape, he would carry on these church activities as a free man among the black community of New Bedford, Massachusetts.[77]

Douglass continued to work hard, saving all the money he could to finance his escape. In the middle of August, Douglass delivered his wages to his master two days late, and an angry Hugh Auld ended their arrangement. Douglass would now have to live with the Aulds and follow Hugh Auld's orders. After thinking over the new arrangement, Douglass resolved once again to escape from slavery. In the three weeks prior to his escape, he made preparations for his journey north. First, he realized that he must not raise the suspicions of his master, and so he became the model, obedient slave. Second, with the help of Anna Murray, a free black and his fiancée, he carefully planned his escape. Anna suggested that Douglass impersonate a sailor. She not only altered the sailor's outfit Douglass had secured from a friend, but provided him with money to help finance his escape. Third, since all free blacks, when traveling, had to carry proof that they were not slaves, Douglass needed to obtain papers that would allow him to pass as a free man. In the days leading up to his escape, he arranged to use, and eventually to return by mail, the papers of a free sailor with whom he had become friends at the shipyard.[78]

On Monday morning, 3 September 1838, Douglass "bade farewell to the city of Baltimore, and to that slavery which had been . . . [his] abhorrence from childhood."[79] Dressed as a sailor, he boarded a train to Wilmington,

Delaware, where he transferred to a steamboat which took him up the Delaware River to Philadelphia. Arriving in Philadelphia, he boarded a train for New York City, where he arrived "safe and sound" the following morning. "The dreams of my childhood and the purposes of my manhood were now fulfilled," Douglass recalled. No longer in the clutches of slavery, he was ready to take the next steps in his career as an orator, a preacher, and an abolitionist.[80]

Notes

1. Frederick Douglass, *My Bondage and My Freedom* (1855; reprint, New York: Dover, 1969), 359.

2. Dickson J. Preston, *Young Frederick Douglass: The Maryland Years* (Baltimore, Md.: Johns Hopkins University Press, 1980), testifies to the reliability and accuracy of Douglass' recollections in his three autobiographies. In his preface, Preston writes:

   From the beginning of my search [for the facts regarding Douglass' Maryland experience] it was evident that, even as a child, Douglass had been a keen observer and a good reporter. Writing from memory without access to records about events that had occurred many years earlier, he had done a remarkable job of recalling them in detail, especially in his second autobiography, *My Bondage and My Freedom*. It was true that he had misspelled names, confused dates—including his own birth date—and in some cases distorted incidents in his antislavery zeal; but in the main his story checked out. Places, happenings, historical events, and people, even down to the identities of obscure slave children he had known only casually, could be verified from existing public and private documents. (xiv)

3. James McCune Smith, introduction to Douglass, *Bondage and Freedom*, xix.

4. Douglass was never certain of the true identity of his father. In his first autobiography, he wrote that his master was rumored to be his father, but admitted that he had no way of knowing "the correctness of this opinion" (Frederick Douglass, *Narrative, of the Life of Frederick Douglass, An American Slave, Written By Himself* [1845; reprint, New York: Signet, 1968], 21-22). In the second autobiography, Douglass again acknowledged that his master could have been his father, but conceded that "it was only a whisper, and I cannot say that I ever gave it credence" (Douglass, *Bondage and Freedom*, 58). In his third autobiography, Douglass simply stated that he knew nothing of his father (Douglass, *Life and Times, of Frederick Douglass* [1892; reprint, New York: Macmillan, 1962], 29).

5. Douglass, *Narrative*, 21; Preston, *Young Frederick Douglass*, 5-6; William S. McFeely, *Frederick Douglass* (New York: Norton, 1991), 3-5.

6. Douglass, *Bondage and Freedom*, 35-40; Preston, *Young Frederick Douglass*, 17; Raymond Gerald Fulkerson, "Frederick Douglass and the Anti-Slavery Crusade: His Career and Speeches, 1817-1861," pt. 1 (Ph.D. diss., University of Illinois, 1971), 12-13; McFeely, *Frederick Douglass*, 9.

7. Douglass, *Bondage and Freedom*, 36-37, 76; Waldo E. Martin, Jr., "Frederick Douglass," in *American Orators Before 1900: Critical Studies and Sources*, ed. Bernard K. Duffy and Halford R. Ryan (New York: Greenwood Press, 1987), 139; Sterling Stuckey, *Slave Culture: Nationalist Theory and the Foundations of Black America* (New York: Oxford University Press, 1987), 336; John W. Blassingame, *The Slave Community: Plantation Life in the Antebellum South* (New York: Oxford University Press, 1979), 127; Richard M. Dorson, ed., *American Negro Folktales* (Greenwich, Conn.: Fawcett Publications, 1967), 48, 51-52; Lawrence W. Levine, *Black Culture and Black Consciousness: Afro-American Folk Thought from Slavery to Freedom* (New York: Oxford University Press, 1977), 88-91. For a thorough discussion of Douglass' family heritage, see Preston, *Young Frederick Douglass*, 3-10. For a detailed discussion of the folk tale, see Levine, *Black Culture*, 88-120.

8. Stuckey, *Slave Culture*, 61; Albert J. Raboteau, *Slave Religion: The "Invisible Institution" in the Antebellum South* (New York: Oxford University Press, 1978), 218, 235-41; E. Franklin Frazier, *The Negro Church in America* (New York: Schocken Books, 1974), 24; Blassingame, *Slave Community*, 131; McFeely, *Frederick Douglass*, 3; Fulkerson, "Frederick Douglass," pt. 1, 12; John W. Blassingame, ed., *The Frederick Douglass Papers, Series One: Speeches, Debates, and Interviews, Volume 1*, 5 vols. (New Haven, Conn: Yale University Press, 1979), 1:xxii.

9. Douglass, *Bondage and Freedom*, 54-56.

10. Blassingame, *Slave Community*, 115, 121, 138; Raymond Hedin, "Muffled Voices: The American Slave Narrative," CLIO 10 (winter 1981): 129; John Lovell, *Black Song, the Forge and the Flame; The Story of How the Afro-American Spiritual Was Hammered Out* (New York: Macmillan, 1972), 37-39, 69; Raboteau, *Slave Religion*, 218, 226; Levine, *Black Culture*, 6-7; Douglass, *Narrative*, 31.

11. Raboteau, *Slave Religion*, 243-50, 264-65; Lovell, *Black Song*, 71-72.

12. Douglass, *Bondage and Freedom*, 97-98; Douglass, *Life and Times*, 54; Douglass, *Narrative*, 31.

13. Douglass, *Narrative*, 31-32; Douglass, *Bondage and Freedom*, 99-100; Levine, *Black Culture*, 8.

14. Douglass, *Narrative*, 35; Douglass, *Bondage and Freedom*, 116-17; Preston, *Young Frederick Douglass*, 57.

15. Douglass, *Narrative*, 36; Douglass, *Bondage and Freedom*, 117; John Sekora, "Comprehending Slavery: Language and Personal History in Douglass' *Narrative* of 1845," *CLA Journal* 29 (December 1985): 164.

16. Fulkerson, "Frederick Douglass" pt. 1, 14.

17. Douglass, *Narrative*, 24-25.

18. Preston, *Young Frederick Douglass*, 81; Fulkerson, "Frederick Douglass" pt. 1, 15-16; Douglass, *Bondage and Freedom*, 134; McFeely, *Frederick Douglass*, 26.

19. Marifrances Trivelli, "'I Knew a Ship from Stem to Stern': The Maritime World of Frederick Douglass," *The Log of Mystic Seaport* 46 (spring 1995): 98; Frank Towers, "African-American Baltimore in the Era of Frederick Douglass," *American Transcendental Quarterly* 9 (September 1995): 169, 170, 174; Dorothy Porter, "The Organized Educational Activities of Negro Literary Societies, 1828-1846," *The Journal of Negro Education* 5 (October 1936): 573.

20. Douglass, *Bondage and Freedom*, 143, 152-53.

21. Ibid., 143, 145; Douglass, *Life and Times*, 78; Preston, *Young Frederick Douglass*, 93; "The Bible Opposes Oppression, Fraud, and Wrong; An Address Delivered in Belfast, Ireland, on 6 January 1846," in Blassingame, ed., *Douglass Papers, Series One*,1:127.

22. Douglass, *Life and Times*, 78-79; Douglass, *Narrative*, 49; Douglass, *Bondage and Freedom*, 145-46.

23. Douglass, *Narrative*, 49-50; Fulkerson, "Frederick Douglass," pt. 1:16.

24. Born in Salisbury, Connecticut, on 15 April 1757, Bingham attended district school and, after graduating, was prepared for college by the local minister. In 1779 he entered Dartmouth. At graduation in 1782 he had the honor of delivering the valedictory address in Latin. After working several years as the master of Moor's Indian Charity School, he moved to Boston and taught in a private school for young ladies. In 1789 he was appointed master of one of the public reading schools, in which capacity he served the city of Boston for seven years. He then became a bookseller and publisher for the next twenty-one years. A pioneer in the writing of textbooks, he published the *American Preceptor* in 1794. Three years later he published the *Columbian Orator*, which was designed as a second part to the *American Preceptor*. For nearly a quarter of a century, these books exceeded in popularity all their competitors. They were more widely used than Webster's readers or any others, and they made Bingham nationally known (*Dictionary of American Biography*, ed. Allen Johnson [New York: Charles Scribner's Sons, 1929], 2:273-74; *The Memorial History of Boston*, ed. Justin Winsor [Boston: J.R. Osgood and Company, 1880-81], 644; Clifton Johnson, *Old-Time Schools and School-Books* [1904; reprint, Gloucester, Mass.: Peter Smith, 1963], 363; Richard L. Johannesen, "Caleb Bingham's *American Preceptor* and *Columbian Orator*," *Speech Teacher* 18 [March 1969]: 139-43).

25. Preston, *Young Frederick Douglass*, 98; Caleb Bingham, ed., *The Columbian Orator* (Boston, Mass.: Manning and Loring, 1797), title page, preface, A2.

26. Douglass is in error here. Bingham's collection does not include a speech delivered by Sheridan on behalf of Catholic emancipation. The only Sheridan

address in the *Columbian Orator* is entitled "Speech in the British Parliament: Mr. Sheridan's Speech Against Mr. Taylor." The speech Douglass appears to be referring to is an oration delivered by O'Connor in the Irish House of Commons, identified by Bingham as a speech "In Favour of the Bill on Emancipating the Roman Catholics, 1795."

27. Douglass, *Bondage and Freedom*, 158; Douglass, *Narrative*, 54-55; Douglass, *Life and Times*, 85.

28. In all three of his autobiographies, Douglass describes this dialogue and provides detailed commentary on its contents. The prominence he gives to the dialogue illustrates how strongly he felt about its message. See Douglass, *Narrative*, 54; Douglass, *Bondage and Freedom*, 157-58; Douglass, *Life and Times*, 84-85. The dialogue was reprinted in John Aikin, *Evenings at Home; or, The Juvenile Budget Opened* (London; reprinted at Salem, Mass.: Thomas C. Cushing, 1799), 4:80-87.

29. Douglass, *Bondage and Freedom*, 157-58; Bingham, ed., *Columbian Orator*, 240-42; Douglass, *Narrative*, 54.

30. Douglass, *Bondage and Freedom*, 158-59; Douglass, *Life and Times*, 85; Douglass, *Narrative*, 54-55; Waldo E. Martin, Jr., *The Mind of Frederick Douglass* (Chapel Hill: University of North Carolina Press, 1984), 8; Philip S. Foner, *Frederick Douglass* (New York: Citadel Press, 1964), 18; Preston, *Young Frederick Douglass*, 99; Bingham, ed., *Columbian Orator*, 240-42.

31. Douglass, *Narrative*, 55; David W. Blight, *Frederick Douglass' Civil War* (Baton Rouge: Louisiana State University Press, 1989), 90.

32. Bingham, ed., *Columbian Orator*, 30-32.

33. Blassingame, ed., *Douglass Papers, Series One*, 1:xxii-xxiii; Preston, *Young Frederick Douglass*, 100.

34. Bingham, ed., *Columbian Orator*, 7-29. To compose this section of his text, Bingham drew extensively from Hugh Blair's *Lectures on Rhetoric and Belles Lettres*. He also drew from the speeches of Cicero and the writings of Quintilian (Johannesen, "Bingham's *American Preceptor* and *Columbian Orator*": 141).

35. Bingham, ed., *Columbian Orator*, 7-10, 13-17.

36. Ibid.,19-23.

37. Ibid., 24.

38. Ibid., 24-29; Douglass, *Narrative*, 54-55.

39. See chapter two of this work.

40. Douglass, *Life and Times*, 84-86, 90; Douglass, *Bondage and Freedom*, 166; Preston, *Young Frederick Douglass*, 97.

41. Douglass, *Bondage and Freedom*, 166-67; Preston, *Young Frederick Douglass*, 97; McFeely, *Frederick Douglass*, 38.

42. Douglass, *Bondage and Freedom*, 51, 168-69; Douglass, *Life and Times*, 29; Martin, *Mind of Frederick Douglass*, 10; Fulkerson, "Frederick Douglass," pt. 1, 18.

43. Douglass, *Bondage and Freedom*, 169.

44. Built in 1773 at Fells Point, the Strawberry Alley church was the second oldest Methodist church in Baltimore. It was given to the black congregation after the Wilkes Street Church was built in 1816. See Henry Elliott Shepherd, ed., *History of Baltimore, Maryland: From Its Founding as a Town to the Current Year: 1729-1898* (Baltimore, Md.: S.B. Nelson, 1898), 382-83.

45. William L. Van Deburg, "Frederick Douglass and the Institutional Church," *Journal of the American Academy of Religion* 45 (June 1977): 468-69; "Boyhood in Baltimore: An Address Delivered in Baltimore, Maryland, on 6 September 1891," in *The Frederick Douglass Papers, Series One: Speeches, Debates, and Interviews*, Volume 5, ed. John W. Blassingame and John R. McKivigan (New Haven, Conn.: Yale University Press, 1992), 5:480.

46. Blassingame and McKivigan, eds., *Douglass Papers, Series One*, 5:480; Van Deburg, "Frederick Douglass": 481; Douglass, *Bondage and Freedom*, 168; Preston, *Young Frederick Douglass*, 96-97. For more information on Reverend Beverly Waugh, see Blassingame, *Douglass Papers, Series One*, 1:388-89.

47. "A Friendly Word to Maryland: An Address Delivered in Baltimore, Maryland, on 17 November 1864," in *The Frederick Douglass Papers, Series One: Speeches, Debates, and Interviews, Volume 4*, ed. John W. Blassingame and John R. McKivigan (New Haven, Conn.: Yale University Press, 1991), 4:39-40; Daniel A. Payne, *History of the African Methodist Episcopal Church* (1891; reprint, New York: Johnson Reprint Corporation, 1968), 16, 19, 112, 232-34; Richard R. Wright, *The Bishops of the African Methodist Episcopal Church* (Nashville, Tenn.: A.M.E. Sunday School Union, 1963), 355; George A. Singleton, *The Romance of African Methodism: A Study of the African Methodist Episcopal Church* (New York: Exposition Press, 1952), 30.

48. Douglass, *Bondage and Freedom*, 165-66; Blassingame and McKivigan, *Douglass Papers, Series One*, 4:40; Blassingame and McKivigan, eds., *Douglass Papers, Series One*, 5:481; McFeely, *Frederick Douglass*, 37-38.

49. Douglass, *Bondage and Freedom*, 169-70, 182-83; Blassingame and McKivigan, eds., *Douglass Papers, Series One*, 5:481.

50. Douglass, *Bondage and Freedom*, 163-64.

51. Ibid., 164-65; Preston, *Young Frederick Douglass*, 101.

52. "The Church is the Bulwark of Slavery: An Address Delivered in Boston, Massachusetts, on 25 May 1842," in Blassingame, *Douglass Papers, Series One*, 1:21-22; Douglass, *Bondage and Freedom*, 165.

53. Douglass, *Bondage and Freedom*, 183-84; Fulkerson, "Frederick Douglass," pt. 1, 20-21; Preston, *Young Frederick Douglass*, 104.

54. Douglass, *Bondage and Freedom*, 187-89, 191-202; Douglass, *Narrative*, 66-67; Fulkerson, "Frederick Douglass," pt. 1, 21.

55. Douglass, *Bondage and Freedom*, 196-97; Douglass, *Narrative*, 67; Van Deburg, "Frederick Douglass": 470.

56. Douglass, *Narrative*, 68; Douglass, *Bondage and Freedom*, 201; "I Have Come to Tell You Something About Slavery: An Address Delivered in Lynn, Massachusetts, in October 1841," in Blassingame, *Douglass Papers, Series One*, 1:3.

57. Douglass, *Bondage and Freedom*, 168, 199-200; Douglass, *Narrative*, 68; "Evangelical Man-Stealers: An Address Delivered in Manchester, England, on 12 October 1846," in Blassingame, *Douglass Papers, Series One*, 1:466.

58. Benjamin Quarles, *Frederick Douglass* (1948; reprint, New York: Atheneum, 1968), 3; Douglass, *Narrative*, 69; Preston, *Young Frederick Douglass*, 105-21.

59. Douglass, *Narrative*, 75; Fulkerson, "Frederick Douglass," pt. 1, 22-23.

60. Douglass, *Narrative*, 76-77. Douglass' apostrophe is repeated verbatim in subsequent editions of his life story. See Douglass, *Bondage and Freedom*, 219-21; Douglass, *Life and Times*, 125-26.

61. Douglass, *Narrative*, 77.

62. Ibid., 77-82.

63. Ibid., 77, 82-83; Douglass, *Bondage and Freedom*, 222-47; William W. Nichols, "Individualism and Autobiographical Art: Frederick Douglass and Henry Thoreau," *CLA Journal* 16 (December 1972): 151; William L. Andrews, *To Tell A Free Story: The First Century of Afro-American Autobiography, 1760-1865* (Urbana: University of Illinois Press, 1986), 143.

64. Douglass, *Bondage and Freedom*, 257-58; Douglass, *Narrative*, 86-87.

65. Douglass, *Bondage and Freedom*, 262-64; Fulkerson, "Frederick Douglass," pt. 1, 23-24; Van Deburg, "Frederick Douglass" 471.

66. Douglass, *Bondage and Freedom*, 263-67; Preston, *Young Frederick Douglass*, 131-32.

67. Douglass, *Bondage and Freedom*, 273-75.

68. Ibid., 276-88; Fulkerson, "Frederick Douglass," pt. 1, 24-25; Preston, *Young Frederick Douglass*, 134-35.

69. Douglass, *Bondage and Freedom*, 286-98; Fulkerson, "Frederick Douglass," pt. 1, 25.

70. Douglass, *Bondage and Freedom*, 298-303; Fulkerson, "Frederick Douglass," pt. 1, 25-26.

71. Douglass, *Bondage and Freedom*, 308-13.

72. Ibid., 312-13; Fulkerson, "Frederick Douglass," pt. 1, 26-27.

73. Caulkers could earn as much as $1.75 per day (Towers, "African-American Baltimore": 175).

74. Douglass, *Bondage and Freedom*, 318-20; Preston, *Young Frederick Douglass*, 145-46.

75. Douglass, *Bondage and Freedom*, 326-28; Fulkerson, "Frederick Douglass," pt. 1, 27.

76. Douglass, *Life and Times*, 111, 150-53; Douglass *Bondage and Freedom*, 319; Martin, *Mind of Frederick Douglass*, 11; Preston, *Young Frederick Douglass*, 148-51; Fulkerson, "Frederick Douglass," pt. 1, 27-28; *New National Era*, 6 July 1871, 2. For a discussion of associational activities of free blacks in urban America, see Leonard P. Curry, *The Free Black in Urban America, 1800-1850* (Chicago: University of Chicago Press, 1981), 201-4; Porter, "Organized Educational Activities of Negro Literary Societies," 557, 573-76.

77. Quarles, *Frederick Douglass*, 11; Edward D. Smith, *Climbing Jacob's Ladder: The Rise of Black Churches in Eastern American Cities, 1740-1877* (Washington, D. C. : Smithsonian Institution Press, 1988), 78; Terry D. Bilhartz, *Urban Religion and the Second Great Awakening: Church and Society in Early National Baltimore* (Cranbury, N. J. : Associated University Presses, 1986), 35-36.

78. Douglass, *Bondage and Freedom*, 328-32; Douglass, *Life and Times*, 189-98; McFeely, *Frederick Douglass*, 70-71; Rosetta Douglass Sprague, "Anna Murray-Douglass-My Mother As I Recall Her," *Journal of Negro History* 8 (January 1923): 95.

79. Douglass, *Bondage and Freedom*, 334.

80. Ibid., 336-37; Douglass, *Life and Times*, 199-201.

✿ *Chapter Two*

Frederick Douglass' New Bedford Experience: Oratory, Preaching, and Abolitionism September 1838-July 1841

HAVING ESCAPED FROM the grasp of slavery, Frederick Augustus Washington Bailey fled first to New York City, and then to New Bedford, Massachusetts. Although the three years Douglass spent in New Bedford have received relatively little attention from his biographers,[1] they were of incalculable importance to his growth as a speaker and his development as an abolitionist. While in New Bedford, Douglass moved primarily within the city's large and thriving black community. Discouraged by the racial prejudice he encountered in New Bedford's white churches, he joined the African Methodist Episcopal Zion Church, in which he became a class leader, an exhorter, and a licensed lay preacher. Simultaneously, he became involved in the movement to abolish slavery by attending and participating in the meetings of New Bedford's black abolitionists. Eventually, he addressed their gatherings and rose to a position of power and influence. He also became exposed to the abolitionist doctrines of William Lloyd Garrison, which helped prepare him for the rhetorical work he would begin as a lecturer for the Massachusetts Anti-Slavery Society in 1841.

I

When Douglass stepped off the train on Tuesday, 4 September 1838, in New York City, he had passed, in fewer than twenty-four hours, from slavery to freedom. He later recalled his feelings at that moment: "A free state around me, and a free earth under my feet! What a moment was this to me! A whole year was pressed into a single day. A new world burst upon my agitated vision." It was, he wrote later, a moment of "joyous excitement" which words could never fully describe.[2]

Those feelings, however, were short-lived. Soon after Douglass' arrival in New York, he unexpectedly met a fugitive slave whom he had known in Baltimore. The fellow fugitive warned Douglass to "trust no man"—black or white—with his secret, for the city was full of "hired men on the lookout for fugitives from slavery, and who, for a few dollars, would betray . . . [him] into the hands of the slave-catchers." The fugitive also cautioned Douglass against going to the wharves to find work, or to black boardinghouses for lodging, "for all such places were closely watched." Deeply discouraged, Douglass wandered the streets of the city for several days with a sense of "loneliness and insecurity."[3]

After nearly a week of living on the streets and feeling he could no longer keep his secret to himself, Douglass felt compelled to disclose his situation to "some one who should befriend me without taking advantage of my destitution to betray me." He chose a sailor, "warm-hearted and generous," who listened to his story with "a brother's interest." The sailor took the distressed fugitive to his home for the night. The next morning, he escorted Douglass to the boardinghouse of David Ruggles, then the secretary of the New York Vigilance Committee, an organization of black men and women who worked to protect fugitive slaves during their stopover in New York City and to direct them to safe refuges in the North or in Canada. In addition, Vigilance Committee members were expected to feed and clothe runaways and send them to points of safety with money and letters of introduction. As a leading member of the Vigilance Committee, Ruggles was among the most daring and active conductors of the Underground Railroad. Douglass later described him as "a whole-souled man, fully imbued with a love of his afflicted and hunted people," who "took pleasure in being to me, as was his wont, 'Eyes to the blind, and legs to the lame.'"[4]

Finding sanctuary in Ruggles' boardinghouse, Douglass wrote a letter to his fiancée, Anna Murray, informing her of his safe arrival and requesting that she leave Baltimore and join him at once. While he anxiously awaited her arrival, Douglass changed his last name from Bailey to Johnson. By assuming a different surname, he hoped to confuse any slave hunter who might travel north in an effort to return him to slavery. Anna finally joined him on 12 or 13 September, and they were married on 15 September by the Rev. James W. C. Pennington, a former Maryland slave and an active abolitionist who was just beginning his career as a Presbyterian minister.[5]

After learning that Douglass was a caulker by trade, Ruggles selected New Bedford, Massachusetts, as the "proper place" for the young fugitive and his wife to live. Ruggles believed that New Bedford, with its thriving shipbuilding and whaling business, was a spot where Douglass could "make a good living."[6] Before Frederick and Anna departed, Ruggles gave them five dollars and a letter of introduction to Nathan Johnson, a prominent black abolitionist in New Bedford. Johnson and his wife, Polly, owned and operated a confectionery business, and their store was an active station on the Underground Railroad.[7]

When the Douglasses arrived in New Bedford, the Johnsons received them "kindly and hospitably" and immediately took a "deep and lively interest" in their welfare.[8] The Johnsons provided food and shelter and advised the young couple on how to secure those necessities for themselves. Nathan Johnson made one other important contribution—he gave Frederick and Anna a new last name. Since his arrival in New Bedford, Douglass had come to realize that the name Johnson was "so numerous as to cause some confusion in distinguishing one [person] from another."[9] Nathan Johnson, who had been reading Sir Walter Scott's *Lady of the Lake*, suggested that Douglass assume the last name of the heroine of the book. The young fugitive readily agreed, and from that point on he was known as Frederick Douglass.[10]

Douglass spent his first afternoon in New Bedford "visiting the wharves and viewing the shipping." The docks, he discovered, were a busy place. Men were engaged in loading and unloading the whaling ships that lined the harbor and brought great wealth and prosperity to the city. Indeed, New Bedford's "solid wealth and grandeur" astonished the newly arrived fugitive. While in slavery, Douglass had "strangely supposed . . . that few of the comforts, and scarcely any of the luxuries, of life were enjoyed at the north, compared with what were enjoyed by the slaveholders in the south." Since northern people owned no slaves, he reasoned, "I supposed that they were about upon the level with the non-slaveholding population of the south." Hence, "in the absence of slaves there could be no wealth, and very little refinement." Douglass quickly discovered he was wrong. New Bedford was a city of "splendid churches, beautiful dwellings, and finely cultivated gardens" in which "every thing looked clean, new and beautiful." Douglass saw "few or no dilapidated houses, with poverty-stricken inmates; no half-naked children and bare footed women," such as he had been accustomed to seeing as a slave in Maryland.[11]

It was the living conditions of the black community, however, that most surprised Douglass. Later in his life he wrote of how he "found many, who had not been seven years out of their chains, living in finer houses, and evidently enjoying more of the comforts of life, than the average of slaveholders in Maryland." His friend Nathan Johnson "lived in a neater house; dined at a better table; took, paid for, and read, more newspapers; better understood the moral, religious, and political character of the nation than nine tenths of the slaveholders in Talbot County, Maryland." Nor was this Douglass' view alone. In July 1837 a correspondent for the *Colored*

American reported that the "people of color" in New Bedford "are, perhaps, according to their number, better off than in any other place; nearly all of them, who are resident citizens, owning their own houses and lots, and many a number of houses, and are quite rich."[12]

New Bedford was a culturally diverse community. Among its 12,000 residents were Wamponoag Indians, Portuguese and other Europeans, Africans, Asians, and Polynesians. The city's guiding influence, however, came from the Quaker ship owners and merchants who believed in hard work, strict self-discipline, complete honesty, and equality and freedom of thought for all. Their names could be found on the boards of directors and among the administrators of nearly all the commercial companies, banks, and social, intellectual, and philanthropic organizations in the city. Later in his life, Douglass noted how the "sight of the broad brim and the plain, Quaker dress . . . greatly increased" his sense of freedom and security in New Bedford.[13]

Frederick and Anna quickly became part of New Bedford's free black community. Not surprisingly, in a port city with a transient population, two-thirds of the black people were men. The black community, which numbered over 1,000, was composed, predominantly, of the descendants of former slaves who had earned their freedom or been emancipated by their owners. There were also Africans from the Cape Verde Islands who had joined crews of whaling ships and later settled in New Bedford. In addition, there were blacks of West Indian descent who, on every 1 August since 1834, had commemorated the abolition of slavery in the West Indies with a parade, speeches, and a festive picnic. Finally, there were fugitive slaves who used New Bedford as a sanctuary for a new life of freedom and economic independence. Taken together, by 1838 the black community of New Bedford had achieved a measure of independence that made this place, according to one historian, "the best city in America for an ambitious young black man."[14]

In New Bedford, Douglass found safe "refuge from the hunters of men." There was strong resolve among the black population to protect one another from the "blood-thirsty kidnapper, at all hazards." This determination, moreover, extended into New Bedford at large. Nathan Johnson assured Douglass that "no slaveholder could take a slave out of New Bedford." The young fugitive, Johnson counseled, need not fear recapture and return to slavery because "there were men who would lay down their lives to save . . . [him] from such a fate." As one nineteenth-century New Bedford historian wrote, "It is said that at one time in the early part of the present century there was hardly a house in the place which had not given shelter and succor to a fugitive slave."[15]

II

As safe and humane a place as New Bedford seemed to be, Douglass quickly discovered that it was not free from racial prejudice. Just four days after arriving, he went in pursuit of a job as a caulker. His quest ended abruptly when, after being hired to caulk a ship fitting out to sea, he was told that "every white man would leave the ship in her unfinished condition" if he proceeded to work on it. Compelled to accept the fact that prejudice against black people was not confined to the South, and quickly realizing he would not be able to practice his trade as a caulker, Douglass was forced to accept any job he could find. Over the next few months he sawed wood, dug cellars, shoveled coal, swept chimneys, rolled oil casks on the wharves, helped load sailing vessels, and worked in a candle factory and a brass foundry.[16]

Douglass not only encountered racial prejudice in his search for employment, but also in the churches. On the first Sunday after arriving in New Bedford, he attended a service at the Elm Street Methodist Church. Although forced on account of his color to sit in the balcony rather than with the predominantly white congregation, Douglass went along with this proscription "as an accommodation of the unconverted congregation who had not yet been won to Christ and his brotherhood." Douglass believed that once he was converted, the white congregation would certainly treat him "as a man and a brother." He soon discovered, much to his "astonishment and mortification," that these "charitable assumptions" were false.[17]

The incident that revealed to Douglass the "exact position" of the Elm Street church on racial matters came one Sunday during the sacrament of Holy Communion. Douglass later described the scene:

> The white members went forward to the altar by the bench full; and when it was evident that all the whites had been served with the bread and wine, Brother Bonney . . . after a long pause, as if inquiring whether all the white members had been served, and fully assuring himself on that important point, then raised his voice to an unnatural pitch, and looking to the corner where his black sheep seemed penned, beckoned with his hand, exclaiming, "Come forward, colored friends!—come forward! You, too, have an interest in the blood of Christ. God is no respecter of persons. Come forward, and take this holy sacrament to your comfort!" The colored members—poor, slavish souls—went forward, as invited. I went *out*, and have never been in that church since, although I honestly went there with a view to joining that body.[18]

Douglass tried other churches in New Bedford "with the same result." So disturbed was he with this treatment that his experiences with northern prejudice in the churches of New Bedford would find their way into many of his early antislavery speeches.[19]

After being rebuffed at several white churches in New Bedford, Douglass joined "a small body of colored Methodists, known as the Zion Methodists," a congregation in the African Methodist Episcopal (A. M. E.) Zion denomination. The A.M.E. Zion Church had been founded by black Methodists in New York City in 1796 in an effort to escape the discriminatory practices that existed within the white church. After meeting in a rented house for four years, the congregation moved to a newly erected edifice which they named the African Methodist Episcopal Zion Church. In 1821 the A.M.E. Zion Church was firmly established when the leaders of the church voted themselves out of the Methodist Episcopal Church and organized a church government of their own. One year later James Varick was elected the first bishop of the church. By the early 1840s, A.M.E. Zion missionaries had extended the church throughout New York, New Jersey, Connecticut, Pennsylvania, Rhode Island, and Massachusetts. Missionaries also helped organize churches in Delaware, Maryland, and the District of Columbia.[20]

The A.M.E. Zion Church became a leader in the struggle to abolish slavery in the United States. Church leaders encouraged members to speak out against slavery and racism, and Zion ministers were often active in the antislavery movement. Slavery and prejudice were often addressed from the pulpit, and a concerted effort was made to keep before the North the injustice and immorality of human servitude. In addition, in a period when few churches would open their doors to the abolitionists for antislavery meetings, the Zion church was never closed to people who wanted to plead for the oppressed. Attracted to the A.M.E. Zion Church by its antislavery philosophy, Douglass found it quite compatible with his own feelings on slavery and freedom.[21]

Soon after joining New Bedford's Zion church in 1838, Douglass distinguished himself as a leading member of the congregation. Later in his life, he credited the pastor, Rev. William Serrington, as the person who attracted him to the small schoolhouse church on Second Street. "I found him a man of deep piety, and of high intelligence," Douglass recalled. "His character attracted me, and I received from him much excellent advice and brotherly sympathy." Under Serrington's guidance, Douglass became active in the church, serving, at various times, in official church capacities as sexton, Sunday school superintendent, steward, class leader, clerk, and exhorter.[22]

As Sunday school superintendent, Douglass was responsible for coordinating and overseeing one of the most important functions of the church—the education of its members. From its beginning, the A.M.E. Zion Church stressed education and training through the church. Sunday school constituted a major part of this effort, and children and adults alike were expected to participate in the school. As superintendent, Douglass was required to monitor the general condition of the Sunday school and report any problems or concerns directly to Reverend Serrington. As a class leader, Douglass had responsibility for the education of at least ten members of the congregation. Any person wishing to become a member of the church was assigned to a class, in which they would learn about Methodism and Christianity. Douglass was expected to meet his class at least one hour each Sunday. In addition, he was required to "pray earnestly" for his students and to "diligently instruct and exhort" them "at their own houses."[23]

Both of these positions—Sunday school superintendent and class leader—elevated Douglass' status within the black community. As superintendent, he was recognized by the congregation and by Reverend Serrington as the leader of the Sunday school—a position of prestige and responsibility. As a class leader, Douglass had many opportunities for oral expression in private, one-on-one situations, as well as in small-group and public settings. Undoubtedly, he took advantage of these instances to practice and improve upon his public speaking skills. Being a class leader also provided Douglass with countless occasions to advance his knowledge of the Bible, of Methodism, and of Christianity in general.

Even more important was Serrington's recommendation that Douglass be licensed as an exhorter, which was the first step toward the ministry. An exhorter was a "religious public speaker," allowed to read a Scripture lesson to the congregation during a church service and to offer a practical explanation and application of the Scripture reading. To become an exhorter, Douglass had to be a member of the church in good standing, be "of good moral and Christian characters," and be recommended by the pastor. In addition, he had to pass an examination by the pastor and deliver an exhortation to the congregation in the presence of the members of the Quarterly Conference, a local court of the church composed of all local preachers, exhorters, traveling preachers, local deacons, elders, class leaders, trustees, stewards, superintendents of the Sabbath school, and the pastor of the church. Douglass easily passed these prerequisites for, in essence, he had been exhorting since his days in Maryland, where he had secretly taught his fellow slaves from the Bible in his own Sabbath schools in St. Michaels and Baltimore. Now, however, he could serve as an exhorter in an official, church-sanctioned capacity, which must have bolstered his confidence as an orator and unquestionably advanced his position within the black congregation. He received his license as an exhorter in 1839. The license was good for one year and had to be renewed annually.[24]

It is impossible to know exactly how often Douglass addressed the congregation in New Bedford's Zion chapel in his capacity as an exhorter, but one of the guidelines in the *Doctrines and Discipline of the African*

Methodist Episcopal Zion Church was that preachers were expected to allow exhorters to speak "often." There is every reason to believe that Serrington permitted Douglass to exhort frequently, for he saw him as a potential minister and leader of the church. Indeed, Douglass was so successful as an exhorter that the next year he was recommended for licensing as a local preacher. The recommendation was made by Rev. Thomas James, who took over as pastor in 1840. A remarkable man, James was born into slavery, escaped at the age of seventeen, and eventually became an ordained A.M.E. Zion minister in 1833. Soon after being ordained, James moved to Rochester, New York, where, in addition to his religious duties, he engaged in a variety of antislavery activities. He organized a local abolitionist society, lectured against slavery throughout New York state, and edited and published a biweekly newspaper called the *Rights of Man*. In 1835 James left Rochester to found a church in Syracuse, where he remained for three years before being transferred to Ithaca, New York. In early 1840 he was transferred to Sag Harbor, Long Island, and then later in the year moved on to New Bedford.[25]

Sometime after his arrival in New Bedford, James was impressed with Douglass' exhorting and public speaking abilities and set him on course to become a local preacher. The process of being licensed as a preacher was similar to that of being licensed as an exhorter. The pastor had to interview Douglass to "ascertain his qualifications for the work." Next, Douglass had to deliver a trial sermon before the congregation and in front of the Quarterly Conference so that all members could observe his qualifications firsthand. After these steps, James was satisfied with Douglass' "gifts, grace, and usefulness," and recommended him to the next Quarterly Conference, which granted him a license to preach the gospel for one year within the local church only.[26]

In the A.M.E. Zion Church, "proclamation of the word" occupied "a place of the highest priority." The congregation could gather as many as three times a day to experience the Scriptures and the sermon. Services could be scheduled in the morning, afternoon, and evening. But regardless of when the service took place, preaching was regarded as the centerpiece of the worship experience. According to one A.M.E. Zion historian, congregations expected the preacher's sermon to engage them totally. The ideal sermon was supposed to "appeal to the intellect (the mind), the emotion (the feeling), and the volition (the will)" of each congregant. As an A.M.E. Zion preacher, Douglass learned to deliver sermons that involved the whole person, a talent he later carried to the abolitionist platform.[27]

Douglass received his first formal training as a public speaker during his time as a licensed A.M.E. Zion preacher. Part of that training came from James who, as pastor of the church, was expected to work closely with Douglass.[28] In addition, Douglass learned about preaching from the

Doctrines and Discipline of the African Methodist Episcopal Zion Church.
A comprehensive guide to the conduct expected of A.M.E. Zion preachers,
the *Doctrines and Discipline* also offered advice on the "Matter and
Manner of Preaching." There were, it counseled, four major steps to
preaching a sermon: first, "to convince"; second, "to offer Christ"; third,
"to invite"; fourth, "to build up, and to do this, in some measure, in every
sermon." The *Doctrines and Discipline* also presented nine additional
directions to follow when preaching to a congregation:

> There are some smaller advices, which may be of use to the
> preachers in general, such as these: 1. Be sure never to disappoint
> a congregation. 2. Begin at the time appointed. 3. Let their whole
> deportment be serious, weighty, and solemn. 4. Always suit their
> subject to their audience. 5. Choose the plainest text they can. 6.
> Take care not to ramble, but keep to the text, and make out what
> they take in hand. 7. Take care of any thing awkward or affected,
> either in their gesture, phrase or pronunciation. 8. Frequently
> read and enlarge upon a portion of scripture . . . 9. Always avail
> themselves to the great festivals, by preaching on the occasion.[29]

According to one church historian, these "advices" were in fact rules that
"were strongly enforced and vigorously encouraged."[30]

In addition, Douglass was expected to strive to meet other expectations
set forth in the *Doctrines and Discipline*. He was required to be "plain in
apparel," for "simple neatness was the general rule." In administering the
word, he was advised to preach with "ministerial earnestness, simplicity,
directness, and spirituality." He should aim his message "to the heart
through the medium of understanding." To accomplish this, he was directed to speak in "plain language" and to use "simple and forcible figures" so
as "to suit the comprehension of the uninformed." We can imagine
Douglass found these rules quite sensible, for they complemented the
advice he had read in Caleb Bingham's *Columbian Orator* to speak naturally, sincerely, and directly.[31] From all indications, Douglass preached
often to the New Bedford congregation. One of James' duties was to give
local preachers frequent "opportunities to preach and to be employed in
the work of the Master's vineyard." According to Douglass, James lived up
to this duty by having him occupy the pulpit on a regular basis—so regularly, in fact, that the *New Bedford Directory* identified Douglass' occupation as "Reverend."[32]

Not only did Douglass participate in New Bedford's A.M.E. Zion Church
by serving as a class leader, exhorter, and local preacher, he also had many
opportunities to witness distinguished black preachers delivering powerful
sermons and antislavery lectures. Besides listening to the preachers
assigned to his own congregation, he took a keen interest in the addresses

of highly talented pulpit orators and antislavery leaders such as Jehiel C. Beman, Dempsey Kennedy, John P. Thompson, and Leven Smith—all of whom spoke at New Bedford's Zion chapel.[33] In addition, Douglass became friends with Christopher Rush, the highly esteemed bishop of the A.M.E. Zion Church. An outstanding preacher with a commanding style, "rare oratorical powers," and "deep piety," Rush was regarded by Zionites "as the ablest preacher of his time." Douglass considered him one of the greatest speakers he ever heard.[34]

Rush and the other distinguished A.M.E. Zion pastors who visited New Bedford strongly influenced Douglass and contributed to his development as a prospective race leader, abolitionist, and orator. Listening to them gave Douglass a sense of the issues, the gestures, the cadences, and the oral style of preaching, and he likely worked to imitate in his own public speaking efforts many of the things he heard and saw in their speeches. "It is impossible for me to tell how far my connection with these devoted men influenced my career," Douglass reflected years later. "No doubt . . . the exercise of my gifts in this vocation, and my association with the excellent men to whom I have referred, helped to prepare me for the wider sphere of usefulness which I have since occupied." Indeed, during a speech in 1870 Douglass recalled that as an exhorter and licensed preacher, he "was as denunciatory of slavery as at any time since."[35]

III

Because most studies of Douglass have overlooked the importance of his activities in the A.M.E. Zion Church, they have tended to overstate the influence of William Lloyd Garrison on Douglass. For instance, according to William S. McFeely, Douglass, after hearing Garrison for the first time in April 1839, "found what he himself would become. He would become an orator—not a playacting orator, privately declaiming the great speeches of other men learned from the *Columbian Orator*, but a man speaking out for himself."[36] Of course, by 1839 Douglass was already speaking out for himself. During his years in slavery and especially in his capacities as class leader and exhorter in New Bedford's A.M.E. Zion Church, he had ample opportunities to speak publicly, and his identity both as an orator and an abolitionist was established well before he heard Garrison speak. Yet there can be no doubt that Garrison did influence Douglass. "It may have been due to my having been a slave, and my intense hatred of slavery," he recalled in 1889, "but no face and form ever impressed me with such sentiments and such hopes as did those of William Lloyd Garrison . . . His power was not in a fine flow of dazzling rhetoric, but in his character, his convictions, and his high moral purpose."[37]

During an April 1839 visit to New Bedford to attend the semiannual meeting of the Bristol County Anti-Slavery Society, Garrison delivered an antislavery lecture before the Young Men's Anti-Slavery Society in the Old Congregational Meetinghouse. One witness recorded that Garrison's lecture, presented on a rainy evening before a "pretty well filled" house, "was interesting and impressive, liberal in the application of denunciatory passages of Scripture to the sin of slavery but generally in a very calm and serious manner." Another member of the audience noted that the address "was listened to with deep and thrilling interest for the space of nearly two hours." Yet another observer wrote that the lecture was replete with "plain facts" and "powerful arguments" that "must rapidly roll on the car of equal rights, and universal freedom."[38]

This marked Douglass' first opportunity to hear Garrison speak, and he did not miss it. "Soon after becoming a reader of the *Liberator*," Douglass recalled in 1892, "it was my privilege to listen to a lecture . . . by William Lloyd Garrison, its editor." Even fifty years after the event, Douglass remembered the main directions of Garrison's message. "His Bible was his textbook, held sacred as the very word of the Eternal Father," Douglass recalled. "He believed in sinless perfection, complete submission to insults and injuries, and literal obedience to the injunction if smitten 'on one cheek to turn the other also.'" Garrison also denounced racial prejudice as "*rebellion against God*," lambasted those ministers "who defended slavery from the Bible" as being fathered by the devil, proclaimed those churches "which fellowshipped with slaveholders as Christians" as "synagogues of Satan," and characterized the United States as "a nation of liars."[39]

Douglass was equally impressed with Garrison's platform presence and delivery. He found the abolitionist leader a "young man of a singularly pleasing countenance, . . . never loud and noisy, but calm and serene as a summer sky, and as pure." His style of speaking, Douglass noted, "would not be called eloquent. There was no fine flow of words, no dazzling sentences framed to tickle and please the ear." Yet, said Douglass, Garrison gave powerful and effective voice to the cause of truth and liberation: "There he stood erect, self-poised, and serene, neither bewailing his hardships, nor glorying in his triumphs—but steadfastly insisting upon the immediate unconditional emancipation as the right of the slave and the duty of the whole country." As Douglass sat in the Old Congregational Meetinghouse listening to Garrison's words, "mighty in truth, mighty in their simple earnestness," he was overwhelmed. "When I heard Mr. Garrison for the first time uttering the thoughts which had struggled to find expression in my own heart," Douglass later recalled, "I saw the deadened hopes of my race resurrected and ascended." He immediately viewed Garrison as "the Moses raised up by God, to deliver His modern Israel from bondage."[40]

Douglass' conversion to Garrisonianism was also advanced by his reading of the *Liberator*. After living in New Bedford for four or five months, he
was solicited to subscribe to Garrison's weekly newspaper. Being that he
had recently escaped from slavery and was "of course very poor and had
no money to pay for it," Douglass declined. The solicitor, however, was
willing to make Douglass a subscriber despite his inability to pay. From
that time forward, Douglass "was brought into contact with the mind of
William Lloyd Garrison."[41]

Although Douglass had proclaimed himself an abolitionist in December
1831, he was, as he noted in later years, "ignorant of the philosophy of the
movement" until he subscribed to the *Liberator*. The paper became
Douglass' "meat and . . . drink." The first lesson he learned from it, he
noted during a speech in 1848, came "from its motto . . . 'My country is the
world—my countrymen, mankind.'" This statement, Douglass revealed,
"was all inspiring. . . . It was a new idea, *and one worthy the cause* to
which the *Liberator* was zealously devoted." The newspaper also filled him
with hope. Its sympathy for the slave, its "scathing denunciations of slaveholders," its exposure of the evils of slavery, and its mighty attacks upon
the upholders of the peculiar institution "sent a thrill of joy" through his
soul. Most important, the paper demanded the complete and immediate
emancipation of the slave. "I *loved* this paper, and its editor," Douglass
recalled. "His words were few, full of holy fire, and straight to the point."
The *Liberator* was published weekly, and each week Douglass made himself "master of its contents." Before long he had "a clear apprehension of
the principles of the anti-slavery movement."[42]

In essence, the *Liberator* became Douglass' textbook on abolition and
Garrison became his teacher. Week after week, Douglass read in the pages
of the *Liberator* Garrison's views on women's rights, nonresistance, and
opposition to political action. Week after week, he drank in Garrison's
harsh, uncompromising language, his strongly worded attacks on the
churches and its ministers, his insistence that slavery was a sin in the sight
of God, and his unyielding demand for unconditional emancipation. He
also found, in Garrison's insistence on the superiority of moral suasion
over political action, confirmation of his own sense of the power of language to bring about social change. Time and again, Garrison expressed his
"faith in the power of truth to overcome the evil that is in the world." He
argued that "Jesus and his apostles had no political power—*they sought
none*—they only 'talked' against idolatry, oppression and all iniquity,
whether legalized or otherwise." They, like abolitionists, relied on preaching, "and yet they accomplished something for the world, even though they
were not politicians." Surely, Douglass was encouraged when he read such
words. By October 1840 he was a licensed lay preacher in New Bedford's
A.M.E. Zion Church, and he knew from his own experience the power of

speech. Moreover, from the *Columbian Orator* he had learned that oratory had the capacity to "scatter the clouds of ignorance and error from the
atmosphere of reason" and to "remove the film of prejudice from the mental eye." In his heart, Douglass knew Garrison was right—that through
preaching the truth something could be accomplished in this world, perhaps even something as revolutionary as the abolition of slavery.[43]

IV

As Douglass was reading the *Liberator* and thinking about the principles of
Garrisonian abolition, he also began attending and participating in the
meetings of New Bedford's abolitionists. Those meetings included regular
monthly gatherings of the New Bedford Young Men's Anti-Slavery Society,
as well as a number of public lectures and gatherings called to deal with
exigent issues and crises.[44] John Bailey, president of the New Bedford Anti-
Slavery Society, invited leaders of New England's abolition movement to
address the monthly gatherings. Among the speakers Douglass recalled listening to were Henry C. Wright, Stephen S. Foster, James N. Buffum,
Edwin Thompson, Nathaniel Whiting, Edmund Quincy, Wendell Phillips,
Parker Pillsbury, and Garrison. These men, he recalled, were "distinguished for their eloquence."[45] In addition, black abolitionists met weekly
at Bailey's home for the purpose of discussing "anti-slavery principles and
events." During these meetings, reported a correspondent to the *National
Anti-Slavery Standard*, "the colored people acquire the habit of thinking
and speaking; a circumstance which may in great measure, account for the
self-possession of their manners, and the propriety and fluency of their
language."[46] Blacks in New Bedford also held special sessions to discuss
pressing issues facing them and the abolition movement and to draft and
pass resolutions expressing their views. All of these meetings presented
Douglass with opportunities to nurture his understanding of abolitionism
and of oratory.

From the outset, Douglass participated in New Bedford's abolitionist
meetings. In his second autobiography, published in 1855, he stated, "All
the anti-slavery meetings held in New Bedford I promptly attended, my
heart burning at every true utterance against the slave system, and every
rebuke of its friends and supporters."[47] In addition, there are several
recorded instances of Douglass speaking at the meetings of black abolitionists, and by June 1841 he had achieved such status among them that
he was elected chair of one of their meetings.

The first recorded instance of Douglass speaking at an antislavery meeting occurred during a gathering of black abolitionists in March 1839 to
protest efforts by the American Colonization Society to revitalize the colonization movement in the North.[48] Facing serious debt in 1838, the

Colonization Society was forced to reorganize or perish. During its annual meeting in August 1838, the society passed a new constitution and appointed a new president, Samuel Wilkeson, a wealthy real estate promoter from Buffalo, New York, who was charged with the tasks of restoring the society's finances and revitalizing the colonization movement. He ordered agents to collect money for the ailing society and to solicit support for colonization over emancipation. The agents sent to New England were Ralph R. Gurley and Elliot Cresson. Gurley was the secretary and general agent of the society. Cresson, a Quaker and a successful merchant from Philadelphia, was considered to be among the society's most outspoken proponents of colonization. Their efforts to revitalize the colonization movement met with strong disapproval from free blacks throughout the North. Blacks in Boston, Philadelphia, New York, New Bedford, and other cities met to denounce the American Colonization Society's revitalization campaign and to formulate responses.[49]

On Tuesday evening, 12 March 1839, an "immense assembly" of New Bedford's black citizens gathered at the Third Christian Church and joined the anticolonization chorus by declaring solidarity with their "brethren in New York, Boston, and elsewhere." Douglass was reported as being one of ten speakers who "ably sustained" resolutions condemning the American Colonization Society. Reverend William Serrington, pastor of New Bedford's A.M.E. Zion Church, was also listed among the names of those who participated. Perhaps his presence inspired Douglass, who had been recently licensed as an exhorter within the church, to speak on this occasion.[50] Although there is no written record of what Douglass said, the resolutions that appear in the minutes offer a sense of what was discussed and debated. During the course of the gathering, the attendants resolved that black people "are *American citizens* born with natural, inherent, just, and inalienable rights." The American Colonization Society, they declared, "shall never entice or drive us from our native soil." The meeting resolved that the current campaign waged by the society "shall have no other effect, than to call into vigorous exercise our dormant energies." In addition, the meeting declared that as long as the agents of the Colonization Society continued to press the "detestable subject" of colonization upon the black citizenry despite their "entreaties, remonstrances and protestations," New Bedford's black population would "continue to reject all future plans with honest *indignation* and *contempt.*" Black people everywhere, they resolved, should "use all just means to hasten the downfall of the now tottering fabric of Colonizationism" and use "the dissemination of anti-slavery principles as an efficient means in bringing it about."[51] These strongly worded resolutions reflected the depth of anger and frustration felt by New Bedford blacks toward the colonizationists' campaign. It is worth noting that the meeting also passed a strong endorsement of Garrison and his moral crusade against slavery. Douglass joined in unanimously adopting a resolution praising Garrison as "the uncompromising advocate of immediate and unconditional emancipation" who "is still deserving of our confidence and support."[52]

Occasionally, a special meeting of New Bedford's black abolitionists would be called to listen to a guest speaker. On Sunday evening, 30 May 1841, Douglass attended a lecture delivered to a meeting of black citizens at the city's forum by Rev. Henry Highland Garnet of Troy, New York. Garnet's audience "listened to an address on slavery, prejudice against color, and colonization," reported a correspondent to the *Liberator*, and he delivered the speech in an "eloquent, forcible and argumentative manner to the satisfaction of the vast assemblage." Garnet made a strong impression on Douglass. Seventeen years later, he recalled that Garnet's address "excited in his breast a new hope for the elevation of his downtrodden race." In 1891 he again recounted the dramatic impact of Garnet's words. "Before hearing him I thought I was a man," Douglass said, "but after hearing him I knew I was a man and a man among men."[53]

Approximately one week after Garnet's appearance, on Monday evening, 7 June 1841, New Bedford's black citizens gathered at the Third Christian Church to pass resolutions honoring Garnet and his address. Having been powerfully affected by Garnet's lecture, Douglass would likely have been in attendance and would have joined in unanimously passing resolutions hailing Garnet's speech "as auspicious in the history of our people, and we feel assured that all who heard the speaker were fully convinced that *mind* has no complexional latitude." Garnet, the meeting resolved, is a "fearless, uncompromising and consistent advocate of universal liberty and equality."[54]

Exactly one month after Garnet's address, at a large "Meeting of Colored Citizens" in New Bedford's Third Christian Church, Douglass chaired a meeting that passed a resolution strongly condemning "the desperate efforts" of a recent convention of the Maryland Colonization Society "to revive their wicked scheme . . . to remove the free colored people out of the State by coercion." The resolution stated that such a scheme to expatriate black people would excite "the public mind to increase the prejudice that now exercises so baneful an influence against" people of color. Douglass' election as chair of the meeting demonstrated his growing prominence in the black community. He also had a special interest in the Maryland Colonization Society's proceedings. He still had close friends in Baltimore who could be directly affected by any plans to expatriate Maryland's free black citizens. In addition, he had been a slave in Maryland and was married to a free black woman from that state. These circumstances, in combination with the anticolonization stand Douglass had taken two years earlier at the 12 March 1839 meeting, may have influenced those present at the meeting to elect him chair. Whatever the reasons for his election, it gave him a say over the final wording of the resolutions and how they were reported to the *Liberator* and other antislavery newspapers.[55]

Besides condemning the proceedings of the Maryland Colonization Society, the meeting passed a resolution expressing its sympathy for the black people of Maryland, "over whose heads the storm of persecution is gathering." Those assembled expressed their hopes that their brothers and sisters would not be "intimidated by threats of expatriation from their native land, but to remain unmoved and place an unwavering reliance upon this omnipotence of truth, and believe that the demands of justice will be heard, and that the voice of bleeding humanity will melt their obdurate hearts, and that God in his mercy will deliver them out of the hands of the spoiler." In another resolution, the meeting condemned the racial prejudice and cruel treatment accorded David Ruggles, who had helped Douglass make the move from New York to New Bedford after his escape from slavery, by the white captain of the steamboat *Telegraph* during a voyage between New Bedford and Nantucket on 19 June 1841. Ruggles had been roughly handled for denouncing and resisting the segregated quarters on the vessel. Unquestionably, Douglass felt a sense of loyalty to Ruggles and a sense of indignation toward the violent manner in which he had been treated. The members of the meeting viewed the "unjust assault" on Ruggles as "an open violation of the laws of this Commonwealth" and as "unworthy of the head or heart of any man who claims an inheritance to the Bay State." The black abolitionists called on the "friends of Liberty to discountenance so insufferable an outrage on equal rights." Although we cannot know the extent to which Douglass was personally responsible for the resolutions, they likely reflected his language and perspective—especially given his role as chair of the meeting and his deep personal involvement in the issues addressed by the resolutions.[56]

Two weeks later, on the evening of Monday, 12 July 1841, New Bedford's black citizens met to "take into consideration the outrage recently committed upon the person of David Ruggles of New-York, at the rail-road depot of this town." Douglass, who had chaired the previous meeting of black citizens that had denounced Ruggles' treatment aboard the steamboat *Telegraph*, most likely attended and participated in this meeting as well. Ruggles, after all, had provided him refuge in New York during his successful escape attempt and had recommended New Bedford as a safe place to settle. After Ruggles had made a few remarks and stated "the facts of the case," the meeting passed a strongly worded resolution condemning the "*inhuman*" assault on Ruggles.[57]

In addition to attending the monthly sessions of the New Bedford Anti-Slavery Society and the meetings of New Bedford's black abolitionists, Douglass likely attended the tumultuous meeting of the Bristol County

Anti-Slavery Society in New Bedford on 16 April 1839. In an effort to break up the meeting, a number of New Bedford residents threw stones "against the house, and into the windows." There was also a cry of "fire" heard. Fifty years later, Douglass recalled attending an abolitionist meeting "not long" after reaching New Bedford in an "old, dilapidated deserted church, at the corner of William and Purchase Streets," where a mob hurled "brickbats, stones, unsavory eggs, and other missiles" at those assembled. He was most likely referring to the 16 April meeting.[58] Among those participating at this turbulent gathering were Garrison, John A. Collins, and Edwin Thompson—all from the Massachusetts Anti-Slavery Society. The minutes state that their presence "roused the *slumbering friends*; gave the meeting a character; created an interest never before manifested, and by their stirring speeches produced an astonishing effect." Although Douglass' name does not appear in the minutes of the meeting, Samuel Rodman, a prominent aristocrat of New Bedford who was present at the meeting, noted in his diary that a number of black people were present. It is likely that Douglass was among them—especially given his recollection of the event, his strong commitment to Garrison, and his attendance at Garrison's lecture at the Old Congregational Meetinghouse the night before. If Douglass did attend the 16 April meeting, it would probably have marked his first, but hardly his last, experience with a violent disturbance of an abolitionist gathering.[59]

Douglass also appears to have taken advantage of periodic public lectures on antislavery, some of which were sponsored by the New Bedford Lyceum.[60] On 28 March 1839, for example, Oliver Johnson, a loyal Garrisonian abolitionist, delivered a lecture on the "Subject of Slavery" at the Elm Street Methodist Church. Douglass was probably in attendance. "One of the first speeches I ever heard," he recalled during an address in 1886, "was from Oliver Johnson."[61] On 23 November 1839, Douglass attended an antislavery lecture delivered by Congressman Caleb Cushing. The address, wrote one observer, was presented with "great earnestness, ability, and effect" to a "crowded" auditory at the Old Congregational Meetinghouse. It must have made a strong impression on Douglass, for he recalled it during a speech thirty-four years later.[62] Douglass may also have been in the audience on 30 December 1839, when George Bradburn presented a lecture entitled "American Slavery" at the Universalist Church, which was "about half full" with a "considerable portion" being people of color.[63] In addition, given Douglass' devotion to Garrison, he surely would have made every effort to attend when the editor of the *Liberator* delivered an "interesting and able lecture on slavery" at the Old Unitarian Church on 25 April 1841.[64] Douglass may have also attended the meetings of the Young Men's Wilberforce Debating Society.[65]

Because records are sketchy, it is impossible to identify with certainty other abolitionist meetings at which Douglass spoke or otherwise participated actively. There were usually no published minutes from the monthly meetings of the New Bedford Young Men's Anti-Slavery Society or the gatherings of black abolitionists. When minutes were printed, the speakers were typically not identified by name. Sometimes only the resolutions were published, with no indication of what took place during the meeting itself. The fact that Douglass was identified as playing a major role on at least two occasions is testimony to his standing among New Bedford's black abolitionists. Even on those occasions when Douglass did not speak, simply by being present he would have been able to absorb the arguments, principles, and stylistic proclivities of the debates and speeches. Indeed, if Douglass took part in only a portion of New Bedford's abolitionist activity, it would have provided ample opportunity for him to advance his understanding of antislavery principles and to refine his public speaking skills.

Later in his life, Douglass identified his three years in New Bedford after escaping from slavery as among the happiest times of his life.[66] Certainly, they were among the most important. By taking advantage of the numerous opportunities New Bedford had to offer, he greatly enhanced his understanding of antislavery principles and rhetorical strategies. He also witnessed dozens of talented public speakers, black and white alike. Listening to black men speak out forcefully against slavery and prejudice most likely added to his confidence and, more important, helped him realize that black people could make a significant contribution to the antislavery movement. By extension, he doubtless realized that he, too, could make a contribution. This realization would soon lead him to emerge as a major figure in Massachusetts abolitionism.

Notes

1. See, for example, James M. Gregory, *Frederick Douglass, the Orator* (1893; reprint, Chicago: Afro-Am Press, 1971), 27; Charles W. Chesnutt, *Frederick Douglass* (1899; reprint, New York: Johnson Reprint Corporation, 1970), 24-28; Benjamin Quarles, *Frederick Douglass* (Washington, D.C.: Associated Publishers, Inc., 1948), 10-12; Philip S. Foner, *Frederick Douglass* (New York: Citadel Press, 1964), 24-26; Nathan Irvin Huggins, *Slave and Citizen: The Life of Frederick Douglass* (Boston: Little, Brown and Company, 1980), 15-17; Waldo E. Martin Jr., *The Mind of Frederick Douglass* (Chapel Hill: University of North Carolina Press, 1984), 20-21; Frederic May Holland, *Frederick Douglass: The Colored Orator* (New York: Funk and Wagnalls Company, 1895), 32-56; John W. Blassingame, ed., *The Frederick Douglass Papers, Series One: Speeches, Debates, and Interviews: Volume 1* (New Haven, Conn.: Yale University Press, 1979), 1:xxiii. Although William S. McFeely and Raymond Gerald Fulkerson provide more detail than the preceding studies on Douglass'

activities in New Bedford, they do not explain how these activities contributed to Douglass' understanding of antislavery principles or to his maturation as an orator. See William S. McFeely, *Frederick Douglass* (New York: Norton, 1991), 74-85; Raymond Gerald Fulkerson, "Frederick Douglass and the Anti-Slavery Crusade: His Career and Speeches, 1841-1861," pt. 1 (Ph.D. diss., University of Illinois, 1971), 32-39.

2. Frederick Douglass, *My Bondage and My Freedom* (1855; reprint, New York: Dover, 1969), 336-37; Frederick Douglass, *Life and Times of Frederick Douglass* (1892; reprint, New York: Macmillan, 1962), 201-2.

3. Douglass, *Life and Times*, 203; Douglass, *Bondage and Freedom*, 338.

4. Douglass, *Life and Times*, 204; Douglass, *Bondage and Freedom*, 341; Fulkerson, "Frederick Douglass," pt. 1, 31; Dorothy B. Porter, "David M. Ruggles, an Apostle of Human Rights," *Journal of Negro History* 28 (January 1943): 23, 32.

5. Frederick Douglass, *Narrative of the Life of Frederick Douglass, An American Slave, Written By Himself* (1845; reprint, New York: Signet, 1968), 112-13; Douglass, *Bondage and Freedom*, 340-41; McFeely, *Frederick Douglass*, 72-73.

6. In 1838 there were 170 vessels in New Bedford's whaling fleet, employing more than 4,000 hands. See Daniel Ricketson, *The History of New Bedford, Bristol County, Massachusetts* (New Bedford, Mass.: Ricketson Publishers, 1858), 373.

7. Douglass, *Narrative*, 113-14; Douglass, *Life and Times*, 205; Barbara Clayton and Kathleen Whitley, *Guide to New Bedford* (Montpelier, Vt.: Capital City Press, 1979), 134.

8. Douglass, *Narrative*, 114; Douglass, *Life and Times*, 206. Nathan and Polly Johnson were also members of the Society of Friends and resided in the first Friends Meeting House of the New Bedford Society. Nathan Johnson, a member of the New Bedford Young Men's Anti-Slavery Society, was one of seven counselors for the society and the only person of color to hold office in the organization. See Judith A. Boss and Joseph D. Thomas, *New Bedford: A Pictorial History* (Norfolk, Va.: Donning Publishers, 1983), 51; Henry H. Crapo, *The New-Bedford Directory* (New Bedford, Mass.: J.C. Parmenter, 1838), 27.

9. According to the 1838 *New-Bedford Directory* (77-78) there were nineteen Johnsons residing in the community, twelve of whom were black.

10. Douglass, *Life and Times*, 206; Douglass, *Bondage and Freedom*, 343; Douglass, *Narrative*, 114-15.

11. Douglass, *Bondage and Freedom*, 343, 345; Douglass, *Narrative*, 115-16; Clayton and Whitley, *Guide to New Bedford*, 13, 21.

12. Douglass, *Narrative*, 116; Douglass, *Life and Times*, 209; *Colored American* (New York), 22 July 1837: 2.

13. Henry H. Crapo, *The New-Bedford Directory* (New Bedford, Mass.: Benjamin Lindsey, 1841), 28; Virginia M. Adams, ed., *On the Altar of Freedom: A Black Soldier's Civil War Letters from the Front/James Henry Gooding* (Boston:

University of Massachusetts Press, 1991), xix-xx; Clayton and Whitley, *Guide to New Bedford*, 22-23; Douglass, *Bondage and Freedom*, 345.

14. Adams, *On the Altar of Freedom*, xix-xx; Douglass, *Narrative*, 116; Mcfeely, *Frederick Douglass*, 76-77. Of the 12,354 people who resided in New Bedford in 1839, there were 709 black males and 342 black females. See the 1841 *New-Bedford Directory*, 28.

15. Douglass, *Narrative*, 117; Douglass, *Life and Times*, 209; Ricketson, *History of New Bedford*, 252-53.

16. Douglass, *Bondage and Freedom*, 349-50; Douglass, *Life and Times*, 209-13.

17. Douglass, *Bondage and Freedom*, 351-52; Helen Pitts Douglass, ed., *In Memoriam: Frederick Douglass* (Philadelphia: John C. Yorston and Co., 1897), 242.

18. Douglass, *Bondage and Freedom*, 353.

19. Ibid.

20. Ibid.; Mcfeely, *Frederick Douglass*, 81-82; Carter G. Woodson, *The History of the Negro Church*, 2d ed. (Washington, D.C.: Associated Publishers, 1921), 78-79, 85; Benjamin F. Wheeler, *The Varick Family* (Mobile, Ala.: n.p., 1907), 5; C. Eric Lincoln, "The Black Church in the Context of American Religion," in *Varieties of Southern Religious Experience*, ed. Samuel S. Hill (Baton Rouge: Louisiana State University Press, 1988), 55; Christopher Rush, *A Short Account of the Rise and Progress of the African Methodist Episcopal Zion Church in America* (New York: Christopher Rush, 1843), 2, 96-97; William J. Walls, *The African Methodist Episcopal Zion Church: Reality of the Black Church* (Charlotte, N.C.: A.M.E. Zion Publishing House, 1974), 43-44, 47-48; James Beverly F. Shaw, *The Negro in the History of Methodism* (Nashville, Tenn.: Parthenon Press, 1954), 69, 73-74.

21. David Henry Bradley Sr., *A History of the A.M.E. Zion Church, pt. 1, 1796-1872* (Nashville, Tenn.: Parthenon Press, 1956), 107-11; Walls, *African Methodist Episcopal Zion Church*, 138; Roy E. Finkenbine, "Boston's Black Churches: Institutional Centers of the Antislavery Movement," in *Courage and Conscience: Black and White Abolitionists in Boston*, ed. Donald M. Jacobs (Bloomington: Indiana University Press, 1993), 175, 185-86.

22. James W. Hood, *One Hundred Years of the African Methodist Episcopal Zion Church* (New York: A.M.E. Zion Book Concern, 1895), 541; Edward D. Smith, *Climbing Jacob's Ladder, The Rise of Black Churches in Eastern American Cities, 1740-1877* (Washington, D.C.: Smithsonian Institution, 1988), 68. Douglass' letter to James W. Hood in 1894 reflecting on his experience in the New Bedford A.M.E. Zion Church is reprinted in William L. Andrews, "Frederick Douglass, Preacher," *American Literature* 54 (December 1982): 596.

23. Walls, *African Methodist Episcopal Zion Church*, 283-84; Rev. G.L. Blackwell, ed., *The Doctrines and Discipline of the African Methodist Episcopal Zion Church* (Charlotte, N.C.: A.M.E. Zion Publication House, 1901), 124; The

Doctrines and Discipline of the African Methodist Episcopal [Zion] Church in America, Established in the City of New York, October 25, 1820, Christopher Rush and George Collins, eds. (New York: Christopher Rush and George Collins, 1820), 69-70.

24. John J. Moore, *History of the A.M.E. Zion Church in America* (York, Pa.: Teachers' Journal Office, 1884), 80; Bishop John B. Small, *Code on the Discipline of the African Methodist Episcopal Zion Church* (York, Pa.: York Dispatch Print, 1898), 130-32.

25. Bradley, *History of the A.M.E. Zion Church, Part 1,* 112-13; McFeely, *Frederick Douglass,* 82; Walls, *African Methodist Episcopal Zion Church,* 148; Hood, *One Hundred Years,* 541; Rush and Collins, *Doctrines and Discipline* (1820), 57-58; Joseph W. Barnes, "The Autobiography of Reverend Thomas James," *Rochester History* 37 (October 1975): 3-6.

26. Walls, *African Methodist Episcopal Zion Church,* 103, 150; Hood, *One Hundred Years,* 541-42; Smith, *Climbing Jacob's Ladder,* 68; Small, *Code on the Discipline,* 132-33. After serving four consecutive years as a licensed local preacher, a person was eligible to be recommended to receive Holy Orders and be ordained a minister (Small, *Code on the Discipline,* 135).

27. Arthaniel Edgar Harris Sr., "Worship in the A.M.E. Zion Church," *A.M.E. Zion Quarterly Review* 97 (July 1986): 34-35; Blackwell, *Doctrines and Discipline,* 48-49.

28. Blackwell, *Doctrines and Discipline,* 103-4.

29. Rush and Collins, eds., *Doctrines and Discipline,* 56-58.

30. Walls, *African Methodist Episcopal Zion Church,* 114.

31. Ibid., 114-15; Caleb Bingham, ed., *The Columbian Orator* (Boston: Manning and Loring, 1797), 10, 14.

32. Hood, *One Hundred Years,* 541; *New-Bedford Directory* (1841), 65; Before 1841, Douglass identified his occupation as "laborer." See Henry H. Crapo, *The New-Bedford Directory* (New Bedford, Mass.: Benjamin Lindsey, 1839), 69.

33. Beman, Kennedy, Thompson, and Smith were considered among the most talented of the African American pulpit orators. A strong leader and organizer, Beman became the first minister of the Boston A.M.E. Zion Church. He began his ministry in Boston in 1838 with seventeen members, and by October 1840 the membership had grown to 140. Deeply involved in Boston's antislavery movement, Beman was also president of the State Temperance Society of Colored People. Dempsey Kennedy was a "pioneer preacher of remarkable skill in stirring up audiences." He divided his time between preaching and delivering antislavery speeches. Leven Smith was a "dauntless pioneer" in the church who organized the Zion church in Providence, Rhode Island, in 1822. See Walls, *African Methodist Episcopal Zion Church,* 128, 129, 141, 144-45, 148; Woodson, *History of the Negro Church,* 173.

34. A full-blooded African and an ardent abolitionist leader within the black community, Rush was born a slave in New Bern, Craven County, North Carolina, in

1777. He escaped to New York City in 1798, where he joined the Zion Church in 1803. He was licensed to preach in 1815 and in 1827 was elected the second bishop of the A.M.E. Zion Church. Active in the Negro Convention Movement and the antislavery movement, in 1833 he organized and became the president of the Phoenix Society of New York City, whose major purpose was to promote the improvement of African Americans in morals, literature, and the mechanic arts. To that end, the society, under Rush's leadership, established a library, schools, and built Phoenix Hall, on West Broadway, in New York City, where educational work was conducted. The hall soon became a center of antislavery activities and conventions. See Hood, *One Hundred Years*, 168-71, 541; Walls, *African Methodist Episcopal Zion Church*, 125, 132, 144-45; Woodson, *History of the Negro Church*, 103; Moore, *History of the A.M.E. Zion Church*, 349-52; Smith, *Climbing Jacob's Ladder*, 67.

35. Hood, *One Hundred Years*, 541-42; "A Reform Absolutely Complete: An Address Delivered in New York, New York, on 9 April 1870," in *The Frederick Douglass Papers, Series One: Speeches, Debates, and Interviews, Volume 4*, ed. John W. Blassingame and John R. McKivigan (New Haven, Conn.: Yale University Press, 1991), 4:263.

36. Mcfeely, *Frederick Douglass*, 84.

37. Frederick Douglass, "Reminiscences," *The Cosmopolitan* 7 (August 1889): 378.

38. Samuel Rodman, *The Diary of Samuel Rodman*, ed. Zephaniah W. Pease (New Bedford, Mass.: Reynolds Printing Co., 1927), 191; *New Bedford Daily Register*, 15 April 1839: 2; *New Bedford Daily Register*, 18 April 1839: 2; *Liberator*, 26 April 1839: 66.

39. Douglass, *Life and Times*, 213-14, mistakenly recalled Liberty Hall as the place where he first heard Garrison lecture. Liberty Hall was the location of the Bristol County Anti-Slavery Society meeting on 9 August 1841, at which Douglass first spoke before a white audience. If Douglass had indeed heard Garrison at Liberty Hall, his first exposure to Garrison would not have been "soon after becoming a reader of the *Liberator*," but two and a half years later.

40. Douglass, *Life and Times*, 213-14; "Recollections of the Anti-Slavery Conflict," in *The Papers of Frederick Douglass* (Washington, D.C.: Library of Congress Photoduplication Service, 1974), reel 18: p. 70; Douglass, *Bondage and Freedom*, 355; "Good Men are God in the Flesh: An Address Delivered in Boston, Massachusetts, on 22 September 1890," in *The Frederick Douglass Papers, Series One: Speeches, Debates, and Interviews, Volume 5*, ed. John W. Blassingame and John R. McKivigan (New Haven, Conn.: Yale University Press, 1992), 5:434.

41. Douglass, *Life and Times*, 213; Douglass, *Narrative*, 118; Douglass, *Bondage and Freedom*, 354.

42. Foner, *Frederick Douglass*, 25; Douglass, *Narrative*, 118; "Colored People Must Command Respect: An Address Delivered in Rochester, New York, on 13 March 1848," in *The Frederick Douglass Papers, Series One: Speeches,*

Debates, and Interviews, Volume 2, ed. John W. Blassingame (New Haven, Conn: Yale University Press, 1982), 2:113-14; Douglass, *Bondage and Freedom*, 165, 354-56; Douglass, *Life and Times*, 213; John W. Blassingame, *Frederick Douglass: The Clarion Voice* (Washington, D.C.: Department of the Interior, 1976), 10; Martin, *Mind of Frederick Douglass*, 20.

43. *Liberator*, 30 October 1840: 175; Bingham, *Columbian Orator*, 31.

44. The *New Bedford Daily Mercury* announced the monthly meetings of the society, but did not publish its proceedings.

45. Douglass, "Reminiscences," 378.

46. *National Anti-Slavery Standard*, 26 August 1841: 46; *New-Bedford Directory* (1841), 32. A correspondent reported to the *Standard* that these meetings were "held every fortnight." However, in a letter written to the *Liberator*, John Bailey indicated that black abolitionists met at his house weekly to discuss antislavery principles (*Liberator*, 30 July 1841: 123).

47. Douglass, *Bondage and Freedom*, 356.

48. The 12 March 1839 issue of the *Liberator* marked the first recorded instance of Douglass' activities in New Bedford's black abolitionist meetings.

49. Douglass, *Bondage and Freedom*, 356; *Liberator*, 12 March 1839: 50; P.J. Staudenraus, *The African Colonization Movement, 1816-1865* (New York: Columbia University Press, 1961), 237-39; Allen Johnson and Dumas Malone, eds., *Dictionary of American Biography, Volume 4* (New York: Scribner's, 1930), 4:540; *Liberator*, 14 December 1838: 199; *Liberator*, 1 February 1839: 17.

50. *New Bedford Daily Register*, 11 March 1839: 2; *Liberator*, 12 March 1839: 50. This issue of the *Liberator* marked the first time Douglass' name appeared in print.

51. *New Bedford Daily Register*, 11 March 1839: 2; *Liberator*, 12 March 1839: 50.

52. *Liberator*, 29 March 1839: 50.

53. *Liberator*, 11 June 1841: 94; *New Bedford Morning Register*, 2 June 1841: 2; "Colored People Must Command Respect, An Address Delivered in Rochester, New York, on 13 March 1848," in Blassingame, ed., *Douglass Papers, Series One*, 2:114-15; "Great is the Miracle of Human Speech: An Address Delivered in Washington, D.C., on 31 August 1891," in Blassingame and McKivigan, eds., *Douglass Papers, Series One*, 5:476.

54. *Liberator*, 11 June 1841: 94.

55. *Liberator*, 9 July 1841: 110. The resolutions of the 30 June 1841 meeting of New Bedford's black citizens were reprinted in the *Pennsylvania Freeman*, 14 July 1841: 3; *National Anti-Slavery Standard*, 15 July 1841: 23.

56. *Liberator*, 9 July 1841: 110; Quarles, *Frederick Douglass*, 12.

57. *Liberator*, 23 July 1841: 118. The case never came to trial. Justice Crapo, of the police court of New Bedford, decided that neither the train company nor its conductors were guilty of any crime against Ruggles (*Liberator*, 23 July 1841: 118).

58. Douglass, "Reminiscences,": 378. The Old Congregational Meetinghouse was located on the corner of William and Purchase Streets (*New Bedford Daily Register*, 15 April 1839: 2).

59. *Liberator*, 12 April 1839: 59; *New Bedford Daily Register*, 13 April 1839: 2; *New Bedford Daily Register*, 19 April 1839: 2; Rodman, *Diary*, 192. The minutes from the 16 April 1839 meeting were published in the *Liberator*, 26 April 1839: 59.

60. New Bedford's Lyceum was organized in 1828 and was one of the oldest institutions of its kind in the country. Among the goals of the Lyceum was the advancement of public education, in the service of which it sponsored paid public lectures. After his return from the British Isles in 1847, Douglass became a Lyceum lecturer. See Ricketson, *History of New Bedford*, 324-25; Leonard Bolles Ellis, *History of New Bedford and Its Vicinity: 1602-1892* (Syracuse, N.Y.: D. Mason and Company, 1892), 637.

61. *New Bedford Daily Register*, 28 March 1839: 2; *Boston Journal*, 13 September 1886.

62. "Recollections of the Anti-Slavery Conflict: An Address Delivered in Louisville, Kentucky, on 21 April 1873," in Blassingame and McKivigan, eds., *Douglass Papers, Series One*, 4:368; Rodman, *Diary*, 198-99.

63. Rodman, *Diary*, 200.

64. *Liberator*, 23 April 1841: 67; Rodman, *Diary*, 220.

65. The Young Men's Wilberforce Debating Society scheduled regular meetings and probably included black citizens in its deliberations. For instance, on 26 August 1839, after the "unhappy division" of the Massachusetts Anti-Slavery Society, the Wilberforce group met "with a large and highly respectable number of . . . colored citizens" to show their support for Garrison. They passed a resolution stating, in part, "That the name of WILLIAM WILBERFORCE, coupled with that of WILLIAM LLOYD GARRISON, be inscribed upon our hearts anew: and that we will teach our children, that their names and their deeds be sainted in their memories" (*Liberator*, 27 September 1839: 156).

66. Hood, *One Hundred Years*, 542.

✿ Chapter Three

The Emergence of an Orator from Slavery: Southern Slavery, Northern Prejudice, and the Church, August - December 1841

WRITING IN 1883, esteemed abolitionist Parker Pillsbury appropriately described the antislavery meetings in New Bedford and Nantucket, Massachusetts, during August 1841 as "memorable in anti-slavery history."[1] It was during these meetings that the Garrisonian abolitionists uncovered a remarkable new voice that would add substance and excitement to the antislavery struggle. This powerful voice could not have emerged at a more fortuitous time. By 1841 many of the local Massachusetts abolitionist societies had grown increasingly apathetic, and the antislavery crusade was sorely in need of revitalization.[2] When William Lloyd Garrison and his colleagues heard Frederick Douglass in New Bedford and Nantucket, they recognized at once that here was a man who could help energize the cause of abolitionism—a fugitive from slavery who could bring to the platform firsthand knowledge of the peculiar institution and who could speak with unquestioned authority about the abuses of the slave system.[3]

This chapter examines Douglass' oratorical activities from the time of his emergence at New Bedford and Nantucket in early August 1841, when he was hired as an agent for the Massachusetts Anti-Slavery Society, through the end of December 1841. The conventional view of Douglass at this stage of his career is that he confined his remarks to a simple narrative of his slave experiences, that he was very much under the wing of Garrison and the Massachusetts Anti-Slavery Society, and that he adhered strictly to Garrisonian doctrine. This view was perpetuated by Douglass himself in his autobiographies, and it has been reiterated by generation after generation of scholars. By following Douglass on a day-by-day basis during this phase of his career, however, a distinctly different view emerges. As we shall see, Douglass did not confine his remarks to his slave experiences. He went beyond recounting his background as a slave to providing thoughtful analyses of southern slavery and northern racial prejudice and their consequences. Among the other subjects he addressed from the platform were the proslavery practices of the church, the supremacy of moral suasion over political action in abolitionism, the dissolution of the Union as a means of ending slavery, and the necessity of petitioning the federal government for the immediate emancipation of the slaves. Moreover, far from merely following Garrisonian doctrine, Douglass at times disagreed with Garrison and other white abolitionists in his speeches and, in general, was discovering his own voice much more rapidly than has been previously understood.

In addition, the few extant speech texts from this period reveal Douglass to be a speaker of considerable eloquence and artistry. Careful study of these early speeches reveals that Douglass was rapidly becoming a skilled orator who regularly elicited powerful, positive reactions from almost all white abolitionist audiences. Listeners consistently commented on his powerful physical presence, his captivating delivery, his forceful voice, and his use of satire, humor, and vivid illustrations to portray the atrocities of southern slavery and the injustice of northern prejudice. Viewed in this light, Douglass' "meteoric" rise as an orator is no less remarkable—but it is understandable.

I

On Monday, 9 August 1841, Douglass attended the annual meeting of the Bristol County Anti-Slavery Society held in New Bedford's Liberty Hall. Garrison was present along with such notable abolitionists as Pillsbury, George Bradburn, John A. Collins, and Edmund Quincy. The meeting was "attended by a choice collection of the friends of human rights, from various parts of the Commonwealth," Garrison reported in the *Liberator*. He also noted that several young black men from New Bedford were in attendance and participated in the proceedings.[4] During the morning session, a resolution condemning the indifference of the church toward slavery was debated. The afternoon session began with the report of a committee appointed to nominate a slate of officers for the society for the coming year. After considerable discussion, the report was adopted. Having resolved this issue, the resolution proclaiming the proslavery nature of the church was again introduced. A correspondent for the *New Bedford Morning Register* reported that "Mr. Garrison opened the fire in a speech supporting the resolution and condemnatory of the church" and its practices. He was followed by Pillsbury, "who spoke on the same side with much earnestness and animation." The names of the abolitionists who followed Pillsbury to the platform were not mentioned in the report.[5] During the evening session, Garrison, Quincy, Collins, Bradburn, "and several col'd individuals" of New Bedford delivered speeches against northern prejudice to a crowded house. Their remarks, an observer wrote, were "principally in relation to the exclusion of col'd people from R.R. cars, cabins of steamboats, body pews of churches, &c." The black speakers also addressed the recent eviction of black abolitionist David Ruggles from a railroad car reserved for white people and the decision of Justice Henry H. Crapo in the case.[6]

Although Douglass claimed in his autobiographies that his first speech before a white audience was given on 11 August 1841 to an antislavery meeting at Nantucket, the evidence strongly suggests that he was one of the "col'd individuals" who spoke at the New Bedford meeting of 9 August.[7] He may not have delivered a formal speech, but he did enter into the discussion, and whatever he said that evening made a distinct impression on Garrison and his colleagues. In his report about the New Bedford meeting, Garrison wrote of how "several talented colored young men from New-Bedford, one of them formerly a slave, . . . were listened to by large and attentive audiences with deep interest."[8] Pillsbury stated that the former slave "spoke so effectively at our meetings that he was invited to go with us to Nantucket, with promise of expenses paid."[9] The next day, Douglass and his wife Anna joined a group of approximately forty abolitionists to travel by steamship to Nantucket.

The trip was not without its difficulties. Upon boarding the steamship *Telegraph*, Douglass and his wife, along with other black abolitionists in attendance, were required to ride in the upper deck, "where they suffered from both sun and rain." The white abolitionists accompanied the black abolitionists to the upper deck, where they held an antislavery meeting. Two resolutions were debated: "that the holding of a fellow-being in bondage was a sin; and that prejudice, on account of complexion, was likewise sinful." The *National Anti-Slavery Standard* reported that Pillsbury "spoke with eloquence and feeling" in supporting the resolutions. He was followed by Collins and James N. Buffum, who offered "appropriate arguments and facts." George Bradburn also spoke "with cool and quiet argument." With this experience behind them, Douglass and his fellow abolitionists arrived at Nantucket Island for the three-day convention.[10]

Douglass listened to Garrison and Quincy speak during the opening session of the Nantucket convention on Tuesday evening, 10 August, but did not speak himself. He also remained silent during the morning and afternoon sessions on 11 August. As Douglass would recall in 1855, "It was enough for me to listen—to receive and applaud the great words of others, and only whisper in private . . . the truths which burned in my breast."[11]

During the evening session of 11 August, Garrison, who had been appointed as a member of the business committee for the convention, presented
the following resolution:

> Resolved, That the people of the North, in cherishing and
> defending a cruel prejudice against those whose skins are not col-
> ored like their own, are putting arguments into the mouths of
> southern task-masters, and acting as the body-guard of slavery;
> that this prejudice is not only unmerciful and wicked, but vulgar
> and unnatural; and that all who would claim the character of sen-
> sible, just, humane or religious men, must divest themselves of it
> at once and forever.[12]

Listening carefully to the resolution, Douglass decided to end his silence.
The minutes from this session indicate that five men spoke in favor of this
resolution. The final orator of the evening was recorded as "_____
Douglas[s], of New-Bedford," who spoke briefly in support of the resolution. His remarks were interrupted because the time for adjournment had
come.[13]

As we saw in the last chapter, dealing with resolutions against northern
prejudice was nothing new for Douglass. While participating in a meeting
of black abolitionists in New Bedford on 12 March 1839, he had "ably sustained" a strongly worded resolution stating, in part, that slavery and prejudice were the "putrifying sores" of the nation.[14] On 30 June 1841, only
weeks before the Nantucket meeting, he had chaired a "Meeting of Colored
Citizens" in New Bedford that passed a resolution strongly condemning the
cruel treatment David Ruggles had received from the captain of the
Telegraph during a voyage between New Bedford and Nantucket. The fact
that Douglass experienced similar treatment aboard the *Telegraph* on his
way to Nantucket may have provided additional motivation for him to
speak in favor of Garrison's resolution against northern prejudice.[15]

In any case, when Douglass rose to speak before the convention at
Nantucket on 11 August 1841, he came to the platform with something to
say and the necessary motivation with which to say it. He had rehearsed
his arguments against northern prejudice at black antislavery meetings, as
well as in private conversations with friends. At Nantucket, however, he
was not only speaking to black abolitionists, but to an audience of whites
as well. It was a memorable moment for Douglass. As he recalled in 1845,
"It was a severe cross, and I took it up reluctantly. The truth was, I felt
myself a slave, and the idea of speaking to white people weighed me down.
I spoke but a few moments, when I felt a degree of freedom, and said what
I desired with considerable ease." This passage reveals the impact of the
Nantucket experience on Douglass. Although he initially allowed himself to
be defined by the receptive white audience, as he continued to speak, he

no longer felt himself a slave. His powers of speech both freed him from slavery and from being defined by another's whiteness. He overcame the silence required of him by his masters during his slave experience and gave full voice to his ideas before a white audience.[16]

At the start of the morning session on 12 August, Douglass was invited to resume his remarks to the convention. Standing before an audience of approximately 1,000 people, he chose not to speak out against northern prejudice as he had the night before. Instead, he related his experiences as a slave. Years later, Douglass recalled the moment vividly:

> He [Coffin] sought me out in the crowd, and invited me to say a few words to the convention. Thus sought out and thus invited, I was induced to speak out the feelings inspired by the occasion, and the fresh recollection of the scenes through which I had passed as a slave. . . . It was with the utmost difficulty I could stand erect, or that I could command and articulate two words without hesitation and stammering. I trembled in every limb.[17]

His nerves notwithstanding, Douglass spoke with great force, conviction, and effect. Although we do not have any record of his exact words, we do have considerable evidence that his remarks electrified the audience. Samuel J. May recalled that Douglass, "after much hesitation . . . rose, and, notwithstanding his embarrassment, he gave evidence of such intellectual power—wisdom as well as wit—that all present were astonished."[18] Another member of the audience described the occasion this way:

> Temperance meetings were held at Nantucket at the same time abolitionists were lecturing: and we indulged the hope that, as they had the testimony of reformed drunkards to sustain their glorious cause, so we might have some repentant slaveholder, or powerful slave to testify 'that which they themselves did know.' The morning of the 12th instant fulfilled our hopes. One, recently from the house of bondage, spoke with great power. Flinty hearts were pierced, and cold ones melted by his eloquence. Our best pleaders for the slave held their breath for fear of interrupting him. Mr. Garrison said his speech would have done honor to Patrick Henry. It seemed almost miraculous how he had been prepared to tell his story with so much power.[19]

Four years later, Garrison recalled "the extraordinary emotion" Douglass' speech excited in his mind. "Never," he wrote, had he "hated slavery so intensely as at that moment; certainly, my perception of the enormous outrage which is inflicted by it, on the godlike nature of its victims, was rendered far more clear than ever."[20] Garrison also recollected the audience's response both during and immediately after Douglass' speech:

I shall never forget . . . the powerful impression it created upon a crowded auditory, completely taken by surprise—the applause which followed from the beginning to the end of his felicitous remarks. . . . As soon as he had taken his seat, filled with hope and admiration, I rose, and declared that PATRICK HENRY, of revolutionary fame, never made a speech more eloquent in the cause of liberty, than the one we had just listened to from the lips of that hunted fugitive. . . . I reminded the audience of the peril which surrounded this self-emancipated young man at the North—even in Massachusetts . . . and I appealed to them, whether they would ever allow him to be carried back into slavery—law or no law, constitution or no constitution. The response was unanimous and in thunder-tones—"NO!" "Will you succor and protect him as a brother-man—a resident of the old Bay State?" "YES!" shouted the whole mass.[21]

On the evening of 12 August, during the final session of the convention, Douglass again came forward and addressed the assembly. "To that time the meetings had advanced with increasing fervor," said Pillsbury, "and, as this was the last session, I began to fear a decline for the close." His fears were eradicated when Douglass, after a slow start, "soon gained self-possession and gradually rose to the importance of the occasion and the dignity of his theme."[22] A witness wrote that Douglass was "listened to by a multitude with mingled emotions of admiration, pity, and horror."[23] Garrison, again inspired by Douglass' remarks, came forward to respond to his speech. "He eulogized, as he deserved, the fugitive who had just spoken," wrote an observer at the meeting, "and anathematized the system that could crush to the earth such men."[24]

At the close of the Nantucket meeting, Garrison and John A. Collins, general agent of the Massachusetts Anti-Slavery Society, "urgently solicited" Douglass to become a full-time lecturer for the society "and to publicly advocate its anti-slavery principles." Fearing that any publicity of his fugitive slave status could lead to his capture and return to slavery, Douglass was hesitant and at first refused. After further consideration, however, he consented to join for a trial period of three months.[25] Fourteen years later, he described his feelings as he accepted the Garrisonians' offer: "Young, ardent, and hopeful, I entered upon this new life in the full gush of unsuspecting enthusiasm. The cause was good; the men engaged in it were good; the means to attain triumph, good. . . . In this enthusiastic spirit, I dropped into the ranks of freedom's friends, and went forth to the battle. For a time I was made to forget that my skin was dark and my hair crisped."[26]

This passage illuminates Douglass' motives for committing himself to the role of abolitionist lecturer. As he spoke at Nantucket, he had experienced a full sense of freedom. By giving voice to truth before white audiences,

Douglass could denounce slavery and slaveholders and, in the process, demonstrate and proclaim his humanity. After his speech at Nantucket, Douglass began to realize the power of his own voice to reach beyond the audiences he had previously addressed in New Bedford. He had spoken to a large, predominantly white audience, and he had been heard. His speeches before the New Bedford and Nantucket antislavery conventions had propelled him into a vocation as an important voice within the antislavery movement. It was, for Douglass, nothing less than a rebirth. Later in his life he recalled that it "was literally the opening upon me of a new Heaven and a new earth—the whole world had for me a new face and life itself a new meaning. I saw myself a new man, and a new and happy future for my downtrodden and enslaved fellow countrymen."[27]

II

During his three trial months as an abolitionist lecturer, Douglass traveled and spoke primarily in Massachusetts. Throughout this period, his lecturing associate was John A. Collins, who was well suited to launch him into the movement. An ardent antislavery advocate and social reformer, Collins was a devoted Garrisonian who firmly believed in "the great and fundamental principle . . . of immediate and unconditional emancipation," and he openly welcomed "people of every sect, country, color, and sex . . . as fellow-laborers in the work."[28] Before joining the Garrisonians, Collins attended Andover Theological Seminary, but left before graduating to become the general agent of the Massachusetts Anti-Slavery Society. He organized the Garrisonian faction which captured control of the American Anti-Slavery Society in 1840, and later that year he traveled abroad in an effort to raise funds for the society.[29] In 1881 Oliver Johnson, a loyal Garrisonian and a friend of Collins, wrote:

> Mr. John A. Collins came to us . . . at the time of the division in Massachusetts. . . . His executive power was remarkable. He did much to infuse courage into our broken ranks, to overcome opposition, to collect funds, and devise and execute large plans of anti-slavery labor. He traveled much at home, and once went to England on a mission in behalf of the cause. A man of tremendous energy, nothing could stagnate in his presence. He could set a score of agents in the field, and plan and execute a campaign on the largest scale. . . . He came to us in a critical hour and his services were exceedingly valuable.[30]

Among Collins' valuable services was guiding Douglass through his first few months as an abolitionist lecturer.

Douglass' success on the lecture circuit was instantaneous, and he awakened a new enthusiasm for the abolition movement in local antislavery societies. One week after his emergence at Nantucket, he spoke in favor of a resolution against prejudice at a quarterly meeting of the Massachusetts Anti-Slavery Society in Millbury. The resolution forwarded by Garrison and the business committee read:

> Resolved, That all those meeting houses in which persons are insulted and degraded on account of their complexion or condition, and compelled to occupy the "negro pew," or a separate seat are (if the requirements of the gospel are binding on mankind, and God is no respecter of persons) under the control of an evil and wicked spirit, against which it is the duty of abolitionists to bear a faithful and consistent testimony.[31]

Douglass' speech in support of this resolution is the first recorded instance of his denunciation of racial prejudice in the church, a topic that would soon become a standard part of his oratorical repertoire.

During the two-day convention at Millbury, Douglass also spoke vividly of his life as a slave. His speech on this topic excited great attention among his auditors and led one, who had also heard Douglass' speech at Nantucket, to write in the *National Anti-Slavery Standard*: "The fugitive, who produced such an interest at Nantucket, again called forth pity and horror at his story. He is shrewd and discriminating, and his deportment is graceful and manly."[32] Another participant saw in Douglass' address a portent of "brighter days" in the crusade against slavery:

> Much interest was added to this occasion by the eloquent and thrilling remarks of a fugitive slave, the audience hanging with breathless silence upon the lips of this faithful representative of the millions in bondage. As he finished, many seemed ready to exclaim woe to the oppressor who would crush the spirit so full of Heavenly fire. May God bless the fugitive Frederick, and bear him forth on his mission to revive the world of abolition. We have strong faith that brighter days are coming.[33]

After the Millbury meeting, Douglass and Collins traveled to Groton at the end of August to attend a two-day meeting of the Middlesex County Anti-Slavery Society. Douglass, "the colored man," the advertisement for the meeting read, "speaks with great power and pathos. He states his own history and the workings of slavery upon his own mind with great eloquence."[34] The minutes from the meeting as reported to the *Liberator* suggest that Douglass, Collins, and Stephen Foster dominated the proceedings. Douglass opened the first session with a prayer and later in the session endorsed a resolution stating that "no person, who is not an avowed and practical abolitionist, ought to be regarded as a patriot, a Christian, or a moral man." Three additional resolutions were introduced and discussed by Collins, Douglass, and Foster. All three resolutions strongly condemned the proslavery practices of the church and its "utter disregard" for slaves and free people of color. The church's position, read the final resolution, "leaves us with no alternative but to assail them by the force of truth, or relinquish hope of the emancipation of the slave, and the salvation of the world."[35]

It is clear, then, that even during his first three weeks on the lecture circuit in August 1841, Douglass spoke on a number of topics other than his personal experiences as a slave. This view is rather different from the one that emerges from Douglass' autobiographies, in which he appears to have exaggerated the restrictions placed upon him during this early period of his career as an antislavery orator.[36] Writing in 1855, he claimed that during his probationary period as a lecturer, he confined his remarks to narrating his personal experiences:

> During the first three or four months, my speeches were almost exclusively made up of narrations of my personal experience as a slave. "Let us have the facts," said the people. So also said Friend George Foster, who always wished to pin me down to my simple narrative. "Give us the facts," said Collins, "we will take care of the philosophy." . . . "Tell your story, Frederick," would whisper my then revered friend, William Lloyd Garrison, as I stepped upon the platform. . . . "Be yourself," said Collins, "and tell your story." It was said to me, "Better have a *little* of the plantation manner of speech than not; 'tis not best that you seem too learned."[37]

According to the historical record, though, only three weeks into his career as an abolitionist lecturer, Douglass was already denouncing the immorality of slavery, the racial prejudice of the North, and the proslavery practices of the church. From the beginning, he expressed his indignation toward what he called the "perpetrators of slaveholding villainy."[38]

Douglass' reputation as an orator grew rapidly in Massachusetts antislavery circles. An announcement for the 4 September quarterly meeting of the Abington Anti-Slavery Society praised his "eloquent and affecting addresses" and the "masterly manner" in which he handled the subject of slavery. Noting that Douglass' "own history" was "full of interest," the account urged that the meeting have "a full attendance."[39] The first of Douglass' addresses at Abington took place the evening before the scheduled one-day antislavery meeting of the Abington Anti-Slavery Society. People gathered at Reverend Alden's Meetinghouse on Friday, 3 September, to hear Collins and Douglass lecture on slavery.[40] Shortly after the Abington Anti-Slavery Society meeting, Samuel Dyer, recording secretary of the society, reported the outcome and strongly praised the oratorical efforts of Douglass and Collins. "Never since the noble-hearted George Thompson publicly lifted up his voice in this town," said Dyer, "have the true friends of the slave felt so deep and lively an interest in the cause as at the present time." According to Dyer, Collins and Douglass had spoken to large audiences at four public meetings in different sections of Abington and had given "a fresh impulse to anti-slavery, which, I trust, will not soon be retarded."[41] Dyer called special attention to Douglass' "eloquent and highly interesting" lectures. "The addresses of friend Douglas[s] have been well received," he reported, and "coming as they did from one who has felt the cruel lash, cannot fail to do for the anti-slavery cause, just what the reformed inebriate is doing for temperance—an immense good."[42]

On Wednesday, 8 September, Douglass and Collins traveled to Dover, New Hampshire, to attend the annual meeting of the Strafford County Anti-Slavery Society. Douglass' first journey away from Massachusetts did not go well. While traveling on an Eastern Railroad train between Newburyport, Massachusetts, and Portsmouth, New Hampshire, Douglass refused to leave his seat next to Collins in the car reserved for whites and was forcefully removed to the Jim Crow car. In a lengthy letter to Garrison, Collins reported that he was "considerably injured in the affray" and that Douglass "suffered some injury to his clothes."[43] When Douglass and Collins finally arrived in Dover, they joined Garrison, Pillsbury, Wendell Phillips, Nathaniel P. Rogers, and Stephen S. Foster. The meeting lasted three days, reported a correspondent to the *Liberator*, and a "respectable number of abolitionists from different parts of the county and State attended."[44] Although Douglass' presence at the Strafford society meeting was noted by the secretary in the minutes, there is no indication that he participated actively in the proceedings.[45]

III

Sometime in the first week of October, Douglass traveled to Lynn, Massachusetts, to deliver his antislavery message. Edward M. Davis, a Philadelphia pacifist, reported in the *Pennsylvania Freeman* that he heard Douglass, "the runaway slave," speak on this occasion. The address, Davis wrote, "was delivered with energy, and evidently from one unaccustomed to make speeches, yet it came so spontaneously that it thrilled through every one present, and compelled them to feel for the Wrongs he endured." Davis was so taken with Douglass that he recorded "the substance, and in some parts the language" of his address, giving the world its first written text of the young fugitive's rhetoric.[46] To this point in time, newspapers had printed only descriptive accounts of Douglass' words from the platform. Now, for the first time, his actual words were transcribed. The text of this speech deserves close attention both for its uniqueness and for what it discloses about Douglass' probable message during the previous six weeks.

In the opening lines of this speech, Douglass placed himself squarely at the center of attention. Expressing his discomfort with addressing a white audience, he began, "I feel greatly embarrassed when I attempt to address an audience of white people. I am not used to speaking to them, and it makes me tremble when I do so, because I have always looked up to them with fear."[47] Considering that Douglass was a former slave who fully understood the stakes when speaking directly and honestly to a white person while in bondage, this statement carried special force. He knew that with the correct words a slave could keep his or her life intact. The wrong words, on the other hand, could cause the slave to be, "without a moment's warning . . . snatched away, and forever sundered, from his family and friends."[48] Douglass' opening statement, therefore, reflected his negative experience with white people while he was in bondage and his lingering fear of their power over him in the present. These lines of the speech also expressed Douglass' respect for his white audience. In the *Columbian Orator*, Caleb Bingham had advised that a speaker should "first settle himself, compose his countenance, and take a respectful view of his audience." The purpose behind this, according to Bingham, was to prepare the audience "for silence and attention."[49] It appears that this was Douglass' aim in the introduction of this speech, for he followed his opening lines by announcing his purpose for speaking. "My friends," he stated, "I have come to tell you something about slavery—what *I know* of it, as I have *felt* it."[50] Douglass' statement of purpose was crucial, for it introduced him as an authentic voice from slavery. He continued in this vein by contrasting his knowledge of slavery with that of white abolitionists. He argued that although white abolitionists knew much about slavery, "were acquainted with its deadly effects," and could "depict its horrors," they could not speak, as he could, "from *experience*." White abolitionists, he said, "cannot refer you to a back covered with scars, as I can; for I have felt these wounds; I have suffered under the lash without the power of resisting. Yes, my blood has sprung out as the lash embedded itself in my flesh."[51]

Having separated himself from the white abolitionists and having centered the audience upon his experiences as a slave, Douglass next introduced the character of his master, the initiator of the cruelty he had experienced, and used an incident drawn from his slave past to illustrate the brutality of his master. He began this section of the speech by declaring that his master had the reputation of being "a pious man and a good Christian" who also "was a class leader in the Methodist church." Yet this religious man cruelly beat his slaves. To demonstrate the irony of the situation, Douglass recounted a scene involving his master and a female slave.

"I have seen this pious class leader," Douglass reported, "cross and tie the hands of one of his young female slaves, and lash her on the bare skin." He then moved to the greatest irony of all—his master justified "the deed by the quotation from the Bible, 'he who knoweth his master's will and doeth it not, shall be beaten with many stripes.'"[52]

In the next section of the speech, Douglass sought to overturn two commonly held misconceptions about slavery. The first misconception was the belief that black people were born to be slaves. While confronting this misconception, Douglass abandoned the intensely personal tone he had used in the opening section of the speech and shifted focus from himself to the slave community. He no longer spoke in the first person singular. Rather, he utilized inclusive pronouns to speak on behalf of all his brothers and sisters in bondage. "Our masters," he exclaimed, "do not hesitate to prove from the Bible that slavery is right, and ministers of the Gospel tell us that we were born to be slaves." As proof for their claims, Douglass said, masters and ministers of the Gospel pointed to the slaves' "hard hands" to "see how wisely Providence has adapted them to do the labor." Then these same people, "holding up their delicate white hands," argued that their hands were "not fit to work." Douglass and other slaves clearly saw through this argument: "Some of us know very well that we have not time to cease from labor, or ours would get soft too."[53]

The second misconception that Douglass confronted concerned the belief that slaves were ignorant of their right to liberty. Douglass attacked this notion by declaring that a "large portion of the slaves *know* that they have a right to their liberty." Slaves, he stated, hear liberty "often talked about" and can also read about it, "for some of us know how to read, although all our knowledge is gained in secret." Douglass then recalled "getting possession of a speech by John Quincy Adams, made in Congress about slavery and freedom, and reading it to my fellow slaves." He recalled how Adams' speech generated "joy and gladness" among the slaves, who were comforted by knowing that "so great, so good a man was pleading for us." By recounting this incident, Douglass placed himself in the company of the few slaves who knew how to read and bolstered his credibility in the minds of his audience. He became the personification of the bridge between ignorance and knowledge in the slave community, for he could read and share his knowledge with his enslaved brethren.[54]

Not only was a prominent politician such as Adams fighting on behalf of the slaves but, Douglass revealed, the slaves of the South had also learned of "a large and growing class of people in the north called abolitionists" who were working for emancipation. This piece of knowledge was "known all through the south, and cherished with gratitude" by blacks, for it "increased the slaves' hope for liberty." Then, addressing his audience directly, Douglass warned: "My friends let it [the agitation against slavery] not be quieted, for upon you the slaves look for help. There will be no out-breaks, no insurrections, whilst you continue this excitement: let it cease, and the crimes that would follow cannot be told." In short, Douglass was suggesting that there was a limit to the slaves' quiet perseverance. As long as politicians and abolitionists agitated against slavery, slaves would be hopeful that one day emancipation would come. If the agitation ceased, slaves would violently rebel against the slave system. If such a violent slave insurrection happened, the full force of the Union would come down upon the slaves and the rebellion would be crushed.[55]

In the next section of the speech, Douglass advanced emancipation as the only "cure for slavery and its evils. It alone will give to the south peace and quietness." Following this utterance, Douglass presented the most impassioned passage of the speech. Emancipation, he claimed, "will blot out the insults we have borne, will heal the wounds we have endured, and are even now groaning under, will pacify the resentment which would kindle to a blaze were it not for your exertions, and, though it may never unite the many kindred and dear friends which slavery has torn asunder, it will be received with gratitude and a forgiving spirit."[56]

In closing his speech, Douglass eloquently addressed the issue of prejudice against people of color. Returning to his own experience as a fugitive in the North, he observed: "Prejudice against color is stronger north than south; it hangs around my neck like a heavy weight. It presses me out from among my fellow men, and . . . I have met it at every step the three years I have been out of southern slavery." As we have seen, racial prejudice consumed much of Douglass' attention during his first two months on the lecture circuit. That he concluded his speech at Lynn with his thoughts on the "heavy weight" of prejudice in the North was significant and reveals how far he went beyond simply dramatizing his slave experiences. Rather, he portrayed himself as a victim both of the system of slavery and of northern prejudice. Slavery was a part of his past, but prejudice was the reality of his present.[57]

Douglass' remarks at Lynn were significant not only because they revealed the content of what he may have been saying in the weeks prior to the speech, but also because they offer evidence of his evolving strategies and skills as an orator. Throughout the speech, Douglass expressed his adherence to Garrisonian doctrine—his belief in the sinfulness of slavery and prejudice, the power of petitioning, and the immediate emancipation of the slaves. Equally important, only weeks into his career as an abolitionist lecturer, Douglass presented himself as the representative voice of all those held in southern bondage. To accomplish this, he used inclusive pronouns to speak implicitly on behalf of all the slaves. In the weeks and months ahead, he would often assume the role of spokesman for his race, slave and free. In addition, a close look at the text reveals Douglass' purposeful use of imagery to transport his auditors into the world of southern slavery and northern prejudice. The images he created provided vivid symbols of the process of dehumanization that black people—North and South—suffered on a daily basis. By creating these scenes, he demonstrated both the power of his own inventiveness and his ability to manipulate language for rhetorical purposes. Moreover, he consistently used his slave experience to move to larger issues. He strategically moved from the personal to the collective, and from the particular to the universal. After listening to Douglass' speech, David N. Johnson, a resident of Lynn, recorded these comments about the orator and his presentation:

> He was more than six feet in height, and his majestic form, as he rose to speak, straight as an arrow, muscular, yet lithe and graceful, his flashing eye, and more than all, his voice, that rivaled Webster's in its richness, and in the depth and sonorousness of its cadences, made up such an ideal of an orator as the listeners never forgot. And they never forgot his burning words, his pathos, nor the rich play of his humor. . . . his eyes would . . . flash with defiance, and . . . grow dim with emotions he could not control; and the roll of his splendid voice, as he hurled denunciations against the infamous system, would pass to the minor key whose notes trembled on his tongue. Then with inimitable mimicry he would give a droll recital of some ludicrous scene in his experience as a slave, or with bitter sarcasm he would tell a tale of insult offered by some upstart who fancied he held his title to manhood by the whiteness of his skin; and then again, with flashing eye, he would hurl his indignant denunciation at "wickedness in high places," against men who, under the pretended sanction of religion, defended the "infernal institution" whose horrors had filled his days with dread, and his night dreams with terror.[58]

It is no wonder, given this description of Douglass' oratorical power, that his address, in Edward Davis' words, "thrilled through every one present" and compelled them to "feel for the wrongs he had endured" both as a slave and as a fugitive.[59]

IV

Unfortunately, the Lynn meeting is the only occasion for which we have a text of one of Douglass' abolitionist lectures during October 1841. We can, however, get a sense of his rhetoric during the rest of this month from newspaper accounts and from the correspondence of those attending the meetings. His next stop after Lynn was on Sunday, 5 October, when he and Collins attended a meeting of the Worcester County South Division Anti-Slavery Society. Douglass dominated the evening session of the meeting with "an address of great eloquence and interest." He had such a powerful effect on the audience that immediately after he concluded his remarks, those assembled at the meeting unanimously passed a resolution stating that "Frederick Douglas[s], who has so eloquently addressed us to-night, notwithstanding he has declared he yet feels himself a slave, is in our opinion 'fitted for freedom,' and is hereby declared to *be free*."[60]

The next day, Douglass and Collins were the guests of the Worcester County North Division Society. "The meetings," reported an observer to the *Liberator*, "which continued through the day and evening, were spirited, and of an interesting character." A total of fifteen resolutions were introduced and "ably and eloquently discussed" by Collins, Douglass, and other abolitionists. Although there are no records of what was said at this meeting, the ninth resolution reflected the powerful impact Douglass' rhetoric had on those in attendance:

> Resolved, That this meeting has listened with feelings of horror, coupled with indignation to the statements of Messrs. Collins and Douglas[s], with respect to the outrages recently committed upon them and others by the Eastern Rail Road Corporation, in forcibly ejecting colored people of both sexes from the first class cars, after they had paid the highest price for their tickets, and dragging from their cars, white people who venture to express their disapprobation of such flagrant violations of constitutional rights, of a decency, of every principle of christianity.[61]

Douglass' name also appeared in the fifth resolution: "Resolved, That the members of this meeting welcome into their midst, Frederick Douglas[s], a fugitive from slavery, and extend to him the right hand of fellowship, as a co-worker in the great cause of human redemption." This resolution concluded with the assurance that abolitionists "make use of all christian means" to prevent Douglass and other fugitive slaves from being returned to slavery.[62]

Six days later, on Sunday, 12 October, Douglass and Collins traveled to Concord to attend a meeting of the Middlesex County Anti-Slavery Society. During the morning session, Douglass, Collins, and others discussed resolutions that had "particular reference to the position occupied by the ministry and the church, at the present time, in relation to slavery." During the afternoon session, Douglass joined Wendell Phillips and Stephen S. Foster in supporting a resolution that called upon "every abolitionist, to throw off the shackles of party, and remember the slave at the ballot box, voting for none but true abolitionists." This marks the first time Douglass publicly endorsed political action by abolitionists on behalf of the slave, a position that he would later renounce. The resolution was voted upon and adopted.[63]

In the evening session, the business committee submitted three resolutions that "excited a very spirited discussion" among the delegates. All three resolutions mirrored those adopted at the Worcester County North Division Anti-Slavery Society meeting the week before in condemning the discriminatory practices of the Eastern Railroad Corporation.[64] According to the *Liberator*, the resolutions were "ably sustained" by Douglass, Collins, Phillips, Garrison, and May and were "unanimously adopted." Douglass and his fellow abolitionists must have spoken impressively. Commenting on the evening session, Garrison wrote that "the subject of prejudice against color, and the brutal conduct of the Eastern R.R. assailants, furnished a fruitful theme for remark, and produced a visible impression upon the audience." In addition, Garrison noted that "impressive and eloquent" speeches were made by Douglass, Phillips, May, and Collins. The minutes of the meeting reported that the entire proceedings "were of a highly interesting character."[65]

The following day, Monday, 13 October, Douglass spoke before the Boston Female Anti-Slavery Society. In her report of the meeting, Maria Weston Chapman wrote, "For Mr. Douglass's encouraging address he received the warm thanks of the society."[66] This was Douglass' first known address to a female antislavery society. An ardent Garrisonian, he accepted women as equal partners in the cause against slavery and, ultimately, he would commit much of his time and energy to the cause of equal rights for women.[67] Toward the end of his career, he wrote: "Observing woman's agency, devotion, and efficiency in pleading the cause of the slave, gratitude for this high service early moved me to give favorable attention to the subject of what is called 'woman's rights' and caused me to be denominated a woman's rights man." Douglass carried the label honestly and proudly. Almost from the start of his antislavery career, he realized that women played an important role in the battle for abolition. "When the true history of the antislavery cause shall be written," he reflected late in his life, "women will occupy a large space in its pages; for the cause of the slave has been peculiarly woman's cause."[68]

On 20 October Douglass, Collins, and Garrison appeared before the quarterly meeting of the Norfolk County Anti-Slavery Society. At this meeting five resolutions were introduced and led to an "animated discussion" in which Douglass took a prominent role. The resolutions condemned slaveholders who professed to be Christians, denounced the formation of a third political party as "inexpedient, and injurious in its tendency to the anti-slavery enterprise," called for abolitionists to interrogate Whig and Democratic candidates for the state legislature "as to their view for the repeal of the marriage law," to help in the circulation of antislavery petitions, and to support a bill preventing the railroad "from proscribing, insulting or assaulting travelers solely on the ground of their complexion."[69] Although we do not know exactly what role Douglass took in these proceedings, we do know that he delivered an address "to a good assembly" during the evening session.[70]

V

During the first two weeks of November 1841, Douglass continued lecturing in Massachusetts. After he and Collins attended the annual meeting of the Hanover Anti-Slavery Society on Monday, 1 November,[71] they rode to Hingham on 4 November to attend a convention of the Plymouth County Anti-Slavery Society, where they were joined by Garrison, George Foster, Edmund Quincy, and escaped slave Lunsford Lane. The proceedings of the convention were chronicled by the editor of the *Hingham Patriot* who, in his words, "went to the Convention, provided with pencil and paper, and noted down the substance of what was said, in the very language of the speakers." Although the texts as recorded by the editor are brief and incomplete, they provide valuable insight into Douglass' thinking at this period of his career and offer further evidence of the subject matter of his early speeches.[72]

The first session of the convention was called to order at 1:30 in the afternoon by Samuel J. May, president of the Plymouth County society. A business committee was appointed and instructed to convene and write a series of resolutions to be used as the basis for debate and discussion. While the committee was preparing the resolutions for the meeting, Foster and Douglass "made a few comments on the progress of the cause," but their remarks were not recorded. When the business committee returned, it presented ten resolutions to the convention. The first resolution asserted the standard Garrisonian conviction of the power of moral suasion over political action:

> Resolved, That our main dependence, under God, for the overthrow of slavery, is *moral suasion*, and the dissemination of our principles; and, relying on the promises of God's word for success, undeterred by legislative proscription or ecclesiastical anathemas, we will continue to press the truth upon the hearts and consciences of slaveholders and their apologists, as opportunity affords, until liberty shall be proclaimed throughout the land, unto all inhabitants thereof.[73]

Edmund Quincy spoke first in favor of the resolution. At the conclusion of his remarks, "a colored man . . . arose, and was introduced to the meeting by Rev. Mr. May, its President, as Mr. Douglas[s]." May presented Douglass as a runaway slave "about whom an interesting story might be told" were it "expedient to make its details public." Douglass then spoke briefly in support of the resolution on moral suasion.[74]

According to the report by the editor of the *Hingham Patriot*, Douglass began with an appeal to all in attendance: "We ought to do just what slave-holders don't want us to do; that is, use *moral suasion*." In Douglass' view, the key to overthrowing slavery was to change people's hearts. The slave-holders "care nothing about your political action; they don't dread the political movement," Douglass declared. "It is the *moral* movement, the appeal to men's sense of right, which makes them and all our opponents tremble." According to Douglass, the most powerful aspect of moral suasion was that it could be practiced by everyone North and South, whereas political action was limited, for the most part, to the North and to men. "One great recommendation of this power of moral suasion," he declared, "is, that every body may exercise it, women as well as men, children as well as adults."[75]

In closing his remarks, Douglass warned that "Slavery is at the North as well as the South: it has interwoven itself in all departments of society but the anti-slavery department, and sometimes I fear I see a little of it there." Douglass' choice of the word "interwoven" was most appropriate and pre-sented a rich image. Slavery was a part of the fabric of American society—even of the antislavery movement itself—and no part of the country was untouched by its insidious influence. One observer reported to the *National Anti-Slavery Standard* that Douglass advocated the resolution, which passed unanimously, "in an eloquent and convincing manner."[76]

The second resolution at Hingham asserted that it was slavery and not abolitionism that threatened to dissolve the Union:

> *Resolved*, That the cry raised, "that the measures of the abolition-ists tend to a dissolution of the Union," is without foundation; that the institution of slavery is the stone of stumbling and rock of offense, which is dashing in pieces our liberties; and those only are the true friends of our country, who are seeking its speedy and peaceful abolition.[77]

Douglass' remarks on this resolution were brief and powerful. He began by pointing to "the fact that the Northern people stand pledged by this union to return runaway slaves." This pledge, he asserted, "constitutes the bul-wark of slavery." Then evoking his personal understanding of the impact of this pledge, Douglass noted that "the slaves are told that if they escape to the North, they will be sent back; and this discourages very many from making any attempts to gain their freedom." Douglass next embraced the Garrisonian doctrine of disunionism: "This is the union whose '*desolation*' we want to accomplish; and he is no true abolitionist, who does not go against this union." The South, he counseled, was not alarmed by how much people "talk and act against slavery as an evil *in the abstract*." Rather, it was the North's pledge to return runaway slaves to the South that mattered most: "It is this pledge binding the North to the South, on which they rely for its support." The minutes reported that Douglass "then alluded, and with considerable wit, to the union between the churches of the North and those of the South." According to one observer, "Douglass demanded, with much rigor, the annihilation of the union between the northern and southern church, and described with much power of sarcasm the spurious piety of both." At the conclusion of his speech, the resolution was passed.[78]

The convention next discussed the case of Lunsford Lane, an escaped slave who was speaking before abolitionist meetings throughout New England to raise money to purchase the release of his wife and six children who were being held in bondage in North Carolina. Both Collins and May stood opposed, "as a matter of principle, to abolitionists contributing to the release" of individual slaves. Douglass openly challenged their views and made "a brief appeal" on behalf of Lane. This is the first report of Douglass publicly taking an opposing view from Collins or any of the white abolitionists, and it reflects his independence of mind even in the earliest stage of his work as an abolitionist agent. Douglass also seized the opportunity to castigate "unmercifully" all "those who called themselves the owners of these slaves." He vividly reported the injustice of slaveholders prospering from the efforts of their chattel:

> They ride about in their carriages . . . with the finest cloth upon their backs, with rings upon their fingers, and in the enjoyment of every luxury that wealth can buy—but who earns it all? whose labor pays for it all? the poor slaves! Their masters bend not a finger in labor, and then are mean enough in soul to pocket the hard earnings of the poor slave, without giving him anything but just bread enough to support life from day to day, that he may still toil on to enrich them.[79]

Despite the lack of a formal resolution on the floor in support of Lane's efforts, the reporter believed Douglass' remarks were important enough to record.[80]

After discussing the Lane case, the convention took up a resolution that urged the towns in Plymouth County "to take prompt and decided measures to circulate the petitions issued by the State Society." The plan was to present these petitions to Congress. After Collins opposed circulating the petitions, Douglass was "requested to state what he knew in relation to the importance of petitioning." Although his comments were brief, Douglass again disagreed with Collins and endorsed the circulation of petitions. "My first knowledge of the abolition movements," he revealed, "was through the petitions for the abolition of Slavery in the District of Columbia." "These petitions," he asserted, "delight the hearts of the

slaves; they rejoice to know that something is going on in their favor."
Douglass' use of the pronoun "they" when referring to slaves in this portion of the speech is noteworthy. When speaking at Lynn just a few weeks
earlier, he had referred to the slaves with the inclusive pronoun "we." Now,
by using "they" to refer to those members of his race in bondage, Douglass
seemed to be distancing himself, consciously or unconsciously, from his
former life as a slave.[81]

Douglass continued his speech by describing how slaves learned about
the abolitionist petitions. His statement, though very similar to the one he
had made at Lynn regarding how slaves knew of their right to liberty, was
far more descriptive and specific:

> Waiters hear their masters talk at table, cursing the abolitionists,
> John Quincy Adams, &c.; the masters imagine that their poor
> slaves are so ignorant that they don't know the meaning of the lan-
> guage they are using; for the slaves always pretend to be very stu-
> pid, they commit all sorts of foolery and act like baboons and wild
> beasts in [the] presence of their masters: but every word is noted
> in the memory.[82]

Here Douglass indirectly attacked the widespread notion that the slaves
were ignorant. Although they acted foolish around their masters for strate-
gic reasons, they were in fact intelligent and used their intelligence deftly
to learn about the antislavery petitions. Once the knowledge of petitions
was attained, Douglass explained, the slaves disseminated their learning
through conversation: "When they get together they talk over what they
have heard—they talk about liberty, and about these petitions." By sharing what they learned, the slaves gained "a vague idea that somebody is
doing something to ameliorate their condition." In fact, Douglass stated, "I
was myself contemplating measures and making arrangements for my own
emancipation, when hearing of these petitions stopped me."[83]

At this stage, Douglass obviously perceived the dangers of his audience
believing that the slaves were being lulled into inactivity by knowledge that
abolitionists were acting on their behalf. Hence, he closed his brief
remarks with a warning: "But, sir, the slaves are learning to read and to
write, and the time is fast coming, when they will act in concert, and effect
their own emancipation, if justice is not done by some other extraneous
agency." In other words, petitions alone were not enough. Douglass wanted to make sure his audience continued their efforts to agitate against slavery and to use every possible means to destroy it.[84]

Douglass' brief, yet poignant remarks had an impact on at least one
observer in his audience:

> As this Douglas[s] stood there in manly attitude, with erect form,
> and glistening eye, and deep-toned voice, telling us that he had

been secretly devising means to effect his release from bondage, we could not help of thinking of Spartacus, the Gladiator; . . . A man of his shrewdness, and his power both intellectually and physically, must be poor stuff . . . to make a slave of.[85]

This unidentified observer clearly comprehended the true meaning of Douglass' remarks, for Douglass was not just stating the importance of petitioning and its impact on the slave—he was also arguing that the slave was an intelligent, shrewd individual, a human being unworthy of being another's property. The observer's remarks also reveal the impact Douglass' physical presence on the platform had on his audience. His "erect form," "glistening eye," and "deep-toned voice" combined with his verbal message to provide a compelling argument against enslaving black people. From the observer's perspective, moreover, Douglass possessed a "manly attitude." During the nineteenth century, being perceived as "manly" in the public forum was equated with being an effective orator. The manly style was driven by reason and appealed to the intellect. At Hingham, Douglass' message was factual, rational, direct, and appealed to reason. Douglass was perceived as a man because he reasoned intelligently and forcefully, and delivered his message in a conventional manly style. By extension, he exhibited manly virtues which overturned racist conceptions that as a black man he was an inferior being.[86]

In the evening session, members of the Plymouth County Anti-Slavery Society gathered to discuss four resolutions that had been postponed from the afternoon session. After three of these resolutions had been passed, Edmund Quincy spoke in support of the fourth, which denounced race prejudice:

> *Resolved*, That the prejudice which prevails so extensively in this country against the colored people is cruel and malignant, utterly at variance with Christianity, in direct violation of the word of God, and justly subjects this nation to the scoffs and reproaches of the civilized world.[87]

Quincy then invited Douglass to share his knowledge of such prejudice. According to the reporter's summation of Douglass' speech, he responded to Quincy's solicitation by reciting a series of examples of northern prejudice "as he had experienced them in his own person." Douglass discussed being dragged from cars on the Eastern Railroad "after paying full fare." He also "told of the obstacles which his complexion threw in the way of his obtaining employment at his trade." Then in a stinging rebuke to the North, Douglass declared, "there was none of this prejudice" in the South. Even though he had been a slave in the South, he could work at his trade and ride the railroad "by the side of his mistress, at her own request." In the South, Douglass proclaimed, "they have no '*Jim Crow pews*' up aloft in their churches."[88]

At this point in the minutes, the reporter stopped paraphrasing Douglass' remarks and proceeded to quote him directly as he moved into a discussion of the oppressive nature of prejudice as it existed in the churches of the North. To reveal the nature of that prejudice, Douglass isolated three incidents he had encountered since escaping from the South. In the first incident, Douglass drew from an experience at New Bedford's Elm Street Methodist Church. After narrating how the bread and wine had been served to all the white members present, Douglass told of what happened next. The "good minister," he stated, "drew a long breath, and looking out toward the door, [where the black people were assembled], exclaimed 'Come up, colored friends, come up! For you know *God is no respecter of persons!*'" Douglass, obviously disturbed by the practice of separating whites from blacks, emphatically stated, "I haven't been there to see the sacrament taken since."[89]

The next two incidents Douglass discussed were drawn from "a great revival of religion" in New Bedford. Here, according to Douglass, "many were converted, and 'received,' as they [whites] said, 'into the Kingdom of Heaven.'" Before relating the incidents, Douglass utilized the power of imagery and allegory to explain that "the kingdom of Heaven is like a net; at least so it was according to the practice of these pious Christians; and when the net was drawn ashore, they had to sit down and cull out the fish; well, it happened now that some of the fish had rather black scales; so these were sorted out and packed by themselves." In this allegory, black people, upon being accepted into the kingdom of Heaven, were singled out and separated from white Christians on the basis of their skin color. Douglass' use of allegory was appropriate to the religious theme he was developing, and it demonstrated his command of rhetorical strategy. Had he simply come forward with his attack, he might have offended his white audience. By clothing his attack against prejudice in an allegory, he demonstrated his sensitivity toward his audience and softened his message without diminishing its meaning.[90]

After the allegory, Douglass presented the second of his specific instances of racial prejudice in the northern church. The incident concerned a young black girl who had somehow slipped through the net of prejudice. Having been "baptised in the same water" with whites, Douglass told the audience, "she thought she might sit at the Lord's table, and partake of the same sacramental elements with the others." The deacon then presented the cup to each of the people present. When he stood before the black girl, "he could not pass her, for there was the minister looking right at him, and as he was a kind of an abolitionist, the deacon was rather afraid of giving him offence; so he handed the girl the cup." The young girl then drank from the cup. Next to her, Douglass revealed, sat a young white lady "who had been converted at the same time, baptised in the same water, and put her hope in the same blessed Saviour; yet when the cup, containing the precious blood which had been shed for all, came to her, she rose in disdain, and walked out of the church. Such was the religion *she* had experienced!"[91]

Douglass then illustrated his point about racial prejudice in the churches with a third incident from the same religious revival. He told the audience a brief story about a young lady who fell into a trance and who, when coming out of the trance, declared she had been to Heaven. An older woman, Douglass related, "inquired of the girl who had the vision, if she saw any black folks in Heaven?" The young girl hesitated, then replied, "*'Oh! I didn't go into the kitchen!*'" This story again illustrated Douglass' point about the supremacy of white people over blacks. In this example, the young white woman who claimed to have been to Heaven had a definite idea of the Heavenly territory black people should occupy. Certainly black people could go to Heaven, but they were banished to the kitchen and placed in a subservient position. Like Douglass' other examples, this incident showed racial prejudice to be a reality blacks in the North faced on a daily basis. Indeed, that prejudice was so severe, he said in drawing this section of his remarks to a close, that some white people found it "disagreeable . . . to even think of going to Heaven, if colored people are going there too!"[92]

Having completed his treatment of prejudice in the North, Douglass next discussed the reasons for such prejudice. "The grand cause," he claimed, was slavery. There were other "less prominent" causes, however, one of which was the way children in the North were "instructed to regard the blacks." According to the editor's report, Douglass was interrupted here by a member of the audience who agreed with this charge: "'Yes!' exclaimed an old gentleman, . . .'When they behave wrong, they are told 'Black man come catch you!'" Seeming to lose his train of thought, Douglass dilated for a moment on the need for white people to keep black people in their proper place. In the process of disclosing his feelings about this issue, he entered into an impassioned attack against "people in general [who] . . . will say they like colored men as well as any other, *but in their proper place.*" He declared:

Who is to decide what is their proper place? *They* assign us that place; they don't let us do it for ourselves, nor will they allow us a voice in the decision. They will not allow that we have a head to think, and a heart to feel, and a soul to aspire. They treat us not as men, but as dogs—they cry "*Slu-boy!*" and expect us to run and do their bidding. That's the way we are liked.[93]

By using the inclusive pronoun "we" in this passage, Douglass implicitly spoke for all black people. At Lynn, he had spoken on behalf of the slaves. Now, at Hingham, he was speaking on behalf of all the members of his race. By using "they" to speak of people who believed black people ought to be kept in their "proper" place, Douglass created a tension he would sustain throughout this portion of his remarks. He also revealed his frustration with being part of an oppressed minority and his belief that the prejudice against his race rested on the assumption that black people were less than human and lacked the abilities to think, feel, and aspire to improve themselves. Although Douglass did not refute that assumption at this point in the speech, his very presence on the platform presented an argument against it. By his eloquence, he demonstrated to his audience that he had a "head to think, and a heart to feel, and a soul to aspire" and that, by extension, other black men and women also possessed these attributes.

At this moment in the speech, Douglass switched his attack from the general "they" to the specific "you," thereby bringing the issue of racial prejudice home to his immediate auditors. "You degrade us," he charged, "and then ask why we are degraded—you shut our mouths, and then ask why we don't speak—you close your colleges and seminaries against us, and then ask us why we don't know more!" Through the use of repetition, parallelism, and antithesis, Douglass here presented a series of stirring contrasts that revealed the glaring contradictions between white people's behavior toward blacks and their expectations of them. He expressed in graphic, biting language the indignation that all black people felt on a daily basis.[94]

Douglass moved from this brief digression to confront what he believed was the true cause of prejudice. "All this prejudice sinks into insignificance in *my* mind," he began, subtly referring to his capacity to think, "when compared with the enormous iniquity of the system which is its cause." Having focused his audience's attention on the system of slavery, Douglass was now poised to attack the "slaveholding ministers." These ministers defended the institution of slavery by endorsing from the pulpit "the divine right of slaveholders to property in their fellow men." Next, Douglass delivered a striking imitation of the message preached by Southern ministers to the slaves. This is the first recorded instance of Douglass' famous "Slaveholder's Sermon." The sermon, most likely drawn from his personal observations from slavery, quickly became the centerpiece of his abolitionist rhetoric:[95]

> Oh! if you wish to be happy in time, happy in eternity, you must be obedient to your masters; their interest is yours; God made one portion of men to do the working, and another to do the thinking; how good God is! Now you have no trouble or anxiety; but ah! you

can't imagine how perplexing it is to your masters and mistresses to have so much thinking to do in your behalf! You cannot appreciate your blessings; you know not how happy a thing it is for you that you were born of that portion of the human family which has the working instead of the thinking to do! Oh! how grateful and obedient you ought to be to your masters! How beautiful are the arrangements of Providence! Look at your hard, horny hands—see how nicely they are adapted to the labor you have to perform! Look at our delicate fingers, so exactly fitted for our station, and see how manifest it is that God designed us to be the thinkers, and you to be the workers—Oh! the wisdom of God![96]

Here Douglass drew upon his slave experience to produce a message dripping with irony and sarcasm. He skillfully used mimicry to denigrate southern ministers and the arguments they used to justify the subjugation of one race to another.[97] Douglass, however, did not just recite the story— he enacted it. In a shrewdly devised turn, he became a southern white minister speaking to the slaves, thereby symbolically transporting his auditors into the southern church and forcing them to confront the same message slaves were asked to believe on a daily basis. In addition, Douglass most likely used a southern dialect and dramatic gestures to bring the irony of the sermon to light. James Monroe, an abolitionist who heard Douglass' slaveholder's sermon "more than once," described it as

a brilliant example of irony, parody, caricature, and *reductio ad absurdum*, all combined. It abounded in phrases which, though innocent in the original preacher, when delivered by Mr. Douglass with suggestive tone and emphasis to a Northern audience, became irresistibly ludicrous. . . . To do him justice . . . you must imagine his marvelous power of imitation and characterization— the holy tone of the preacher—the pious snuffle—the upturned eye—the funny affectation of profound wisdom . . . and the tearful sympathy with which the speaker dwelt upon the helpless condition of his hearers in case they should cease to be the property of slaveholding masters.[98]

In closing his remarks at Hingham, Douglass kept the audience immersed in his slave experience by particularizing the slaveholder rendered above and giving him a concrete form. To achieve this, Douglass repeated, nearly in its entirety, a section from his address at Lynn. He talked of his former master, "a class leader" in the Methodist church, a man who "could pray at morning, pray at noon, and pray at night," yet tie up Douglass' "poor cousin by . . . [her] two thumbs" and "inflict stripes and blows upon . . . [her] bare back, till the blood streamed to the ground!"

Worse yet, while committing this violent offense against his slave, Douglass' master quoted the "scripture for his authority."[99]

Immediately after Douglass' speech, Garrison rose to take advantage of the impression made by it, saying:

> I am almost afraid to speak now, lest I should undue the impression made by our friend Douglas[s]—a noble man indeed! fitted to adorn any station in society! And such a man by slaveholders is called a "*thing*," and treated as a beast! He is a miracle! a proof of what man can do and be, in spite of station or condition. He is not a picked man, sent here to show off; he is the creature of accident, one who has had no previous advantages, and who is but a specimen of what thousands, now bound down by the yoke of oppression, might be, if they were only blessed with the precious boon of liberty.[100]

Following Garrison's brief and poignant comments, a vote was taken and the resolution denouncing racial prejudice passed unanimously.

As Garrison's comments indicate, Douglass' speech at the Hingham convention evoked strong reactions. Increase S. Smith, secretary of the meeting, reported that Douglass "produced a very powerful effect."[101] Another observer reported to the *National Anti-Slavery Standard* that Douglass had spoken "admirably with regard to prejudice against color."[102] Evelina Smith, a local abolitionist, wrote that although some people of Hingham were "very mad" with Douglass because of his "impudence," she thought he had "great talent" and "gave great interest to the meeting here."[103] The editor of the *Hingham Patriot* informed his readers that Douglass was "very fluent in the use of language" and spoke as well "as men who have spent all their days over books. He is forcible, keen and very sarcastic; and considering the poor advantages he must have had as a slave, he is certainly a remarkable man."[104]

VI

Except for a short trip to New Hampshire in early September, Douglass had done all his speaking in Massachusetts. After the Hingham meeting, however, he traveled with William Lloyd Garrison and John A. Collins to Providence to assist in the campaign regarding black suffrage in Rhode Island. With one exception—an appearance at Fall River, Massachusetts, on 23 November—this campaign would occupy him for the remainder of 1841.[105]

Suffrage in Rhode Island had traditionally been limited to white males who owned property worth at least $134 and to their eldest sons, who were exempt from the property requirement. Although these suffrage qualifications were not literally specified under the outdated charter issued by

Charles II in 1663, they were generally considered to be constitutional. The people of Rhode Island wanted a new constitution that would abolish the property requirement for voting. Since 1839 the disenfranchised majority of the state's citizens had worked to create such a constitution. Although their efforts had heretofore proved unsuccessful, they were gaining force by the end of 1841.[106]

In October of that year, a so-called People's Convention had met at Providence and drafted a new constitution which removed the property qualification and extended the right to vote to all white male citizens of the state but denied it to black citizens.[107] Garrison's response was swift. "What meanness, hypocrisy, oppression!" he cried in the *Liberator*. "Let the most determined opposition to this despicable proscription be made by the people."[108] The *Liberator* also summoned the Rhode Island abolitionists to action:

> The abolitionists of Rhode Island should resolve, as one man . . . that the next annual meeting of their State Society, (which is near at hand) shall witness such a gathering on their part as has not been seen since the standard of immediate emancipation was unfurled to the breeze. They have long been slumbering, . . . and it is time for them to wake out of sleep, and wrestle mightily with a corrupt public sentiment which is crushing humanity to the dust, and making merchandize of the image of God. Especially should they act in a spirited and united manner, at this time, when an attempt is making Rhode Island, by the pseudo friends of political reform, to make the rights of a man dependent on the hue of his skin![109]

The notice closed with a promise: Garrison and other Massachusetts abolitionists would travel to Rhode Island to attend the annual meeting of the state's antislavery society.

From 11-13 November the Rhode Island Anti-Slavery Society assembled at Franklin Hall in Providence. The society's executive committee had set the mood for the convention by issuing a circular immediately after the People's Convention "calling on the abolitionists to make a combined and vigorous effort against the proposed Constitution."[110] As promised, Garrison, along with Collins and Douglass, journeyed from Massachusetts for the meeting. Judging from the minutes of the convention, Douglass played a prominent role. On 11 November, during the evening session, he was one of six blacks who spoke in favor of the resolutions relating to prejudice against people of color. The minutes noted that these resolutions "were ably discussed . . . in presence of a large audience by Frederic[k] Douglas[s], recently a slave." His remarks to the convention "were listened to with great attention by a crowded house, and served to remove, in some degree at least, that vulgar prejudice which measures the capacity of a man's mind by the color of his skin."[111] A correspondent for the *Narragansett Chief* noted that "a colored man by the name of Douglas[s], made the most gentlemanlike speech which we heard during the session; betraying both an ease of delivery and a brilliancy of thought truly remarkable."[112] A reporter for the *Suffrage Examiner* wrote: "We wish the hall had been ten times as large, and all our 'negro haters' could have heard them. They would have learned, if they did not know it before, that 'the colored man,' as *Douglass* beautifully expressed it, 'had a head to think, a heart to feel, and a soul to aspire to like other men.'" Reporting the impact of Douglass' message on the assembly, the correspondent stated, "Many of those who attended the meeting, left the hall that night ashamed of their treatment towards this oppressed class."[113]

Not only did Douglass stir the local abolitionists on the first day of the convention with his remarks concerning prejudice, but his remarks on suffrage on the second day appear to have impressed them as well. A correspondent to the *Suffrage Examiner* reported that a "free discussion" concerning suffrage dominated the Friday sessions. Garrison, Nathaniel P. Rogers, "and others" participated in the proceedings.[114] Douglass was among those abolitionists who entered into the discussions to condemn the proposed constitution and denounce "the course pursued by the Suffrage party." Rogers, a prominent abolitionist editor from Concord, New Hampshire, heard Douglass speak during one of the Friday sessions and reported his reaction in his newspaper, the *Herald of Freedom*:

> The fugitive Douglass was up when we entered. This is an extraordinary man. He was cut out for a hero. . . . A commanding person—over six feet, we should say, in height, and of most manly proportions. His head would strike a phrenologist amid a sea of them in Exeter Hall, and his voice would ring like a trumpet in the field. . . . As a speaker he has few equals. It is not declamation—but oratory, power of debate. He watches the tide of discussion with the eye of a veteran, and dashes into it at once with all the tact of the forum or the bar. He has wit, sarcasm, pathos—all that first-rate men show in their master efforts. His voice is highly melodious and rich, and his enunciation quite elegant; and yet he has been but two or three years out of the house of bondage.[115]

Douglass' impact on the convention can be gauged by his appointment to two important assignments growing out of the Friday meeting. Toward the end of the afternoon session, a special suffrage committee resolved that the Rhode Island society "call a series of meetings during the fall and winter, in different parts of the State" at which abolitionist lecturers could agitate against the proposed constitution. The special committee also recommended that a committee be appointed to go before the adjourned People's

Convention, to be held in Providence the next week, "to protest, in the name of the abolitionists of this State, against the insertion of the word 'white' in their new constitution." This meeting was a continuation of the People's Convention held in Providence in October. Both of the actions taken by the special committee involved Douglass. Not only was he appointed as one of the team of lecturers to campaign across Rhode Island, but he and Abby Kelley were the only members of the twelve-person protest committee appointed by the meeting not to hail from Rhode Island.[116]

One week later, on 18 November, Douglass, Kelley, and the other ten members of the protest committee appeared before the People's Convention in Providence. Their appearance did not go well. Kelley informed the *National Anti-Slavery Standard* that they were "not treated . . . by the adjourned convention with that courtesy which they might expect." The lack of courtesy extended to the abolitionists by the People's Convention was only a foreshadowing, however, of what was to come.[117]

The team of lecturers appointed by the Rhode Island Anti-Slavery Society to campaign throughout the state against the new constitution included Douglass, Kelley, John A. Collins, Stephen S. Foster, Parker Pillsbury, and Abel Tanner. They were assigned to visit every town and village in the state "without delay" and to organize six conventions "to be held before the days set apart for voting on the constitution." Since the vote on the constitution was scheduled for 27-29 December, there was little time to organize the conventions, six of which were hastily scheduled for Woonsocket, North Scituate, Fiskville and Phenix, Kingston, Newport, and Providence.[118]

From the beginning, Douglass and his colleagues were denounced as intermeddlers and told to mind their own business. Supporters of the new constitution and neutrals alike were incensed by out-of-state abolitionists intruding in the internal affairs of Rhode Island. The *New Age*, the newspaper of the Suffrage Party, charged that the abolitionists' main goal was "to break down all organizations of both the Church and State, and convert people to *transcendentalism*." The newspaper accused them of being "against all governments regulated by law" and attacked them as a "class of disorganizers." The people of Rhode Island, the newspaper declared, "will not suffer themselves to be libelled by persons from other States as *murderers, manstealers, hypocrites*, and *adulterers*." Everywhere Douglass and his colleagues sought to speak they were greeted by mobs determined to break up their meetings. This marked the first time in his abolitionist career that Douglass encountered mob resistance.[119]

Following their instructions, Douglass and his fellow lecturers sought to establish conventions in each of the six scheduled locations. The first convention was held in Woonsocket Falls on 2-3 December and was fraught with difficulties.[120] Upon arriving, the abolitionists had trouble finding a suitable meeting place. Once they found a hall, their first session was "thinly attended." The evening session "brought a crowded house" but was broken up by "a mob, whose watchword was 'nigger voting.'" The next day's sessions proceeded without disruption until "just before the time for adjournment in the afternoon," when the people in charge of the hall informed the meeting that the doors would be closed against them for the evening session. The proprietors of the hall feared the house would be damaged by a mob. Unable to secure a meeting place for the evening, the convention ended.[121]

The second convention was held in North Scituate on 7-8 December.[122] Again Douglass and his colleagues had difficulty finding a meeting place. Only after "agreeing nothing should be discussed but the subject of slavery," they were permitted to convene in the Freewill Baptist Church. According to one eyewitness account, during the evening session, Stephen S. Foster, ignoring the agreement with the leaders of the church, introduced a resolution denouncing the "white Suffrage Constitution" as "more odious and repugnant to the true principles of freedom than the old charter; and cannot receive the support of any true republican or genuine Christian." According to the observer, Douglass, "a runaway slave" and a "man of some natural talent," rose to support Foster's resolution, declaring that "he was bound by the laws of God, to oppose any Constitution" that would be in accordance with the old charter. A brief debate followed his remarks until "one of the committee of the house" reminded the abolitionists that the church "was not engaged for such discussion" and declared the meeting dissolved. Nevertheless, Foster took the floor and began speaking against the new constitution. The reaction was violent. A mob "repeatedly disturbed the meeting," Kelley reported, "and the tumult was wild and fierce." The next day's sessions were also "much disturbed by the suffrage mob."[123]

The third convention convened at Phenix and Fiskville on 14 December, apparently with the same results.[124] At the request of "friends from East Greenwich," the convention adjourned to that place on 15 December.[125] The meeting at the Court House in East Greenwich marked the first time Douglass and his associates were "able to go through a regular routine of business, and pass resolutions." Even during the course of this convention, however, "there were frequent interruptions and outbreaks."[126]

After holding a convention at Kingston on 21-22 December, Douglass and his colleagues traveled to Newport, where the pattern of intolerance and intimidation emerged once again.[127] When notice was given that a convention would convene there on 24-25 December, "many threats of violence were thrown out."[128] On 24 December, during the opening session at Armory Hall, the convention was interrupted "with great confusion and

disturbance" by "persons of standing." The second meeting was also interrupted and "closed by the clamor of the mob," which followed some of the
abolitionists to their lodgings. The following day, two meetings were scheduled. The morning session proceeded "quietly," but the afternoon session
never met because "the hall was full of rioters." With "all hope of obtaining a hearing being vain," the abolitionists withdrew.[129]

The final convention was held on 27-28 December in Providence,
"where the whirlwind . . . was completely up during the meetings."[130] The
hall where the convention convened was reported to have been "much
injured by the rioters." Meetings were filled with "boisterous and malig-
nant" crowds "determined to drown every voice that was raised." The anti-
abolitionists threw "snowballs and other missiles" at the lecturers, and at
the conclusion of one of the meetings, a crowd of people accompanied
Abby Kelley home with "howls and snow-balls."[131] The turbulent final session, held on the evening of 28 December, was described by William Alpin,
the recording secretary of the state society:

> The discussion was commenced about 7 o'clock by S. S. Foster,
> who addressed the meeting without interruption, until nearly the
> close of his remarks, when he was interrupted by the stamping and
> shouting of a large number of men and boys, who had filled the
> house to overflowing . . . for the purpose of breaking up the meet-
> ing. The mobocratic elements which had raged with so much
> vehemence at the previous conventions in different parts of the
> State, appeared to be here congregated, *en masse*, and burst forth
> into an irresistible outbreak, which continued without intermis-
> sion and with increasing violence until a late hour. The mob had
> entire possession of the Hall, defying even the power of the police
> present to quell the riot. During the evening, the audience was
> addressed by Frederick Douglas[s], Parker Pillsbury, Thomas
> Davis, and Abel Tanner, appealing to the friends of order to sustain
> freedom of speech, but without success, and this series of conven-
> tions of the Rhode Island Anti-Slavery Society was adjourned
> amidst a scene of confusion and uproar never before witnessed by
> the friends of free discussion in this city.[132]

With their tactics of intimidation and intolerance, the mob had succeeded
in muffling debate over the new constitution for the moment, but ultimately the voice of reason would triumph. Before the end of 1842, the conservatives of the state would write and ratify a constitution abolishing the
racial and property qualifications for voters.[133]

The arduous Rhode Island campaign further matured Douglass as an
orator, and he returned home to Massachusetts in January 1842 a seasoned abolitionist lecturer. From the beginning of his agency in mid-
August though the end of December, he had traveled more than 3,500

miles, visited more than sixty towns and parishes, delivered nearly 100
lectures, and attended at least twenty-four county meetings and conventions throughout Massachusetts, New Hampshire, and Rhode Island. He
had demonstrated his courage by remaining calm before angry, boisterous,
threatening mobs. He had proven his endurance and tolerance by riding in
the cold, comfortless "nigger cars" on trains and by maintaining a demanding speaking schedule in spite of severe hardships.[134] His three-month trial
period had ended in November, and his value to the antislavery crusade
could not be questioned. In a letter to Garrison in January 1842, Collins
reflected on the new agent's work during the previous months:

> Frederic[k] Douglas[s], a fugitive from slavery, has travelled
> much of the time with me. Though he has never been favored with
> the advantages of an education, his style of speaking is chaste, free
> and forcible—his enunciation clear and distinct—his manner
> deliberate and energetic, alike free from tameness and ranting
> vehemence. His descriptions of slavery are most graphic, and his
> arguments are so lucid, and occasionally so spiced with pleasantry,
> and sometimes a little satire, that his addresses, though long, are
> seldom tedious, but are listened to with the most profound atten-
> tion. He is capable of performing a vast amount of good for his
> oppressed race.[135]

As Collins understood, in Douglass the Garrisonian abolitionists had
uncovered a remarkable new voice that added substance and excitement
to the antislavery struggle. From the outset, Douglass told the story of his
slave past and fugitive present with such force that it enabled him to speak
with an authenticity unequaled by even the most talented white abolitionists. While white abolitionists could only talk about the evils of slavery,
Douglass drew from his own background to produce vivid illustrations of
slavery and freedom as he had experienced them. Contrary to the usual
accounts of Douglass' life, however, he quickly moved beyond recounting
the story of his slave and fugitive experiences and broadened the scope of
his subject matter. Within weeks of the Nantucket meeting in August, he
was denouncing northern racial prejudice, attacking the church as proslavery, advocating petitioning, discussing the supremacy of moral suasion
over political action, calling for dissolution of the Union, and denouncing
the pledge of the North to return fugitive slaves to the South. Contrary to
the conventional view that he was entirely under the wing and influence of
Garrison and the Massachusetts Anti-Slavery Society, Douglass at times
disagreed with his traveling partner, Collins, and other white abolitionists
in his speeches. By the end of 1841, Douglass' oratorical abilities had
helped him to emerge from obscurity to become a powerful abolitionist
lecturer—a spokesman for his race, slave and free. In January 1842 the

Massachusetts Anti-Slavery Society hired him as a full-time lecturer, in which capacity he would soon be moving throughout Massachusetts to deliver his antislavery message.

Notes

1. Parker Pillsbury, *Acts of the Anti-Slavery Apostles* (Rochester, N.Y.: Claque, Wegman, Schlicht, and Company, 1883), 324.

2. Raymond Gerald Fulkerson, "Frederick Douglass and the Anti-Slavery Crusade: His Career and Speeches, 1817-1861," pt. 1 (Ph.D. diss., University of Illinois, 1971), 46.

3. *The Life and Writings of Frederick Douglass, Volume 1*, Philip S. Foner, ed. (New York: International Publishers, 1950), 1:45-46.

4. *Liberator*, 20 August 1841, 134-35.

5. *New Bedford Morning Register*, 10 August 1841, 2.

6. *Liberator*, 23 July 1841, 118; Samuel Rodman, *The Diary of Samuel Rodman*, ed. Zephaniah W. Pease (New Bedford, Mass.: Reynolds Printing Company, 1927), 224.

7. Frederick Douglass, *Narrative of the Life of Frederick Douglass, An American Slave, Written By Himself* (1845; reprint, New York: Signet, 1968), 118-19; Frederick Douglass, *My Bondage and My Freedom* (1855; reprint, New York: Dover, 1969), 357-58; Frederick Douglass, *Life and Times of Frederick Douglass, Written by Himself* (1892; reprint, New York: Macmillan, 1962), 215.

8. *Liberator*, 20 August 1841, 134-35.

9. Pillsbury, *Acts*, 325.

10. Foner, *Life and Writings*, 1:26; Pillsbury, *Acts*, 325; *National Anti-Slavery Standard*, 26 August 1841, 46.

11. Douglass, *Bondage and Freedom*, 356.

12. *Liberator*, 20 August 1841, 135.

13. Ibid.

14. *Liberator*, 29 March 1839, 50.

15. *Liberator*, 9 July 1841, 110.

16. Douglass, Narrative, 119; Peter F. Walker, *Moral Choices: Memory, Desire, and Imagination in Nineteenth-Century American Abolition* (Baton Rouge: Louisiana State University Press, 1978), 241. See also Houston A. Baker, *The Journey Back: Issues in Black Literature and Criticism* (Chicago: University of Chicago Press, 1984), 44.

17. Douglass, *Bondage and Freedom*, 357-58.

18. Samuel J. May, *Some Recollections of Our Anti-Slavery Conflict* (Boston: Fields, Osgood, and Co., 1869), 294.

19. *National Anti-Slavery Standard*, 26 August 1841, 46.

20. Douglass, *Narrative*, vi.

21. Ibid., vi-vii.

22. Pillsbury, Acts, 326.

23. *National Anti-Slavery Standard*, 26 August 1841, 46.

24. Ibid.

25. Douglass, *Bondage and Freedom*, 358-59; Fulkerson, "Frederick Douglass," part 1, 46; Benjamin Quarles, *Frederick Douglass* (1948; reprint, New York: Atheneum, 1968), 14.

26. Douglass, *Bondage and Freedom*, 359-60. According to Walker, *Moral Choices*, 244, "This passage is Douglass' enduring summary statement about the way he felt as he entered the abolitionist enterprise, once he was able to see what the experience had really meant for him."

27. "Recollections of the Anti-Slavery Conflict," in *The Papers of Frederick Douglass* (Washington, D.C.: Library of Congress Photoduplication Service, 1974), reel 18, frame 190.

28. *Liberator*, 4 June 1841, 89.

29. Quarles, *Frederick Douglass*, 19; Allen Johnson and Dumas Malone, eds., *Dictionary of American Biography* (1929; reprint, New York: Scribner's, 1958), 2:307-8.

30. Oliver Johnson, *W. L. Garrison and His Times* (1881; reprint, Miami, Fla.: Mnemosyne Publishing Company, 1969), 300. See also Garrison's letter to Collins of 1 April 1841, in *The Letters of William Lloyd Garrison, Volume III*, ed. Walter M. Merrill (Cambridge, Mass.: Belknap Press, 1973), 3:20.

31. *Liberator*, 27 August 1841, 139.

32. *National Anti-Slavery Standard*, 2 September 1841, 50.

33. *Liberator*, 10 September 1841, 146. Writing in 1897, the abolitionist James Monroe recalled that he had met Douglass for the first time at the Millbury meeting: "In the summer of 1841 . . . I went from my home in Connecticut to Millbury, Massachusetts, to attend an anti-slavery convention. There, for the first time, I met Mr. Douglass. . . . The tall, straight, well-built youth, with a strong head, eyes and face full of humor, and a certain frank manliness of bearing, won from me, at once, a kindly esteem which grew in strength for more than half a century. . . . When I saw him at Millbury, I did not know that he was a great man; but even then there was something in his manner of thought and expression, that might have led me to suspect it. He was genial and affable and prone to laugh at his own deficiencies. He could read and write, and had acquired some general knowledge. On a table near him was a leaf of paper on which were scrawled perhaps two-dozen words. 'What is this?' I said. 'That,' he replied with a laugh, 'is my speech'" (James Monroe, *Oberlin Thursday Lectures Addresses and Essays* [Oberlin, Edward J. Goodrich, 1897], 57-58).

34. *Liberator*, 27 August 1841, 138.

35. *Liberator*, 6 August 1841, 127.

36. Blassingame draws a similar conclusion. See John W. Blassingame, ed., *The Frederick Douglass Papers, Series One: Speeches, Debates, and Interviews, Volume 1* (New Haven, Conn.: Yale University Press, 1979), 1:xlviii.

37. Douglass, *Bondage and Freedom*, 361-62.

38. Ibid., 362.

39. *Liberator*, 3 September 1841, 153.

40. Blassingame, ed., *Douglass Papers, Series One*, 1:lxxxvii, does not include the lecture of 3 September in its itinerary of Douglass' speaking activities.

41. *Liberator*, 24 September 1841, 153.

42. *Liberator*, 3 September 1841, 143; *Liberator*, 24 September 1841, 153.

43. *Liberator*, 15 October 1841, 165.

44. Blassingame, ed., *Douglass Papers, Series One*, 1:lxxxvii, mistakenly indicates that Douglass attended a meeting in Georgetown, Massachusetts, on 10 September. Since Douglass was in Dover, New Hampshire, on 10 September attending the annual meeting of the Strafford County Anti-Slavery Society, he could not have been in attendance at the Georgetown meeting.

45. *Liberator*, 1 October 1841, 158. Blassingame, ed., *Douglass Papers, Series One*, 1:lxxxvii, erroneously states that the Stratford County meeting of 8-10 September took place on 8 September only.

46. *Pennsylvania Freeman*, 20 October 1841, 1-2; Blassingame, ed., *Douglass Papers, Series One*, 1:3.

47. "I Have Come to Tell You Something About Slavery: An Address Delivered in Lynn, Massachusetts, in October 1841," in Blassingame, ed., *Douglass Papers, Series One*, 1:3.

48. Douglass, *Narrative*, 35; John Sekora, "Comprehending Slavery: Language and Personal History in Douglass' Narrative of 1845," *CLA Journal* 29 (December 1985): 164.

49. Caleb Bingham, ed., *The Columbian Orator* (Boston, Mass.: Manning and Loring, 1797), 25.

50. Blassingame, ed., *Douglass Papers*, Series One, 1:3.

51. Ibid.

52. Ibid. In 1845, Douglass published this same story in his *Narrative of the Life of Frederick Douglass, An American Slave, Written By Himself*, 68-69.

53. Blassingame, ed., *Douglass Papers*, Series One, 1:3-4.

54. Ibid., 1:4.

55. Ibid.

56. Ibid.

57. Ibid., 1:5.

58. David N. Johnson, *Sketches of Lynn* (1880; reprint, Westport, Conn.: Greenwood Press, 1970), 230-31.

59. *Pennsylvania Freeman*, 20 October 1841, 1.

60. *Liberator*, 15 October 1841, 166.

61. *Liberator*, 29 October 1841, 175. For a complete disclosure of this incident, see the letter from Collins to Garrison, 8 September 1841, published in the Liberator, 15 October 1841, 165. See also Douglass, *Bondage and Freedom*, 398-400; Douglass, *Life and Times*, 224-25.

62. *Liberator*, 29 October 1851, 175.

63. *Liberator*, 22 October 1841, 171.

64. The first resolution strongly denounced the actions of the railroad "in forcibly ejecting persons of both sexes solely on account of their complexion, and in hauling out and mistreating white people for venturing to remonstrate against such flagrant violations of law, decency and good order." The second resolution called upon the state legislature to "define the limits granted to Rail Road Corporations, [so] that persons travelling on their respective roads shall not be insulted and proscribed merely on the ground of their complexion." The third resolution "recommended to all persons travelling from Boston to Portland, to patronize the Rail Road known by the name of the 'Upper Route,' in preference to the Eastern Rail Road," because people of color were "treated by this corporation as equal human beings" (*Liberator*, 22 October 1841, 171).

65. *Liberator*, 15 October 1841, 167; *Liberator*, 22 October 1841, 171.

66. *Liberator*, 29 October 1841, 174.

67. Quarles, *Frederick Douglass*, 131-32; Waldo E. Martin, Jr., *The Mind of Frederick Douglass* (Chapel Hill: University of North Carolina Press, 1984), 136-37.

68. Douglass, *Life and Times*, 469, 472.

69. *Liberator*, 29 October 1841, 175. Garrison had begun agitating against the marriage law, a law that barred marriages between whites and blacks, in one of the first issues of the *Liberator*. Thereafter, abolitionists attacked the law with an unrelenting editorial assault and a continuous flow of petitions to the Massachusetts legislature, which finally repealed it in February 1843. See Leon F. Litwack, *North of Slavery: The Negro in the Free States, 1790-1860* (Chicago: University of Chicago Press, 1961), 105-6.

70. *Liberator*, 29 October 1841, 175.

71. *Liberator*, 22 October 1841, 171. There were no minutes published from the Hanover meeting, which Blassingame, ed., *Douglass Papers, Series One*, 1:lxxxvii, fails to include in his itinerary of Douglass' speaking activities. Moreover, Blassingame incorrectly states that Douglass attended the quarterly meeting of the Plymouth County Anti-Slavery Society at South Scituate on 5 November. The source of his confusion is most likely the announcement in the *Liberator*, 22 October 1841, 171, that the Plymouth County convention would

meet on 5 November in South Scituate. The following week, however, the paper announced that the meeting had been rescheduled for Hingham on 4 November. See the *Liberator*, 29 October 1841, 175.

72. *Hingham Patriot* in the *Liberator*, 26 November 1841, 189; Raymond Gerald Fulkerson, "Frederick Douglass and the Anti-Slavery Crusade: His Career and Speeches, 1817-1861," pt. 2 (Ph.D. diss., University of Illinois, 1971), 440-41.

73. *Liberator*, 12 November 1841, 182.

74. *Hingham Patriot* in the *Liberator*, 26 November 1841, 189. See also Fulkerson, "Frederick Douglass," pt. 2, 442.

75. *Hingham Patriot* in the *Liberator*, 26 November 1841, 189.

76. Ibid.; *National Anti-Slavery Standard*, 18 November 1841, 94.

77. *Liberator*, 12 November 1841, 182.

78. Blassingame, ed., *Douglass Papers, Series One*, 1:6; *National Anti-Slavery Standard*, 18 November 1841, 94. The text of Douglass' speech was published in the *Hingham Patriot*, 13 November 1841; *Liberator*, 26 November 1841, 189; *Liberator*, 3 December 1841, 193; *Liberator*, 10 December 1841, 197. It is also available in Fulkerson, "Frederick Douglass," pt. 2, 443-47.

79. Blassingame, ed., *Douglass Papers, Series One*, 1:6-7.

80. It is impossible to discern from the published proceedings of the meeting the impact Douglass' remarks had on those in attendance.

81. Blassingame, ed., *Douglass Papers, Series One*, 1:7-8.

82. Ibid.

83. Ibid.

84. Ibid.

85. *Liberator*, 3 December 1841, 193.

86. Ibid.; Kathleen Hall Jamieson, *Eloquence in an Electronic Age: The Transformation of Political Speechmaking* (New York: Oxford University Press, 1988), 76-79.

87. *Liberator*, 10 December 1841, 197.

88. Blassingame, ed., *Douglass Papers, Series One*, 1:9-10. For a full exposition of Douglass' encounters on the Eastern Railroad, see John A. Collins to William Lloyd Garrison, 4 October 1841, in *Liberator*, 15 October 1841, 165. See also Douglass, *Bondage and Freedom*, 399-400. For an account of Douglass' problems in obtaining employment as a caulker in New Bedford, see Douglass, *Bondage and Freedom*, 348-49; Douglass, *Life and Times*, 207-11.

89. Blassingame, ed., *Douglass Papers, Series One*, 1:10-11.

90. Ibid., 1:11.

91. Ibid.

92. Ibid., 1:11-12.

93. Ibid., 1:12.

94. Ibid.

95. Ibid., 1:17n, suggests that Douglass' sermon was based in part on his experiences in slavery "and apparently in part" on Thomas Bacon's sermons to servants and slaves in the South. Bacon, a minister of the Protestant Episcopal Church in Maryland, published his sermons in a manual, the second part of which contained two addresses to the slaves. The first of these addresses taught servants and slaves to be obedient to their masters and mistresses, and was based on the same biblical quotation as Douglass' slaveholder's sermon. Here the similarities between the two sermons end. Although it is certainly possible that Douglass was familiar with Bacon's sermon, there is no firm evidence that he was. For Bacon's text, see William Meade, ed., *Sermons Addressed to Masters and Servants, and Published in the Year 1743, by the Rev. Thomas Bacon, Minister of the Protestant Episcopal Church in Maryland, Now Republished with Other Tracts, and Dialogues On the Same Subject, and Recommended to All Masters and Mistresses to be Used in Their Families* (Winchester, Va.: John Heiskell, 1813), 87-111, especially 104-11.

96. Blassingame, ed., *Douglass Papers, Series One*, 1:12.

97. This is the first recorded instance of Douglass' use of the rhetorical device of mimicry. He would use this device repeatedly throughout his career as an abolitionist.

98. Monroe, *Oberlin Thursday Lectures*, 84-90. Although Monroe's description was not penned specifically about Douglass' use of the sermon at Hingham, there is no reason to doubt that it would apply to that occasion.

99. Blassingame, ed., *Douglass Papers, Series One*, 1:12-13.

100. *Liberator*, 10 December 1841, 197.

101. *Liberator*, 12 November 1841, 182.

102. *National Anti-Slavery Standard*, 18 November 1841, 94.

103. Evelina Smith to Caroline Weston, 12 December 1841, Weston Family Papers, Boston Public Library, reprinted in Fulkerson, "Frederick Douglass," pt. 1, 47.

104. *Liberator*, 3 December 1841, 193.

105. On 23 November 1841, Douglass traveled to Fall River, Massachusetts, where he, Collins, Foster, and Kelley attended the quarterly meeting of the Bristol County Anti-Slavery Society. Although we have no texts of Douglass' speeches at this one-day convention, we know that he spoke in favor of three resolutions. The first declared that "any man who will go to the polls and vote for a slave-owner, or any other than an out-spoken and a out-acting abolitionist, proves most conclusively that he has no more regard for principle than an Algerine buc[c]anier." The second resolution condemned "the venomous prejudice against color," while the third was a strongly worded denunciation of the church. The first of these resolutions dominated both the morning and

afternoon sessions, as well as part of the evening, before being tabled. The second resolution passed, apparently without great debate. The third never came to a vote, perhaps because there was little time left to discuss it (*Liberator*, 24 December 1841, 205).

106. Fulkerson, "Frederick Douglass," pt. 1, 51-52; Quarles, *Frederick Douglass*, 21; Foner, *Life and Writings*, 1:48; Arline Ruth Kiven, *Then Why the Negroes: The Nature and Course of the Anti-Slavery Movement in Rhode Island: 1637-1861* (Providence, R.I.: Urban League of Rhode Island, 1973), 58. See also J. Stanley Lemons and Michael A. McKenna, "Re-enfranchisement of Rhode Island Negroes," *Rhode Island History* 30 (winter 1971): 2-13.

107. For an account of the proceedings at the People's Convention, see *National Anti-Slavery Standard*, 21 October 1841, 77.

108. *Liberator*, 29 October 1841, 175. This issue of the *Liberator* also contained an account of the People's Convention in Rhode Island. In a letter from Garrison to Edmund Quincy on 9 November 1841 urging Quincy to attend the Rhode Island Anti-Slavery Society convention, Garrison wrote, "It is really a crisis with our anti-slavery friends in Rhode-Island, and they need all the aid and encouragement we can give them at the present time" (Merrill, *Letters of Garrison*, 3:38).

109. *Liberator*, 29 October 1841, 175.

110. *National Anti-Slavery Standard*, 4 November 1841, 86. The circular was printed in the *Suffrage Examiner* (Providence, R.I.), December 1841, 1.

111. *National Anti-Slavery Standard*, 23 December 1841, 113. See also *Liberator*, 31 December 1841, 210.

112. *Narragansett Chief* (Providence, R.I.), 19 November 1841, 2.

113. *Suffrage Examiner*, December 1841, 3.

114. Ibid.

115. *Herald of Freedom*, 3 December 1841, 162-63.

116. *National Anti-Slavery Standard*, 23 December 1841, 113-14.

117. Ibid., 114.

118. Douglass, *Life and Times*, 221; *National Anti-Slavery Standard*, 23 December 1841, 114; *Suffrage Examiner*, December 1841, 2.

119. Douglass, *Life and Times*, 221; Fulkerson, "Frederick Douglass," pt. 1, 54; *National Anti-Slavery Standard*, 23 December 1841, 114; *Suffrage Examiner*, December 1841, 2; *New Age and Constitutional Advocate* (Providence, R.I.), 10 December 1841, 2-3.

120. Blassingame, ed., *Douglass Papers, Series One*, 1:lxxxviii, misdates this meeting as occurring "c. 18-20 November."

121. *National Anti-Slavery Standard*, 23 December 1841, 114.

122. Blassingame, ed., *Douglass Papers, Series One*, 1:lxxxviii, fails to include this meeting in its itinerary of Douglass' speaking activities.

123. *New Age and Constitutional Advocate*, 10 December 1841, 3; *National Anti-Slavery Standard*, 23 December 1841, 114.

124. Blassingame, ed., *Douglass Papers, Series One*, 1:lxxxviii, does not include this meeting in its itinerary of Douglass' speaking activities.

125. Ibid. indicates that a meeting took place in East Greenwich in December, but he does not include the date of the meeting in its itinerary of Douglass' speaking activities.

126. *National Anti-Slavery Standard*, 30 December 1841, 118.

127. Although I have been unable to uncover a record of the proceedings at Kingston, I assume that a convention was held there as announced in the *Suffrage Examiner*, December 1841, 2. If a convention was not held at Kingston, it would be the only instance in which Douglass and his colleagues did not meet a scheduled appointment in Rhode Island. Blassingame, ed., *Douglass Papers, Series One*, 1:lxxxviii, indicates that a meeting took place in Kingston in December, but does not include the dates of the meeting in its itinerary of Douglass' speaking activities.

128. Blassingame, ed., *Douglass Papers, Series One*, 1:lxxxviii, indicates that a meeting took place in Newport in December, but does not include the dates of the meeting in its itinerary of Douglass' speaking activities.

129. *National Anti-Slavery Standard*, 13 January 1842, 126; *Providence Daily Journal*, 31 December 1841, 2.

130. Blassingame, ed., *Douglass Papers, Series One*, 1:lxxxviii, indicates that a meeting took place in Providence in December, but does not include the dates of the meeting in its itinerary of Douglass' speaking activities.

131. *National Anti-Slavery Standard*, 13 January 1842, 126.

132. *Liberator*, 14 January 1842, 5.

133. Fulkerson, "Frederick Douglass," pt. 1, 55.

134. For a sharp description of the hardships Douglass encountered while traveling on the railroads in Rhode Island, see George Foster to Lydia Marie Child, 20 December 1841, in *National Anti-Slavery Standard*, 6 January 1842, 122.

135. *Liberator*, 21 January 1842, 11.

✒️ *Chapter Four*

Oratory of Power and Eloquence:
From Local Notoriety to Regional Prominence,
January - August 1842

AFTER COMPLETING the tumultuous lecture tour of Rhode Island in December 1841, Frederick Douglass returned to Massachusetts a seasoned veteran of the abolitionist crusade and an emerging leader within the anti-slavery movement. His probationary period as a lecturer had expired in November 1841, and his growing importance to the movement was undeniable. Everywhere he went, he attracted large and enthusiastic audiences and infused excitement into the crusade against slavery. In January 1842 he was employed by the Massachusetts Anti-Slavery Society as a full-time lecturer. For the next eight months, he traveled extensively throughout the Bay State delivering his antislavery message. His rhetorical activities included impressive speaking performances at county, state, regional, and national antislavery meetings, as well as a solo lecture tour of Massachusetts. In addition, he played a crucial role in a lecture tour of Cape Cod, in which he traveled with William Lloyd Garrison, Henry C. Wright, and George Bradburn. In all of these activities, Douglass strengthened his standing as a powerful voice in the struggle for immediate abolition.

Throughout this period, Douglass became increasingly Garrisonian in his approach to abolitionism. In November 1841 he had spoken in favor of compensating slaveholders for freeing their slaves. During a speech in May 1842, he reversed his position and subscribed to the Garrisonian view of no compensation to slave owners for the emancipation of their slaves. During his first ten months as an agent for the Massachusetts Anti-Slavery Society, he had supported the slaves' efforts to assert their liberty through the use of force. In June 1842 he endorsed the Garrisonian principle of

nonresistance as essential to the overthrow of oppression. Equally important, during this time Douglass' rhetoric became progressively moral in
tone. His crusade against slavery became increasingly centered on the
immorality of southern slavery and northern racial prejudice, the
hypocrisy of the proslavery church and clergy, and the iniquity of participating in the political process. Unquestionably, he was a man on a moral
crusade as he passionately expressed his devotion to overthrowing the
slave system by moral means.

I

Only one week after attending the final antislavery meeting of the Rhode
Island campaign, Douglass resumed a rigorous speaking schedule. On 5-6
January 1842, he attended the annual meeting of the Worcester County
South Division Anti-Slavery Society with John A. Collins, Charles Lenox
Remond, Samuel May, and Abby Kelley. The two-day meeting was impor-
tant because it brought together Douglass and Remond for the first time.[1]

During the 1830s Charles Lenox Remond had proved to be among abo-
lition's most effective speakers. In fact, he was the first black man to take
the platform as an antislavery lecturer and was the most talented African
American representative until the emergence of Douglass in the 1840s.
Consequently, Remond was chosen by the American Anti-Slavery Society
in 1840 as one of its four delegates to attend the first World Anti-Slavery
Convention in London. After the convention, he remained in the British
Isles for nineteen months. During that time, he lectured in favor of temperance and spoke out passionately against slavery, colonization, and
racial prejudice. His speaking itinerary was crowded and his lecture tour a
resounding success. He returned to Massachusetts in December 1841
ready to resume his antislavery activities.[2]

As ardent abolitionists, Remond and Douglass presented a striking contrast. Remond was born free; Douglass was born a slave. Remond was from
an established black family in Salem, Massachusetts; Douglass was of
obscure parentage. Remond was "small in stature, thin-faced, dark-
skinned, and suffered from consumption"; Douglass was "a six-feet tall
mulatto, broad shouldered with long hair, eyes deep set and steady nose,
well formed lips, and skin bronze colored."[3] Remond identified himself as
the representative educated free black man and often alluded to the fact
that "not a drop of slave blood" ran through his veins; Douglass prided
himself as the representative black man, both slave and free.[4] Both men,
however, shared the common goal of elevating their race and securing full
equality for all black people. It is not surprising, then, that a correspondent
for the *Liberator* described the Worcester County South Division meeting
at which both Douglass and Remond participated as "an effective one"

where "many were led to see the wrongs which slavery and proslavery prejudice inflict on their victims everywhere."[5]

During the first day of the Worcester meeting, Douglass and Remond were silent. The issue under consideration was the admission of Texas to the Union. On the second day of the meeting, Douglass broke his silence and offered the following strongly worded resolution condemning the proslavery character of the American church: "Resolved, That the sectarian organizations of this country, called churches, are, in supporting slavery, upholding a system of theft, adultery, and murder; and it is the duty of abolitionists to expose their true character before the public." Douglass then made a speech in support of the resolution. He was followed by four speakers— including Remond and Collins—supporting the resolution. The debate consumed the rest of the day and culminated in the resolution's adoption.[6]

The next day, 7 January, Douglass and Abby Kelley traveled to Barre, Massachusetts, to attend a meeting of the Worcester County North Division Anti-Slavery Society. During the one-day meeting at the Town Hall, Douglass and Kelley spoke in favor of resolutions supporting the "principles promulgated by the American Anti-Slavery Society" and condemning the prejudice that "exists in this country against the colored population." This prejudice, read the resolution, was "wicked in its nature, nefarious in its influence, and . . . is the legitimate fruit of slavery." The resolutions were unanimously adopted. During the evening session, Douglass delivered a stirring antislavery lecture "which was listened to with intense interest for about two hours, by a large and respectable audience." A correspondent to the *Liberator* described Douglass as a "warm-hearted and truly eloquent brother" who, "having been himself a slave, and felt upon his own person the scorpion lash of this terrible monster, . . . was abundantly prepared to portray to his hearers the evil of American slavery."[7]

During the final week of January, Douglass was in Boston to attend the tenth annual convention of the Massachusetts Anti-Slavery Society.[8] For Douglass and his fellow abolitionists, the annual convention offered an opportunity to reflect on past successes of the movement, to renew their commitment to it, and to discuss its most pressing issues and challenges for the coming year. Because the meetings were carefully conducted to ensure vigorous debate and discussion, they were often spirited and exciting. This was the first time Douglass participated in a convention of a major antislavery society, and it marked an important step for him. For the first time, abolitionists from all over the North had the opportunity to hear him speak, and he did not squander the opportunity. He spoke several times during the course of the meeting and, judging from the reviews of his speeches, he spoke impressively.[9]

The meeting commenced in Boston on Wednesday morning, 26 January, at the "spacious and commodious Melodeon on Washington

Street," with roughly 1,000 persons in attendance.[10] The morning session was spent appointing a business committee to draft resolutions for the meeting to discuss, forming a nomination committee to put forward potential officers for the ensuing year, and reading the Treasury Report. In the afternoon, the business committee introduced a series of resolutions asserting that moral suasion was superior to political action in the struggle against slavery. "Appeals to conscience—arguments—the spreading of information," read the first resolution, "in a word, the formation of a correct public opinion—are the best and only sure means of effecting our object." The second resolution condemned the formation of a third political party and declared such efforts "a waste of means, which, in the present state of our enterprize, is ruinous—a misdirection of effort, whose least evil results will be the retarding of our cause." The third resolution demanded that the Massachusetts society seize "this opportunity to renew its testimony against any attempt to form a third political party" and to strengthen its resolve to "bear a constant and faithful testimony in word and deed against a mistake freighted with ruin." Because there was not enough time to discuss these resolutions, debate on them was deferred until the evening session.[11]

When the evening session convened, Nathaniel P. Rogers opened debate on the resolutions regarding the superiority of moral suasion over political action by arguing that the "anti-slavery enterprise is strictly a moral enterprise" and that "the revolution it seeks to accomplish is moral and peaceful." He was followed by Dr. Thomas Jinnings, a black dentist from Massachusetts, and Jonathan Peckham Miller, an abolitionist from Vermont, both of whom advocated political action. Their arguments are important because they inspired Douglass to respond. Although there are no complete texts of what these two men said, there are published accounts that summarize their speeches.[12] One account summarizing Miller's speech appeared in the *Herald of Freedom*. According to the *Herald*, Miller spoke with "genuine warrior spirit" in favor of political action. "The fetters of the slave," he argued, "ought to be knocked off by the strong hand—if they won['t] come off without."[13] A second account, written for the *Liberator* by Maria Weston Chapman, characterized the views of Jinnings and Miller this way:

> It had been argued "that third party was a road to abolition and that so that end were attained, what signified the road? That governments were necessary for the making of laws, and that the penalty annexed to breaking those laws should not give the government the character of physical force, rather than that of moral power. That if punishment were called force, the government of God himself was liable to the charge. That the interrogation system [of political candidates] did but suggest to men to tell falsehoods,

for the sake of securing the votes of the abolitionists. Whatever has been done for the cause has been done through political action. By going against third party, you array abolitionists against each other. Get a man to deposit a liberty ticket, and you do much. He cannot do it without being made to think. The third party is a *liberty party*; and if all men go for it, will not immediate emancipation be effected?"[14]

After Jinnings and Miller had spoken, Douglass came forward to deliver an intensely personal and impassioned discourse against political action.[15] He began unpretentiously, saying: "I am no debater, Mr. President [Francis Jackson], and I dislike to feel called upon to dispute the gentleman last up. But it happens so that we differ, for once." This carefully stated opening line performed two important functions. First, Douglass created a personal and respectful tone for the remarks that were to follow. Second, by denying his efficacy as a debater, he sought to lower the expectations of his audience. This was his first appearance before the convention, and most certainly he understood the importance of making a favorable impression.[16]

Having set the tone and purpose of his remarks, Douglass stated: "The great difficulty with [a] third party [Liberty Party] is, that it disposes men to rely entirely on political, and not moral action." At this point, Miller interrupted Douglass and stated that "he did use and appreciate moral action." Graciously accepting Miller's clarification, Douglass responded: "My friend says, however, that all that has been accomplished for this cause has been accomplished through the instrumentalities of political action. I do not believe it." Douglass then used his personal experience to refute Miller's position: "I ask you what this Legislature has done that has caused you to recognize my humanity? Yet there are those in Massachusetts who do recognize it, and treat me like a man and a brother. I ask, was it political action that removed your prejudices, and raised in your minds a holy zeal for human rights? No one will say this." According to Douglass, it was the power of moral suasion—not political action—that had helped abolitionists recognize Douglass' humanity.[17]

Douglass' strategy for refutation was simple and direct. He introduced Miller's argument, denied its veracity, and moved to a series of questions and answers during which he led his audience to see the exception to the argument and, most important, to understand the superiority of moral suasion over political action. Douglass' strategy for refuting his opponent's arguments was outlined in Caleb Bingham's *The Columbian Orator*. "In confutation," advised Bingham, "the arguments of the adverse party ought first to be repeated in a plain and distinct manner that the speaker may not seem to conceal, or avoid the force of them." Once the adverse party's position was stated, Bingham counseled, the speaker should offer a "serious answer" to its position. In addition to following Bingham's refutational strategy, Douglass used his own experience to point out the flaws in the argument on political action. He then moved from the personal to the universal—from his experience with being recognized by some as a human being to the grand movement for human rights for all. Finally, by using questions, he engaged his audience and forced them to confront the weakness of his opponent's claim—all the while maintaining the respectful, personal tone established in the opening. The audience must have appreciated Douglass' argument in this section of the address, for they responded with applause.[18]

In the next section of the speech, Douglass raised the claims of those who supported a third party and summarily dismissed each one. He began by bringing forth the arguments of those who supported the formation of a third party. Maintaining the personal tone he had established earlier in the speech, he announced: "I have seen something of the operation of third party in the town where I have been lately." There, the Liberty Party claimed "that all who are conscientiously opposed to voting at all, are proslavery men." Being a staunch Garrisonian, Douglass supported not voting in elections. The audience certainly realized that he stood against slavery, yet according to the claim made by the third party, he would be considered proslavery—obviously a ludicrous claim. In essence, Douglass became the argument against those who supported political action, thereby helping to expose the weakness in the position taken by supporters of political action.[19]

In this section of the speech, Douglass also raised Miller's claim that "we had better not ask political candidates what they think about abolition, for it only tempts them to pretend to be abolitionists." Douglass believed abolitionists must question candidates regardless of the risk of being deceived. In so doing, he was following Garrisonian doctrine. "I had rather take my chance about that," Douglass reasoned, "than be obliged to take a man I know nothing about, upon the mere nomination of the third party." He closed his argument by raising doubts about the soundness of the practice of not questioning candidates: "When I see men I know have never been active abolitionists, setting up other men who were never before heard of in the cause, *and no questions asked*, I inquire, why am I to suppose this man is an abolitionist any more than the candidate of the other parties?" Certainly, candidates of all parties must be interrogated, especially those of the third party.[20]

Douglass continued his argument by explaining the basis for his suspicion of Liberty Party candidates. He urged his audience to "look at the root of this third party. Those who were active once in the cause, and begun to find out that it led to more sacrifice than they wanted to make, got it up when they found their plans to put down the old Society failed." Here Douglass called into question the motives of the men who originally founded the Liberty Party. He believed the true motive of the party and, by implication, of third-party candidates in general, was to undermine the Garrisonian wing of the crusade against slavery and to replace moral suasion with political action. He also questioned the character of the men who had formed the third party by intimating that they were looking for a solution that did not demand the sacrifices required by moral suasion. "Much as I respect the sincerity of some who are engaged in" the Liberty Party, he concluded, "I see the plan itself, to begin with, is only new organization new organized." Douglass was linking efforts to organize a third party to the "new organization"—the American and Foreign Anti-Slavery Society—which had split off from the American Anti-Slavery Society in 1840 and which provided the nucleus of the Liberty Party.[21]

Although by this time in his career as an abolitionist Douglass had delivered hundreds of impromptu speeches, the address to the Massachusetts Anti-Slavery Society convention is the first written account which records his simple, direct confutational style. This style of bringing forth his adversary's argument and then refuting it with personal experience, personal testimony, Garrisonian doctrine, and carefully reasoned discourse demonstrated Douglass' increasing prowess as a debater and platform speaker. Although we know little about the impact of Douglass' remarks, Maria Weston Chapman did record her reaction. In her summary of the proceedings, she wrote, "it is interesting to see with how few words a man of color, like Douglas[s], can beat down the mountain of prejudice, which a white man might work a day in vain to pile up proofs against."[22]

The following day, the convention reconvened at the Melodeon, but Douglass was quiet during the morning and afternoon sessions. He was an active participant, though, in the evening session held at the Representatives' Hall in the State House. "It was, by far, the largest annual meeting the society ever held," reported a correspondent to the *Liberator*. "Every spot in the hall was densely filled."[23] The meeting began with the reading of resolutions relating to the marriage law, the exclusion of people of color from railroad cars throughout Massachusetts, and the connection of Massachusetts with slavery. Following the reading of the resolutions, Douglass was among the "nine able and interesting speakers" who addressed the "immense" gathering with "thrilling effect."[24] Garrison introduced Douglass, in a "peculiarly arousing manner," as "a thing from the South!" One observer noted that Douglass then "came forward modestly, but self-possessed, in obedience to a general call, and was saluted with a round of applause." Douglass dramatically opened his speech by declaring: "I appear before the immense assembly this evening as a thief and a robber. I stole this head, these limbs, this body from my master, and

ran off with them." As he uttered these striking phrases, reported a correspondent to the *Lynn Record*, his "eye flashed as he spoke in tones of
appalling earnestness and significancy." The remainder of the speech was
"a stern denunciation of slavery, such as became a man who had endured
its unutterable indignities."[25] Although we have no text of Douglass' words,
a correspondent for the *Herald of Freedom* summarized his remarks.
Because there is no record of Douglass' speech in any of his published
papers, the *Herald's* summary is worth quoting in full:

> He spoke with an indignation approaching to anger, which it was
> most satisfying and refreshing to hear. He denounced the North, as
> well as the South, as the chief sustainers of the slave system. He
> charged upon the whole country the infliction of slavery on him-
> self and his brethren. He spoke of the southern clergy in the most
> withering sarcasm and with admirable mimickry took off their
> slaveholding gospel as they preach it to master and to slave in the
> southern sanctuary. And the North preached the same thing, he
> sternly said, from pulpit and theological seminary—in meeting
> house, and in stage, and rail-road car, and every where. He spoke
> of his own master, a miserable wretch of a Methodist class leader,
> who, we should suppose, would make one of the most insolent and
> impudent of all the slaveholding tyrants. That ecclesiastical
> department is a capital training for the berth of an overseer and
> driver. He had known him, he said, [to] whip his female slave,
> cousin to the speaker—till the blood stood in a pool at her feet!
> And then he would go off and groan and howl at class meeting . . .
> so as to be heard over several plantations![26]

According to the *Bay Street Democrat*, Douglass made "the best speech
of the evening," and he returned to his seat "amid the cheerings of the people." Indeed, his remarks were reported in the newspapers more compre-
hensively than any of the other speakers that evening, which included
such accomplished orators as George Bradburn, Jonathon Peckham Miller,
Wendell Phillips, Abby Kelley, and Charles Lenox Remond. Of all the
aspects of his speech, his imitation of how slaves were preached to in the
South received the greatest attention. His mimicry of the "matter and
manner in which religious instruction is conveyed to the slaves by ministers," wrote a correspondent in the *Lynn Record*, "was believed to be
excellent. It was certainly very laughable." A correspondent to the *Bay
Street Democrat* agreed: "He showed great imitative powers and gave an
amusing exhibition of the southern style of preaching to the slaves, and the
corresponding practice, which seemed to interest the meeting greatly. His
active talents are evidently of a high order."[27]

The next day, Friday, 28 January, the Massachusetts society returned to the Melodeon for the final day of the convention. During the morning session, Douglass took an active role in the proceedings, speaking in favor of the resolutions condemning the proslavery character of the church and affirming the supremacy of moral suasion over political action. The last formal action of the meeting was the adoption of a resolution expressing the "sincere conviction" of those gathered "of the personal worth and anti-slavery fidelity of WILLIAM LLOYD GARRISON." Concluding her report to the *Liberator*, Maria W. Chapman wrote: "Taking the whole three days of the meeting, I never witnessed so much high-toned feeling, triumphant enthusiasm, and complete satisfaction, as on these occasions. Such spiritual communion is ennobling and a lovely thing; and it was here as pure as disinterestedness and hope could make it."[28]

That evening, a "large and overwhelming meeting of the citizens of Boston" was held in Faneuil Hall "favorable to the immediate abolition of slavery in the District of Columbia." The meeting also centered on the antislavery significance of the "Address From the People of Ireland to Their Countrymen and Countrywomen in America," which Remond had brought to the United States from Great Britain in December. The mammoth address, containing the signatures of Irish statesman Daniel O'Connor, temperance advocate Father Theobald Matthew, and 60,000 other Irish, called "upon all true-hearted Irishmen" in the United States "to make common cause with the American abolitionists, and to rally as one man under the banner of immediate and universal emancipation." A correspondent for the *Liberator* reported that the Hall, which could "contain 5000 persons, . . . was full at 7 o'clock, when the meeting was called to order by Francis Jackson." The galleries were "crowded with ladies," reported a correspondent in the *New Hampshire People's Advocate*, "and the floor with hundreds of the sons of Erin." In reporting the scene to the *National Anti-Slavery Standard*, James C. Fuller wrote: "I wish that I could convey a description of this enthusiastic meeting. My pen is insufficient for the task, and pictorial representation inadequate to the scene. It must be seen, to be appreciated."[29]

Once the meeting was called to order, Garrison was unanimously elected to preside. After a brief speech, he presented twelve resolutions for the meeting to consider. These resolutions condemned the presence of slavery in the nation's capital, denounced Congress for refusing to receive antislavery petitions, praised John Quincy Adams for his defense of the right of petition, and called for Massachusetts senators and representatives, when "deprived of liberty of speech" in Congress "and prohibited from defending the right of their constituents to petition that body in a constitutional manner," to withdraw immediately and return to their homes. Garrison's resolutions also called for the dissolution of the Union, demanded that Massachusetts "cease to give her countenance and support to the southern slave system by allowing the slave hunter to seize his prey on her soil," and called for the people of Massachusetts to flood both houses of the state legislature with petitions demanding "that every bondman shall become free on arriving within her jurisdiction." Douglass was among the nine speakers who inveighed in favor of the resolutions.[30]

Douglass was introduced by Garrison, who stated: "It is recorded in holy writ that a beast once spoke. A greater miracle is here tonight. A chattel becomes a man." Douglass then made his way to the platform and was received with applause. "I rejoice to be permitted, as well as to be able to speak upon this subject tonight," he began. Indeed, this was the high point of Douglass' young oratorical career. He was speaking against slavery in historic Faneuil Hall before the largest assembly he had ever addressed. After his opening sentence, Douglass reinforced Garrison's introductory remarks by reminding his audience of his slave status: "I will not detain you long, for I stand here a slave." Upon hearing this declaration, the audience responded with a resounding, "No!" Quickly adjusting to their objection, Douglass rephrased his statement, "A slave at least in the eye of the Constitution." Again, the audience replied, "No! no!" Searching for the right phrase, Douglass offered another: "It is a slave by the laws of the South, who now addresses you." The audience, comfortable with this statement, answered, "That's it!"[31]

Having established his status to the satisfaction of the audience, Douglass focused his remarks on his slave past, a past he wished to make vivid and immediate for his listeners. "My back," he declared, "is scarred by the lash—that I could show you. I would, I could make visible the wounds of this system upon my soul." By establishing that he had personally experienced the cruelties of slavery on both a physical and spiritual level, Douglass established his credibility as someone who could speak with unquestioned authority on behalf of the slave. In addition, he introduced the central theme of his speech. It was the wounds of the slave system upon his soul and the souls of all slaves that he would work to "make visible" for his auditors this evening.[32]

In doing so, Douglass said, he stood before the audience as the representative of "the two and half millions remaining in that bondage from which I have escaped. I thank God for the opportunity to do it. Those bondmen, whose cause you are called to espouse, are entirely deprived of the privilege of speaking for themselves." With these lines, Douglass not only portrayed himself as the spokesman for the slaves, but also began to separate himself from his white audience. He then reminded the abolitionists of their duty to the bondmen of the South. He used "you" to place the responsibility of ending slavery squarely on their shoulders. The "cause you are called to espouse," Douglass chided, was the cause of the slave. His "call" was to voice the concerns of the slave. Hence, Douglass' role in the antislavery movement was distinct from that of white abolitionists. His duty was to represent the interests of the slave; that of white abolitionists was to put an end to slavery.[33]

Equally important, by declaring himself the spokesman for the slaves, Douglass may have been distancing himself from Remond. Douglass was working to claim the voice of all slaves as his own. Certainly, Remond could speak on behalf of free blacks in the North, but only Douglass, a fugitive slave, could speak with authority on behalf of his enslaved brethren. In the past, he had intimated his representative slave status to the audience. Now he was proclaiming his representative slave status to all in attendance. Whatever Douglass' motives for declaring himself the spokesman for the slaves, he next provided the reason slaves were not allowed to speak for themselves. In so doing, he reinforced the necessity of his role as spokesman for this brethren in bonds. "They are goods and chattels," he declared, "not men." Because slaves were considered property, he argued, they were denied the privilege of the liberty of speech, "denied the privileges of the Christian," "denied the rights of citizens," and "not allowed the rights of the husband and father." Douglass concluded this section of the address by reminding the abolitionists of their responsibility to the slaves: "It is to save them from all this, that you are called."[34]

Douglass followed these remarks with an emotional plea to the abolitionists to act decisively on behalf of the slave. "Do it!" he demanded, "and they who are ready to perish shall bless you! Do it! and all good men will cheer you onward! Do it! and God will reward you for the deed; and all your consciences will testify that you have been true to the demands of the religion of Christ." Through the skillful use of repetition and parallelism, Douglass worked to rally his audience to action. He also revealed to his listeners his view of God and Christianity. His God was a benevolent being, a God who rewarded good and righteous deeds. Douglass believed God looked kindly upon the acts of the abolitionists because they were fighting for the slaves' release from bondage and were thus being true to their moral consciences and to the "demands of the religion of Christ." Douglass' appeal must have been heard and appreciated because the audience responded with applause at this juncture of the speech.[35]

Having rallied the audience to the cause of the slave, Douglass was now ready, at the end of his address, to deliver what he had "been called upon to describe"—the style in which religion was preached to the master and the slave in the South. Looking up at the gallery of Faneuil Hall, he symbolically transformed the hall into a southern church and himself into a white southern minister. The text of the speech, as reprinted in the *Liberator*, captured both Douglass' words and manner, as well as the reactions of his audience:

Looking high up to the poor colored drivers and the rest, and spreading his hands gracefully abroad, he [the minister] says, (mimicking,) "And you too, my friends, have souls of infinite value—souls that will live through endless happiness or misery in eternity. Oh, *labor diligently* to make your calling and election sure. Oh, receive into your souls these words of the holy apostle— 'Servants, be obedient unto your masters.' (Shouts of laughter and applause.) Oh, consider the wonderful goodness of God! Look at your hard, horny hands, your strong muscular frames, and see how mercifully he has adapted you to the duties you are to fulfil! (continued laughter and applause) while to your masters, who have slender frames and long delicate fingers, he has given brilliant intellects, that they may do the *thinking*, while you do the *working*." (Shouts of applause.)[36]

This is the most complete written version of Douglass' famous "Slaveholders Sermon," which he recited in many of his early abolitionist lectures, often, as on this occasion, at the request of his audience.

Reactions to Douglass' address were effusive. A correspondent in the *National Anti-Slavery Standard* wrote, "it is saying but little that in the Melodeon, as well as the State House, and Faneuil Hall, he shone brightly." Writing in the *Herald of Freedom*, Nathaniel P. Rogers compared Douglass to Samuel Adams: "Think of that, ye miserable flesh mongers that are trying to excommunicate the venerable John Quincy Adams from your infamous Congress—a *fugitive* playing the Sam Adams before a *Boston* audience in Faneuil Hall . . . and all amid the most enthusiastic cheering!"[37] Half a century later, most likely recalling this meeting at Faneuil Hall, Elizabeth Cady Stanton wrote of her initial reaction to Douglass' eloquence:

> Trained in the severe school of slavery, I saw him first before a Boston audience, fresh from the land of bondage. He stood there like an African prince, conscious of his dignity and power, grand in his physical proportions, majestic in his wrath, as with keen wit, satire and indignation he portrayed the bitterness of slavery, the humiliation of subjection to those who in all human virtues and capacities were inferior to himself. His denunciation of our national crime, of the wild and guilty fantasy that men could hold property in man, poured like a torrent that fairly made his hearers tremble. . . . Around him sat the great anti-slavery orators of the day, watching his effect on that immense audience, completely magnetized with his eloquence, laughing and crying by turns with his rapid flights from pathos to humor. All other speakers seemed tame after Douglass.[38]

That evening in Faneuil Hall, Douglass indeed "shone brightly" as his eloquence filled the "Old Cradle of Liberty." His reputation as an orator was significantly advanced by this and his previous speaking performances during the Massachusetts Anti-Slavery Society convention. Truly, he had lived up to Garrison's dramatic introduction—Douglass the "chattel" had become a man, a man who courageously declared that he was the representative of his enslaved brethren. Douglass had boldly seized the moment to enact the right his fellow bondmen and women could only dream about—the right of speaking for themselves.

II

During February and March 1842, county antislavery meetings consumed most of Douglass' time and energy. On 8 February, for example, Douglass traveled to Andover to attend a meeting of the Essex County Anti-Slavery Society. "The roads were excessively bad," wrote a correspondent to the *Liberator*, "and the traveling tedious." Despite the inclement weather and poor road conditions, however, the meeting was "the largest anti-slavery meeting" ever held in the county. The gathering lasted for two days and the deliberations "were of a deeply interesting character."[39] At the center of discussion was a series of resolutions presented by Garrison calling for dissolution of the Union. Throughout the proceedings, Douglass, Garrison, Phillips, Bradburn, Remond, Pillsbury, and Kelley were reported to have spoken "with great ability."[40]

One week later, Douglass traveled to Hubbardston to attend the Worcester County North Division Anti-Slavery Society meeting. During the morning session, he spoke in favor of a resolution condemning slavery as "a system of oppression, at war with the dearest rights of humanity," and demanding "its immediate removal." The resolution was adopted. Douglass opened the afternoon session with a prayer, after which resolutions condemning the church as "the great 'bulwark of American Slavery'" were discussed. Douglass and Phillips were among those who spoke in support of the resolutions. "This discussion," reported J.T. Everett to the *Liberator*, "was one of deep and solemn interest."[41]

On Friday, 25 March, just three weeks after the birth on 3 March of his second son, Frederick, Jr., Douglass traveled to South Scituate to attend the quarterly meeting of the Plymouth County Anti-Slavery Society.[42] A correspondent reported to the *Liberator* that the meeting "was well attended, notwithstanding the severe inclemency of the day, and the proceedings were of a most spirited and satisfactory character." Three issues were debated—the *Creole* incident, the people's right to petition Congress, and the abolition of slavery in the District of Columbia. Douglass participated only in the debate over the *Creole* incident. On 25 October 1841, the brig

Creole had left Norfolk, Virginia, bound for New Orleans with 135 slaves on board. During the voyage the slaves, led by Madison Washington, carried out a successful mutiny and forced the ship to put into port at the British territory of Nassau. Subsequently, the U.S. government demanded that the British government return the slave mutineers to the United States for trial. The British government refused to extradite the slaves or to indemnify their owners. There was agitation, especially in the South, urging the United States to declare war against Great Britain over the case. Abolitionists had little sympathy with any government efforts to repossess the slaves of the *Creole*, and the resolutions discussed at the Plymouth County meeting reflected their contempt.[43]

The first resolution heralded the heroism of Madison Washington and his comrades on board the *Creole* "who, to obtain their liberty, threw off a yoke of oppression." The second resolution declared that if the United States and Britain should become embroiled in a conflict over the return of the slaves, the "government must expect no aid, no countenance from this quarter, but may be assured that we of the North shall do all that we may, by moral means, to discourage and paralyze those who would go to enforce the wrong." The strongly worded resolution vowed that abolitionists would not fight, and would work to "dissuade others from fighting, for the protection of slavery or of the slave-trade, either foreign or domestic." Samuel J. May, president of the Plymouth society, reported that the "resolutions elicited a very serious and animated debate." Douglass was among the ten men who actively participated in the discussion. Immediately following the debate, a vote was taken and the resolutions passed unanimously.[44]

At the end of March, Douglass' attention shifted from attending county antislavery meetings to presenting formal antislavery lectures throughout eastern and central Massachusetts. In a letter to Garrison published in the *Liberator*, John A. Collins, general agent of the Massachusetts Anti-Slavery Society, announced that Douglass and five other agents of the society were currently traveling in different parts of Massachusetts delivering lectures on slavery.[45] Douglass, Collins announced, "is now lecturing in Harvard, on his way from Groton to Dedham, and will pass through and lecture in Bolton, Berlin, Northborough, Westborough, Upton, Milford, Medway, Bellingham, Franklin, Wrentham, Foxborough, Sharon, and Canton." Before this, Douglass had always spoken in conjunction with Collins, Garrison, or other abolitionist speakers. Now he was on his own in his first solo lecture tour.[46]

Douglass' tour began on Thursday, 31 March, in Groton. From 31 March through 8 May, he spoke against slavery seven days a week and sometimes presented two lectures a day. In the month of April he visited at least thirty-two different towns and villages and delivered approximately thirty-seven lectures. All told, he spoke twenty-three of the thirty days of April, despite being ill for three days and not being able to keep any of his other appointments. During the first eight days of May, he visited ten different locations, giving at least one lecture in each.[47]

Although there is only one surviving account of Douglass' speeches on this tour, it is possible to reconstruct his typical pattern of activity in the towns he visited.[48] He arrived in the scheduled place early in the day and immediately sought out the most prominent abolitionist of the town. Once he located the appropriate person, Douglass would identify himself and his mission and solicit the person's help in securing a place to speak. Usually Douglass was permitted to speak at a church, town hall, or school. "As a general rule," he recalled in 1892, "there was in New England after 1840 little difficulty in obtaining suitable places where I could plead the cause of my people." This was not always the case, however. Not all towns were friendly to the cause of the abolitionists, particularly Garrisonian abolitionists. Consequently, Douglass was at times forced to speak outdoors, usually in a town square or park.[49]

After securing a place to speak, Douglass would publicize his lecture. In Grafton, for instance, he posted notices all over town. The notice read: "Frederick Douglass, a fugitive slave, will lecture on Grafton Common this evening at 8 o'clock. All who wish to hear of the workings of Slavery from one of its own recipients are invited to attend." In addition to posting written notices, Douglass would, at times, walk through town announcing his evening lecture. In Grafton, he acquired a small hand bell and, ringing the bell, strolled through the streets and "cried his own meeting." In towns friendly to the abolitionist cause, church bells would ring to signal that a lecture was about to take place.[50]

At the appointed time, Douglass would deliver his lecture, which usually lasted over an hour. On 4 April in Lanesborough, the one speech from the tour for which we have a written account, he began the meeting by praying for the "two million & a half of his inhabitants in the United States who are in Chains." Following the prayer, he introduced the subject of his lecture, asking those gathered "'What is Slavery?'" After asking the question, he worked to establish the character of American slavery and to illustrate its harms on the South and the North. To accomplish this, Douglass relied on anecdotes drawn from his experiences in slavery and his life as a fugitive in the North. He told the story of his "very pious master who was so pious" that he would take Douglass' cousin Henny "and whip her till the blood ran." Douglass also shared with his auditors how he "had a very pious mistress who . . . would set down & cry because 'my master would not let her whip me when she wanted.'"[51] Douglass concluded the lecture with his slaveholder's sermon. Following the sermon, he demanded that his listeners withdraw all support from slavery. He then solicited donations to help finance the efforts of the Massachusetts Anti-Slavery Society.[52]

Although we do not know if Douglass used the same speech at all stops during his tour, we can be sure that he asked for donations everywhere he appeared. Moreover, those donations provide one measure of his rhetorical effectiveness—especially when compared with the donations received by his fellow agents. During the month of April, Douglass raised approximately $116 for the Massachusetts Anti-Slavery Society. In comparison, during the same period, Leach raised $6.25 and Tanner collected $61.44. Collins collected $1,042.31, but $1,000 of that came from a single donation.[53]

Once Douglass was finished speaking in a town, he would travel by stagecoach, train, horseback, or foot to the next location, where he would begin the process all over again. It was an arduous enterprise, fraught with hardships and dangers. Like all agents, Douglass had to endure a demanding speaking schedule. As a fugitive slave, he faced the added danger of being captured and returned to the South. As a black man, he faced racial prejudice on public transportation and in public housing. Nevertheless, he remained committed to the antislavery campaign and spoke against slavery to anyone who would listen. As he traveled from town to town, he awakened an interest in the abolition of slavery and worked to bring to light his slave experience for the people of Massachusetts. As one local abolitionist wrote after hearing him lecture, "Although an abolitionist before, yet never have I had my sympathy touched so sensibly for the slave as when hearing him."[54]

III

After delivering the final lecture of his solo tour in Webster on 8 May 1842, Douglass traveled to New York City to attend the ninth annual meeting of the American Anti-Slavery Society, scheduled to begin on Tuesday, 10 May.[55] More than 3,000 persons crowded into the Broadway Tabernacle to attend the gathering. The main topic of the meeting was the duty "of the North, in relation to her continuance in the Union." This topic was "discussed with great freedom," Lydia Marie Child reported in the *National Anti-Slavery Standard*, "and earnestness sometimes rose to a most excellent indignation." Attended by the most powerful and influential antislavery leaders, the meeting gave Douglass a chance to speak before a national abolitionist audience.[56]

Although Douglass did not play a prominent role in the deliberations of the meeting, he did speak on at least three occasions. On Wednesday, the second day of the convention, he spoke in support of a resolution advocating the questioning of "all candidates for legislative office" as to their stand in relation to "the holding of human beings in slavery." He was the final speaker to address the resolution. A vote followed and the resolution was adopted "with one dissenting voice."[57]

On the morning of Thursday, 12 May, Douglass followed Lunsford Lane, "a noble looking colored man, who had purchased himself and wife, and seven children" out of slavery, to the platform. Lane, a correspondent to the *National Anti-Slavery Standard* reported, told "the story of his sufferings, his wrongs, and his perils, with a dignified simplicity and pathos, that deeply touched the sympathies of his hearers. . . . The whole audience were melted to tears."[58] Douglass followed Lane with "some thrilling remarks" about "his enslaved brothers and sisters, toiling in the rice swamps of the South." In addition, he took issue with Lane by opposing efforts to purchase the freedom of slaves. "I would rather see fifty dollars paid into the treasury of the anti-slavery society," he declared, "than fifty thousand dollars spent in buying up slaves. Mr. Garrison was in the right when he said he did not want to spend time and strength in breaking off a few leaves, or even boughs; he wanted to ascertain how many strokes at the root would make the whole tree fall."[59] Although in November 1841 Douglass had spoken at Hingham, Massachusetts, in favor of Lane's endeavor to purchase his family's freedom, now—six months later—he reversed his position and adopted the Garrisonian position of no compensation to slave owners for the freeing of slaves.

Douglass' final speech at the convention was presented during the afternoon session of 12 May, when the dissolution of the Union was discussed "with considerable activity." Douglass joined Collins, Henry Highland Garnet, and James McCune Smith in supporting a resolution that required the executive committee of the American Anti-Slavery Society "to appropriate $2,000 for the purpose of testing, in the Supreme Court of the United States, whether the citizens of each State shall be allowed the privileges and immunities of citizens in the several States." Although this resolution was tabled "after some discussion," and although Douglass had played no more than a minor role in the four days of the convention, his presence was noted in the minutes and he had made a positive impression on the delegates, thereby furthering his standing among abolitionists as the representative voice of his enslaved brethren.[60]

Two weeks later, Douglass traveled to Boston to attend the annual meeting of the New England Anti-Slavery Society. His name, which had not appeared in advertisements for the annual meetings of the Massachusetts and American Anti-Slavery Societies, was included in the advertisements urging abolitionists to attend the New England meeting. The presence of his name on the listing of those men and women "expected to participate in the proceedings" suggests that Douglass was no longer being overshadowed by Remond as the premier black abolitionist of the cause. Certainly, Douglass' recent performances at the Massachusetts and American Anti-Slavery Society meetings, and his lecture tour and fundraising activities as an agent for the Massachusetts Anti-Slavery Society, had elevated his status in the eyes of the leaders of the movement—particularly Garrison who, for the first time, spelled his name correctly in the *Liberator*'s advertisement for the New England Anti-Slavery Society convention.[61]

The convention met from 24 to 27 May 1842 in Boston's Chardon Street Chapel. A correspondent for the *Boston Daily Ledger* exclaimed, "There is nothing equal to this Convention, in interest in the city," while the *Liberator* reported the proceedings as "most interesting" and the speeches as "eloquent and impressive." Referring to the nature of the deliberations and the quality of the speeches, the *Daily Ledger* wrote: "Everything is discussed here of a moral, civil, religious, political, physical character, and the speakers hail from all portions of the country, and belong to both sexes. Here is great talent, and eccentricity, and great fanaticism and some tremendous moral truths uttered in a tremendously powerful manner." According to the *Herald of Freedom*, "the Convention in New-England would have satisfied the world's representatives. . . . It surpassed in interest, power and *liberty*, even all its predecessor anniversaries." Nowhere else, said the *National Anti-Slavery Standard*, could one "find such life and eloquence."[62]

According to the minutes of the convention, Douglass spoke four times and, from all accounts, with great effect. Although he was quiet the opening day, during which Garrison, Nathaniel P. Rogers, and Stephen S. Foster introduced a series of resolutions endorsing moral suasion and condemning the proslavery character of the American church, on the second day he joined the debate over these resolutions. According to one account, he spoke "with great fluency and correctness" as he set out to prove, "by fact and argument," that the Christian church was the "bulwark of slavery and the great obstacle in the progress of human liberty." Although we do not have a text of Douglass' remarks, his speech had a profound impact on at least one member of the audience:

> We have seldom heard a better speech before a popular assembly—better, we mean, as to the language and the manner. Many of the speakers who followed him, and of a lighter complexion, men who boasted that they were ministers, and who had, doubtless, the advantage of education, which the man of color could never have enjoyed, might well be desirous of emulating the appropriateness of his elocution and gesticulation, and the grammatical accuracy of his sentences.[63]

After several other speeches had been delivered, reported a correspondent for the *Boston Courier*, Douglass "again took the floor, to state some facts, which occurred at New-Bedford, the place of his residence." According to the reporter's account, Douglass shared several anecdotes "in a sort of sarcastic tone, showing the inconsistency of the professions of many of the Christian Churches which rail against slavery and uphold it by their practice." In the process, he cited a personal experience from New Bedford, an experience he had mentioned in previous speeches. On this occasion, however, he went beyond describing the experience and enacted it for his listeners by imitating the New Bedford preacher addressing his congregation. "He stated that at an administration of the Lord's Supper in the Methodist Episcopal Church at New-Bedford, the elements were not administered to the colored people, until *all* the white people had been served; that *then* the minister invited the colored ones to come forward and partake, 'for that God is no respecter of persons.'" Ironically, Reverend Bonney, the minister Douglass was likely imitating, was identified by the *Courier* as being present in the audience that day in Boston and apparently sat near Douglass while he uttered this statement.[64] "The tone and manner with which Douglass pronounced this quotation," the reporter for the *Courier* reflected, "imitating, apparently, the voice and manner of the Methodist minister, must have cut like a two-edged sword."[65]

Douglass then offered another anecdote from his experiences at New Bedford. In this case the anecdote assumed the form of an allegory that he had used in previous speeches. On this occasion, however, instead of leaving the minister within the allegory anonymous, Douglass identified him by name. Elder Knapp, he charged, "got up a great revival, and among its subjects were some colored ones; for you know . . . when Brother Knapp throws his net into the sea, he cannot expect to catch all white fish; there will be some black ones, but he culls them out after he draws the net to the shore." This separation based solely on the color of a person's skin by a professed Christian minister deeply troubled Douglass, but he chose not to expand upon the racial slight and instead continued his argument by extending the racial prejudice experienced at the hands of northern ministers to white congregations in the North.[66]

Douglass was reported to have related other incidents illustrating his claim that "the Church, *so called*, was an obstacle in the progress of the abolition movement." Unfortunately, the correspondent recording Douglass' message did not report or summarize these remarks. He did, however, reflect on Douglass' talent as a speaker. "We left the chapel, and left him speaking," the correspondent wrote, "but not without a sentiment of respect for his talent, his good sense, and his zeal in a cause, in which, at least, he and his unfortunate race must be commended to the good wishes of the world."[67] In another account of the same speech, a correspondent for the *Boston Daily Ledger* wrote how Douglass, "formerly a slave, . . . showed up the inconsistency of southern slaveholding Christians, in great style," and "proved that they were supported by the great body of Christians in the North, in the way of communion and fellowship."[68]

Douglass spoke on two additional resolutions during the New England Anti-Slavery Society meeting. The first was Collins' resolution condemning the "bigoted sectarianism, and deep rooted hostility of free discussion and equality of fellowship, which have marked the clerical abolitionism of our country." The second was Edmund Quincy's proposition that abolitionists should "extend their anti-slavery fellowship to those bodies of professing christians, who have expressed their abhorrence of the sin of American slavery" and who have excluded slaveholders, ministers, and church members "who are not out-spoken and uncompromising abolitionists."[69] Unfortunately, no texts of Douglass' remarks in support of these resolutions have been located. The *Liberator* expressed its regret "that no reporter was secured to report the many eloquent and impressive speeches that were made in support of the various resolutions adopted by the Convention." Similarly, a correspondent for the *Herald of Freedom* wrote, "It is a pity there had not been a reporter to have saved the whole of the speeches. Anti-slavery must have reporters. . . . The eloquence of our meetings must not be any longer lost to the reader." Despite the lack of speech texts, however, there can be little doubt that the New England convention added to Douglass' reputation as an orator. He had spoken out against the proslavery church before the most powerful and influential antislavery leaders in New England. Applauding the addresses of both Douglass and Remond, a reporter for the *Herald of Freedom* believed that these black speakers had "already made color not only honorable but enviable. . . . If they were politicians or divines, the press would stretch itself to speak of them, and magnify their eloquence."[70]

IV

After the conclusion of the New England convention, Douglass returned to the field as a lecturer for the Massachusetts Anti-Slavery Society. From 3 to 9 June 1842, he delivered a series of lectures in and around Northbridge, Massachusetts. On Friday, 3 June, he spoke in the Congregational Church at Northbridge to a "very respectable and attentive audience." On Sunday he delivered two lectures in Reverend Stacy's church in Millville "to very large audiences." On Monday, 6 June, and Thursday, 9 June, he returned to Northbridge and lectured at Holbrook's Village.[71] Although there are no texts from any of these lectures, we can glean valuable information about what Douglass said and to what effect from a letter published in the *Liberator* written by a person who attended the speeches at Holbrook's Village. Because this account of Douglass' speech has been overlooked by previous scholars, it should be examined closely here.[72]

According to the letter writer's account, audiences were most impressed by Douglass' intellectual capacity. "In none of these efforts," observed the writer, "did he manifest any of that deficiency of mental power, which is said, by many, to be characteristic of the African race. On the contrary, the

universal opinion of those who heard him is, that he gave evidence of intellectual greatness, of which any man might be proud." Considering that
Douglass was a fugitive slave, the writer continued, "less than four years
from the lands of whips and thumbscrews," his intellectual ability was a
cause for "absolute astonishment."[73]

The letter writer went on to discuss the content and style of Douglass'
lectures. "It was the object of the lecturer," he reported, to establish "the
character of 'American slavery, stript of its concomitants and collaterals,'
to use his own words; to shew its cardinal principle—that without which,
it does not and cannot exist, viz., the principle of chattelism, and to run
that principle out into its natural and legitimate results." For Douglass, the
"cardinal principle" of slavery was treating human beings as property, a
practice which had a profound impact on the "pecuniary interests of the
country, especially that of the North." According to the writer's account,
Douglass argued that the responsibility for slavery was "not of the South
only, but of the whole country, and the North in particular." Hence, slavery was a national problem, and it was the North that had to lead the way
to put an end to the "existence of the whole accursed system."[74]

Not only did Douglass address the nature of the problem, he also proposed a solution. "All he asked of the people of the North," revealed the
writer, "was just to undo what they have done—just to make it known
throughout the length and breadth of the land, that, henceforth and forever, they, one and all, withdraw all countenance and support from the institution of slavery." Douglass called on his listeners to carry this out regardless of the consequences: "Compact or no compact, Constitution or no
Constitution, Union or no Union, they [the people of the North] will never
again restore the slave to his master, and . . . they will never lift a finger to
crush the slave, should he rise and assert his liberty by force of arms."[75]
Apparently, Douglass was calling upon his auditors to make a commitment
to protecting fugitive slaves from being returned to slavery and, more important, to support the slaves' efforts to "rise and assert" their liberty through
the use of force. This was a startling position, for it stood in direct disagree-
ment with the Garrisonian doctrine of nonresistance. As a slave, Douglass
had physically resisted the cruelties of slavery. Now it seems that he was calling for the North to support slave insurrections should they occur.

According to the letter writer's account, Douglass buttressed this and
other claims with "a course of reasoning as transparent as light itself, and
from the force of which, it was admitted, on all hands, there was no way of
escape." The writer concluded his letter to the *Liberator* with a stirring
tribute to Douglass' speaking ability:

> It has been my fortune to hear a great many anti-slavery lectur-
> ers, and many distinguished speakers on other subjects; but it has
> rarely been my lot to listen to one whose power over *me* was

greater than that of Douglass, and not over me only, but over all who heard him. May he live to prosecute his labors with unabated ardor, and constantly increasing power, until the air shall be rent with the mighty shout of Freedom's Jubilee![76]

V

One week after his Northbridge lectures, Douglass joined Garrison, George Bradburn, and Henry C. Wright for a series of antislavery and nonresistance meetings on Cape Cod. These meetings, which ran from 16 June through 22 June, were important for Douglass because they marked the first time he toured with Garrison, who came away with a profound respect and admiration for Douglass both as a person and as an orator.[77] Although there are no surviving texts of the Cape Cod speeches, Garrison chronicled the tour in the *Liberator* and offered a day-by-day account of the activities at each of the seven stops. Neither Douglass' nor Garrison's biographers have taken notice of Garrison's chronicle, yet it provides valuable information both about the tour in general and about Douglass' speeches and their impact on his audiences.[78]

The first meeting of the Cape Cod tour began at Barnstable, on Thursday, 16 June, and was dedicated to the subject of nonresistance. It got off to a rocky start. Wright was expected to attend the meeting, "but was detained by his appointments in Maine." Garrison, who traveled from Boston to Barnstable by boat, arrived two hours late "owing to poor winds, gales, dead calm, thunder and lightning, torrents of rain, [and being] grounded on a sandbar at the entrance of the harbor." Despite his tardiness, Garrison wrote, "the audience behaved with exemplary patience" and "appeared to take deep interest in the discussion."[79]

After Garrison spoke "at some length," Douglass followed as one of two "witnesses on the side of non-resistance." Douglass, who had "the most cause to repudiate the doctrine, if it be dangerous to adopt it in practice," seems to have pleasantly surprised and deeply impressed Garrison with his public support of nonresistance:

> He stood there as a slave—a runaway from the southern house of bondage—not safe for one hour, even on the soil of Massachusetts—with his back all horribly scarred by the lash—with the bitter remembrances of a life of slavery crowding upon his soul—with every thing in his past history, his present condition, his future prospects, to make him a fierce outlaw, and a stern avenger of outraged humanity! He stood there, not to counsel retaliation, not to advocate the right of the oppressed to wade through blood to liberty, not to declaim after the manner of worldly patriotism—O no!—but with the spirit of christian forgiveness

in his heart, with the melting accents of charity on his lips, with the gentleness of love beaming in his eyes! His testimony was clear and emphatic. The cause of non-resistance he declared to be divine, and essential to the overthrow of every form of oppression on earth. It was so plain to his vision, it was so palpably in accordance with the genius of Christianity, that he found it difficult to argue the question.[80]

Douglass' compassion toward the oppressed deeply affected Garrison. "I could not help thinking," reflected Garrison, "how incomparably superior was this 'chattel,' in all the great qualities of the soul, to any warrior whose deeds are recorded on the page of history; and that here was a remarkable instance of christian magnanimity, and martyr-like devotion to the cause of humanity." Certainly, slaves would be "justified in resisting their relentless tyrants unto blood." Yet Douglass, a former slave who wore the brutality of slavery on his person and who had actively resisted his slave master, was preaching forgiveness and love and advocating nonresistance as essential to the overthrow of oppression. According to Garrison, the speaker who followed Douglass to the platform was so moved by his remarks that she commended his Christian ways and "held up his example for the imitation of others."[81]

The next day, Douglass, Garrison, and Bradburn held an antislavery meeting at Yarmouth Port. "The audiences," reported Garrison, "were respectable in point of number as well as character, but not large." The timing of the meetings was not opportune, for "a large portion" of the men were out at sea. "The winter," advised Garrison, "is the time to secure large gatherings." Still, this meeting, and the meetings that occurred throughout the tour, Garrison noted, helped to "diffuse light" and to "excite interest" in the antislavery movement.[82]

On Saturday, 18 June, the company moved to Centreville, where the meeting began at 1 P.M. and lasted until 10 P.M. Unlike their experience in Yarmouth, Garrison, Douglass, and Bradburn found the "interest in these appearances to be very great in the mind of the people." During the meeting, reported Garrison, "a large mass of important facts [were] presented to show how slavery is hurrying the country down to destruction." In recording his reactions to Douglass' speeches on this occasion, Garrison suggested the range of Douglass' oratory. Douglass, he wrote, delivered a speech "of great power and eloquence" in which he "exposed the guilt and servility of the North, in a manner not less effective than original—'from gay to grave, from lively to severe.'"[83]

The following day, Douglass, Bradburn, and Garrison traveled to Osterville to hold nonresistance meetings. Both the afternoon and evening sessions were "well attended." All three men spoke in favor of a resolution that declared "a Christian cannot fight, with carnal weapons, against his enemies, or the enemies of others; nor take the life of his fellow-man, nor assist or empower others to take it, either in self-defence or as a penalty for crime." Garrison spoke first and was followed by Bradburn. Douglass spoke last and received the most attention in Garrison's summary of the meeting. Douglass, Garrison reported, "displayed the power of an unsophisticated mind and the glow of an earnest heart, in support of the resolution." Reflecting on the impact of Douglass' message, Garrison wrote: "How charming, how powerful is truth, uttered in love, and clothed with simplicity! His remarks were exceedingly pertinent, and made a visible impression on the countenances of the audience."[84]

On 20 June two antislavery meetings were held in the Baptist Meeting House at Hyannis. "The audience," reported Garrison, "was highly respectable, on the score of numbers and character." The speakers, who included Douglass, Bradburn, Wright, and Garrison, examined "nearly all the bearings of slavery, in a religious and political point of view." Douglass played an especially important role during the meeting. According to Garrison's account, a sea captain rose to give testimony that he had seen the slave system at work in "various parts of the slave states." The captain stated that he had never seen a slave flogged, and he insisted that the slaves were not treated "so bad as was generally represented." Douglass "then rose to give his testimony—to state what his own eyes had seen, his own ears had heard, and he himself had suffered." He also read "a large amount of evidence . . . given by southern men . . . proving the entire slave system to be diabolical."[85]

This is the first recorded instance of Douglass coupling his personal testimony with a written work. He most likely read from Theodore Weld's *American Slavery As It Is: Testimony of a Thousand Witnesses* (1839), a graphic catalogue of the horrors of slavery.[86] Weld cited southern slave laws and statutes, newspaper accounts, eyewitness accounts, and advertisements from southern newspapers. His work was an important resource in the abolitionist campaign. By reciting it, Douglass doubtless strengthened his credibility and buttressed his argument against slavery. In addition, Garrison's report lends credence to Douglass' claim in his second autobiography that "It was impossible for me to repeat the same old story month after month, and to keep up my interest in it, . . . for I was now reading and thinking. New views of the subject were presented to my mind." Those views came from many sources—including orators such as Garrison, Wright, Collins, Remond, Kelley, and Phillips—but they also came from books such as Weld's monumental work. Douglass' speech at Hyannis shows that he was reading about slavery and thinking about how best to persuade audiences of its barbarity.[87]

From Hyannis the company traveled to North Dennis for a meeting on 21 June. "Our first meeting" there, reported Garrison in the *Liberator*, "was the most impressive and interesting of the whole series."[88] Although the weather was "intensely warm," the audience was large for the afternoon session "and more earnest attention to the thoughts that were uttered could not have been given." Douglass was one of five speakers who addressed the assembly.[89] Although Garrison did not offer any commentary on Douglass' speeches, an eyewitness account of his Tuesday evening antislavery lecture appeared in the *Nantucket Islander* in early July. This account, like Garrison's chronicle, is especially telling because it was written by a person who was not an abolitionist and who openly acknowledged that he was "a bundle of prejudices" before attending the lecture.[90]

Although the letter writer admitted that his motive for attending the lecture was "amusement and recreation," what he found, much to his surprise, was an "eloquent negro." According to this account, Douglass was "chaste in language, brilliant in thought, and truly eloquent in delivery. His mind seemed to overflow with noble ideas, and they always came forth in suitable garb. He is a remarkable man." Douglass, the observer continued, "gave us a good proof of the freedom of his mind . . . [and] his wit and power of sarcasm . . . are remarkable." The writer also quoted a small portion of the speech, during which Douglass imitated the minister of the Methodist church in New Bedford speaking to the black members of the congregation:

> "Brethren," said the meek pastor in New-Bedford, addressing his colored friends, "Brethren, you should be meek and lowly; you should not complain that you are seated in the 'Jim Crow Pew,' or placed in the lowest seat in the synagogue! You should be humble!" *What meekness was there!* said Douglass.[91]

Certainly, for Douglass, the northern ministers of religion were the champions and sustainers of racial prejudice. He was clearly angered over the contradiction between Christian theory and practice where African Americans were concerned. Douglass' message made a strong impression on the observer. His words, say the letter, showered down "like 'manna from heaven,'" and the writer left the hall that evening "with a mountainload of prejudice tumbling from his back."[92]

The Cape Cod tour came to a close on Wednesday, 22 June, in Brewster, "where two meetings were held to break open the doors of the southern prison-house, and to set the captives free." The audiences "were not large," reported Garrison, "but no little excitement was produced in the course of the proceedings." For Garrison and his company, the tour was a success. "I trust something has been done by this tour," wrote Garrison, "to diffuse light, and to excite an interest in the anti-slavery movement." Certainly, Douglass played an important part in the success of the tour. He delivered speeches of great power and eloquence, in which he impressed

Garrison and other listeners with his passionate endorsement of nonresistance and his devotion to the cause of humanity. It is no wonder that Garrison concluded his commentary of his experience on Cape Cod with this reflection: "Long shall I remember, if my life be spared, my first anti-slavery trip to Cape Cod."[93]

VI

In late July, Douglass was appointed by the general agent of the Massachusetts Anti-Slavery Society as its delegate to attend the annual meeting of the Eastern Pennsylvania Anti-Slavery Society, a meeting scheduled to coincide with the commemoration of the anniversary of the abolition of slavery in the British West Indies.[94] One week later, he was appointed a delegate of the American Anti-Slavery Society for the same meeting. These twin appointments mark Douglass' growing prominence as an abolitionist orator. The advertisements for the Eastern Pennsylvania Society meeting heralded Douglass' plans to attend. "It would be worth a travel of many miles to the meeting," read advertisements in the *Pennsylvania Freeman* and the *Liberator*, "if it were for no other object than to hear Douglas[s]." Coincidentally, Douglass had also been invited to speak at antislavery meetings in Providence, Rhode Island, on the same day. The advertisement for this meeting exclaimed, "Frederic[k] Douglas[s], the eloquent *self*-emancipated [slave], will address the meetings; and should any abolitionists walk twenty miles to hear him, they will never regret the trouble."[95] Douglass chose to attend the Eastern Pennsylvania meeting, which ran for three days and was held at the Baptist meeting house in Norristown.[96] The audience of approximately 1,000 people was reported to have been "highly respectable." The hall "was crowded each day of the meeting," and Douglass was among the "several talented speakers" to address the convention, though, unfortunately, there are no surviving accounts of his speeches or of the convention in general.[97]

After returning to Massachusetts from Pennsylvania, Douglass went back into the field as an agent for the Massachusetts Anti-Slavery Society. During the second week of August he attended the annual series of meetings in New Bedford and Nantucket, which one year earlier had been the site of his emergence as an abolitionist orator. The New Bedford meetings of 8 and 9 August focused on the proslavery position of the American church. The topic, reported Garrison in the *Liberator*, "excited not only a highly animated discussion in the meeting, but a most tremendous sensation out of it." Garrison identified Douglass as one of the abolitionists who attended the meeting, which was disrupted in the evening of the second day by an anti-abolitionist mob that shouted down the speakers and produced what one observer called a "foul disgrace" upon the character of the people of New Bedford "which years cannot efface."[98]

The violence the abolitionists experienced at New Bedford, however, was only a prelude to what was to come in Nantucket. The resolution condemning the church as the bulwark of American slavery was brought forward for discussion and, according to Garrison, "produced even a greater sensation than at New-Bedford." The Nantucket convention began in the Great Hall of the Atheneum at 2 P.M. on Wednesday, 10 August, and remained in session until Monday evening, 15 August.[99] The minutes from the meeting describe the audience as "large and intelligent" and "deeply interested" in the proceedings. The convention began with the election of officers for the meeting and with the appointment of a business committee. Douglass, possibly for the first time in his career with the Massachusetts Anti-Slavery Society, was appointed to the business committee. As a member of the committee, he would have influence over the direction of the convention. It is noteworthy that the four resolutions introduced by the business committee centered on slavery as an American institution and on the proslavery nature of the Christian church, two subjects about which Douglass felt most strongly.[100]

During the evening session on Wednesday, a resolution declaring that "the existence of slavery in this country is incompatible with the preservation of northern rights and interests" was brought forward for discussion. Charles Lenox Remond spoke in favor of the resolution, working to show "the incompatibility of slavery at the South with the property of the North." Next Douglass came forward and, in characteristic fashion, "endeavored to prove that we have no right to talk of northern liberty and southern slavery, while all parts of the country are equally involved in the guilt of slaveholding." In addition, he denounced the church, "both at the North and the South," as proslavery. Douglass reportedly "spoke of the southern clergy in terms of the most withering sarcasm." In so doing, "he evinced great imitative powers, in an amusing exhibition of their style of preaching to the slaves, which greatly interested the audience." According to the minutes of the proceedings, Douglass' "graphic mimickry of southern priestly whining and sophistry was replete with humor and apparent truth, which elicited tremendous applause."[101]

The following morning, Thursday, 11 August, the discussion of the business committee's resolutions continued. Garrison, Collins, Foster, and Douglass were among the speakers supporting the resolutions. Douglass reportedly commented on the "spurious character" of religion. He did not participate in the afternoon or evening sessions, the latter of which were "annoyed by noisy and riotous proceedings of persons assembled around the Hall." The mob, "by hooting, screeching, throwing brick-bats and other missiles, manifested their determinations not to listen to the truth."

Fortunately, those people assembled within the hall "kept as quiet as possible," and the meeting was able to "proceed in its deliberations, without material interruptions."[102]

At the opening of the morning session on Friday, 12 August, Garrison introduced three resolutions condemning the riots which had occurred in Philadelphia on 1 August during the public observance of the anniversary of the abolition of slavery in the West Indies.[103] Toward the end of this session, Douglass spoke to one of Garrison's resolutions. "The ferocious assault upon the colored population of Philadelphia," read the resolution, "grew out of hatred and contempt of a colored skin." Douglass was reported to have described the effects of racial prejudice "in exciting mobs against the colored people—preventing them from taking their places in society as equal members—excluding them from lucrative and varied employments—and, finally, in furnishing the strongest defense of slavery itself."[104]

On Friday evening, "the mob rallied in great numbers, and attempted in vain to break-up the meeting." According to the minutes of the meeting, the mob "was making a hideous noise without, stamping and whistling, flinging brickbats and stones, in response to the powerful arguments urged by the speakers." Despite all the noise and the throwing of bricks and "other missiles into the windows," the speakers, "too confident of the integrity of their cause to be intimidated by such rebuffs," continued, and the meeting adjourned at the usual hour of ten o'clock. Still, the violence was enough to lead the trustees of the Atheneum building to insist that the convention meet elsewhere for the rest of its sessions unless it would guarantee the safety of the hall "and make good on any damage which it might receive at the hands of the mob." When the leaders of the convention refused to make such a guarantee, the abolitionists moved to Franklin Hall, where the convention continued.[105]

Douglass actively participated in the Saturday evening session at Franklin Hall. He joined Bradburn, Foster, and Collins in supporting a series of resolutions declaring the importance of the crusade against slavery in restoring "two and a half millions of our fellow countrymen to their liberties." The other resolutions called for helping the American Anti-Slavery Society raise funds to "scatter agents throughout the free States" and for encouraging the interest of children in the antislavery enterprise. Unlike the previous two evenings, the convention was not disturbed by the mob until late in the proceedings when, wrote a correspondent for the *Nantucket Inquirer*, it was "assailed by a shower of rotten eggs, in such an exceedingly nauseous and offensive state of putrefaction" as to cause "a sudden and somewhat precipitous adjournment."[106]

On Sunday afternoon, 14 August, the convention convened at the Town Hall, where Douglass addressed a "large audience."[107] The convention then adjourned until evening, and it concluded the next day.[108] Douglass had been active throughout the proceedings. As a member of the business committee, he was able to influence the direction of the convention. During the deliberations, he charged the North and the South with being equally involved in the guilt of slaveholding, denounced the proslavery character of the American church, examined the spurious character of religion, described the effects of racial prejudice on black people in the North, and declared his allegiance to the crusade against slavery. The meeting had presented Douglass with the opportunity to speak on the subjects about which he felt most strongly, and he had not wasted the chance.

After the Nantucket convention, Douglass returned to the field as a lecturer for the Massachusetts Anti-Slavery Society. Sometime after returning from Nantucket, he lectured twice in Sutton and several times in Grafton. Theron E. Hall, a local abolitionist who attended Douglass' lectures in Sutton and Grafton, reported to Garrison in a letter published in the *Liberator* that "any one who heard him will justify me in saying, that he gave good satisfaction."[109] There is no doubt that Douglass' lecture had a powerful effect on Hall, as he explained to Garrison:

> Although an abolitionist before, yet never have I had my sympathy touched so sensibly for the slave as when hearing him. I would that those who say, "the slave is happy in his present condition," could hear this "nigger," as by some the colored man is contemptuously called, and I think that this argument would be silenced at once. "Why, (say they,) you know nothing of the condition of the slave—therefore, let him alone—he is happy in his present condition"! But when one comes to them with his back scarred by the ruthless lash of the slave-driver, can they say, "he knows nothing of slavery"?[110]

According to Hall, Douglass' oratory "awakened such an interest in Sutton as will have an abiding effect, and in a few years, and I think I may say months, you may consider this strong hold of slavery as an anti-slavery town."[111]

Before leaving Massachusetts for a lecture tour of western New York, Douglass returned home to Lynn, where he attended a nonresistance meeting. The meeting convened on 21 August in the basement rooms of the Lyceum Hall.[112] So many people attended, however, that the meeting had to be moved upstairs into the Great Hall, where the assembly was "elegantly addressed" by Douglass, Henry C. Wright, and John A. Collins. Douglass, noted Nathaniel P. Rogers, "was especially eloquent and powerful." In a departure from his usual attack on the organized religion of the North, Douglass spoke of prayer. "His illustration of prayer," reflected Rogers, "was very happy and forcible." Rogers paraphrased Douglass' remarks:

Prayer was *doing* he said, and not *saying*. He had prayed in words, but his prayers were never answered. He had observed that. He had often prayed, after the fashson of our worship, but never knew that any of his prayers had been granted. He had often prayed for freedom, he said, when he was a slave—but freedom never came. At length he *run away after it*, and he found it. That was the effectual sort of prayer—DOING![113]

As a slave, Douglass realized that praying was not going to free him from slavery. Only through the act of running away could he attain his freedom. By escaping the bonds of slavery, he demonstrated his belief that God was not wholly responsible for freeing him from slavery. Although emancipation required faith, it also required suffering and struggle. Now, as a fugitive, he was not merely praying for the end of slavery, but was using the power of oratory to help bring it to an end.[114]

The eight-month period from January to August 1842 was a crucial stage in Douglass' career as an antislavery lecturer and Garrisonian abolitionist. As 1842 marched forward, his oratory became more biting and sarcastic, his message more universal, eloquent, and refined. By the end of August 1842 he had distinguished himself as a leading Garrisonian abolitionist orator with a growing reputation throughout northern antislavery circles. His next challenge would be to venture into New York state, where the conviction that slavery could be abolished only through political action was gaining strength at the expense of Garrisonianism and where the state's local and county antislavery societies, active during the 1830s, had all but disappeared in the 1840s. It would prove to be one of the most trying campaigns of his career.

Notes

1. *Liberator*, 11 February 1842, 22. John W. Blassingame inaccurately dates this meeting as occurring on 5 January only. See John W. Blassingame, ed., *The Frederick Douglass Papers, Series One: Speeches, Debates, and Interviews, Volume 1* (New Haven, Conn.: Yale University Press, 1979), 1:lxxxviii.

2. Benjamin Quarles, *Black Abolitionists* (New York: Oxford University Press, 1969), 131-32; John Daniels, *In Freedom's Birthplace: A Study of Boston Negroes* (Boston: Houghton Mifflin, 1914), 47; Patrick G. Wheaton and Celeste M. Condit, "Charles Lenox Remond (1810-1873), Abolitionist, Reform Activist," in *African-American Orators: A Biocritical Sourcebook*, ed. Richard W. Leeman (Westport, Conn.: Greenwood, 1996), 302-3.

3. William Edward Ward, "Charles Lenox Remond: Black Abolitionist, 1838-1873" (Ph.D. diss., Clark University, 1977), 119-20.

4. William Wells Brown, *The Rising Son: The Antecedents and Advancement of the Colored Race* (Boston: A.G. Brown, 1874), 403.

5. *Liberator*, 11 February 1842, 22.

6. Ibid.

7. *Liberator*, 21 January 1842, 9.

8. According to Blassingame, ed., *Douglass Papers, Series One*, 1:lxxxviii, Douglass attended the 11 January quarterly meeting of the Essex County Anti-Slavery Society at Rockport, and the 19 January meeting of the Norfolk County Anti-Slavery Society at Dedham. However, Douglass' name does not appear in the records of either meeting and there is no way to place him definitively at either. For the minutes from these meetings, see the *Liberator*, 21 January 1842, 11; *Liberator*, 28 January 1842, 15.

9. Benjamin Quarles, *Frederick Douglass* (Washington, D.C.: Associated Publishers, 1948), 22; Raymond Gerald Fulkerson, "Frederick Douglass and the Anti-Slavery Crusade: His Career and Speeches, 1817-1861," pt. 1 (Ph.D. diss., University of Illinois, 1971), 56.

10. Blassingame, ed., *Douglass Papers, Series One*, 1:lxxxviii, erroneously states that the Massachusetts Anti-Slavery Society meeting convened on 26 January only, when in fact it ran from 26-28 January.

11. *Herald of Freedom*, 11 January 1842, 202; *National Anti-Slavery Standard*, 3 February 1842, 138; *Liberator*, 11 February 1842, 22; *Tenth Annual Report of the Board of Managers of the Massachusetts Anti-Slavery Society* (Boston: Dow and Jackson's Press, 1842), 1-3.

12. *Liberator*, 11 February 1842, 22, 23; Blassingame, ed., *Douglass Papers, Series One*, 1:13.

13. *Herald of Freedom*, 11 February 1842, 202; Blassingame, ed., *Douglass Papers, Series One*, 1:13.

14. *Liberator*, 11 February 1842, 22; *National Anti-Slavery Standard*, 24 February 1842, 149; Blassingame, ed., *Douglass Papers, Series One*, 1:13.

15. The text of this speech is in Blassingame, ed., *Douglass Papers, Series One*, 1:13-15.

16. Ibid., 1:14.

17. Ibid.

18. Caleb Bingham, ed., *The Columbian Orator* (Boston: Manning and Loring, 1797), 26; Blassingame, ed., *Douglass Papers, Series One*, 1:14.

19. Blassingame, ed., *Douglass Papers, Series One*, 1:14.

20. Ibid., 1:14-15

21. Ibid., 1:15; Dwight L. Dumond, *Antislavery: The Crusade for Freedom in America* (Ann Arbor: University of Michigan Press, 1961), 285-87.

22. *Liberator*, 11 February 1842, 22.

23. *Tenth Annual Report*, 5-6; Liberator, 11 February 1842, 23. The *Lynn Record* described the meeting as "grand and imposing" and reported that a large number of people who wished to attend "were unable to gain admittance" (*Lynn Record* in the *Herald of Freedom*, 11 February 1842, 201).

24. The other eight speakers were Bradburn, Garrison, Phillips, Remond, Jonathon Peckham Miller, Nathaniel P. Rogers, James C. Fuller, and Abby Kelley (*Lynn Record* in the *Herald of Freedom*, 11 February 1842, 201; *Herald of Freedom*, 11 February 1842, 202).

25. *Lynn Record* in the *Herald of Freedom*, 11 February 1842, 201.

26. *Herald of Freedom*, 11 February 1842, 202.

27. *Lynn Record* in the *Herald of Freedom*, 11 February 1842, 201; *Bay Street Democrat* in the *Liberator*, 18 February 1842, 25. Douglass was followed to the platform by Abby Kelley. Next Garrison took the stand and, referring to Douglass' speech, addressed the audience: "They had heard that fugitive slave speak before them, he said. He now asked of the meeting, and he would thank them to answer him, if they deemed him a man, and capable of taking care of himself? YES! was the prompt reply. Well then, he cried, is he entitled to his Liberty? YES! shouted the multitude. Will you aid the southern bloodhounds, if they should come here after him, to seize him and carry him back to slavery? NO! thundered the multitude, in a voice that made the old Hall ring again" (*Herald of Freedom*, 11 February 1842, 202).

28. *Tenth Annual Report*, 8-9; *Liberator*, 11 February 1842, 22.

29. *Liberator*, 7 January 1842, 3; *New Hampshire People's Advocate* in the *Liberator*, 18 February 1842, 26; *Liberator*, 4 February 1842, 18; *National Anti-Slavery Standard*, 3 February 1842, 138; Blassingame, ed., *Douglass Papers, Series One*, 1:15; Raymond Gerald Fulkerson, "Frederick Douglass and the Anti-Slavery Crusade: His Career and Speeches, 1817-1861," pt. 2 (Ph.D. diss., University of Illinois, 1971), 452.

30. *Tenth Annual Report*, 9-18; Blassingame, ed., *Douglass Papers, Series One*, 1:16. The text can also be found in the *Liberator*, 4 February 1842, 19; *National Anti-Slavery Standard*, 17 February 1842, 146; *Tenth Annual Report*, 18-19; Fulkerson, "Frederick Douglass," pt. 2, 453-54.

31. Blassingame, ed., *Douglass Papers, Series One*, 1:16.

32. Ibid.

33. Ibid.

34. Ibid.

35. Ibid. For a discussion of Douglass' religious views, see Frederick Douglass, *Narrative of the Life of Frederick Douglass, An American Slave, Written By Himself* (1845; reprint, New York: Signet, 1968), 120-26; William L. Van Deburg, "Frederick Douglass and the Institutional Church," *Journal of the American Academy of Religion* 45 (June 1977): 465-87; William L. Van Deburg, "Frederick Douglass: Maryland Slave to Religious Liberal," *Maryland Historical Magazine* 69 (Spring 1974): 27-43; David W. Blight, *Frederick Douglass' Civil War: Keeping Faith in Jubilee* (Baton Rouge: Louisiana State University Press, 1989), 8-11.

36. Blassingame, ed., *Douglass Papers, Series One*, 1:16-17.

37. *National Anti-Slavery Standard*, 3 February 1842, 138; *Herald of Freedom*, 4 February 1842 in the *Liberator*, 18 February 1842, 26.

38. Helen Pitts Douglass, ed., *In Memoriam: Frederick Douglass* (Philadelphia: John C. Yorston and Co., 1897), 44.

39. Blassingame, ed., *Douglass Papers, Series One*, 1:lxxxviii, misdates the 8-9 February meeting at Andover as taking place on 8 February only.

40. *Liberator*, 25 February 1842, 30. The preamble and resolutions presented by Garrison calling for the dissolution of the Union were reprinted in the *Liberator*, 25 February 1842, 30.

41. *Liberator*, 11 March 1842, 38.

42. Blassingame, ed., *Douglass Papers, Series One*, 1:lxxxviii, does not include this meeting in its itinerary of Douglass' speaking activities.

43. *Liberator*, 1 April 1842, 51; John Hope Franklin, *From Slavery to Freedom*, 3d ed. (New York: Alfred A. Knopf, 1967), 249; Quarles, *Black Abolitionists*, 225; Waldo E. Martin Jr., *The Mind of Frederick Douglass* (Chapel Hill: University of North Carolina Press, 1984), 52. For a detailed description of the *Creole* incident, see *Emancipator and Free American*, 7 January 1842, 144.

44. *Liberator*, 1 April 1842, 51.

45. The other five agents were Abel Tanner, George C. Leach, Jeremiah B. Sanderson, George Bradburn, and John A. Collins (*Liberator*, 1 April 1842, 51).

46. *Liberator*, 1 April 1842, 51.

47. Ibid.; *Liberator*, 8 April 1842, 54; *Liberator*, 22 April 1842, 63; *Liberator*, 13 May 1842, 75. The itinerary of Douglass' tour in Blassingame, ed., *Douglass Papers, Series One*, 1:lxxxviii-lxxxvix, contains several errors. It does not account for his lectures in Lanesborough on 4-5 April, and it erroneously states that Douglass was in Berlin on 4 April and in Northborough on 5 April, when in fact he spoke in Lanesborough on these dates. A complete itinerary of the tour is printed as part of appendix A of this work.

48. I have contacted every town in which Douglass spoke during this period and have located only one account of his lecture activities. That account, recorded by a ten-year-old boy, contains only a brief sketch of his remarks at Lanesborough on 4-5 April. See Danforth Comstock Hodges, "'Formerly a Slave': Frederick Douglass Comes to Lanesborough," ed. Terry Alford *New England Quarterly* 60 (March 1987): 86-88.

49. *Herald of Freedom*, 19 August 1842, 103; Frederick Douglass, *Life and Times of Frederick Douglass* (1892; reprint, New York: Macmillan, 1962), 223.

50. *Herald of Freedom*, 19 August 1842, 103; Douglass, *Life and Times*, 224.

51. Douglass is likely referring to Rowena Auld, the wife of his master, Thomas Auld. See Frederick Douglass, *My Bondage and My Freedom* (1855; reprint, New York: Dover, 1969), 187.

52. On Monday, 4 April 1842, Danforth Comstock Hodges recorded in his diary that he had gone to Lanesborough's Talcott School to listen to a lecture on slavery delivered by Douglass. The next evening, Hodges attended a lecture Douglass delivered on gradualism (Hodges, "'Formerly a Slave'": 86-88).

53. *Herald of Freedom*, 19 August 1842, 103; *Liberator*, 13 May 1842, 75.

54. *Liberator*, 9 September 1842, 142. Occasionally, Douglass departed from his lecture tour to attend other abolitionist meetings. On 26 April, for instance, he interrupted his tour to attend the Middlesex County Anti-Slavery Society meeting in Lexington. During the meeting, seven resolutions were debated. The first three demanded the "repeal of the Union between North and South." The fourth and fifth praised John Quincy Adams and Joshua Giddings for their fight in Congress to uphold free speech and the right of petition, while the sixth condemned the proslavery nature of the Christian church. The final resolution urged members of the society to attend the upcoming national meeting of the American Anti-Slavery Society in New York City. "These resolutions," reported a correspondent to the *Liberator*, "elicited a most serious, animated and highly interesting discussion." Phillips, Garrison, Samuel J. May, Remond, and Douglass were among the speakers who participated. See the *Liberator*, 29 April 1842, 67.

55. Blassingame, ed., *Douglass Papers, Series One*, 1:lxxxix, misdates this meeting, which took place on 10-13 May, as occurring on 10 May only. For another account of this meeting, see *New York Herald*, 14 May 1842.

56. *National Anti-Slavery Standard*, 19 May 1842, 198.

57. Ibid., 199.

58. For a text of Lane's remarks, see *Liberator*, 3 June 1842, 86; *National Anti-Slavery Standard*, 9 June 1842, 1.

59. *National Anti-Slavery Standard*, 19 May 1842, 199.

60. Ibid.

61. *Liberator*, 20 May 1842, 79. Whenever Douglass' name had appeared in the Liberator, prior to this issue, it was misspelled, usually as "Frederic Douglas" or "Frederick Douglas."

62. *Liberator*, 27 May 1842, 83; *Boston Daily Ledger* in the *Liberator*, 3 June 1842, 86; *Herald of Freedom*, in the *Liberator*, 10 June 1842, 90; *National Anti-Slavery Standard*, 9 June 1842, 1-2.

63. Blassingame, ed., *Douglass Papers, Series One*, 1:18. Another version of this text may be found in *National Anti-Slavery Standard*, 9 June 1842, 2.

64. *Boston Courier* in Blassingame, ed., *Douglass Papers, Series One*, 1:19. In 1855 Douglass shared this anecdote with his readers and identified Reverend Bonny, the pastor of the Elm Street Methodist Church, as the person who addressed the black congregants in this manner (Douglass, *Bondage and Freedom*, 351-52).

65. Blassingame, ed., *Douglass Papers, Series One*, 1:19-20.

66. Ibid., 1:20.

67. Ibid.

68. Ibid., 1:18-19; *Boston Daily Ledger* in the *Liberator*, 3 June 1842, 86.

69. *Liberator*, 3 June 1842, 87.

70. *Liberator*, 27 May 1842, 83; *Herald of Freedom* in the *Liberator*, 10 June 1842, 90.

71. Blassingame, ed., *Douglass Papers, Series One*, 1:lxxxix, does not include the lecture of 9 June in its itinerary of Douglass' speaking activities.

72. *Liberator*, 17 June 1842, 94.

73. Ibid.

74. Ibid.

75. Ibid.

76. Ibid.

77. Blassingame, ed., *Douglass Papers, Series One*, 1:lxxxix, mistakenly dates the Cape Cod tour as taking place from 1 to 21 July. In addition, it does not include the meetings of 16 June, 19 June, or 21 June in its itinerary of Douglass' speaking activities.

78. For Garrison's report, see *Liberator*, 1 July 1842, 102; *Liberator*, 8 July 1842, 107; *Liberator*, 15 July 1842, 110; *Liberator*, 22 July 1842, 114.

79. *Liberator*, 1 July 1842, 102.

80. Ibid.

81. Ibid.

82. Ibid.

83. Ibid.

84. *Liberator*, 8 July 1842, 107.

85. *Liberator*, 15 July 1842, 110.

86. For a detailed discussion of Weld's work see Stephen H. Browne, "'Like Gory Spectres': Representing Evil in Theodore Weld's *American Slavery As It Is*," *Quarterly Journal of Speech* 80 (August 1994): 277-92.

87. Douglass, *Bondage and Freedom*, 361. Theodore Weld, *American Slavery As It Is: Testimony of a Thousand Witnesses* (New York: American Anti-Slavery Society, 1839). Douglass often paraphrased and quoted directly from Weld's work. For instances see Blassingame, ed., *Douglass Papers, Series One*, 1:42, 51-52, 75, 254, 275, 279-80, 281, 322, 485.

88. Blassingame, ed., *Douglass Papers, Series One*, 1:lxxxix, incorrectly locates Douglass at a meeting of the Essex County Anti-Slavery Society at Danvers, Massachusetts, on 21 June.

89. *Liberator*, 22 July 1842, 114.

90. *Liberator*, 8 July 1842, 106. Although the letter does not identify the date of Douglass' speech, it states that the correspondent, "having a leisure hour on

Tuesday evening . . . was seduced into hearing Frederick Douglass, the fugitive slave." The speech in North Dennis is the only Tuesday evening antislavery lecture by Douglass in June 1842 of which I am aware.

91. *Liberator*, 8 July 1842, 106.

92. Ibid.

93. *Liberator*, 1 July 1842, 102; Liberator, 22 July 1842, 114.

94. Douglass' activities in July 1842 are impossible to determine. Weekly issues of the *Liberator*, 17 June-16 September 1842 reveal little about Douglass' activities in July.

95. *Liberator*, 22 July 1842, 115. Liberator, 29 July 1842, 119; *National Anti-Slavery Standard*, 28 July 1842, 31.

96. Blassingame, ed., *Douglass Papers, Series One*, 1:xc, misdates this meeting, which ran from 1-3 August, as occurring on 1 August only.

97. *National Anti-Slavery Standard*, 11 August 1842, 38; *National Anti-Slavery Standard*, 1 September 1842, 49. Unfortunately, I have not been able to locate minutes of the Norristown meeting in either the *Liberator*, the *Herald of Freedom*, or the *National Anti-Slavery Standard*.

98. *Liberator*, 19 August 1842, 131; *Herald of Freedom*, 19 August 1842, 103; *Herald of Freedom*, 2 September 1842, 112; *Morning Register* (New Bedford), 12 August 1842, 2. Neither the *Liberator*, the *Herald of Freedom*, nor the *National Anti-Slavery Standard* published minutes from the New Bedford meeting. The *New Bedford Morning Register* focused its reports of the convention on the Tuesday evening riot.

99. Blassingame, ed., *Douglass Papers, Series One*, 1:xc, places Douglass at the Nantucket convention on 10 August, but mistakenly represents the meeting as lasting one day rather than six. Douglass was present at least until the fifth day and, most likely, until the end.

100. *Liberator*, 2 September 1842, 138.

101. Ibid.

102. Ibid.

103. On 1 August 1842 a large number of whites broke up a parade of black people who were marching in celebration of the anniversary of the abolition of slavery in the British West Indies. The mob attacked the marchers and burned the new African Hall and Colored Presbyterian Church. The situation became so serious that state troops had to be called to assist the police in calming the city. A grand jury placed the blame for the riots on the provocative nature of the black procession, while others charged that the attack was premeditated and strengthened by unemployed white workers. See Franklin, *Slavery to Freedom*, 235; Leon F. Litwack, *North of Slavery: The Negro in the Free States, 1790-1860* (Chicago: University of Chicago Press, 1961), 102.

104. *Liberator*, 2 September 1842, 138.

105. *Liberator*, 19 August 1842, 131; *Nantucket Islander* in the *Liberator*, 26 August 1842, 134; Liberator, 2 September 1842, 138.

106. *Liberator*, 2 September 1842, 138; *Nantucket Inquirer* in the *Liberator*, 26 August 1842, 134.

107. Upon deciding to leave Atheneum Hall, the abolitionists had applied to the Nantucket authorities for use of the Town Hall. Their request was granted, and they were allowed to convene in the hall for the Sunday sessions (*Liberator*, 2 September 1842, 138).

108. *Liberator*, 2 September 1842, 138.

109. I have been unable to determine the precise dates of the Sutton and Grafton lectures. Assuming that the letter dated 18 August 1842 from Hall to Garrison was written soon after Hall heard Douglass, the most likely dates for the lectures were 16-17 August. Blassingame, ed., *Douglass Papers, Series One*, 1:xc, does not include either the Sutton or the Grafton meetings in its itinerary of Douglass' speaking activities.

110. *Liberator*, 9 September 1842, 142.

111. Ibid.

112. Blassingame, ed., *Douglass Papers, Series One*, 1:xc, fails to include this meeting in its itinerary of Douglass' speaking activities and erroneously states that Douglass was in western New York on a lecture tour with Abby Kelley by mid-August.

113. *Herald of Freedom*, 26 August 1842, 106.

114. Van Deburg, "Frederick Douglass": 34-35; Blight, *Frederick Douglass' Civil War*, 9.

✍ Chapter Five

Tumultuous Times: Douglass as Abolitionist Orator, Agitator, Reformer, and Optimist, August 1842 - June 1843

AS FREDERICK DOUGLASS' oratorical reputation increased during the first half of 1842, so did the demand for his services. The period from August 1842 through June 1843 was one of intense agitation and antislavery activity, the likes of which he had not experienced during his brief career as an abolitionist lecturer. In early August 1842, the executive committee of the American Anti-Slavery Society recognized Douglass' potential as a drawing card and hired him as one of eight agents to tour western and central New York from the end of August to the end of October. As the tour was winding down, George Latimer, a fugitive from slavery, was arrested and jailed in Boston and threatened with the prospect of being returned to the South and enslaved. Douglass immediately traveled to Boston and joined Charles Lenox Remond, William Lloyd Garrison, and Wendell Phillips in the battle for Latimer's release. In December the Rhode Island Anti-Slavery Society hired Douglass as a lecturer, and he spent much of the next four months in Rhode Island organizing conventions and lecturing against slavery. During the spring of 1843 he returned to Massachusetts and, under auspices of the Massachusetts Anti-Slavery Society, embarked on a brief lecture tour of eastern Massachusetts with Remond and Latimer. During the months of May and June he also attended the American, Connecticut, and New England antislavery societies' annual conventions, at which he spoke eloquently and with great effect.

During all these activities Douglass demonstrated his deep and abiding commitment to the antislavery movement. He weathered unfriendly audiences, health problems, inclement weather, and assaults on the abolitionist cause. To the repertoire of issues he had developed to date he added a

135

lecture on the progress of the abolitionist cause, spoke in favor of the elevation of his race, defended freedom of speech, denounced the fugitive slave law, addressed the connection between colonization and slavery, and assailed the degrading influence of colonization on the black race. When his voice failed him, instead of resting quietly, he responded by writing the first public letter of his career, thereby uncovering another path to argue against slavery. In all these rhetorical activities, Douglass advanced his standing as a leader among the Garrisonian abolitionists and his reputation as an orator from slavery continued to flourish.

I

In July 1842 the executive committee of the American Anti-Slavery Society hired John A. Collins as its general agent. Collins, an ardent Garrisonian, had organized numerous lecture tours for the Massachusetts Anti-Slavery Society. Now he planned to organize a major lecture tour through western and central New York. The purpose of the tour was to "plead the cause of the slave" and to revive the antislavery movement in New York, where "party interest" had taken precedence over Garrisonian abolition. Every effort was to be made to rebuild the local and county antislavery societies that had been active in the 1830s but had largely disappeared after the 1840 split of the American Anti-Slavery Society into the American Anti-Slavery Society and the American and Foreign Anti-Slavery Society. Collins hired eight agents for the tour—Douglass, Abby Kelley, E.C. Smith, J.N.T. Tucker, H. Weed, Erasmus D. Hudson, Jacob Ferris, and Nelson Bostwick. They were chosen, Collins announced in the *Liberator*, because of their "ability, zeal, efficiency, and disinterestedness."[1]

The three-month campaign would begin in Buffalo, New York's westernmost city, and move steadily eastward until it concluded in Cooperstown. The tour was scheduled from mid-August to the end of October and included stops in twenty-four counties. Two conventions were scheduled each week, one beginning on Tuesday, the other beginning on Friday, with each convention lasting two or three days. The eight agents were divided into three teams. Smith, Tucker, and Weed were appointed to speak at the Tuesday conventions. Hudson, Ferris, and Bostwick were appointed to lecture at the Friday conventions. Douglass and Kelley were expected to attend both the Tuesday and Friday meetings. Collins predicted that during the twelve-week tour, more than 600 lectures would be delivered.[2]

In announcing the tour in the *Liberator* and the *National Anti-Slavery Standard*, Collins emphasized that, for the tour to be successful, New York abolitionists would have to make every effort to secure "a good house to speak in, and a large audience to hear" the addresses of the agents. "I entreat you," Collins wrote, "to have large and overwhelming County meetings." Douglass was advertised as the centerpiece of the tour. "It is well worth a journey of forty miles," Collins announced, "to listen to the eloquent pleadings of FREDERICK DOUGLASS, the fugitive from our *'Peculiar Institutions.'*" Collins, of course, could speak with authority. He had traveled extensively with Douglass during his three-month probationary period in 1841 and had experienced firsthand the powerful effects of his oratory.[3]

Douglass, however, did not emerge as the celebrity of the tour. Rather, it was Kelley who attracted the most attention and created the most controversy. Throughout the tour her name dominated the news reports and minutes from the proceedings. Her lectures were most frequently quoted and commented upon. Opponents and friends alike of the Garrisonian wing of abolition were captivated by her appeals and presence on the platform. For all of his talent and oratorical prowess, Douglass became part of Kelley's supporting cast. Her appearance as an antislavery lecturer occurred at a time when society demanded silence and submission from women. The church and the press were particularly hostile toward women speaking in public forums with men. Throughout the New York tour, Kelley, a powerful and eloquent speaker, addressed mixed audiences and ventured into meeting houses where no woman had publicly spoken before. Consequently, she attracted enormous attention and created controversy wherever she went.[4]

Though Douglass played a supporting role in the New York tour, it was important for him. He actively participated in debates and discussions, defended the integrity of the abolitionists with whom he traveled, and faced hostile and friendly audiences alike with grace and dignity. Equally important, by experiencing firsthand the criticism and prejudice directed toward a woman speaking before assemblies of men and women, Douglass was forced to recognize the oppression of women in the United States on a daily basis. His subsequent devotion to the cause of woman's rights is understandable in light of his experiences on the road with Abby Kelley. In addition, this phase of Douglass' early career has been overlooked by all previous students of Douglass' oratory, as well as by historians of abolitionism in general.[5] By giving close attention to his activities in western New York, we can gain insights into his message and the challenges he confronted daily as an abolitionist.

The tour of New York began on Tuesday, 9 August, in Buffalo, and was dominated by Kelley from the start.[6] To prepare the way for the first convention, Kelley spoke on the evenings of 6 and 7 August without the services of Douglass, who was attending the New Bedford antislavery meetings,. Both lectures were well attended. On the first evening, she lectured an hour and a half. "We never listened with more interest than upon this occasion," reported a correspondent to the Buffalo *Commercial Advertiser and Journal*, "and never certainly with less danger of conversion." The Sunday evening lecture was crowded to capacity and many people had to be turned away. "There was nothing brazen" in Kelley's demeanor, the correspondent wrote, "yet she was confident and self possessed." The antislavery crusade "could hardly have a more determined or able advocate," wrote the correspondent, "nor one more ultra in opinion. She speaks evidently with great ease and freedom, and evinces a perfect familiarity with abolition arguments." Although Kelley used "strong language" and her manner of speaking was "uncompromisingly hostile, even bitterly so, to the sentiments of all who do not think as she does," her "eloquence, her good looks, her full mellow voice, and her evident sincerity," the correspondent concluded, "make the auditor listen with interest."[7] Erasmus D. Hudson, who was present throughout the proceedings, characterized the meeting as a success and attributed its triumph to Kelley's efforts. "A glorious gathering took place in Buffalo," he reported to the *National Anti-Slavery Standard*. "Such a revival of spirit was produced by the powerful application of truth to the consciences of the people during the convention, by Abby Kelley, as was never before known in Buffalo."[8]

From Buffalo, the tour moved to Lockport on 9 August, to Leroy on 16 August, to Albion on 19 August, and to Perry on 21 August.[9] Finally, on Friday, 26 August, Douglass and Collins joined Kelley and Hudson for the Rochester meetings, which convened in the Third Presbyterian Church. Again, Kelley became the focus of controversy. Although only "a few had assembled" for the morning session, recorded Hudson in his journal, the discussion was lively. During the course of a debate over whether or not "a crier with a bell" should go through the streets of Rochester to "ring the people out," the "virtuous Christians and clergy" were attacked. Upon hearing the attack, and seeing Kelley stand to address the meeting, observed Hudson, a minister of the church "ran and gathered . . . the Council and soon reappeared with a letter" ordering the abolitionists "to quit the house forthwith as they could not allow Abby Kelley to speak in the Church for humanity." The other reason given for demanding the abolitionists to leave, Hudson reported, was that "discussions had already been held, which the trustees considered subversive of the cardinal principles of Christianity." The convention then disbanded and reconvened at Bethel Church, where the remainder of the sessions were held. In reporting on the convention, the *Rochester Daily Democrat* focused on Kelley and her speeches. "Miss Abby Kelley is present," it reported, "and participates largely in the proceedings. . . . Her style is forcible and pointed, and at times eloquent." Neither Douglass' presence nor his contributions to the debate were noted by the *Daily Democrat*.[10]

Douglass did participate, however. During the morning session on the second day of the convention, Collins and Hudson were "pounced upon" by a Mr. Johnson, who charged them with having a "bad spirit." Douglass rose to reply. Hudson recorded in his journal that Douglass did Johnson "all up: reading and commenting on Christ's woes to scribes, Pharisees and hypocrites, vipers, Lawyers, whited sepulchres and making *Congregational* prayers." This is the first recorded instance of Douglass reading from the Bible in an abolitionist speech. Like Christ, he argued, abolitionists were ridiculed and assailed by the leaders and followers of organized religion. Like all true reformers, "who were uncompromising for the truth," abolitionists were causing upheaval with their moral crusade to end slavery and, in the end, their cause would prevail.[11] During the evening session, a resolution on "slave-labor produce" and prejudice against people of color "was discussed by several to a full audience." Douglass most likely was among those who discussed the resolution. Following the long session, he joined Collins, Hudson, and others at the home of Isaac and Amy Post, two locally prominent abolitionists, where they spent the night. This marked the beginning of an important relationship for Douglass. During the years ahead, he and the Posts would become close friends and allies in the crusade against slavery.[12]

After attending a convention at Genesee on 30 August, Kelley, Collins, and Douglass met Hudson at the Presbyterian meeting house in Victor on Friday, 2 September, for a two-day convention. "The meeting was well attended," wrote a correspondent to the *National Anti-Slavery Standard*, "and much interest has been awakened here on the subject of slavery." Douglass played a prominent role at Victor, where he was appointed to the business committee to help draft resolutions for discussion in the convention. All told, the committee drafted fourteen resolutions. Although similar resolutions were probably drafted at each convention, those from the Victor meeting are the only ones that survive from the New York tour. It is important, therefore, to summarize them here—especially because Douglass had a hand in their composition.[13]

The first three resolutions reflected Douglass' most strongly held interests. The first resolution was a strong denunciation of slavery. "The relation of master and slave," it read, "must be, under all circumstances, wrong; and can be justified on no principle of justice, republicanism, humanity, or Christianity." The second and third resolutions denounced racial prejudice and called for abolitionists to work toward the elevation of people of color. The fourth and fifth resolutions called for supporters of the antislavery crusade to subscribe to the *National Anti-Slavery Standard* and to contribute money to the American Anti-Slavery Society. The sixth resolution denounced political action and advocated the "immediate and complete overthrow" of slavery. The seventh resolution declared that slavery could not be abolished "until the American people have their minds enlightened, in relation to all the bearings upon all our institutions, by which they shall see that it wars upon all their rights and interests." The eighth resolution insisted on the correctness of the abolitionist cause as being "in accordance with the doctrines of Christianity." The ninth resolution vowed that abolitionists would not be "disheartened by the opposition" to their cause. The tenth and eleventh resolutions declared the intent of the abolitionists to reach out to the children of America and interest them in the cause. The twelfth resolution labeled the church as the great bulwark of American slavery, and the thirteenth endorsed the American Anti-Slavery Society's decision to hold "three great State Conventions" in New York on the first of November. The final resolution instructed the secretaries to "furnish the papers in this region with the proceedings of this meeting."[14]

According to the minutes of the meeting, Douglass and his fellow speakers "advocated and enforced the sentiments contained in these resolutions, upon the minds of the people, in a very able manner." Collins, Kelley, Hudson, and Douglass were reported to have "cheered and encouraged" the "friends of the cause . . . to engage, with renewed zeal and energy, in the cause of the oppressed." The traveling agents, the report continued, induced their auditors "to look at slavery as it is, at the relation it sustains to our country and its institutions, and at its blighting influence upon them." Douglass and his company, the minutes concluded, "may look for much good, as the result of their labors among us."[15]

Although the supporters of Garrisonian abolition offered positive reports of the meetings in the *Liberator* and *National Anti-Slavery Standard*, Liberty Party supporters and nonabolitionists were not as positive. The political wing of the antislavery movement perceived the lecture tour as an encroachment on their territory and, consequently, declared war on the Garrisonians. A correspondent for the *Emancipator and Free American* claimed:

> If our Massachusetts friends are anxious to try their patent mode of dissolving the Union by moral suasion in this State, nearly the whole Eastern section is open to them. Let them try their experiment on the North River counties. There they will, at least, not build on another's foundation, nor tear down what others have toiled years to erect. But, if Mr. Garrison is for picking a quarrel with the Liberty Party in this State . . . then, regret it though we may, yet we shall promptly rally at the call of duty, and shall oppose with such weapons as become the contest, all who throw themselves in the way of the Liberty cause. . . . Let Liberty men stand to their arms. Our ranks are compact, and those who would break them must take the blows.[16]

Despite such negative reactions, Douglass and the other speakers pressed on. From Victor, Douglass, Kelley, and Collins traveled to Penn Yan for a convention on 6 September. The *Yates County Whig's* announcement of their arrival reflected Kelley's predominance on the tour and Douglass' supporting role: *"Miss Abby Kelley*, a distinguished Quaker woman of Boston, gives notice . . . that she will address the people of this county in this village on Tuesday the 6th of September. . . . A fugitive slave, by the name of *Douglass*, said to be one of nature's Orators, is one of the Company." As was the case during the previous meetings, the focus of the Penn Yan convention was on the church. According to a report published in Auburn's *Northern Advocate*, Douglass, Kelley, and Collins, having attracted an audience, proposed to pass resolutions or deliver speeches instilling "the doctrines that the churches were apostate, the ministers of christian churches corrupt, and finally, . . . that all church organization, since the days of the apostles, has been a conspiracy against Christianity." The writer of the report strongly condemned the meeting. "We need not say," the correspondent concluded, "that such proceedings must prove as detrimental to all consistent anti-slavery movements as to the church of God."[17]

On Friday, 9 September, Douglass, Collins, Kelley, and Hudson organized a convention in Palmyra. Once again, the company had difficulty securing a place to hold their meeting. "All the meeting houses shut up," recorded Hudson in his journal, "save the Methodist, which, being small, poorly accommodated us." Nevertheless, the meetings went on as scheduled, lasted two days, and were well attended. The proceedings, concluded Hudson, were "full of intense interest."[18]

The next convention convened in Ithaca's Methodist Church at 10 a.m. on 13 September. Kelley, Douglass, Collins, and Hudson were among the abolitionists who attended the two-day proceedings. All three of the local newspapers that carried the announcement for the meeting heralded the appearance of Kelley, whose name appeared first, and of Douglass, "the eloquent fugitive from slavery." But despite the publicity, the audiences were disappointingly small. "This place is dead," lamented Hudson in his journal, and "uprooted as to any living principle." Throughout the convention, Douglass and his colleagues were threatened with mob violence, which reached its climax during the second day. Having held the morning and afternoon sessions in the Baptist meetinghouse, the abolitionists were forced outdoors, into the courthouse square, for the evening session due to a "notice that the meeting house would not be open in the evening unless the Abolitionists would be responsible for damage done by the Mobocrats." The company declined to accept responsibility for the church and "adjourned into God's house—the open air," where the abolitionists "had a good auditory."[19]

One of the local people attending the convention offered this unflattering eyewitness account of Douglass on the platform:

A clay-colored gentleman, a kind of neutral tint, but who was counted with the blacks, lamented exceedingly that he had been refused the sacrament in some Methodist Church, which he thought a burning shame, as he was ready to prove that *Jesus Christ, the Saviour of the world, was a Negro.* This was the highest flight of fancy we heard on the subject, and which if sufficient to deprive him of communion here, should entitle him to full communion in a much warmer region. This fellow styles himself a fugitive from slavery, he undoubtedly is a fugitive from justice, and prides himself so highly on his escape, that he openly declared he would keep company with only a choice assortment of the blacks, and not with more than one in every nine, of the whites.[20]

Although the observer did not name the "clay colored" orator, there can be no doubt that he was describing Douglass. Douglass was a mulatto, and his speeches often included references to his fugitive status, his escape from slavery, and his being refused the sacrament in New Bedford's Methodist Church. There is no previous or later record of him claiming that Christ was a black man. Nor is there any record of him stating that he would be selective as to the company he kept, black or white. These statements were uncharacteristic of his rhetoric and most likely he never made them. The report better reflects the capacity for distortion due to racial prejudice in the mind of the observer. If Douglass in fact made these statements at Ithaca, they may reflect the effects of the strenuous lecture tour on his oratory. Or he may have deliberately said these things to get a rise out of the audience. If this was the case, he certainly caught the attention of at least one auditor.

From Ithaca, the company traveled to Waterloo. There, on Friday morning, 16 September, they held a convention in the courthouse and attracted "a very good audience." In the evening they gathered in the Baptist meetinghouse, "which was thronged." Hudson, Douglass, and Kelley were among the speakers. At the conclusion of the Waterloo convention, Hudson left the tour for two weeks to travel with James C. Fuller. The rest of the company probably traveled to Millport on 20 September, and then to Ledyard on 23 September.[21]

On Monday, 26 September, Kelley and Douglass organized an antislavery convention in Port Byron. Although this was an unscheduled stop, the demand to have a convention at that place was too strong to ignore. J.N.T. Tucker reported to the *National Anti-Slavery Standard* that a "very great desire had existed among the friends of the liberty party in Port Byron to hear the far-famed, eloquent Abby Kelley, and Frederic[k] Douglas[s]; but more especially Abby Kelley." Once again, Kelley emerged as the center of attention. The day before the convention, after Kelley and the abolitionists had been denied use of the Presbyterian and Baptist meeting houses, she lectured to an audience of more than 400 people at the National Hotel. More than one hundred people had to be turned away because the "room was not sufficiently large to accommodate all who came." Kelley also lectured the next evening to a boisterous and crowded house, although "a continual hissing and murmuring was kept up" by some members of the audience the entire time she spoke. All told, the two-day meeting was a resounding success. "A very large number of persons has generally attended the meetings," reported Tucker, "and a great amount of misapprehension and prejudice has been removed from the minds of the people, especially, the friends of the liberty party, during the discussions."[22]

After holding conventions in Cato Four Corners on 29-30 September and Cortland on 4-5 October, Douglass, Collins, and Kelley traveled to Syracuse where, prior to holding their convention on 7-8 October, Hudson, Collins, Tucker, and most likely Douglass attended the Liberty Party convention taking place in the city on 5-6 October.[23] During that convention, William Goodell, who had helped to organize the Liberty Party, presented an address that attacked the American Anti-Slavery Society and urged abolitionists "not to patronize the . . . Society, its publications or agents, or *identify themselves with their meetings*." When Tucker rose to defend the American Anti-Slavery Society, he was precluded from doing so. The gag, he wrote later, exposed the Liberty Party's "spirit of imbridled intolerance—a love of dominion—the lust of power—a sectarian persecution." The Liberty Party convention also drew the ire of Garrison. "The meeting could not endure free speech," he wrote in the *Liberator*. "It had an object to accomplish, which was incompatible with a fair and full discussion—and that was, the destruction of the American Anti-Slavery Society."[24]

On 7-8 October Douglass, Tucker, Kelley, and the rest of their company met at the Congregational Church in Syracuse. "It was," wrote Tucker to the *National Anti-Slavery Standard*, "a very pleasant and profitable session." Unlike the Liberty Party convention the day before, "all [were] invited to attend and participate." Again, Douglass did not play a prominent role in the convention, which was dominated by Kelley and Collins. The first day's proceedings were packed and, according to Hudson, "quite an interest [was] elicited." On Friday evening, the church was crowded to hear Collins and Kelley, "who addressed the meeting with great power."[25]

After the meeting in Syracuse, the abolitionists moved to Chenango County for a convention in Oxford on 11 October and then traveled to Oswego County, where they convened in Pulaski on 14 October.[26] Douglass and his companions then lectured "in the intervening and adjacent towns." At all the meetings in Oswego County, reported Tucker, "whether at a single lecture or in discussion, we have enjoyed full houses and attentive audiences." Additional meetings were scheduled in Cazenovia, Rome, and Cooperstown. Following the Cooperstown convention on 25 October, the lecture tour ended and the company disbanded.[27]

It had been a grueling twelve weeks. In courthouses, town halls, churches, and town squares, Douglass, Kelley, Hudson, Collins, and the rest of the lecturers advanced the cause of the slave and revitalized local and county branches of the American Anti-Slavery Society in western and central New York. Even before the New York tour was over, abolitionists were declaring it a victory for Garrisonian abolition and the American Anti-Slavery Society. "The labors of Abby Kelley and Frederick Douglass," reported Garrison in the *Liberator*, "have been crowned with signal success." According to Tucker, "there is an acknowledged consciousness that her [Kelley's] efforts, as also the others who are laboring in conjunction with her, are doing a very great amount of service to the cause of the slave in this state." In a letter to Garrison, Kelley stated: "The American Society did wisely in sending her agents here. Such franknes[s], such readiness to receive the truth, and to follow it, is rarely found." Third-party prejudice against Garrisonian abolition, she continued, "vanishes like the damps of night before the sun of the morning." Collins echoed Kelley's sentiments. "It is truly marvelous to see into what a perfect commotion this whole region of country is thrown," he wrote. The county conventions, reported Collins, "are crowded to the very last. Many of our conventions continue for three days." Due to the "tremendous work" of the devoted agents of the American Anti-Slavery Society, he opined, the "influence of third party is fast becoming weakened. It has nothing to live on."[28]

Although Douglass was overshadowed by Kelley throughout the tour, his presence on the platform drew people to the meetings, and he no doubt continued to develop his oratorical skills and to hone his abolitionist ideas. Equally important, traveling with Kelley doubtless advanced his thoughts and feelings toward women as an oppressed group. Churches had been closed to her, men had jeered her as she addressed audiences, and reporters had denounced her presence on the platform as being outside of woman's sphere. Douglass surely noted the prejudice against Kelley and identified with it. In observing her devotion and determination on behalf of abolition, he could not have helped but admire her efforts, and we can assume with some confidence that the New York tour was an important factor in stimulating his long commitment to equal rights for women.[29]

II

As the tour through western and central New York drew to a close, Douglass and his fellow Garrisonians discovered an issue that would consume their attention and energies in the months ahead. In early October

George Latimer, "a very light" mulatto from Norfolk, Virginia, escaped the bonds of slavery. He immediately fled to Boston with his wife and child. On 19 October he was arrested and jailed. The arrest was made on a written order to the jailor of Suffolk County from James B. Gray, of Norfolk, Virginia, who claimed that Latimer was his fugitive slave. Abolitionists rallied to Latimer's defense and demanded his release. Their petition for a writ of habeas corpus, however, was denied by Chief Justice Shaw of Massachusetts, who ruled that Gray had the right to come to Boston and seize Latimer and have him jailed until he could prove that the fugitive was his slave. Shaw's decision enraged the abolitionists, who quickly organized a public meeting for 30 October at 6 P.M. in Faneuil Hall "for the rescue of liberty." Douglass was invited to speak at the meeting, and he eagerly accepted.[30]

On Sunday evening, 30 October, more than 4,000 people crowded into Faneuil Hall. According to a reporter for the *Boston Daily Bee*, "the body of the Hall was crowded, while the galleries literally groaned beneath the weight of the assembled multitude." A correspondent for the *National Anti-Slavery Standard* reported that the hall was "crowded to suffocation." Well before the meeting was to start, "the throng was immense," reported a correspondent to the *Liberator*, "and multitudes were unable to gain admittance." As the audience filed into the hall, the speakers—Douglass, Garrison, Phillips, Remond, and Stephen S. Foster—were seated on the platform. Each was introduced to the meeting and received applause. The meeting was called to order by Francis Jackson, who had chaired the committee of arrangements. Samuel E. Sewell, Latimer's legal counsel, was called upon to chair the meeting. After Sewell made a brief address explaining the purpose of the meeting, Joshua Leavitt, one of the secretaries appointed to record the proceedings, read a series of eighteen resolutions. A portion of the audience was loud and uncooperative from the beginning. "A more shameless, debased, lawless set of rogues and ruffians never intruded themselves upon a decent audience," reported a correspondent to the *Liberator*. About halfway through the reading of the resolutions, "the audience had become so noisy," wrote a correspondent to the *Boston Daily Bee*, "that scarce a word of the speaker's could be caught by us, though we stood very near the platform."[31]

The resolutions denounced slavery as a crime and the arrest of Latimer as a "sad and revolting spectacle." Latimer was portrayed as embodying the "the rights and immunities of all people." One of the resolutions declared that Massachusetts was a "free and independent State" that "cannot be polluted by the foot-print of slavery, without trampling on her bill of rights, and subjecting herself to infamy." Another resolution condemned the federal fugitive slave law, which granted that "a slaveholder has a legal right to seize his runaway slave, in any of the free states, and drag them from thence by force without bringing him before any court or magistrate." This law, the abolitionists asserted, "ought to be repealed." Moreover, they claimed the clause of the U.S. Constitution requiring the surrender of fugitive slaves should not be "morally binding upon the American people, and should be disregarded by all who fear God and love righteousness."[32]

Edmund Quincy spoke first in support of the resolutions. The audience in the hall continuously interrupted him "with loud outcries and cat-calls." Joshua Leavitt followed Quincy. "Though his voice is very loud," reported a correspondent to the *National Anti-Slavery Standard*, "the uproar was so great, that I lost what he said." His remarks were received "with shouts of laughter and derision from the centre of the hall." Remond was then introduced to the meeting, "but a small number of turbulent persons on the floor of the hall created so great a clamor" that he could not be heard. His remarks were drowned out by "groans, hisses, and [calls of] 'down with darkey'—'sell the nigger.'" Phillips followed Remond to the platform, and the uproar continued.[33]

Douglass was next, and he confronted the same difficulties as the previous speakers. "He gesticulated to the noisy audience for about twenty minutes," reported a correspondent to the *Daily Mail*, "but one word in a hundred he uttered was heard." A correspondent to the *National Anti-Slavery Standard*, who was able to hear at least some of what Douglass said, wrote that he "tried to tell them *he* was a slave, and what were his fears for *himself* and hundreds of his brethren if the decision of the Supreme Court were not reviewed and altered." The audience continued to be noisy, however, and Douglass was "powerless before the unfeeling hirelings." At nine o'clock, "the noise having somewhat abated," the resolutions were put to a vote and adopted. The meeting then adjourned, "and soon the vast assembly quietly retired."[34]

Douglass' harsh treatment at Faneuil Hall did not deter him from continuing his campaign to free Latimer. Indeed, the meeting at Faneuil Hall was followed by a series of "Latimer meetings" throughout the state. During the first week of November, Douglass and Remond took Latimer's case to the people of New Bedford. On Friday evening, 4 November, they spoke at the Universalist Society meetinghouse, which was filled for the occasion.[35] After Douglass and Remond addressed the assembly, seven resolutions were introduced. All but one of the resolutions were selected from those presented at the Faneuil Hall meeting. The first resolution, however, was new. It quoted the Declaration of Independence and asserted that no person born in America should be born into slavery and that "to reduce any man to servitude, is a high handed act of robbery and impiety." It also declared that "if all men are made of one blood, and have a common Father, then they are not distinct races, but members of one common family." All the resolutions were adopted by "a rising vote."[36]

On Sunday, 6 November, Douglass and Remond held three meetings in New Bedford's new Town Hall. In the first public letter of his career, Douglass reported to Garrison and the readers of the *Liberator* what transpired during these meetings. In the morning session, Douglass was listened to by a large and attentive audience for approximately an hour "on the question as to whether a man is better than a sheep." The afternoon session drew a "mighty" crowd. "They needed no bells to remind them of their duty to bleeding humanity," Douglass wrote. "They were not going to [the] meeting to have their prayers handsomely said for them, or to say them, merely themselves; but to pray, not in word, but in deed and in truth." As Douglass gazed upon the crowded auditory, his "soul leaped for joy." After having faced hostile crowds in New York and Boston in the recent past, he found New Bedford's residents friendly, sympathetic, and fervent—a significant change from August, when he had encountered an angry mob in the same city. The highlight of the afternoon session was a speech by Remond, "who addressed the meeting in his usual happy and deeply affecting style."[37]

For the evening session, benches had to be brought in to accommodate the large number of people. "The splendid hall was brilliantly lighted," wrote a delighted Douglass, "and crowded with an earnest, listening audience." In fact, so many people attended that "a large number had to stand during the meeting." Douglass then described what he saw from the platform. "I could see the entire audience," he wrote, "and from its appearance, I should conclude that prejudice against color was not there, . . . we were all on a same level, every one took a seat just where they chose; there were neither men's side, nor women's side; white pew, nor black pew; but all seats were free, and all sides free." After Douglass briefly addressed the meeting, he was followed by J.B. Sanderson, an agent of the Massachusetts Anti-Slavery Society, and finally by Remond. "When they had concluded their remarks," reported Douglass, "I again took the stand, and called the attention of the meeting to the case of bro[ther] George Latimer, which proved the finishing stroke of my present public speaking." Douglass reported that upon returning to his seat, he was "seized with a violent pain" in his chest followed by a cough and shortness of breath. He had lost his voice and was "unfit for public speaking, for the present."[38]

Unable to carry forward his campaign on behalf of Latimer from the podium, Douglass was forced to resort to the pen. "My heart is full," he wrote, "and had I my voice, I should be doing all that I am capable of, for Latimer's redemption. I can do but little in any department; but if one department is more the place for me than another, that one is before the people." Although this was an unhappy development for Douglass, it was fortunate for students of his oratory, for it led him to write out a portion of his Town Hall speech in the second half of his public letter to Garrison.

Although this portion of Douglass' letter to Garrison has gone largely unstudied by historians and rhetoricians alike,[39] it is important both because it reveals the message he most likely delivered during the campaign to free Latimer and because it illustrates his ability to craft finely polished prose at this early stage of his career. Time and again during the early 1840s his auditors noted the power and refinement of his language, but there are few surviving texts to indicate exactly what he said. As one of those texts, his defense of Latimer requires close examination.[40]

Douglass' controlling rhetorical strategy was to use language so as to allow his audience to visualize Latimer's brutal capture and incarceration. To accomplish this, he related the facts of the case in the form of a narrative. To engage his audience, he demanded that they see how slavery had landed in their "very midst and commenced its bloody work." He wished his auditors to feel perilously close to Latimer's situation and wanted to alert them of its seriousness and motivate them to act on behalf of the jailed fugitive. To enable his audience to experience the episode on an emotional level, Douglass linguistically brought the fugitive Latimer before them:

> Just look . . . here is George Latimer, a man—a brother—a husband—a father, stamped with the likeness of the eternal God, and redeemed by the blood of Jesus Christ, out-lawed, hunted down like a wild beast, and ferociously dragged through the streets of Boston, and incarcerated within the walls of Leverett-st. jail.[41]

Douglass captured the barbarity of the event by casting Latimer first in human, Christian terms and then by transforming him into a fugitive from the law who was treated as a hunted beast. His word choice reinforced the ruthlessness of the act. Once a free man, Latimer was now treated as a brute, "hunted down," "ferociously" dragged through the streets of Boston, and caged like a "wild beast." The fact that this event had occurred in Boston did not escape Douglass' wrath, for the irony of a slave being hunted down in the streets of "liberty-loving, slavery-hating Boston—intellectual, moral, and religious Boston" was all too clear.[42]

In the next section of the discourse, Douglass asked, "What crime had George Latimer committed?" Nothing more, he answered, than "the crime of availing himself of his natural rights, in defence of which the founders of this very Boston enveloped her in midnight darkness, with the smoke proceeding from their thundering artillery." For Douglass, the irony was clear. Latimer had escaped slavery to pursue his natural rights as a free man, the same rights the citizens of Boston had died defending during the American Revolution. Now, Douglass charged, Boston had "become the hunting-ground of merciless men-hunters and man-stealers." "Henceforth," Douglass exclaimed, "we need not portray to the imagination of northern people, the flying slave making his way through thick and dark woods of the South, with white fanged blood-hounds yelping on his blood-stained track; but refer to the streets of Boston, made dark and dense by crowds of professed christians."[43]

Wishing to make the scene even more vivid, Douglass took his audience inside the northern slavehunt for Latimer. In doing so, he transformed the slave hunter into the beast and generated sympathy for the victim of the hunt, Latimer:

> Take a look at James B. Gray's new pack, turned loose on the track of poor Latimer. I see the blood-thirsty animals, smelling at every corner, part with each other, and meet again; they seem to be consulting as to the best mode of coming upon their victim. Now they look sad, discouraged—tired, they drag along, as if they were ashamed of their business, and about to give up the chase; but presently they get a sight of their prey, their eyes brighten, they become more courageous, they approach their victim unlike the common hound. They come upon him softly, wagging their tails, pretending friendship, and do not pounce upon him, until they have secured him beyond possible escape. Such is the character of James B. Gray's new pack of two-legged blood-hounds that hunted down George Latimer, and dragged him away to the Leverett-street slave prison but a few days since.[44]

Latimer, helplessly deceived by Gray's "two-legged blood-hounds," was captured. Douglass presented Latimer's capture in the present tense and described the action of the hunt in visual terms. He wanted his audience to see the action—to experience it firsthand—as if it were happening in the present, thereby making the situation more immediate and real. In the process, he conveyed the idea that slavery had indeed come to Boston, an idea he amplified in vivid hues:

> We need not point to the sugar fields of Louisiana, or to the rice swamps of Alabama, for the bloody deeds of this soul-crushing system, but to the city of the pilgrims. In [the] future, we need not uncap the bloody cells of the horrible slave prisons of Norfolk, Richmond, Mobile, and New Orleans, and depict the wretched and forlorn condition of their miserable inmates, whose groans rend the air, pierce heaven, and disturb the Almighty; listen no longer at the snappings of the bloody slave-driver's lash. Withdraw your attention, for a moment, from the agonizing cries coming from hearts bursting with the keenest anguish at the South, gaze no longer upon the base, cold-blooded, heartless slave-dealer of the South, who lays his iron clutch upon the hearts of husband and

wife, and, with one mighty effort, tears the bleeding ligaments apart, which before constituted the twain of one flesh. I say, turn your attention from all this cruelty abroad, look now at home.[45]

Having moved his audience from the condition of slaves in the South to the presence of this "soul-crushing system" in the home of the pilgrims, Douglass next took his listeners to the Boston courtroom, where he urged them to "mark him who sits upon the bench." The judge, said Douglass, "may, or he may not . . . tear George Latimer from a beloved wife and tender infant." In this way Douglass equated the judge with "the heartless slave-dealer" he had described earlier. The parallels between the North and the South were abundantly clear. Like the South, Boston had its own version of slave hunters and slave dealers. Also like the South, Boston had its own slave prison. "Let us take a walk to the prison in which George Latimer is confined," Douglass wrote. "Inquire for the turn-key; let him open the large iron-barred door that leads you to the inner prison." As Douglass took the audience into the inner prison, he demanded they stop and listen to the cries of a fugitive from slavery: "Hear the groans and cries of George Latimer, mingling with which may be heard the cry—my wife, my child—and all is still again." In the stillness, Douglass became the voice for Latimer and linguistically carried the audience into the thoughts and fears of the imprisoned fugitive slave:

A moment of reflection ensues—I am to be taken back to Norfolk—must be torn from a wife and tender babe, with the threat from Mr. Gray that I am to be murdered, though not in the ordinary way—not to have my head severed from my shoulders, not to be hanged—not to have my heart pierced through with a dagger—not to have my brains blown out. No, no, all these are too good for me. No: I am to be killed by inches. I know not how; perhaps by cat-hauling until my back is torn all to pieces, my flesh is to be cut with the rugged lash, and I faint; warm brine must now be poured into my bleeding wounds, and through this process I must pass, until death shall end my sufferings. Good God! save me from a fate so horrible.[46]

Moving out of the character of Latimer, Douglass resumed his own voice and abruptly declared, "You have heard enough." Now he called upon the husbands and fathers of Massachusetts to place themselves in Latimer's position and to act accordingly. "Feel his pain and anxiety of mind," he demanded. "Give vent to the groans that are breaking through his fever-parched lips, from a heart emersed in the deepest agony and suffering; rattle his chains; let his prospects be yours, for the space of a few moments." Pressing his audience to action, Douglass urged them to "make up your minds to what your duty is to George Latimer, and when you have made your minds up, prepare to do it and take the consequences." Recalling a time when, as a slave, he himself was jailed for planning to escape from slavery, Douglass concluded, "I can sympathize with George Latimer, having myself been cast into a miserable jail, on suspicion of my intending to do what he is said to have done, viz., appropriating my own body to my use." In essence, Douglass was doing what he had asked his audience to do—he was working to free Latimer.[47]

Douglass' discourse provided strong evidence of his rhetorical artistry. Arranging the discourse in narrative form allowed him to unfold the events of Latimer's capture and imprisonment in a dramatic, chronological structure. By drawing sharp parallels between southern slavery and Latimer's treatment in Boston, Douglass brought the evils of slavery home to the city of Boston. He used vivid imagery to make the situation immediate and real for his audience. In addition, his artistic use of metaphor, simile, parallelism, repetition, irony, ridicule, imagery, and foreshadowing demonstrated his understanding of time-proven rhetorical devices, devices he used to gain sympathy for Latimer and to motivate his audience to action. The discourse also reveals Douglass' confidence and control. He commanded the audience's senses and directed their experience by telling them what to think, see, hear, and feel. Although he claimed that he could not "write to much advantage, having never had a day of schooling in my life," Douglass produced powerful, controlled prose on behalf of Latimer—prose that prefigured the more refined, developed artistry of his discourse during the 1850s.[48]

III

In the middle of November, Douglass, still in poor health, left Lynn and traveled to Providence, Rhode Island, to attend the seventh annual meeting of the Rhode Island State Anti-Slavery Society.[49] The three-day meeting, scheduled to begin Tuesday, 16 November, was an important gathering.[50] Since the last annual meeting in November 1841, the focus of Rhode Island abolitionists had been on the state constitution and the suffrage question. "The great excitement" generated by the agitation of the suffrage question, wrote George L. Clarke, corresponding secretary for the Rhode Island Anti-Slavery Society, had "almost entirely precluded discussion of anti-slavery." Now with the "excitement . . . partially subsided," the executive committee of the Rhode Island society hoped abolitionists would "lay aside their party feelings, allow reason to assume her throne, and with one heart and mind labor earnestly in behalf of the oppressed."[51]

The purpose of the annual meeting was to decide whether the society should cease its efforts "or with renewed strength and zeal, go on." The decision, asserted the executive committee, rested with the state's abolitionists. To attract a large audience, the executive committee invited Garrison, Phillips, Remond, Rogers, Parker Pillsbury, and James Boyle. There is no record of Douglass having been invited—perhaps because of his health problems. Nevertheless, notwithstanding his poor health, he did travel to Providence, where he was appointed to the business committee and delivered one speech to the convention, despite being "under painful affliction of the lungs and at hazard of renewing" the bleeding he had "lately suffered." His speech dealt with a resolution that charged the church with being the bulwark of American slavery. According to a correspondent for the Providence *Daily Evening Chronicle*, debate on this resolution was conducted in a "warm, acrimonious style" that was hardly in accordance with a "true christian like spirit." In contrast to the other abolitionists, Douglass impressed the correspondent with his dignity and restraint, as well as with his oratorical talents. The correspondent judged Douglass' address "the most gentlemanlike speech which we heard during the session; betraying both an ease of delivery and a brilliancy of thought truly remarkable."[52]

Five days after the Providence meeting, Douglass joined George Latimer, who had recently been released from jail, at an assembly in Salem. Latimer had been freed on 18 November after a group of abolitionists paid Gray $400. After his release, the excitement generated over his case did not abate, and Latimer meetings continued to be held throughout the state.[53] The purpose of the Salem meeting was to express sympathy for the suffering Latimer had experienced during his incarceration in Boston and to consider "the encroachments of the Slave Power upon the rights and interests of the sovereign State of Massachusetts." The meeting convened on Monday evening, 21 November, at Mechanics' Hall which, the *Boston Daily Bee* reported, "was well filled at an early hour." Although Latimer was not an effective speaker, he told his story well enough to make an impression on the audience. Douglass, apparently recovered from his health problems, was at his best at the meeting. He "made a very amusing speech of more than an hour in length," reported a correspondent to the *Daily Bee*, during which he "was rather severe upon the church . . . and ended with a sermon in imitation of a southern preacher, which . . . put the audience in high good humor with the speaker."[54] A correspondent for the *Salem Register* offered this account:

> The most wonderful performance of the evening was the address of Frederick Douglass, himself a slave only four years ago! His remarks and his manner created the most indescribable sensations in the minds of those unaccustomed to hear *freemen* of his color speak in public, much more to regard a *slave* as capable of such an effort. He was a living, speaking, *startling* proof of the

folly, absurdity and inconsistency . . . of slavery. Fluent, graceful, eloquent, shrewd, sarcastic, he was without making any allowances, a fine specimen of an orator. He seemed to move the audience at his will, and they at times would hang upon his lips with staring eyes and open mouths, as eager to catch every word, as any "sea of upturned faces" that ever rolled at the feet of Everett or Webster to revel in their classic eloquence.[55]

On 26-27 November Douglass attended a meeting of the Essex County Anti-Slavery Society at the Universalist Meeting House in Essex.[56] The meeting was important for Douglass. Having regained his energy and zeal after his illness, he engaged almost every issue brought forward at the meeting. Most important, for the first time in his career, he publicly endorsed the actions of abolitionists who attended church services with the intention of disrupting them to demand to speak on behalf of the slave. His endorsement of this practice demonstrated his increasing desire to reach and influence as many people as possible. For Douglass, these were extraordinary times that demanded drastic action.[57]

Sometime in November 1842 the executive committee of the Rhode Island Anti-Slavery Society invited Douglass to become an agent and authorized him to lecture and collect funds on its behalf. The executive committee hoped he could infuse new life into the state's languishing antislavery campaign. Hiring him as an agent, the committee wrote, was the "best manner of advancing the interests of the anti-slavery cause."[58] Douglass accepted the offer, and although we do not know his exact itinerary, he appears to have spent much of December 1842 and January 1843 delivering antislavery lectures and collecting donations in Rhode Island.[59]

Toward the end of January, Douglass interrupted his work in Rhode Island and returned to Massachusetts to attend the eleventh annual meeting of the Massachusetts Anti-Slavery Society in Boston at Faneuil Hall. "The attendance of delegates and friends is large," reported a correspondent to the *Liberator*, "and all seem to be animated by the right spirit." On the first day of the meeting, Wednesday, 25 January, Douglass was silent during the morning and afternoon sessions but spoke during the evening in support of a resolution that advocated the dissolution of the Union. The next day, he again spoke in support of this resolution, which was passed after considerable discussion and debate. That evening, the society gathered at the State House, where Douglass delivered his slaveholder's sermon in support of a resolution that charged Massachusetts with behaving like a slave state. "His illustrations of the doctrine inculcated from the pulpits of the South," recorded one of the secretaries in the minutes of the meeting, "drew forth the loudest applause." After speeches by Remond, Garrison, Rogers, Phillips, and George Bradburn, the resolution for dissolution of the Union was "adopted by acclamation."[60]

On Friday, 27 January 1843, the society reconvened in Faneuil Hall. During the morning session, Douglass sat silently while other abolitionists reconsidered the dissolution of the Union resolution. During the afternoon, he spoke in favor of a resolution by Wendell Phillips calling for abolitionists to withdraw their support from all ministers and churches that refuse "to treat the sin of slaveholding." Douglass did not participate in the evening session.[61]

After the Massachusetts Anti-Slavery Society meeting, Douglass returned home to Lynn, where he attended a meeting of the Society of Universal Inquiry and Reform from 28-31 January. "The meetings were fully attended," reported Collins to the *Liberator*, "and the debates were animated, and deeply interesting up to the close of the last session." Douglass was reported to have been among those who took part in the discussions. His participation in the meeting demonstrated his increasing interest in a broadening of reform activities.[62]

Before returning to Rhode Island, Douglass journeyed to Princeton, Massachusetts, to attend the Worcester County North Division Anti-Slavery Society meeting. The meeting was held on Wednesday and Thursday, 1-2 February, at the Baptist Meetinghouse, and Douglass dominated its proceedings.[63] During the Wednesday afternoon session, he spoke in favor of a resolution that declared the antislavery enterprise "is virtually and essentially a *Christian* enterprise, and is, therefore, imperative in its claims on the regard, sympathy and cooperation of the professedly christian churches of our land." That evening, he addressed the audience "on various topics kindred to the cause."[64]

The next morning, after Douglass and Remond had been added to the business committee, Douglass introduced the following resolution for discussion: "Resolved, That the hands of the American church are full of blood, and that she is not, while she continues thus, what she assumes to be, the heaven-appointed instrumentality for reforming the world." According to the minutes of the proceedings, Douglass spoke to the resolution by proving conclusively "the instrumentality of the church in the support of this great evil" of slavery. Using an allegory to illustrate his point, he charged the proslavery clergy and their followers with refusing to acknowledge the "pit of slavery." Douglass commanded his audience to observe how the priest and his deacons "on their way to the . . . mountain, to discuss some new topic, or gain some new truth," when passing the pit of slavery, "spread over this pit" the priest's "pontifical robe." Douglass believed the church ignored the evil nature of slavery and desired slavery to remain contained in its pit, veiled from view, outside the domain of society and the world.[65]

That afternoon, Douglass opened the session with a prayer. After Remond discussed a resolution calling for the dissolution of the Union,

Douglass followed with a speech "in his usual free and interesting style." According to the minutes, he alluded to the recent meeting of the Massachusetts Anti-Slavery Society and discussed "the progress of the cause, from William Lloyd Garrison . . . to the present time." During the evening session, Douglass, Remond, and others discussed resolutions that demanded the dissolution of the Union, denounced political action, called for abolitionists to support the efforts of the American and Massachusetts antislavery societies, and promised that as abolitionists they would do all they could do within their power "to hasten the hour" of the slaves' emancipation.[66]

Douglass returned to Rhode Island in early February. Shortly thereafter, the executive committee of the state's antislavery society requested that he deliver a series of speeches in Providence. He responded by presenting a Sunday evening lecture series that ran from mid-February through early April. Although we do not have texts from any of the lectures, it appears that Douglass not only spoke against slavery, but also addressed the progress of the antislavery cause and the degrading influence of colonization on blacks. Clearly, he was broadening the breadth of the subjects he addressed from the antislavery platform.[67]

The opening lecture of the series took place on Sunday, 19 February, at Franklin Hall. Douglass informed Garrison and readers of the *Liberator* that attendance for the first lecture was very encouraging. The hall, which could hold approximately 500 persons, "was crowded to overflowing" and "many went away who could not get in." Douglass delivered his second lecture in Westminster Hall, which he characterized as "the largest and most splendid in the city." Again, he was pleased with the attendance. "It was crowded with a highly respectable and intelligent audience," he reported, "and it is estimated that not less than a thousand went away, who could not get in." The people of Providence, he continued, "seize upon morsels of anti-slavery which are presented to them, with great avidity."[68] Douglass' third lecture was delivered in Franklin Hall on Sunday, 5 March, and drew a very large audience. "So great was the desire to hear him," reported the executive committee, "that hundreds were obliged to leave for want of room." At the close of the speech, a collection was taken "to defray the expenses of the lectures."[69]

Midway through the lecture series, the executive committee announced its intention to solve the problem of turning people away from Douglass' speeches by selling "tickets of admission," which they hoped would be "favorably received and prove successful."[70] Douglass, in the meantime, returned to Massachusetts to deliver a lecture on "Slavery, as actually existing at the South," on Monday, 6 March, at Boston's Armory Hall and to attend the Essex County Anti-Slavery Society meeting at Lynn on 9-11 March.[71] He then returned to Providence where, on 19 March, he delivered his fourth Sunday antislavery lecture. One week later, on 26 March, he presented his fifth lecture, entitled "Colonization and its connexion with slavery, and the degradation of the colored people of the United States." Apparently, the executive committee's plan to sell tickets in advance had not proven successful, for the advertisement publicizing this speech reported that admittance was free. At the close of the lecture, a collection was taken "in aid of the cause."[72] Douglass delivered his final lecture of the series on Sunday, 2 April, on the subject of the "progress of the cause." Once again, admission was free and a collection was taken at the end of the lecture "in aid of necessary expenses."[73]

The lecture series was finished and Douglass had done his best to revitalize the sagging antislavery movement in Providence. Still, it was clear by mid-March that the movement was in trouble. In early February a meeting of abolitionists at the West Baptist Church in Providence voted to form a new state organization. At the end of March the executive committee of the Rhode Island State Anti-Slavery Society authorized Douglass and George L. Clark to call a special meeting of the society to determine whether or not its office in Providence should be closed. With no money in the treasury and the society "still somewhat in debt," a meeting was planned at East Greenwich on 12 and 13 April to determine if the society should continue or be disbanded. Happily for Douglass and other abolitionists, enough money was raised and pledges received at this meeting to keep the society afloat.[74]

IV

At the end of April, Douglass returned to Massachusetts to resume his activities as an agent for the Massachusetts Anti-Slavery Society. On Thursday, 20 April, he attended the annual meeting of the Norfolk County Anti-Slavery Society at Dedham.[75] "A large number of abolitionists were in attendance from all parts of the county," Edmund Quincy reported to the *Liberator*, "notwithstanding the unfavorable aspect of the weather." Douglass joined Phillips, Remond, Collins, Boyle, Quincy, and others in a discussion over resolutions condemning slavery and prejudice and declaring that abolitionists "can recognize no person as a consistent Christian, or good moral citizen, who refuses to exert his influence" for the removal of slavery. Other resolutions declared the abolitionists' support of fugitive slaves and celebrated the removal of the "Colored Car" from the Eastern Railroad. During the evening session, Douglass, Remond and Edwin Thompson addressed a "crowded" Town Hall "with much effect." The meeting, reported Quincy, was "the most successful meeting ever held in Dedham—and it is believed will have a most happy effect upon the advancement of the cause."[76]

Following the Norfolk County meeting, Douglass joined Latimer and Remond on a brief lecture tour of eastern Massachusetts.[77] One of the stops was in Lowell, where the trio delivered a series of antislavery lectures at the Appleton Street Church on Monday, 24 April, and Tuesday, 25 April.[78] "At every meeting we had crowded houses," reported H.W. Foster to the *Liberator*, and "many went away" without getting inside. At the Monday evening meeting, Latimer spoke first and delivered "an account of his escape from Mr. Gray, and his adventures subsequently." Latimer told his story "in a simple and artless manner," reported a correspondent to the *Lowell Journal*, "which makes it attractive. . . . His tale exhibits strikingly the degradation to which the system of slavery reduces its victims, and the native manliness and vigor of the man, which no oppression could entirely stifle, and which shines out in spite of all efforts to destroy it." The correspondent compared Latimer with Douglass. Douglass, he reported, "is a man of a higher order; he was once a slave, having escaped four or five years ago." The correspondent quoted Douglass directly and described his dramatic opening comments to the meeting. "I am one of the *things* of the South," Douglass reportedly said. Then "drawing himself up to his full height, and spreading his arms wide," Douglass exclaimed, "*Behold the thing!.*'" He was "not merely a story-teller," the correspondent continued. "He can speak of the workings of the slave system from observation, but that is not all—he is a man of strong mind and quick thought, and occasionally powerful eloquence. In his speeches are occasionally passages of great power."[79]

The following evening, Douglass delivered his slaveholder's sermon. "His introductory remarks before the sermon were the best we heard him make," reported the *Lowell Journal*'s correspondent, "and the sermon itself was very good—just such a one as we should suppose would be preached where slavery exists, and where the master patronizes religious teachers for his slaves, principally for the sake of keeping those 'things' in order." All told, Douglass and his colleagues made a strong impression on the Lowell community. "In Frederick Douglass and George Latimer," the correspondent for the *Journal* concluded, "the people of the North have a specimen of the serfs of the South . . . *par excellence.* . . . We fancy people will soon become divested of the idea that slavery is the natural and proper position of such men as these; and they will clamor louder and louder for their release from bondage, and the recognition of their rights." H.W. Foster reported to the *Liberator* that the lectures in Lowell "were like tornadoes, which broke up the ground of public sentiment in this city; and at the last meetings, Douglass, Remond and Latimer sowed the genuine seed of anti-slavery."[80]

Douglass continued to tour eastern Massachusetts with Remond and Latimer until the beginning of May, when he left to attend the tenth anniversary meeting of the American Anti-Slavery Society in New York City. Garrison summoned the readers of the *Liberator* to the meeting: "Let us resolve, abolitionists! . . . to stand shoulder to shoulder, hand to hand, heart to heart—to assemble at our great anniversary, from all parts of the country in which freemen are allowed to exist, that we may look upon each other's countenances, take each other by the hand, listen to each others voices, and be refreshed by the interview." The three-day meeting began at the "beautiful and spacious" Apollo Saloon on 9 May.[81] "The hall," reported Garrison in the *Liberator*, was "densely occupied by a most attentive and evidently delighted assembly." According to the *New York Herald*, the audience "was chiefly composed of the fair sex." In addition, there were "methodist preachers and class leaders" present. A correspondent for the *New York Daily Express* noted the presence of Quaker women and "sable-complexioned sons of Africa" in the audience. A correspondent for the *New York Daily Tribune* estimated the crowd at 1,500 persons.[82]

The American Anti-Slavery Society customarily used the opening session of its annual meeting to celebrate its anniversary. Subsequent sessions were reserved for considering the business of the society. Since abolitionists and nonabolitionists attended the opening session, and since the speeches at this session were often reported in the New York newspapers, the society typically invited four or five of its most eloquent and effective orators to speak on the occasion. It is telling, therefore, that Douglass was one of the speakers in 1843. He shared the honor with Kelley, James Monroe, Garrison, and Phillips.[83]

The anniversary meeting was called to order at 10 a.m. on Tuesday, 9 May. In the absence of Lindley Coates, the president of the society, Francis Jackson, one of the vice presidents, chaired the meeting. After a prayer and the reading of the annual report of the executive committee and the treasurer's report, Monroe spoke "at great length on the state and prospects of the Anti-Slavery cause." He was followed to the platform by Douglass, whom the *New York Herald* described as "a tall sturdy mulatto."[84] The most detailed account of his address comes from a report by a correspondent for the *Daily Express*. Although primarily a condensed summary of the speech, the account succeeded in capturing a portion of Douglass' words and quoting them directly.[85]

In the opening section of the speech, Douglass set out to establish himself as an authentic voice from slavery. To accomplish this, he began with a pronouncement of his former slave status: "I have myself been a slave." Douglass then worked to lower the expectations of the audience. "I do not expect to awaken such an interest in the minds of this intelligent assembly," he declared, "as those have done who spoke before me." He next disclosed why he felt insecure before his audience: "I have never had the advantage of a single day's schooling in all my life." Moreover, he explained, as a former slave, he had instilled into his "heart a disposition" he never could "quite shake off, to cower before white men." Slavery had deprived him of a formal education, instilled in him a fear of white people, and taught him to be humble in their presence.[86]

Having established his slave identity and the reasons for his uncertainty over his abilities as a speaker, Douglass was ready to announce the subject he believed he could address confidently and competently. "But one thing I can do," he declared, "I can represent here the slave—the human chattel, the despised and oppressed, for whom you, my friends, are laboring in a good and holy cause." As he had done in many previous speeches, Douglass identified his role in the abolitionist crusade as the representative of the plight of the slave. "As such a representative," he stated, "I do not fear that I shall not be welcome to all true-hearted abolitionists."[87]

Douglass was now ready to announce the central idea of his speech, which he communicated in the form of a resolution stating that "the antislavery movement is the only earthly hope of the American slave." According to Douglass, the truth of this resolution was "almost every where, and by almost every body, denied." Instead of viewing antislavery agitation as "a powerful aid to abolition," he said, "it is far too generally viewed as retarding that event." But this, he claimed, "was a grievous error." "I know," he boldly asserted, "for I speak from experience." He then proposed to draw upon his experience as a slave to prove that the antislavery movement was a "powerful aid to abolition."[88]

"It has been imagined," he began, "that the slaves of the South are not aware of the movements made on their behalf, and in behalf of human freedom, every where, throughout the northern and western States." This, he said, "is not true. They do know it." Moreover, they had known of the abolitionists' efforts from the beginning: "They knew it from the moment that the spark was first kindled in the land. They knew it as soon as you knew it, sir, in your own New England." Douglass then shifted from declarative sentences to rhetorical questions and from discussing the slaves as a distant "they" to a more immediate and personal "we":

> Did not petitions by thousands, immediately go forth for the abolition of slavery in the District of Columbia, and in the territories, and for the overthrow of the internal slave trade? Heard we not of that? And in the curses of our masters against the abolitionists, did we not feel instinctively that these same abolitionists were our friends? And in every form of opposition to the great cause, did we not hear it?[89]

Before the onset of abolitionism, Douglass continued, the slaves languished in "darkness and despair . . . and not a ray of light was thrown across." But when word came of the antislavery movement, "hope sprang up in my mind, and in the minds of many more." At that moment, Douglass said, "I knew, I felt, that truth was above error, that right was above wrong, that principle was superior to policy; and under the peaceful and beneficent operation of abolitionism, I felt that I should one day be free." The audience must have been moved by these remarks, for they responded with "loud and protracted applause."[90]

In the next section of the speech, Douglass continued to show how the antislavery movement was the only hope for the slave. "There was," he contended, "no hope for the slave in Church, or State, or in the working of society, framed as it now is: nothing whatever in any of the institutions of the day." The slaves' only chance was the American Anti-Slavery Society, where "the slave sees an exposition of his true position in the scale of being." There, Douglass believed, the slave discovered "that he is, indeed, a Man—admitted, recognized as such, as he is by them." As a result of this recognition, Douglass argued, the slave "goes on, calmly and quietly, hoping in his chains that the day may come, when by their aid, he shall be relieved from his thraldom!"[91]

Having established the American Anti-Slavery Society as the only institution that would recognize the slave's humanity, Douglass sought to prove that the American Anti-Slavery Society was superior to the church or state. "This society," Douglass asserted, "is above either Church or State; *it is moving both*, daily, more and more." To demonstrate the progress the movement had made in changing the proslavery practices of the state, he cited the recent action taken by the Massachusetts legislature in response to the petition campaign launched by Garrison and the Massachusetts Anti-Slavery Society to protest Latimer's arrest and incarceration, a campaign in which Douglass had played an important part. As a result of this campaign, Douglass stated, Massachusetts had "closed her gaols, and her court-rooms, against the slave-hunters, and has bidden them to look for no aid at the hands of her people, in this unholy work. Thus is the great work going on!"[92]

Douglass then returned to the impact the antislavery movement had on the slaves in the South. "The slave," he said, "sees that God has raised up a mighty work in his behalf, among the people of the North, when he observes the reluctance with which the slave owner now makes his tours to the North." If the master does decide to take his slave North, Douglass explained, he "soon finds his 'property' among the missing," and when he returns to the South, he "curses the abolitionists of the North" and the slaves "begin to feel that they have friends, and that the time will come, when the exertions of such will be used for their liberation, as well as that of their brethren." Consequently, Douglass concluded, abolitionists should "go on, in the confidence of a good cause, to the breaking of bonds, the unloosening of shackles, and the liberation of the enchained, the enthralled, and the oppressed."[93]

Douglass returned to his seat. Precisely focused, carefully reasoned, and vividly expressed, Douglass' speech was an optimistic, uplifting portrayal of abolitionism and its achievements, and it elicited "a very warm and enthusiastic applause." Indeed, a correspondent to the *Cincinnati Philanthropist* noted that "there seemed to be one continual roar of applause from beginning to end." Garrison reported in the *Liberator* that Douglass "spoke in a very feeling and impressive manner, as the representative of his enslaved brethren and sisters." Assuming the role of spokesman for those in bondage, he had explained the impact that the antislavery movement had on him and his brethren in slavery. In so doing, he left little doubt that the antislavery campaign was the slaves' only earthly hope for liberation. It was, as the *Daily Express* opined, an "extraordinary" speech.[94]

Two days after his speech at the American Anti-Slavery Society meeting, Douglass traveled by boat to Hartford for the anniversary meeting of the Connecticut (American) Anti-Slavery Society. It would turn out to be a turbulent three days. On Sunday morning and afternoon, 14 May, one day before the anniversary meeting was scheduled to begin, Douglass addressed a gathering of abolitionists in Gilman's Hall. His speech, as reported by Hudson, contrasted "the true and false religion of the day; the one, love, peace on earth, good will to man; good news to the poor—balm to the wounded heart. The *other*, chattelizing men, women, and children—baptizing the system into the name of the Father, Son, and Holy Ghost. The latter was . . . the religion of the churches generally, at the South and North!"[95] That evening, also in Gilman's Hall, Douglass lectured to a "large audience," including many nonabolitionists, "on the moral character of slavery, and the support it received from Church influence especially." His speech was not well received. Hudson reported that it elicited "hissings" from the audience, who found his ideas "insufferable, coming from a 'nigger!'"[96]

The next day, the Connecticut Anti-Slavery Society meeting tried to convene at Gilman's Hall, but found it closed to them. In a letter published in the *Liberator*, Sydney Howard Gay explained the circumstances. According to Gay, when the owner was asked why he refused to allow the abolitionists to meet in the hall, he replied that "he could not allow his property to be used for the dissemination of such principles as were advanced by DOUGLASS, in a lecture there the night before." According to Gay, Douglass had charged the Hartford churches with being "pro-slavery, and therefore unchristian." "Holding the views of Douglass unsound and wrong" and fearing "mob outrages," the proprietor felt justified in breaking his contract with the Connecticut Anti-Slavery Society "and denying to them the right of free speech."[97]

Unable to secure a meeting place anywhere in the city, the abolitionists were forced to meet "on the sidewalk, in Main-street, under the shadow of the Rev. Dr. Hawes's 'steep house.'" Prior to the afternoon session, "the time and place of meeting were cried through the city." When it began, "a respectable assembly" had gathered. The men in the audience were forced to stand, while two settees were secured from the local firehouse for the women. A "rough deal-box" was procured for a rostrum.[98]

Once the meeting was under way, Stephen S. Foster was the first speaker, followed by Douglass and Abby Kelley. According to Hudson, all three "made eloquent and powerful addresses to the large multitude, which had gathered at so novel a spectacle." Not all listeners were enthralled, however, and the speeches were "met with occasioned hisses from the men . . . and a gallant pelting of the women with pebbles and bits of mortar." Some listeners "threw stones and eggs" in an effort to deter the abolitionists. In his speech, Douglass "referred to the conduct of Mr. Gilman . . . and exonerated him from the blame which otherwise might seem to be attributed to him." Douglass believed Gilman "could only be looked upon as the slave of the Hartford people, who not only refused the right of free speech, but denied each other the right of using their property as each should choose."[99]

Before the afternoon session ended, Foster announced that he and Douglass would lecture that evening from the stone steps of Dr. Hawes's church. At the appointed time a large crowd had assembled, but when Foster and Douglass tried to speak, they were prevented from doing so by a mob that "rendered it impossible." There were "shouts, and hurres and hisses," Gay reported. "Every abolitionist that was recognized was surrounded, and hustled about, till he escaped from among them." Fortunately, no one was injured in the confrontation.[100]

Undaunted, the abolitionists met in the same place on Tuesday morning, 16 May, at nine o'clock, to hear speeches by Douglass, Foster, Monroe, and Kelley. "A large audience gathered," wrote Hudson, "and listened, for the most part, quite attentively, to the speakers," though "a few were busily engaged in trying to disturb us with stones and eggs." During the afternoon session, some members of the audience grew more unruly as they tried, in vain, to break up the meeting. "The speakers were frequently interrupted," noted Gay, "and the most obscene and disgraceful language was sometimes used."[101]

It had been a stormy three days. Douglass and his colleagues' addresses were met with repeated interruptions. Their listeners hissed and shouted vulgarities during their meetings and tried to bring the sessions to an end by throwing stones and eggs at the speakers. Through it all, Douglass and his companions remained true to their abolitionist principles and refused to be silenced or intimidated.

After the tumultuous proceedings in Hartford, Douglass returned to Massachusetts in time to attend the annual meeting of the New England

Anti-Slavery Society, which convened on Tuesday morning, 30 May, at Boston's Miller Tabernacle on Howard Street. Douglass was extremely active throughout the three-day meeting. During the opening session, he was appointed to the business committee, and on Wednesday evening, during a meeting at Faneuil Hall, he spoke to a crowd of 5,000 people in favor of Garrison's "Address to the Slaves of the South," which informed the slaves that their masters were tyrants and hypocrites and advised them to run away at the first opportunity. Although we do not have a text of Douglass' remarks, they appear to have been well received. The *Liberator* reported that Douglass' speech "elicited the most rapturous applause," while a correspondent for New York's *Herkimer Journal* praised the address as possessing "a very high order of talent and character."[102]

The most important aspect of the meeting with respect to Douglass, however, was the passage of a resolution proposing a six-month lecture tour through Vermont, New York, Ohio, Indiana, and Pennsylvania. Known to history as the Hundred Conventions tour, it was to be a major event in Douglass' career. In an address announcing the tour and Douglass' appointment as one of the agents, Francis Jackson, president of the Massachusetts Anti-Slavery Society, stated that Douglass' "keen intellect, sound judgment, readiness in debate, and broad comprehension of the cause of freedom" had earned "him the admiration and esteem of all eastern abolitionists" and qualified him for the Hundred Conventions tour. As one of the team of lecturers, Douglass was expected to carry the antislavery campaign into the western part of the United States, where once again his devotion to the antislavery crusade would be severely tested.[103]

Notes

1. *Liberator*, 19 August 1842, 131; Oliver Johnson, *W. L. Garrison and His Times* (1881; reprint, Miami, Fla.: Mnemosyne Publishing Company, 1969), 300; Dorothy Sterling, *Ahead of Her Time: Abby Kelley and the Politics of Antislavery* (New York: Norton, 1991), 151-52.

2. *Liberator*, 19 August 1842, 131.

3. Ibid., 103.

4. Sterling, *Ahead of Her Time*, 1-3, 93; Allen Johnson and Dumas Malone, eds., *Dictionary of American Biography* (New York: Scribner's, 1931), 6:542-43; Edward T. James, ed., *Notable American Women, 1607-1950, A Biographical Dictionary* (Cambridge, Mass.: Harvard University Press, 1971), 1:647-50; Karlyn Kohrs Campbell, ed., *Women Public Speakers in the United States, 1800-1925: A Biocritical Sourcebook* (Westport, Conn.: Greenwood, 1993), xii-xiii; William S. McFeely, *Frederick Douglass* (New York: Norton, 1991), 99.

5. Blassingame notes that Douglass was lecturing with Abby Kelley in western New York from mid-August through late October 1842 under the auspices of the American Anti-Slavery Society, but he does not identify any of the places they traveled. As we shall see, Blassingame's itinerary of Douglass' speaking dates also leaves out other important meetings that he attended from August 1842 through June 1843 (John W. Blassingame, ed., *The Frederick Douglass Papers, Series One: Speeches, Debates, and Interviews: Volume 1* [New Haven, Conn.: Yale University Press, 1979], 1:xc). Fulkerson treats the New York tour in a similar way. He observes that Kelley and Douglass traveled together through western New York, but he does not document their activities. He does identify most of Douglass' other speaking engagements during the period, but due to the scope of his project, he provides little analysis of Douglass' activities (Raymond Gerald Fulkerson, "Frederick Douglass and the Anti-Slavery Crusade: His Career and Speeches, 1817-1861," pt. 1 [Ph.D. diss., University of Illinois, 1971], 58-62). Nor do other authors take more than a brief look at the period from August 1842 through June 1843. See, for example, McFeely, *Frederick Douglass*, 99-100; Benjamin Quarles, *Frederick Douglass* (1948; reprint, New York: Atheneum, 1968), 27-29; Philip S. Foner, ed., *The Life and Writings of Frederick Douglass, Volume 1* (New York: International Publishers, 1950), 1:53-55; Sterling, *Ahead of Her Time*, 152-53.

6. I have been able to locate records of the proceedings from all of Douglass' stops on the tour except for the meetings of 9 August (Lockport), 16 August (Leroy), 19 August (Albion), 21 August (Perry), 30 August (Genesee), 20 September (Millport), 23 September (Ledyard), 29-30 September (Cato Four Corners), 4-5 October (Cortland), 18 October (Cazenovia), 21 October (Rome), and 25 October (Cooperstown).

7. Despite these positive comments about Kelley as a speaker, the correspondent regretted that "a lady with such advantages of person and talent should not have found a more appropriate sphere of action—one more befitting her sex" (*Commercial Advertiser and Journal*, 8 August 1842, 2).

8. *Commercial Advertiser and Journal*, 8 August 1842, 2; *National Anti-Slavery Standard* 25 August 1842, 47.

9. *Liberator*, 19 August 1842, 131; *National Anti-Slavery Standard*, 25 August 1842, 47; *National Anti-Slavery Standard*, 8 September 1842, 54.

10. Erasmus D. Hudson, Journal, 26 August 1842, Special Collections and Archives, University Library, University of Massachusetts, Amherst; *National Anti-Slavery Standard*, 15 September 1842, 59; *Rochester Daily Democrat*, 27 August 1842.

11. Later in his antislavery career, Douglass read from the Bible. See, for instance, "The Free Church of Scotland and American Slavery: An Address Delivered in Dundee, Scotland, on 30 January 1846," in Blassingame, ed., *Douglass Papers, Series One*, 1:146-47.

12. Hudson, Journal, 27 August 1842; *National Anti-Slavery Standard*, 15 September 1842, 59.

13. *National Anti-Slavery Standard*, 22 September 1842, 62.

14. Ibid.

15. Ibid.

16. *Liberator*, 2 September 1842, 137. Also see *Liberator*, 21 October 1842, 165.

17. *Yates County Whig*, 6 September 1842, 3; *Liberator*, 21 October 1842, 165.

18. Hudson, Journal, 9-10 September 1842.

19. Hudson, Journal, 14 September 1842; *Ithaca Journal and General Advertiser*, 7 September 1842, 3; *Tompkins Volunteer*, 6 September 1842, 2; *The Ithaca Chronicle*, 7 September 1842, 2.

20. *Tompkins Volunteer*, 27 September 1842, 2.

21. Hudson, Journal, 16-29 September 1842; *National Anti-Slavery Standard*, 18 August 1842, 43.

22. *National Anti-Slavery Standard*, 13 October 1842, 74.

23. Although Hudson did not mention Douglass by name in his journal entry on the Cato Four Corners meeting, I have no reason to believe that he was not in attendance (Hudson, Journal, 29 September 1842).

24. *American Citizen in the Liberator*, 21 October 1842, 166; *Liberator*, 28 October 1842, 170. Tucker's letter to Garrison is in the *Liberator*, 28 October 1842, 170. Goodell's address against the American Anti-Slavery Society was reprinted in the *Liberator*, 4 November 1842, 173.

25. *Liberator*, 28 October 1842, 170; *National Anti-Slavery Standard*, 27 October 1842, 82; Hudson, Journal, 6 October 1842.

26. *National Anti-Slavery Standard*, 6 October 1842, 71.

27. *National Anti-Slavery Standard*, 27 October 1842, 82. As reported in the *National Anti-Slavery Standard*, 13 October 1842, 75, the scheduled date of the Cazenovia meeting was 18 October, while the Rome meeting was slated for 21 October.

28. Garrison's report and the letters from Kelley and Collins were printed in the *Liberator*, 30 September 1842, 155; Tucker's letter is in the *National Anti-Slavery Standard*, 13 October 1842, 74.

29. *National Anti-Slavery Standard*, 13 October 1842, 75.

30. Samuel J. May, *Some Recollections of Our Antislavery Conflict* (1869; reprint, New York: Arno Press, Inc., 1968), 305-8; John Daniels, *In Freedom's Birthplace: A Study of the Boston Negroes* (Boston: Houghton Mifflin Company, 1914), 58; Benjamin Quarles, *Black Abolitionists* (New York: Oxford University Press, 1969), 193; *Liberator*, 4 November 1842, 174; *Liberator*, 25 November 1842, 186. For a detailed description of the proceedings before Chief Justice Shaw, see the *Liberator*, 28 October 1842, 171.

31. *Boston Daily Bee* in the *Liberator*, 4 November 1842, 174; *Liberator*, 4 November 1842, 175; *Emancipator and Free American*, 3 November 1842, 107; *National Anti-Slavery Standard*, 10 November 1842, 91.

32. *Emancipator and Free American*, 3 November 1842, 107; *Liberator*, 4 November 1842, 174.

33. *Emancipator and Free American*, 3 November 1842, 107; *Liberator*, 4 November 1842, 174; *National Anti-Slavery Standard*, 10 November 1842, 91.

34. *Emancipator and Free American*, 3 November 1842, 107; *National Anti-Slavery Standard*, 10 November 1842, 91; *Liberator*, 4 November 1842, 174.

35. *Liberator*, 11 November 1842, 179. Blassingame, ed., *Douglass Papers, Series One*, 1:xc, incorrectly states that Lynn, Massachusetts, was the location of the 4 November meeting. There was a Latimer meeting in Lynn on 4 November, but Douglass spoke at the gathering in New Bedford on that date.

36. *Liberator*, 11 November 1842, 179; *Liberator*, 18 November 1842, 182, 183; *Emancipator and Free American*, 17 November 1842, 115.

37. *Liberator*, 18 November 1842, 182.

38. Ibid.

39. Blassingame, ed., *Douglass Papers, Series One, Volume 1*, does not include the letter in its collection of Douglass' speeches. Foner, *Life and Writings*, 1:105-9, reprints part of the letter without commentary or analysis. Fulkerson, "Frederick Douglass," pt. 1, 59-60, also reprints a segment of the letter, but does not discuss its style or content. The full text of the letter is reproduced in appendix B of this work.

40. For other instances of the rhetorical criticism of public letters, see Malinda Snow, "Martin Luther King's 'Letter from Birmingham Jail' as Pauline Epistle," *Quarterly Journal of Speech* 71 (August 1985): 318-34; F. Forrester Church, "Rhetorical Structure and Design in Paul's Letter to Philemon," in *Rhetorical Dimensions in Media: A Critical Casebook*, ed. Martin J. Medhurst and Thomas W. Benson (Dubuque, Iowa: Kendall Hunt, 1984), 280-95; Richard P. Fulkerson, "The Public Letter as a Rhetorical Form: Structure, Logic, and Style in King's 'Letter from Birmingham Jail,'" *Quarterly Journal of Speech* 65 (April 1979): 121-36.

41. *Liberator*, 18 November 1842, 182.

42. Ibid.

43. Ibid.

44. Ibid.

45. Ibid.

46. Ibid.

47. Ibid.

48. Ibid. Douglass' letter to Garrison adumbrates the rhetorical techniques he used in a number of later speeches, including his masterful "What to the Slave is the Fourth of July?" In this address, delivered on 5 July 1852, he symbolically transported his audience to the sights and sounds of the internal slave trade and the slave auction. In the same manner, while defending Latimer, he had

visualized the scene of the fugitive's arrest and incarceration so vividly that listeners could experience its sights, sounds, and emotions. See "What to the Slave is the Fourth of July?: An Address Delivered in Rochester, New York, on 5 July 1852," in *The Frederick Douglass Papers, Series One: Speeches, Debates, and Interviews: Volume 2*, ed. John W. Blassingame (New Haven, Conn.: Yale University Press, 1982), 2:372-73. For a rhetorical analysis of Douglass' address, see John Louis Lucaites, "Abolitionist Discourse: The Case of Frederick Douglass's 'What to the Slave is the Fourth of July?'" in *Rhetoric and Political Culture in Nineteenth-Century America*, ed. Thomas W. Benson (East Lansing: Michigan State University Press, 1997), 47-69.

49. Douglass moved from New Bedford to Lynn, Massachusetts, sometime in 1842. Speculation as to the precise time he moved varies greatly. McFeely claims he moved in late 1841, Blassingame places him in Lynn in 1842, and Fulkerson speculates that he moved in the fall of 1844. See McFeely, *Frederick Douglass*, 103; Blassingame, ed., *Douglass Papers, Series One*, 1:xxiii; Fulkerson, "Frederick Douglass," pt. 1, 73. My research suggests that Blassingame's 1842 date is probably most accurate.

50. Blassingame, ed., *Douglass Papers, Series One*, 1:xc, incorrectly states that this meeting took place on 16 November only.

51. *National Anti-Slavery Standard*, 10 November 1842, 91.

52. Ibid.; *National Anti-Slavery Standard*, 12 January 1843, 127; *Herald of Freedom*, 25 November 1842, 158-59; *Daily Evening Chronicle*, 18 November 1842, 2. For another account of this meeting, see *Providence Daily Journal*, 14 November 1842, 2.

53. For a detailed discussion of Latimer's incarceration and release, see *National Anti-Slavery Standard*, 24 November 1842, 99; *National Anti-Slavery Standard*, 1 December 1842, 103; Quarles, *Black Abolitionists*, 194; May, *Recollections*, 308-9.

54. *Daily Bee*, 24 November 1842, 2; *Liberator*, 9 December 1842, 194; Quarles, *Frederick Douglass*, 28.

55. *Salem Register* in the *Liberator*, 9 December 1842, 194. This review of Douglass' performance was also reprinted in the *National Anti-Slavery Standard*, 15 December 1842, 111.

56. Blassingame, ed., *Douglass Papers, Series One*, 1:xc, incorrectly states that this meeting took place on 26 November only.

57. *Liberator*, 9 December 1842, 194.

58. *National Anti-Slavery Standard*, 12 January 1843, 127. The announcement also appeared in the *Liberator*, 13 January 1843, 7.

59. The *Liberator* and the *National Anti-Slavery Standard* did not report on Douglass' work during this period, and scholarly accounts of his efforts vary greatly. Fulkerson, "Frederick Douglass," pt. 1, 61, claims that Douglass began his antislavery activities in Rhode Island in the latter part of December. Blassingame, ed., *Douglass Papers, Series One*, 1:xc, has Douglass attending

Latimer meetings in Massachusetts from 15-30 December, but says nothing about his activities during the first three weeks of January 1843. Blassingame also states that Douglass attended the Windham County Anti-Slavery Society meeting at Hampton, Connecticut, on 13-14 December, but James Monroe reported to the *National Anti-Slavery Standard* that Douglass was not present at that meeting (*National Anti-Slavery Standard*, 22 December 1842, 114). Quarles, *Frederick Douglass*, 29, states that after agitating on behalf of Latimer's release, Douglass spent three months in Rhode Island, which overstates his presence in that state by at least one full month.

60. *Liberator*, 20 January 1843, 11; *Liberator*, 27 January 1843, 15; *Liberator*, 3 February 1843, 18.

61. *Liberator*, 3 February 1843, 18.

62. *Liberator*, 17 February 1843, 28.

63. Blassingame, ed., *Douglass Papers, Series One*, 1:xc, does not include this meeting in its itinerary of Douglass' speaking activities.

64. *Liberator*, 10 March 1843, 38.

65. Ibid.

66. Ibid.

67. *Liberator*, 24 March 1843, 46.

68. Ibid.

69. *Providence Daily Journal*, 4 March 1843, 2; *Providence Daily Journal*, 18 March 1843, 2. Blassingame, ed., *Douglass Papers, Series One*, 1:xc, does not include this speech in its itinerary of Douglass' speaking activities.

70. *Providence Daily Journal*, 17 March 1843, 2; *Providence Daily Journal*, 18 March 1843, 2.

71. The speech that Douglass delivered in Boston's Armory Hall on 6 March 1843 was part of a series of lectures organized and sponsored by the Boston Female Antislavery Society. Garrison, Phillips, Samuel J. May, Edmund Quincy, John Pierpont, Remond, and Bradburn also participated in the series, which began on 13 February and ended on 3 April. During the course of the Essex County meeting at Lynn on 9-11 March, Douglass served on the business committee and spoke in favor of resolutions supporting the right of free speech and denouncing the proslavery character of the church and the U.S. government. See *Liberator*, 3 February 1843, 19; *Liberator*, 31 March 1843, 50. Blassingame, ed., *Douglass Papers, Series One*, 1:xc, incorrectly states that the Essex County meeting of 9-10 March convened on 9 March only.

72. *Liberator*, 20 January 1843, 11; *Liberator*, 3 February 1843, 19; *National Anti-Slavery Standard*, 9 February 1843, 142; *Liberator*, 31 March 1843, 50; *Providence Daily Journal*, 25 March 1843, 2.

73. *Providence Daily Journal*, 1 April 1843, 2. Blassingame, ed., *Douglass Papers, Series One*, 1:xc, does not include the lectures of 26 March or 2 April in its itinerary of Douglass' speaking activities.

74. *Liberator*, 10 February 1843, 23; *National Anti-Slavery Standard*, 30 March 1843, 171; *National Anti-Slavery Standard*, 27 April 1843, 186; *Liberator*, 5 May 1843, 69.

75. Blassingame, ed., *Douglass Papers, Series One*, 1:xci, does not mention this meeting in its itinerary of Douglass' speaking activities.

76. *Liberator*, 28 April 1843, 66.

77. Details of the tour are sketchy. Neither the *Liberator* nor the *National Anti-Slavery Standard* published an itinerary detailing the dates and locations of the meetings scheduled for April and May.

78. *Liberator*, 12 May 1843, 74. Blassingame, ed., *Douglass Papers, Series One*, 1:xci, incorrectly dates the Lowell speeches as taking place on 26 April.

79. *Lowell Journal* in the *Liberator*, 12 May 1843, 74. Foster's letter to Garrison is reprinted in the *Liberator*, 12 May 1843, 75.

80. *Lowell Journal* in the *Liberator*, 12 May 1843, 74; *Liberator*, 12 May 1843, 75.

81. Blassingame, ed., *Douglass Papers, Series One*, 1:xci, erroneously states that the meeting occurred on 9 May only.

82. *Liberator*, 5 May 1843, 71; *Liberator*, 12 May 1843, 75; *New York Herald*, 10 May 1843, 1; *New York Daily Tribune*, 10 May 1843, 4; *Daily Express* in the *Liberator*, 19 May 1843, 78.

83. Raymond Gerald Fulkerson, "Frederick Douglass and the Anti-Slavery Crusade: His Career and Speeches, 1817-1861," pt. 2 (Ph.D. diss., University of Illinois, 1971), 456; *National Anti-Slavery Standard*, 11 May 1843, 195.

84. *National Anti-Slavery Standard*, 18 May 1843, 198; *New York Daily Tribune*, 10 May 1843, 4; *New York Herald*, 10 May 1843, 1; *Liberator*, 12 May 1843, 75.

85. The *New York Daily Express* account of Douglass' speech was reprinted in the *National Anti-Slavery Standard*, 18 May 1843, 198, and the *Liberator*, 19 May 1843, 78. Other texts of this speech may be found in the *New York Morning Express*, 10 May 1843; *New York Herald*, 10 May 1843; *New York Tribune*, 10 May 1843; Fulkerson, "Frederick Douglass," pt. 2, 458-59. I will follow the text as reprinted in Blassingame, ed., *Douglass Papers, Series One*, 1:20-23.

86. Blassingame, ed., *Douglass Papers, Series One*, 1:21.

87. Ibid.

88. Ibid.

89. Ibid., 1:21-22.

90. Ibid., 1:22.

91. Ibid.

92. Ibid.

93. Ibid., 1:23.

94. Ibid.; *Cincinnati Philanthropist*, 12 July 1843, 1; *Liberator*, 12 May 1843, 75; *Daily Express* in the *Liberator*, 19 May 1843, 78. For another reaction to Douglass' speech, see the *New York Daily Tribune*, 10 May 1843, 4.

95. *National Anti-Slavery Standard*, 8 June 1843, 2.

96. Ibid.

97. *Liberator*, 26 May 1843, 82; *Christian Freeman*, 19 May 1843, 3.

98. *National Anti-Slavery Standard*, 8 June 1843, 2; *Liberator*, 26 May 1843, 82.

99. Ibid.

100. Ibid.

101. Ibid.

102. *Liberator*, 2 June 1843, 89; *Herkimer Journal* in the *Liberator*, 16 June 1843, 94.

103. *Liberator*, 16 June 1843, 95; *National Anti-Slavery Standard*, 22 June 1843, 11; *Twelfth Annual Report, Presented to the Massachusetts Anti-Slavery Society, By its Board of Managers, January 24, 1844* (1844; reprint, Westport, Conn.: Negro Universities Press, 1970), 34-35.

✿*Chapter Six*

The Hundred Conventions Tour of the West: Independence and Restlessness, June-December 1843

THE HUNDRED CONVENTIONS tour of the West was a milestone in the development of abolitionist rhetoric. Garrisonian abolitionists intended to awaken northern sympathy and arouse the national conscience by holding a series of 100 antislavery conventions that included meetings in Vermont, New York, Ohio, Indiana, and Pennsylvania. Frederick Douglass was chosen by the Massachusetts Anti-Slavery Society's board of managers as one of six agents who would conduct the six-month tour. Others selected were George Bradburn, Charles Lenox Remond, John A. Collins, Jacob Ferris, and James Monroe. In addition, William A. White of Watertown, Massachusetts, and Sydney Howard Gay, managing editor of the *National Anti-Slavery Standard*, volunteered to join the crusade, which began on 13 July 1843 and lasted until 7 December.[1]

Although the Hundred Conventions tour was a major event in the history of abolitionism, neither it nor Douglass' role in it have been closely studied.[2] In addition, most scholars have overlooked Douglass' other rhetorical activities during the last seven months of 1843, most notably his activities in New Hampshire and in the vicinity of New Bedford, Massachusetts, in June and early July, and his participation in the National Convention of Colored Citizens in Buffalo, New York, in mid-August, where he distinguished himself as an eloquent orator and reformer before a national audience of African Americans. By examining these activities, this chapter provides a detailed account of Douglass' ventures during the last six months of 1843, a period of great importance for him and for abolitionism in general.

171

I

As the Hundred Conventions tour approached, Douglass attended anti-slavery meetings in New Hampshire and in the area around New Bedford, Massachusetts. During these meetings, none of which has been discussed by previous scholars, Douglass continued to agitate for the abolition of slavery and solicited support for the Hundred Conventions tour. Although we do not have texts of Douglass' speeches at these meetings, we can reconstruct many of his activities from newspaper accounts and private letters.

In early June, Douglass journeyed to Concord to attend the annual meeting of the New Hampshire Anti-Slavery Society, scheduled to begin on Wednesday, 7 June.[3] During the three-day convention, he addressed the meeting several times, speaking in support of resolutions extolling the virtues of the men and women committed to the abolition of slavery and denouncing the proslavery clergy as "deadly foes to freedom and christianity." The meeting, Douglass wrote to Abby Kelley, "was a strange gathering. I never saw anything like it." It was at once "disgraceful, mortifying, alarming, divided, united, glorious, and most effective."[4]

In the middle of June, Douglass returned to Massachusetts, and on 14 June he traveled to Lunenburg to attend the Worcester County North Division Anti-Slavery Society meeting.[5] During this one-day gathering, he joined abolitionists Charles Lenox Remond and Cyrus Burleigh in supporting resolutions denouncing prejudice as "un-christian, cruel, and savage," demanding protection for people of color on the railroads, and calling on slaves "to fly from their oppressors, and take refuge in Massachusetts." After lecturing in Fall River on 19 June, Douglass traveled to New Bedford to attend the Bristol County Anti-Slavery Society meeting.[6] On Tuesday, 20 June, an "eager and attentive" audience crowded into the new Town Hall to listen to Douglass, Nathaniel Rogers, James Monroe, Edmund Quincy, Stephen S. Foster, and others speak in favor of resolutions calling on the people of the North to abolish slavery and endorsing the Hundred Conventions tour of the West. Other resolutions that were discussed during the two-day meeting denounced political parties, demanded that all "non-slaveholding states" repeal any laws "which in any manner infringe upon the rights of free citizens of the United States on account of color," and called on abolitionists to remove their support from churches and ministers "who refuse to treat the crime of slaveholding and its perpetrators or apologists" with the same rebuke and discipline with which they treat the crimes that "go to make it up, and those that commit or defend them." Unlike the year before, when the speakers at the Bristol County meeting were "drowned in shouts of riot and misrule," the 1843 gathering proceeded without incident.[7]

Two days later, on Friday, 23 June, Douglass attended the opening of a three-day antislavery convention at Nantucket's Atheneum Hall.[8] On the first day of the convention, during the afternoon session, Douglass spoke in favor of a resolution denouncing the proslavery church and clergy. The following day, after listening to George Bradburn, a former member of the Massachusetts legislature, argue that the Constitution was not a proslavery document, Douglass, adhering to Garrisonian principles, contended that it was. Unhappy at being contradicted by a black man, Bradburn, left the convention floor rather than speak in reply to Douglass.[9] Douglass' willingness to disagree publicly with white men on the platform was an indication of things to come—as was Bradburn's indignation. As we shall see during this period of Douglass' career, his growing freedom of thought, independence of action, and personal confidence increasingly created conflicts with some of his white antislavery companions.

On Tuesday, 27 June, Douglass returned to Fall River to attend an antislavery convention.[10] The principal speakers were Douglass, Remond, and Burleigh. According to a report in the *Liberator*, the discussion centered around two questions: "the intimate connection of the northern churches and ministry with southern slavery, and the proslavery character of the United States Constitution." According to a correspondent from the *Fall River Argus*, Douglass and Remond spoke with great effect:

> Mr. Douglass spoke on both these questions, and very eloquently too. In fact, we have heard but few *white* men who surpassed him in genuine oratory. And yet this man is but four and a half years from servitude, never attended school a day in his life, and is a negro. If there are those who contend the colored race is inferior to the white, let them but listen to the glowing strains of Frederick Douglass and Charles Lenox Remond—the one a full-blooded negro, and the other a mulatto—and say whether they think *these* below the white man in point of intellect.[11]

The correspondent also shared with his readers an anecdote Douglass used to attack the proslavery character of the northern church and its followers. "I was engaged at a particular time, in collecting funds for the antislavery cause, in and about Worcester," Douglass reportedly told the Fall River audience, when "I one day called on Mrs. Waldo, belonging to a wealthy family which had erected a church at its own expense." After hearing that Douglass was a slave, Mrs. Waldo said, "I suppose you want money to buy yourself with?" Douglass responded with an emphatic no and further explained that he was a runaway slave. "Then I cannot give you any thing," Mrs. Waldo responded. The woman explained how she believed Douglass had done his master "a *great wrong*" when he "ran away from him." Next, the woman questioned Douglass as to how much money he "would have brought at the South." He answered, "Perhaps a thousand dollars." "Then you have robbed your master of a thousand dollars," was Mrs. Waldo's response. To Douglass, the irony was clear, and he shared it with his audience. "All this," Douglass said, "was spoken in a very pious tone, for Mrs. W. was a member of the church, and an exceedingly godly woman."[12]

During the same meeting, Douglass also told a story to capture the nature of the proslavery church in the South. Drawing from his slave experience, he told the tale of a convention in Baltimore of Baptist ministers that was "composed almost wholly of slaveholders." During the course of the meetings, Douglass explained, numerous clergy who were slaveowners participated: "A *thief* preached the sermon—a *thief* made the prayer—a *thief* administered the sacrament, and then this pack of thieves all stood up together and sang in unison—'Lo! What an entertaining sight, For brethren to agree!'" This is the only recorded instance of Douglass using this striking anecdote with its obvious and powerful irony and its powerful denunciatory language.[13]

One week later Douglass attended the annual meeting of the Plymouth County Anti-Slavery Society at Kingston on the 4th of July. Remond and Sydney Howard Gay also participated. The significance of the day did not go unnoticed, as Douglass joined Gay, Remond, and others who spoke in support of a resolution that declared the determination of abolitionists to "obey the 'living God' and finish peaceably the work" begun by the Founding Fathers. Those attending the meeting also heard Douglass share his views on "the position of the church and clergy, in regard to the institution of slavery."[14]

II

Following the Kingston meeting, Douglass returned to Lynn to prepare for the Hundred Conventions tour. He was excited about being involved in "a real campaign" that would require nearly six months to complete. It was an "honor to be chosen one of the agents to assist in these proposed conventions," Douglass recalled, "and I never entered upon any work with more heart and hope." He believed that all "the American people needed . . . was light. Could they know slavery as I knew it, they would hasten to the work of its extinction." The plan of the Hundred Conventions tour, as Collins conceived it, was to put as strong a force of lecturers into the field as the board of managers of the Massachusetts Anti-Slavery Society could assemble. The lecturers—Douglass, Bradburn, Remond, Monroe, Collins, and Ferris—"were all masters of the subject, and some of them able and eloquent orators." They were divided into two groups, which were to hold a series of simultaneous meetings in different places along the route of the conventions. In addition, the groups would come together occasionally to convene a "grand" meeting. The goal of the campaign was to hold over 100 conventions, thus laying "the truth before from three to five hundred thousand" people. The abolitionists of each city, village, and town on the convention circuit were expected to provide food, lodging, publicity, meeting places, and transportation for the traveling lecturers. When suitable meeting places could not be obtained, Collins expected local abolitionists to build "temporary structures along the route."[15]

In the middle of July, Douglass, Collins, and Bradburn left Massachusetts and began making their way west. Traveling north, they headed for Middlebury, Vermont, to conduct a two-day meeting, scheduled to begin on Thursday, 13 July.[16] Things did not go well from the beginning. For part of the trip, Douglass and his colleagues were transported by stage, during which Douglass, on account of the color of his skin, was treated with contempt by the other passengers.[17] When the group arrived at Middlebury, they met an "intensely bitter and violent" response. Before they arrived, Douglass recalled, "college students had very industriously and mischievously placarded the town with violent aspersions of our characters and the grossest misrepresentations of our principles, measures, and objects." Douglass was portrayed as an escaped convict from the state penitentiary, while the other lecturers "were assailed not less slanderously." As a result of the negative publicity, few people attended the meeting and "little was accomplished by it." Fortunately, when the trio moved northward on 17 July to neighboring Ferrisburg, they held a successful a two-day meeting that generated a "more favorable" response and a more sympathetic hearing.[18]

From Vermont, Douglass, Collins, and Bradburn traveled westward into New York, where they encountered "apathy, indifference, aversion, and sometimes mobocratic spirit . . . all along the Erie Canal, from Albany to Buffalo." The indifference of New York's abolitionists to the Hundred Conventions campaign can be attributed in part to the efforts of Alvan Stewart, one of the leaders of New York's antislavery movement and co-organizer of the state's Liberty Party. In a letter to the *Liberty Press* in early July of 1843, Stewart urged the abolitionists of central and western New York to boycott the Hundred Conventions tour. The Massachusetts agents, Stewart charged, were "no human government" men who were "opposed to the liberty party, and *secretly* opposed to voting, or petitioning the government to abolish slavery" and, as a result, were "actually prolonging the slave's bondage." Stewart advised New York abolitionists to give neither of their money nor of their time to the convention tour.[19]

On 27 July Douglass and his colleagues arrived at Utica, where they were scheduled to hold a three-day meeting.[20] A correspondent for the *Herkimer Journal* reported that they addressed "a limited audience," which the reporter attributed to Stewart's notice advising New York abolitionists not to attend. Upon seeing the low turnout, the lecturers decided to limit the convention to one day. During the meeting, Douglass reportedly "occupied much of the time in detailing his own painful experience and observation as a bondman, and in exposing and castigating the conduct of the Church and the State, which in his view are the chief agencies that uphold the reign of despotism in this country." Douglass must have spoken well, for he made a favorable impression on the reporter from the *Herkimer Journal*. "Douglas[s] is an able and effective speaker," the correspondent wrote, "and we wish the whole American people could hear him. He is surely destined, if he lives, to make his influence widely felt toward the overthrow of the accursed system of Slavery."[21]

From Utica, Douglass headed west to Syracuse. Rather than travel with him, Bradburn briefly left the tour to visit Gerrit Smith in Peterboro. Collins, a recent convert to Fourier communitarianism, a reform that opposed all individual ownership of property, decided to remain in Utica to conduct an anti-property meeting. Douglass, therefore, traveled alone. When he arrived in Syracuse at the end of July, he could not secure a place in which to hold meetings. Undaunted, and with the help of Stephen Smith, "an eminent citizen," he held his first gathering on Sunday morning, 30 July, in a park in front of Smith's house under the shade of a small tree with an audience of five persons. By the close of the afternoon session, he had attracted an audience of "not less than five hundred." Before the evening session, he was offered the shelter of a run-down, abandoned church. That evening he spoke at the old Congregational Church, where the meeting continued for the next two days.[22]

On the last day of the Syracuse convention, Douglass was joined by Collins, who was in such poor health that he "took little part" in the meeting.[23] Bradburn also arrived in Syracuse on the last day of the meeting, but he decided to travel on to Skaneatles. Rather than hold an evening session on the last day, Douglass elected to bring the convention to a close in the afternoon so to give the abolitionists an "opportunity to attend a collation that [was] given by the ladies at the antislavery fair" that night. At the collation, Charles Lenox Remond, who had arrived in Syracuse late that afternoon, was called upon to address the crowd. He complied with the request and delivered, in Douglass' words, "a short but happy speech." According to Douglass, following Remond's speech, two conflicting announcements were made. Notice was given that a property convention would meet the next day in the old Congregational Church—the same place Douglass' antislavery convention had met the previous three days. A short time later, another notice was given that Douglass and Remond would be holding an antislavery meeting the next day in the afternoon at the old Congregational Church. The stage was set for a confrontation.[24]

The next morning, Douglass, Remond, and Abby Kelley attended Collins' antiproperty meeting. Toward the end of the morning session, Douglass sensed that Collins had no intention of giving his meeting over to the abolitionists, and "arose and inquired if it was understood that there would be an anti-sl[avery] meeting there in the afternoon." Collins replied in the negative and then continued by making a long speech "respecting the bigotry and narrowmindedness of abolitionists" and charging them with being selfish and having little concern with universal reform. Remond responded briefly to Collins, charging him "with weakening the antislavery cause" and using it "as a mere stepping stone to his own favorite theory of the right of property." Collins, now angry, rose and defended his character. In addition, according to Douglass' account of the meeting, Collins declared that the antislavery cause was "a mere dabbling." If slavery were abolished and the private ownership of property continued to exist, he charged, abolition would exist "only . . . in form" and would "remain in fact." "To recognize property in the soil," said Collins, was worse than enslaving people. In his view, the universal reform movement would "do more for the Slave than the antislavery movement."25

After Collins finished his speech, Douglass asked to be heard. "I felt that the anti-slavery cause had been wantonly assailed," he reported in a letter to Maria Weston Chapman, "and by one to whom I had looked up to as its warmest protector." After speaking for a few minutes, Douglass "gave way for adjournment" with the understanding that he would be allowed to continue in the afternoon. To be certain of responding to each of Collins' positions, he took time during the recess to "write out the remarks" he intended to make. At the beginning of the afternoon session, he was given the floor. After a few preparatory remarks, he defined the issue for the audience. "It was not that Mr. Collins had not a right to be a property man," Douglass argued. "Nor was it that he had not the right to devote one half of his time to the one, and the other half to the antislavery cause. No. This was the question: whether it was just or honorable for Mr. Collins to labor in the one at the expense of the other." Having defined the issue, Douglass proceeded to examine Collins' position. After only a few minutes, however, he was interrupted and told he was out of order. The audience quickly came to Douglass' defense and demanded that he be heard. Douglass then continued for approximately twenty minutes and concluded his speech by saying that if the board of managers of the Massachusetts Anti-Slavery Society sanctioned such behavior from Collins, its general agent, he would resign his agency in carrying out the Hundred Conventions campaign.26

Maria Weston Chapman, corresponding secretary of the Massachusetts Anti-Slavery Society, was inundated with letters from the involved parties. In his letter to Chapman, Douglass detailed "the whole facts in the case, as they transpired," and again threatened to resign if Collins continued as general agent. Kelley's letter corroborated Douglass' version of the incident. She reported that Douglass had "merely inquired" of Collins if his property meeting would give way for an antislavery meeting in the afternoon. Douglass, she wrote, made "the proposition cooly and gentlemanly." Thereupon, "Collins became angry," as did Remond and Douglass, and harsh words were exchanged among the three of them. The two black men were not altogether right, Kelley wrote, but neither was Collins who, in her judgment, "was not fit for the work to which he is appointed. His nervous irritability alone, was sufficient to disqualify him—I presume the Conventions get on better without than with him." To Kelley, as to Douglass and Remond, Collins was disrupting the Hundred Conventions campaign for the benefit of his other reform interests.[27]

Collins, of course, perceived the issue differently. In a lengthy letter to Chapman, he reported that "Douglass groaned and looked sad" while he was speaking in support of property reform. As soon as he had finished his last sentence, Collins charged, "Remond was upon his feet, and with an agitated frame, half stifled, angry and furious delivery, disposed of the property question as humbug and moonshine." After Remond spoke for nearly an hour, Collins recounted, he was followed by Douglass, who "sustained Remond in all his charges" and insisted that Collins be replaced as general agent. After Douglass was finished with his speech, he and Remond left the meeting, followed by "some fifteen or twenty" supporters. Collins reported that he then took the platform and defended himself "as well as possible from their assaults." He also tried to apologize for his colleagues' actions. In a tone that sounded paternalistic and condescending, Collins stated he could forgive Douglass and Remond inasmuch as the one was a fugitive from slavery and the other was "writhing under" the effects of prejudice "against people of his color." "Any cause presenting higher claims than Anti-slavery," he explained, "should necessarily excite their jealousy and opposition." Collins, however, was not as charitable toward Kelley. He portrayed her as instigating the entire incident by stirring Douglass and Remond "into a frenzied state." "She hates the property question, as the slaveholder hates antislavery," Collins charged. "She is intolerant beyond degree."[28]

Ultimately, Chapman and the board of managers of the Massachusetts Anti-Slavery Society ruled on the side of Collins. Collins still had her "entire confidence and esteem," she wrote to Kelley, although she, too, wished he would not call property meetings. Considerate as Chapman was toward Kelley, she was harsh with Douglass and sharply reprimanded him for being insubordinate to his superiors. "This was a strange and distressing revelation to me," Douglass recalled later in his life, "and one of which I was not soon relieved. I thought I had only done my duty." Although Douglass publicly passed off the reprimand as stemming from the board's fear of how the Liberty Party press would use his "seeming rebellion against the commanders of our antislavery army" to discredit the Garrisonian crusade, he knew there was considerably more at stake, for the reprimand implied that it was inappropriate for him, as a black man, to challenge senior white abolitionists. For Douglass, this would not do. The antiproperty meeting at which he had spoken, he argued in his response to Chapman, "was professedly a free meeting, where anybody might speak whenever and whatever they pleased. I felt I was violating no rule directly nor indirectly by insisting on my right *there* to defend the cause which had been *there* assailed." It was difficult to escape the fact that the leadership of the Massachusetts Anti-Slavery Society was imposing a double standard of conduct—one for white abolitionists and another for black abolitionists. While white abolitionists preached independence and equality for black people, the leaders of the abolition movement, at least in this incident, could not tolerate the behavior of a black man who acted in an independent and equal manner with whites.[29]

Contrary to his threat, however, Douglass did not resign his agency. The antislavery crusade was his vocation and, although wounded by Chapman's reprimand, he continued on the Hundred Conventions tour. His growing independence of mind, his increasing confidence on the platform, and his unwavering commitment to the abolition of slavery would not permit him to quit. Therefore, after the Syracuse debacle, he traveled westward to Rochester, where he participated in the annual meeting of the American Anti-Slavery Society of Western New York. There he met Jacob Ferris, Bradburn, who had been lecturing in Waterloo, New York, and Collins, who was in such poor health that he did not participate in the meeting, which convened on 3 August at Bethel Church. According to a report in the *Rochester Democrat*, Douglass played a dominant role throughout the four-day convention.[30] On the opening day, he introduced and "spoke eloquently" in support of a resolution proclaiming abolition as the "application of Christianity to the system of slavery." The next day, during the afternoon session, he "spoke of the proslavery position of the great church organizations." On Saturday, he "entertained the congregation with an abolition song" and introduced and spoke in support of a resolution declaring "the press and the living speaker [as] the only means by which to advance the cause of abolition." All told, the convention was a rousing success, so much so that on Saturday evening the abolitionists of Rochester voted to continue it one more day. Unable to secure a meeting place, Douglass, Bradburn, and Ferris held the extra meeting at the public square. Despite being scheduled at the last minute, reported Sydney Howard Gay to the *Liberator*, the session "was a grand one, and very fully attended."[31]

Pleased with their success in Rochester, Douglass and Bradburn traveled to Buffalo, where a Mr. Marsh, a local abolitionist, unable to secure a church or hall for their meetings, had to settle for an "old dilapidated and deserted room, formerly used as a postoffice." On 7 August Douglass and Bradburn went to the abandoned post office building to conduct the first session of a scheduled three-day convention. When they arrived, they "found seated a few cabmen in their coarse, everyday clothes," Douglass recalled, "whips in hand, while their teams were standing on the street waiting for a job." As Bradburn looked over the "unpromising audience," he decided not to stay and address "such a set of ruffians." Feeling that the Hundred Conventions tour was proving far from successful, he took the first steamer out of Buffalo to visit his brother in Cleveland.[32] Once again, Douglass was left to conduct the meetings alone. Determined to succeed without the aid of Bradburn, throughout the next several days he spoke in the rundown hall to "constantly increasing" audiences.[33] One of his listeners recalled the event years later. This eyewitness account offers a rare sketch of Douglass' message at the time and attests to his power in attracting and holding an audience:

> In the early autumn of 1843, at an anti-slavery meeting in Buffalo, I first had the happiness to hear Frederick Douglass make a speech. . . . It was a poor little meeting—the odds and ends of the city—not a soul there I had ever seen. I had never heard a fugitive slave speak, and was immensely interested to hear him. He rose, and I soon perceived he was all alive. His soul poured out with rare pathos and power. Among other things, he told how a slave-holder would preach to an audience of slaves and take the text: "*Servants, be obedient to your masters,*" and then proceed to say, "The Lord in His Providence sent pious souls over to Africa—dark, heathen, benighted Africa—to bring you into this Christian land, where you can sit beneath the droppings of the sanctuary and hear about Jesus! The Lord has so established things that only through the channel of obedience can happiness flow.["] For instance, Sam, the other day, was sent out by his master to do a piece of work that would occupy about two hours and a half. At the expiration of that time, Sam's master went out; and, lo! and behold! there lay Sam's hoe in one place, and Sam in another, fast asleep! The master remembered the words of Scripture: "He that knoweth his master's will, and doeth it not, shall be beaten with many stripes." So Sam was taken up and whipped, so that he was disabled from doing any work for the short space of three weeks and a half. "For only through the channel of obedience can happiness flow."[34]

Around 10 August, Remond arrived in Buffalo and immediately joined Douglass. During the next five days, people crowded to listen to the two eloquent black men. When the audiences became too large for the old post office, a Baptist church was thrown open for their meetings. By Sunday, 13 August, the church had become too small, so Douglass and Remond moved outside to an open park, where they "addressed an assembly of four or five thousand persons." The meetings, Remond reported to Garrison, "succeeded . . . beyond our expectations in making a strong interest in our cause." "Hundreds were in daily attendance," Remond wrote, and participated in the deliberations of the convention. One of those participants was William Wells Brown, an escaped slave from Kentucky. A resident of Buffalo at the time, Brown was a conductor on the Underground Railroad and was on the verge of starting a distinguished career as a lecturer in the antislavery movement. After hearing the "eloquence and enthusiasm" of Douglass and Remond for the first time, Brown wrote a letter to the *National Anti-Slavery Standard* praising their efforts. The two men, Brown reported, "called thousands to hear them" and were greeted with "thunders of applause." According to Brown, they "tore the veil of prejudice from the eyes of the whites of the city" and "with their mighty voices" opened the barred doors of the churches to the antislavery cause.[35]

Although Douglass and Remond surpassed the expectations of the board of managers by speaking in Buffalo eight days instead of the planned three, they were not yet through with their activities in the city. Instead of traveling west to Ohio to the scheduled meetings of the Hundred Conventions tour, they decided to stay in Buffalo to attend the National Negro Convention. "Frederick and myself," Remond informed Garrison, "intend remaining during the sitting of the Convention of the people of color, and shall join our respective parties in Ohio with all possible despatch." The two independent black men did not ask permission to stay—they simply informed Garrison that they intended to do so. By extending his time in Buffalo, Douglass missed appointments in Cleveland, Oberlin, Mansfield, Woodbury, and Green Plain, Ohio.[36]

The National Convention of the Colored Citizens of the United States, the first such convention since 1835, planned to convene on the third Tuesday of August. Its avowed purpose was to "deliberate on those questions that pertain to the colored man's rights, and to adopt such measures as will effectually secure to him the privileges of an American citizen." The convention was organized by black abolitionists in New York who were loyal to the Liberty Party and the American and Foreign Anti-Slavery Society. Indeed, although Douglass and Remond had been elected as delegates from Massachusetts during a meeting of Boston's black citizens in July, many black abolitionists loyal to Garrison had expressed opposition to an exclusively black convention. Black Garrisonians in Boston, New Bedford, and Philadelphia protested strongly against the convention, and Pennsylvania blacks did not send any delegates to the meeting.[37]

Despite this opposition, the convention held its opening session on Tuesday, 15 August, and did not adjourn until Saturday, 19 August.[38]

Douglass and Remond—the only delegates representing Massachusetts and the only Garrisonians present—joined delegates from Maine, Connecticut, New York, Ohio, Michigan, Illinois, Virginia, North Carolina, and Georgia. Of the seventy-three delegates, thirty-six were from New York state, and most of those were members of the American and Foreign Anti-Slavery Society and supporters of the Liberty Party.[39] The tone of the meeting was set from the start. At the beginning of the morning session, Buffalo's Samuel H. Davis was elected chairman, pro tem. He opened the proceedings with a speech extolling the Constitution of the United States as a document "which guarantees freedom and equal rights to every citizen" and hinting at the need for militant antislavery action by calling on black people "to rise up and assert" their "rightful claims." Although Davis did not detail what he meant by such statements, his speech left room for the delegates to suggest how black people could rise up and assert their rights. During the afternoon session, Douglass was elected as one of seven vice presidents of the convention. On Tuesday evening, the convention convened for "public meetings" at the Park Presbyterian Church. Douglass joined Remond, Henry Highland Garnet, and Charles B. Ray in addressing the "largely attended" meeting.[40]

During the afternoon session of the second day, Garnet thrilled the convention with his "Address to the Slaves of the United States of America," today one of the most acclaimed speeches in American history. Garnet, like Douglass, had formerly been a slave. He was born in December 1815 on a plantation near New Market in Kent County, Maryland. His grandfather was said to have been a chieftain and warrior in the Mandingo Empire of West Africa. When Garnet was nine years old, he and his family escaped from bondage and made their way to New York City, where his father, after securing employment, enrolled him in the African Free School. After graduation, Garnet and three other black students enrolled in the Noyes Academy of New Canaan, New Hampshire. In 1836, after an angry mob of white men destroyed the academy, Garnet entered Oneida Theological Institute, at Whitesboro, New York. He completed his studies in 1839, and one year later took up residence in Troy, New York. There he divided his time between preaching and abolition activities. He was employed as an agent of the American Anti-Slavery Society and soon earned distinction as a preeminent black abolitionist. In 1840 he was one of eight black men among the founders of the American and Foreign Anti-Slavery Society and became one of the most ardent supporters of the Liberty Party.[41]

Garnet's "Address to the Slaves," while not directly advocating violence against slaveholders, alluded pointedly to the possibility of bloody slave insurrections. Although Garnet proposed that slaves take action which in itself was nonviolent, he believed their action would most likely lead whites to respond with violence. His plan advised the slaves to go to their masters and demand their freedom. If this approach failed, he instructed the slaves to refuse to work. "Do this," he urged, "and for ever after cease to toil for the heartless tyrants, who give you no other reward but stripes and abuse. If they then commence the work of death, they, and not you, will be responsible for the consequences. You had far better all die—*die immediately*, than live slaves, and entail your wretchedness upon your posterity." Further, Garnet declared, "However much you and all of us may desire it, there is not much hope of Redemption without the shedding of blood." It was better, Garnet claimed, to "*die freemen, than live to be slaves*."[42] He concluded by saying:

> In the name of God we ask, are you men? Where is the blood of your fathers? Has it all run out of your veins? Awake, awake; millions of voices are calling you! Your dead fathers speak to you from their graves. Heaven, as with a voice of thunder, calls on you to arise from the dust.

> Let your motto be RESISTANCE! RESISTANCE! RESISTANCE! No oppressed people have ever secured their liberty without resistance. What kind of resistance you had better make, you must decide by the circumstances that surround you, and according to the suggestion of expediency. Brethren, adieu. Trust in the living God. Labor for the peace of the human race, and remember that you are three millions.[43]

Following Garnet's address, Charles Ray moved that it be sent to a revision committee, which would include Garnet as chair. Speaking in support of his motion, Ray expressed his desire to have the address closely and critically examined and, "perceiving some points in it that might in print appear objectionable," to have it "somewhat modified." Garnet immediately "arose to oppose the motion" and delivered a "masterly" speech. The "whole convention, full as it was," recorded the secretary in the minutes, "was literally infused with tears." After Garnet's speech, a reporter wrote in the *Buffalo Commercial Advertiser*, "it would have been dangerous to a slave-holder to have been in sight."[44]

Douglass immediately rose to respond to Garnet. Standing before the convention, he expressed his opposition to "certain points in the address" and advocated its referral to a committee. For Douglass, a proponent of Garrison's nonresistance doctrine and a moral suasionist, "there was too much physical force" both in the address and in Garnet's speech defending it. According to the minutes, Douglass "was for trying the moral means a little longer." Clearly, he did not wish to be involved in advocating action that could lead to slave insurrection. "Such a catastrophe," he argued, should be avoided. He wanted emancipation to come in a "better way," and he believed that it would. In the end, the meeting voted "by a large majority" to refer the address to the revision committee, which included both Garnet and Douglass. Ultimately, a toned down version of the address returned to the convention floor where, after two days of heated debate, a proposal to distribute it was rejected by a narrow vote of 19-18.[45]

In speaking against Garnet's address, Douglass demonstrated his determination to reform public opinion in order to abolish slavery. For Douglass, the crusade to end slavery was moral rather than revolutionary. When faced with the choice between peaceful reform and violent revolution, he chose peaceful reform. As he had thought before the Hundred Conventions campaign, "All that the American people needed . . . was light." He believed that if people came to know slavery as he knew it, "they would hasten to the work of its extinction." Although he would modify his stance in later years, at the time of Garnet's address, Douglass rejected militant action and put his hopes in Garrison's peaceful moral crusade to end slavery.[46]

Another point of contention involving Douglass arose during the afternoon session on Thursday, 27 August, over a resolution stating that "it is the duty of every lover of liberty to vote the Liberty ticket so long as they are consistent to their *principles*." Douglass led the opposition against its adoption. He was followed by Remond, William Wells Brown, and two other men. In summarizing their arguments against the resolution, the convention secretary recorded that "our friends from Massachusetts" stated "they would not accept the Liberty party" because they believed it was imprudent to align abolitionists with any political party, all of whom were "verily and necessarily corrupt." Further, according to E. A. Marsh's report in the *Liberator*, Douglass and his allies contended that the convention, "professing to represent the colored people, had no right to commit itself to any sect or party." Even in the face of overwhelming opposition, Douglass once again demonstrated his unwavering belief in Garrisonian doctrines and methods. Presented with an opportunity to endorse political action over moral suasion, he earnestly defended moral suasion as the most effectual way to achieve emancipation of the slave and the attainment of equal rights for people of color. On this resolution, however, Douglass and others of similar mind were greatly outnumbered. Garnet, Ray, Theodore Wright, and others spoke in support of the resolution, which was adopted with only seven dissenting votes.[47]

Not all the issues addressed during the convention were as contentious as the resolutions endorsing slave rebellion and the Liberty Party. Douglass and Remond joined with the majority of delegates in supporting resolutions denouncing the proslavery church, supporting the "happy effects" of the temperance movement, condemning the American Colonization Society, proclaiming America as the black person's native land, endorsing the work of the abolition movement in the United States, supporting the "education and moral training of the young and rising generation" as the means for "elevating" all black people, stressing the value of the mechanical arts and agriculture, attributing the condition of blacks—North and South—to the evils of slavery, and calling for another national convention for the people of color.[48]

This was Douglass' first opportunity to attend a national convention of African Americans, and he made the most of it. Throughout the sessions, he ably debated ideas and resolutions with the foremost black leaders, and accounts of the convention indicate that he earned distinction among his peers as an eloquent orator. The *National Anti-Slavery Standard* cited Garnet, Ward, Remond, and Douglass as "most distinguished" among the speakers. The *Buffalo Daily Gazette* wrote that the convention exhibited "a great amount of talent of [the] first order" and pointed to Garnet, Remond, Douglass, and Wright as "men of decided talents. . . . In speaking they have few, or no superiors in our city." Douglass, the Gazette continued, "who was once a 'chattel personal' fully sustains his claims to be considered a MAN among his fellow men, by the powerful and sensible manner in which he handles the subjects which come up before the convention for consideration."[49]

III

Following the National Convention of Colored Citizens, Douglass and Remond remained in the Buffalo-Rochester area for ten days. Remond reported to the *Liberator* that he and Douglass continued to speak "to large and increasing audiences, more than twice a day." At Mendon, a small town outside Rochester, the two men addressed "many in front of the Friend's meeting-house," which had been closed against them. According to Remond, they then moved on to another part of Mendon "and addressed one of the most crowded audiences I ever saw, in the Christian meeting-house; and I think an excellent impression was made." On Friday morning, 1 September, Douglass and Remond left Buffalo and began their journey to Oakland, Ohio, where they hoped to reunite with their colleagues on the Hundred Conventions tour at the first anniversary meeting of the Ohio American Anti-Slavery Society.[50]

Unfortunately, Douglass and Remond did not make it to the Ohio meeting in time. Being unexpectedly detained, they arrived in Oakland on 7 September, the day after the convention adjourned.[51] "There has been one thing to mar our pleasure," William A. White reported to the *Liberator* at the conclusion of the convention, "that Charles and Frederick have not been with us."[52] Before moving on to Indiana to canvass that state, Douglass and Remond held an impromptu meeting in Oakland. "Immediately on their arrival," a reporter wrote to the *Clinton Republican*, "notice was given that they would address the people and in about two hours a large crowd assembled." Abraham Brooke, corresponding secretary of the Ohio American Anti-Slavery Society, estimated that the meeting attracted over 1,000 people. Douglass and Remond, "though weary with their recent journey," the *Clinton Republican* correspondent reported, "walked up to their subject and into the understandings, and consciences, and hearts of their hearers, with a boldness and power which I had never seen surpassed." Douglass reportedly moved the audience with his "keen, withering satire" and "ineffably scalding-shrivelling sarcasms." Brooke wrote to Garrison that Douglass and Remond "would disarm the opposition to our cause in Ohio in one year, were they to traverse the State." The correspondent for the *Clinton Republican* declared, "What a loathsome, soul sickening ineffably contemptible thing is this American prejudice against color. Charles Lenox Remond and Frederick Douglass! yours is a noble and glorious work, and nobly and gloriously are you performing it. God speed you!" At the conclusion of the meeting, the participants unanimously adopted resolutions denouncing prejudice against people of color and praising Douglass and Remond for their eloquent addresses on behalf of the slave.[53]

From Ohio, Douglass and Remond parted company and headed for their scheduled conventions in Indiana, a state in which almost all of their experiences would be unpleasant. "The roughest handling we received anywhere was in the State of Indiana," Douglass later recalled. "Many of its inhabitants were from Virginia and North Carolina, and felt that in loyalty to their native states they must suppress the antislavery agitation. So we were met everywhere with opposition and often with mobs."[54] At Cambridge on 11 September, Douglass rejoined Bradburn and William A. White for a two-day meeting.[55] They next traveled to Richmond, where they were mobbed and pelted with rotten eggs.[56] From Richmond, Douglass and his companions traveled to Pendleton, where "this mobocratic spirit was even more pronounced." They arrived on Thursday evening, 14 September, and were informed by their host, Dr. Fussell, secretary of the Indiana State Anti-Slavery Society, that a mob had threatened to travel from Columbus, "a miserable, rum-drinking place, about six miles distant," to disrupt their meetings.[57]

Determined not to be intimidated by a mob, Douglass, Bradburn, and White held their first meeting the next day in the Baptist Church. "Frederick spoke," White reported to Garrison, "and there was no interruption, though I observed a great number of men, such as do not usually attend our meetings." Prior to the afternoon session, Douglass and his colleagues learned that the trustees of the Baptist Church, fearing the building would be damaged if the meetings continued there, were closing its doors to them. When the three men arrived outside the church, an intoxicated mob of thirty or more people had gathered to greet them and were, according to White, "very much excited." The crowd, wrote Bradburn to the *National Anti-Slavery Standard*, was composed of "sundry unshaven, lantern-jawed, savage looking loafers" who made "murderous threats, and blasphemous oaths, against abolitionists and 'niggers.'" In an effort to calm the crowd, Douglass, Bradburn, and White "went in among them, and talked in a conversational way for some time." Believing the mob was now subdued enough to begin the meeting, Bradburn mounted the steps in front of the church and began speaking "on the rights of our northern working-men" without interruption for approximately fifteen minutes until rain came and the meeting had to be stopped. That evening, a group of citizens met and passed resolutions disapproving the actions of the mob and "expressing a determination to resist it." The resolutions were ordered to be "posted up about the town." White and Bradburn spoke briefly to those attending, and the abolitionists "hoped we should have no more trouble."[58]

Their hopes, however, were short-lived. The next morning brought more mob action, chaos, and violence. Unable to secure a lecture hall, Douglass, Bradburn, and White conducted their meeting in the woods on the outskirts of town where, according to White, "seats and stands had been arranged." Douglass recalled that "quite a large audience assembled" for the morning session. Also present was a mob that White estimated at eleven people. For the moment, at least, the mob was quiet, and the meeting began without incident. "We opened the meeting with a song," White reported to the *Liberator*, "after which I made a few remarks, and was followed by Bradburn." During the course of Bradburn's remarks, White wrote, "the mob continued to collect, but were quiet." After a while, the mob withdrew into the woods.[59]

A few moments later, there was a shout, and the mob emerged from the woods and headed toward the meeting. White calculated the mob at this time to be "thirty or more in number," marching two-by-two in a straight line. "Coatless, with shirt-sleeves rolled up," the mob was "well supplied with brick-bats, stones, and 'evangelical eggs.'" When the mob stopped "at the outskirts of the assembly," members of the audience, now numbering 130, rose and were about to retreat when White appealed to them to be seated, "which some of them did" while others left. The leader of the mob, wearing a coon-skin cap, ordered his comrades to surround the meeting. The mob encircled the audience and some stood in front of the platform. Now in place, the leader of the mob ordered the abolitionists to "be off." His command, reported White, "was followed by a volley of eggs and stones." No one was hurt in the barrage and those audience members who decided to remain boldly stood their ground. Douglass and his companions did not move from the platform.[60]

For the moment the mob, seemingly surprised at the resolve of the abolitionists, was at a loss as to what to do next. One of the members of the mob, a man named James Jackson, asked the abolitionists why they did not go to the South to deliver there. Bradburn replied and Jackson offered an answer. White thereupon invited Jackson up to the platform to continue the debate. Jackson complied, White reported later, and "made a most ridiculous spectacle, interlarding his speech with copious oaths, and ending off by saying he could not talk, but he could fight—that he had too much good blood in his veins to let us go on." One of the members of the mob, apparently having had enough talk, jumped up on the platform and stated that nothing was going to be done unless he did it. He then proceeded to overturn the speakers' table, and began to pull the stand to pieces. The rest of his friends joined him in the destruction of the platform, and much pushing and shoving followed.[61]

Meanwhile, Douglass had been taken aside and was safe among several of the members of the audience. But not seeing White and hearing that his friend was in danger, Douglass abandoned his Garrisonian nonresistance principles, seized a club, and rushed into the crowd. His club was immediately taken from him, White reported, and "finding he had attracted their anger against himself, fled for his life." Shouts of "kill the nigger" followed him. The leader of the mob soon overtook Douglass, "knocked him down and struck him once with a club, and was raising a second time to level a blow which must have been fatal had it fallen." White arrived in time to throw himself on the man "and stop him from his murderous purpose." During the tumult that followed, Bradburn reported, White was struck by a stone on the back of the head, "making a gash in the scalp two inches long, and quite down to the skull." Douglass was also struck on the head by a stone, "which raised a protuberance nearly as large as a hen's egg, though without breaking the skin."[62]

When the violence finally ended, an unconscious and bruised Douglass was transported by wagon about three miles to the home of Neal Hardy, "a kind-hearted member of the Society of Friends," where he was cared for by his wife, Elizabeth, and nursed back to health. Although Douglass seemed initially to have been "seriously injured," White wrote, "he soon recovered." Besides suffering a lump on the head, Douglass had broken his right hand. Because the bones "were not properly set," he later recalled, his hand "never recovered its natural strength and dexterity." More mob violence was feared when rumors circulated through the town that the mob was going to return to Pendleton that evening and destroy Dr. Fussell's home. The citizens of Pendleton responded by arming themselves, but the mob never returned. "This was the most brazen, dare-devil mob I ever knew," Bradburn wrote to the *National Anti-Slavery Standard*. "They perpetrated their damning deeds before all the people, and in the light of a noon-day's sun; and then, before leaving town, paraded themselves on horseback through its principal streets."[63]

Douglass always remembered what happened that morning at Pendleton. Three years later, while touring the British Isles, he wrote to White from Edinburgh, disclosing how he would "never forget those days" in the summer of 1843 when he and White, "like two very brothers were ready to dare—do, and even die for each other." The whole event was "tragic awfully so," he said, "yet I laugh always when I think how comic I must have looked when running before the mob, darkening the air with the mud from my feet. How I looked running you can best describe but how you looked bleeding I shall always remember." In his letter, Douglass praised White for leaving "a life of ease and even luxury" to "do something toward breaking the fetters of the slave and elevating the despised black man"—all "against the wishes of your father and many of your friends." Your blood, "so warm so generous," Douglass told his friend, "was too holy to be poured out by the rough hand of that infernal mob." Douglass ended his reminiscence by writing tenderly to the man who probably saved his life, "Dear William, from that hour you have been loved by Frederick Douglass."[64] Fifty years after the event, Douglass wrote to Richard Josiah Hinton that he had abandoned his nonresistance principles that day at Pendleton. "I was a Non Resistant till I got to fighting with a mob in Pendleton, Ind[iana] in 1843," he confessed. "Nature in that case proved more powerful than grace. I fell never to rise again, and yet I cannot feel that I did wrong. The impulse to fight at the moment seemed to be devine [sic]."[65]

From Pendleton, Douglass, White, and Bradburn traveled the twenty miles to Noblesville, Indiana, where they conducted a one-day meeting on 17 September.[66] From Noblesville, the abolitionists journeyed to Jonesboro, where they attended the annual meeting of the Indiana Anti-Slavery Society, which was scheduled to begin on 21 September. Douglass, White, and Bradburn joined Sydney Howard Gay, Charles Lenox Remond, and James Monroe for the three-day anniversary meeting. In a letter to Garrison, Gay reported that the sessions "were not characterized through-out by the best spirit. There seemed to be a lurking suspicion in the minds of some of the Indianans of the eastern agents; and though it broke out in no overt act which really caused alienation among us, it seemed to pervade the meeting like an unwholesome atmosphere, and gave rise, occasionally, to momentary inflammation." Ohio abolitionist Abraham Brooke made a similar observation in a letter to Maria Weston Chapman, except he attrib-uted the tension at the meeting to "a want of harmony among our Eastern friends who were with us."[67]

The tensions came to a head during a heated confrontation involving Douglass, Remond, Bradburn, and Daniel Worth, the chair of the meeting. During one of the afternoon sessions of the convention, Bradburn offered a resolution decrying the negative influence of slavery upon the northern people. According to Brooke, instead of speaking on his resolution, Bradburn chose to answer "some objections to the anti-slavery cause, some twenty of which he had noted down." Bradburn's speech on the objections consumed the afternoon session, and he had covered only five objections on his list. The following morning, Worth read Bradburn's resolution and gave him the floor. Douglass interrupted Bradburn in the midst of his long speech, demanding that he yield the floor because he was speaking on a subject tangential to the resolution currently under consideration. Bradburn, reported Brooke, insisted "that according to parliamentary usage he had an undoubted right to go on." Douglass reportedly denied Bradburn's right to continue and appealed to the chair, who "decided in favor of Bradburn." Remond immediately took the floor and came to the support of Douglass. After calling the chairman a "jackass," Remond reportedly "made a long, hot speech and appealed to the meeting," which sustained the decision of the chair. In response, Remond reportedly remarked there "must be a set of monkeys out here in the West."[68] Bradburn took the floor and, according to Brooke, "made some very offensive personal remarks—alluding to them [Douglass and Remond] as *colored* men, [and] styled their conduct monkeyism." To add insult to injury, when Bradburn finally concluded his speech, the meeting called Monroe, an abolitionist from Connecticut, to the stand, bypassing Douglass who was scheduled to speak next.[69]

This unsightly confrontation troubled several western abolitionists. One white antislavery man, quoted in a letter from Brooke to Maria Weston Chapman, believed that if Douglass and Remond "do not do more hurt than good before they get out of the state, he would feel thankful." In his judgment, the two black men were "a disgrace to abolition." Other abolitionists, Brooke reported, complained that Remond and Douglass chose "to be the lions of the party and are unwilling to be directed by others or restrained by common parliamentary usage." Brooke believed the two black men needed to be brought under control. "Talented and glorious specimens of the 'fallen' humanity as they are," he wrote, Douglass and Remond "still are but unregenerate men. The antislavery reform is but a partial reform after all." It was appropriate for Douglass and Remond to assail slavery, said Brooke, but they were overlooking the fact that such attacks were only part of what should be the exposition of "the higher sentiments and intellectual powers of our nature." Brooke drew an important lesson from the public clash between the abolitionists. He suggested that "the plan of calling conventions at which shall be collected several of the prominent speakers in the antislavery ranks is a bad one." In these situations "each cannot be *the* lion he is accustomed to be when laboring alone and as a consequence, these jealousies and ugly ruptures" will sometimes happen.[70]

While Brooke's perception of the situation may be accurate, he captured only part of the problem. Douglass had been laboring on his own for part of the Hundred Conventions tour and indeed may have grown accustomed to being the "lion" during his conventions. But in addition, he probably was angry with Bradburn for having abandoned him in Buffalo, leaving him to lecture to the city alone. These two issues most likely contributed to Douglass' decision to interrupt Bradburn at the Jonesboro convention. In addition, as we have seen throughout this chapter, Douglass was developing an independent voice. He viewed the antislavery crusade as the most important of all reform movements and was prepared to challenge any reformer, regardless of color or status, who allowed other causes to distract from it.

After the incident at Jonesboro, Douglass once again asserted his independence and decided to take a temporary leave from the Hundred Conventions tour.[71] He returned alone to Clinton County, Ohio, where he lectured "most ably and successfully" to large and enthusiastic audiences through the end of October.[72] "Frederick has been doing a grand work in this neighborhood the past week," Brooke reported in early October. "I hope . . . the American [Anti-Slavery] Society may be able to make an arrangement with Frederick to spend a year in our state before long. He could not operate in a more fruitful field."[73]

While Douglass was lecturing in Clinton County, his colleagues continued to hold conventions in Indiana until 3 October, when they headed eastward for Ohio.[74] Toward the end of October, Douglass reunited with Remond, Gay, and Monroe on the Hundred Conventions campaign. He joined them with great energy and enthusiasm, and accounts of his oratory dominated the published reports of the conventions in Ohio and Pennsylvania. On 30 October, for example, Douglass and his companions arrived in Lloydsville, Ohio, for a two-day meeting.[75] According to the *Cincinnati Philanthropist*, Douglass fully engaged and controlled the audience's emotions. "He soon obtained the command of their feelings," the correspondent reported, "and set them to laughing or weeping at will."[76] At New Lisbon, Douglass and his colleagues addressed "a tolerably full and very attentive audience." Again, the focus of the press was on Douglass. His efforts, a correspondent reported to the *New Lisbon Advocate*, "made a permanent impression. . . . Mr. D. gave proof positive, intellectual proof, that, although he has been under the iron hoof of oppression, and though he has not the orthodox constitutional skin, he is a MAN; a man of very extraordinary mental powers." Douglass, the correspondent continued, spoke "manfully" against slavery "and those who advocate its dishonest claims to perpetuity." In concluding his article, the reporter praised Douglass' powerful platform skills:

> The speaker is every thing for ability and eloquence that the eastern papers have represented him to be. Notwithstanding, he

has never been educated, he is a workman that need not be ashamed. Nature has effected much for him; he need fear no man in argument who might attempt to justify slavery, no, not the great demigod of whiggery, Henry Clay himself. Indeed, he used up some of Clay's favorite and cherished slavery doctrines most effectually. And if Clay had been there, and felt the force of some of the sarcasm and argument of this man, once a slave, he would have crept through an inch auger-hole to get out of hearing.[77]

Due partly to accounts such as these, Douglass' fame as an orator spread quickly throughout Ohio. Wherever the lecturers traveled, Bradburn reported to Collins, "the people wanted to hear Douglass."[78]

From Ohio, the lecturers traveled by horseback to Pennsylvania.[79] Upon arriving in Pittsburgh, Douglass and his companions temporarily parted company. Douglass traveled by steamboat to New Brighton to conduct a two-day convention on 3-4 November.[80] He addressed a crowded house at the Presbyterian Church, "the only one that could be had in the place." In a letter to Garrison, Milo A. Townsend praised Douglass and related the impact of his message on the audience:

> Much interest was manifested to hear this able advocate of human rights; and as the result of hearing him, the unbelieving have been converted, the sluggish have been aroused, the faltering have been strengthened, and the faithful have been cheered, and their hopes renewed. Frederick Douglass is a speaker of great power and eloquence, surpassed, I think, by few, if any, in the nation.[81]

Townsend also provided a vividly detailed account of Douglass' message and rhetorical method at this stage of the Hundred Conventions tour. According to Townsend, Douglass began his address with a "somewhat minute examination of the doings of the churches on the slave question, proving to every candid and discriminating mind, that they are emphatically the 'bulwarks of slavery.'" Douglass "hurled the thunderbolts of Truth against this spiritual wickedness in high places, and against gilded villainy and ecclesiastical wrong-doing." According to Townsend, Douglass appealed to the audience's senses—particularly sound—to capture the brutal reality of the connection between the American church and the slave plantations of the South. "He proved," Townsend reported, "that 'the churches hold the keys of Slavery's dungeons;' and that they are responsible for the throbs of anguish, the sighs of sorrow, the shrieks of agony, and the wailings of despair, which are ascending night and day from the plantations of the South 'as swift witnesses before the living God.'" Douglass concluded his address by preaching the slaveholder's sermon.[82]

From all accounts, the speech made a strong impact on Douglass' audience. "The truth flashed its light upon the minds of many," Townsend wrote, "and they went away believing; though sorrowing that such was the state of the professedly christian bodies of this land." Others in the audience reportedly "gnashed their teeth and howled," and one person walked out during the Slaveholder's Sermon "muttering *pious* wrath" and complaining that Douglass was "making a mock of holy things." Douglass' harsh treatment of the church particularly "aroused the ire" of a Methodist minister who, at the conclusion of the speech, declared that the Methodist Church "'had been misrepresented'" and that he was ready "'to prove it at a suitable time.'" Douglass reportedly invited the minister to do so immediately, but the minister declined.[83]

From New Brighton, Douglass returned to Pittsburgh to reunite with his colleagues. When he arrived, Monroe, Gay, Bradburn, and White were too ill to conduct the meetings scheduled for 6-7 November. Consequently, Douglass and Remond were left to lecture to the city of Pittsburgh by themselves, and they did so with great effect. They held a weeklong series of meetings and reportedly addressed their audiences "most eloquently."[84] Douglass and Remond, said the *Pittsburgh Spirit of Liberty*, "have at least convinced most, if not *all* who heard them, that, in the language of one of the first speakers and *the* most talented man in our city, 'there are few or none more eloquent in the Union.'" The same newspaper summarized the impact of Douglass' and Remond's oratory:

> The meetings have been full—many of them crowded—and the enthusiasm most grateful. We may say, without fear of contradiction, that more has been done during the past week by Douglass and Remond . . . to push forward the great and glorious cause, than could have been hoped for in months, by any other instrumentality. We have heard of *many*, very many converts already made, and are assured that hundreds, if not *thousands*, have been awakened by the appeals of these orators.[85]

Years later, one of these converts recalled that during one of the Pittsburgh meetings Douglass used his powers of impersonation and ridicule to dramatize the immorality of slavery. According to this observer, Douglass symbolically brought U.S. Senators Henry Clay and John C. Calhoun, and Daniel Webster, the secretary of state, before the audience: [86]

> Douglass put them all upon the stage before us. . . . Half an hour we held our places, fidgeting at first, then frightened, into the cutting consciousness of a somehow participated culpability in the villainies charged home upon our Constitution and our color. . . . There in that charmed atmosphere the magician reared the National Capitol, opened the Senate Chamber, and represented to a miracle the men we had thought were without a model or a shadow. It was even terrible to our sympathies, so deeply enlisted, to witness the

daring of that unlettered slave, attempting the personification of Clay, Calhoun, and Webster, in action, thought, and utterance. Gracefully athletic in his flow of thought as Clay in his happiest mood, when he presented him arguing the right of restitution— terribly concentrative as Calhoun in vindicating the international obligation, and ponderously logical as Webster in expounding the doctrine of the demand. His astounding power of transformation, his perfect clearness of discrimination, and his redundant ability in the execution, more than justified the audacity of the design. To see one man with all the varied capacity of these three, mixing them up, without confusion or mistake, in the puppet-show of his imagination, and playing upon them at his pleasure, was verily a sight to see . . . and we have an earnest doubt if any man in that assembly has lost a tone of that wondrous voice, or a tingle of the nerves, which he touched with pain and shame and rage and ridicule that night.[87]

The observer's recollection shows Douglass using his power of mimicry in a manner he had not used it before. In the past, he had used his imitative powers to bring the slaveholder, the southern preacher, and the northern minister before the audience for the purpose of exposing and shaming their behavior. By impersonating Clay, Calhoun, and Webster, Douglass moved from ridiculing and disgracing the slaveholder and the ministers of the church to dishonoring the great triumvirate. As he worked to capture their words, delivery, and character for his auditors, he seemingly transformed himself into each of them. In so doing, he hoped to inspire his auditors to pay closer attention to what these men were doing and saying and to deliberate more carefully over the government officials' behavior. Through mimicry, ridicule, and powerful delivery, he was able to elicit from his auditors a rousing emotional response that made a lasting impression on at least one of the listeners who experienced his discourse that evening. This appears to be the only recorded instance of Douglass impersonating these three men.

After the Pittsburgh conventions, Douglass traveled alone by horseback to Fallston, where he conducted "a most enthusiastic" antislavery meeting. "The Convention," reported a correspondent to the *New Lisbon Aurora*, "was large and continued two days, [and was] addressed most of the time by the fugitive, Douglass."[88] At the end of November, Douglass rejoined Bradburn and White at West Chester.[89] According to a report in the *National Anti-Slavery Standard*, Douglass made a dramatic entrance at the 25 November meeting. "Just as William White was closing his opening speech, in the morning, and in sad tones was offering reasons for the absence of Douglas[s]," reported the correspondent, "that moment, a stir was seen amidst the crowd at the door, and the next, Douglas[s] himself stood before them!" A very excited White, the reporter continued, "sprung forward," grasped Douglass' hand, "and at once introduced him to the audience." At that time, Douglass made only "a few prefatory remarks," but in the afternoon he presented a full address "to the great interest and satisfaction of the audience."[90]

From West Chester, the company of lecturers traveled eastward toward Philadelphia for a 4 December meeting commemorating the tenth anniversary of the American Anti-Slavery Society, a meeting that also was intended to be the climax of the Hundred Conventions tour. Held in Philadelphia's Second Independent Universalist Church, the three-day meeting was chaired by Robert Purvis, president of Philadelphia's Vigilance Committee, an organization which sheltered runaway slaves. Purvis was also a conductor on the Underground Railroad and had been a participant in the first meeting of the American Anti-Slavery Society ten years earlier.[91]

Douglass participated actively throughout the convention. On Monday, 4 December, during the opening session, after Purvis had made a short speech and White had read the Declaration of Sentiments adopted by the society in 1833, Douglass joined White, Lucretia Mott, Cyrus Burleigh, Thomas Earle, and Rev. Henry Grew in speaking for a resolution extolling the success of the American Anti-Slavery Society over the past ten years. Before the session ended, Douglass was appointed as a member of the business committee for the convention. On the second day of the convention, he spoke in favor of an amendment to a resolution that substituted the phrase "withdrawal of fellowship and support" for "total separation." The amended resolution called for the "withdrawal of fellowship and support from proslavery parties and sects" as being "essential to the speedy triumph of our cause." The amendment passed, but the resolution was tabled. The next day, Douglass addressed the convention in support of a resolution declaring that the American Anti-Slavery Society would "not undertake to proscribe to its members, what course of political action they shall pursue, further than that they vote for none" until they "publicly avow themselves favorable to the abrogation of all laws and constitutional provisions which require the aid of public officers or private citizens for the retaining of human beings in a state of slavery." The resolution was adopted by the convention. The following day, Douglass was the final person to speak in favor of a resolution proposed by Collins urging that the executive committee of the American Anti-Slavery Society "be instructed to suspend the publication of the *Standard* after the issuing of four more numbers, and to close the anti-slavery office, relinquish its lease, and go to no further expense on account of the society until its debts are liquidated."[92]

Although we do not have texts of any of these speeches by Douglass, they seem to have made a positive impression on the audience. According to a report in the *Philadelphia Weekly Cultivator*, those gathered at the convention were especially interested in and attentive to Douglass. "He was a slave only five years ago," the *Weekly Cultivator* wrote, and "is quite an extraordinary man." As an orator, the newspaper continued, Douglass "is graceful, winning, fluent, argumentative, logical and convincing; his inimitable anecdotes are so happily and appropriately interspersed, and his appeals to humanity so graphic and touching, that he can transport his hearers to the regions of rapture, or of comus, and lower them into the deepest feeling, for suffering humanity; and he has the faculty to penetrate the inmost chords of philanthropy, 'ad libitum.'"[93]

The tenth anniversary meeting ended on 7 December and with it the Hundred Conventions tour of the West. Declaring the tour a success, the board of managers of the Massachusetts Anti-Slavery Society exulted that "We doubt whether there has ever been, in the history of the cause, so great an amount of wholesome agitation produced at so small an expense, or accomplished in so short a time. . . . Tens of thousands, perhaps hundreds of thousands of minds have been reached, and consciences stirred, as to their duty to the slave." After the tour was over, Gay reflected that the "stirring eloquence" of the agents "made an impression on the western people which will not easily be effaced." Throughout the 3,000 mile journey, he wrote, the agents kept their "eyes as steadily fixed upon the object of our mission as the fugitive fixes his upon the North star." Douglass, as one of the "faithful advocates" of the Hundred Conventions tour, had played a crucial part in reaching and stirring the hearts and minds of thousands of people. Now he would return to Massachusetts where, once again, he would be called upon to awaken the interest of the people of the Bay State in the crusade to end slavery.[94]

Notes

1. The genesis of the Hundred Conventions tour can be traced to February 1843, when the executive committee of the Ohio Anti-Slavery Society invited Douglass, Bradburn, Remond, and Abby Kelley to organize a series of county conventions throughout the state beginning in June or July and ending in the fall. By the time of the American Anti-Slavery Society meeting in May, the plan had become more ambitious. During that meeting, a proposal was considered to hold a series of 100 conventions in the western states, but action on the proposal was postponed until the New England Anti-Slavery Society meeting later that month, at which time the tour was approved. The New England Anti-Slavery Society then authorized the board of managers of the Massachusetts Anti-Slavery Society "to take the necessary measures" to put the tour into operation. See the *Liberator*, 16 June 1843, 95; *National Anti-Slavery Standard*, 2 March 1843, 155; *Twelfth Annual Report, Presented to the board of managers, January 24, 1844* (1844; reprint, Westport, Conn.: Negro Universities Press, 1970), 34-35.

2. Blassingame, for example, includes the tour in his itinerary of Douglass' speaking activities, but he does not identify all the places visited and numerous times misdates meetings. Fulkerson provides an account of the campaign, but does not discuss its impact on Douglass' career or on his thinking about such issues as slave insurrection, political action, or abolitionism in general. McFeely identifies some of the places Douglass and his colleagues visited on the tour and discusses briefly its effect on Douglass' career. See John W. Blassingame, ed., *The Frederick Douglass Papers, Series One: Speeches, Debates, and Interviews, Volume 1* (New Haven, Conn.: Yale University Press, 1979), 1:xci-xcii; Raymond Gerald Fulkerson, "Frederick Douglass and the Anti-Slavery Crusade: His Career and Speeches, 1817-1861," Pt. 1 (Ph.D. diss., University of Illinois, 1971), 62-69; William S. McFeely, *Frederick Douglass* (New York: Norton, 1991), 104-13.

3. Blassingame, ed., *Douglass Papers, Series One*, 1:xci, does not include this meeting in its itinerary of Douglass' speaking activities.

4. *Herald of Freedom*, 23 June 1843, 71; Frederick Douglass to Abby Kelley, 19 June 1843, Kelley-Foster Papers, American Antiquarian Society.

5. Blassingame, ed., *Douglass Papers, Series One*, 1:xci, does not include this meeting in its itinerary of Douglass' speaking activities.

6. Ibid. does not include the Fall River lecture of 19 June in its itinerary of Douglass' speaking activities.

7. *The Morning Register* (New Bedford), 20 June 1843, 2; *Liberator*, 23 June 1843, 98; *Liberator*, 30 June 1843, 102; Frederick Douglass to Abby Kelley, 19 June 1843, Kelley-Foster Papers, American Antiquarian Society; *Daily Evening Bulletin* (New Bedford), 21 June 1843, 2. Blassingame, ed., *Douglass Papers, Series One*, 1:xci, incorrectly states that the 1843 New Bedford convention of 20-21 June met on 20 June only.

8. Blassingame, ed., *Douglass Papers, Series One*, 1:xci, incorrectly states that this convention met on 23 June only.

9. *Liberator*, 14 July 1843, 110.

10. Blassingame, ed., *Douglass Papers, Series One*, 1:xci, does not include this meeting in its itinerary of Douglass' speaking activities.

11. *Fall River Argus* in the *Liberator*, 7 July 1843, 106.

12. *Liberator*, 7 July 1843, 106.

13. Ibid.

14. *Liberator*, 14 July 1843, 111.

15. Frederick Douglass, *Life and Times of Frederick Douglass, Written by Himself* (1892; reprint, New York: Macmillan, 1962), 226; *Twelfth Annual Report*, 34-35; *Liberator*, 16 June 1843, 95.

16. Blassingame, ed., *Douglass Papers, Series One*, 1:xci, includes this meeting in its itinerary of Douglass' speaking activities, but does not indicate the date of the meeting.

17. For a brief account of the treatment Douglass received while a passenger on the stage to Vermont, see "I Am Here to Spread Light on American Slavery: An Address Delivered in Cork, Ireland, on 14 October 1845" in Blassingame, ed., *Douglass Papers, Series One*, 1:45.

18. Douglass, *Life and Times*, 226-27; *Liberator*, 16 June 1843, 95; Fulkerson, "Frederick Douglass," pt. 1, 63. Blassingame, ed., *Douglass Papers, Series One*, 1:xci, includes the Ferrisburg meeting in its itinerary of Douglass' speaking activities, but does not indicate its date.

19. Douglass, *Life and Times*, 227; *National Anti-Slavery Standard*, 27 July 1843, 30; *Liberator*, 4 August 1843, 121. Alvan Stewart was a lawyer and an abolitionist. Born in 1790 in South Granville, New York, he entered the University of Vermont in 1809. He left the university to teach in Canada, returning to the United States to study law. After earning a distinguished reputation as a lawyer, in 1834 he joined the American Anti-Slavery Society and immediately took the lead in establishing antislavery organizations throughout New York state. The next year, he led the effort to form the New York State Anti-Slavery Society and was elected its first president. An early proponent of an independent political party, Stewart joined Myron Holley, the leading political abolitionist in New York, in calling for an antislavery political convention. The convention met in Albany, New York, on 1 April 1840, with Stewart as presiding officer. The convention organized the Liberty Party and nominated Stewart for governor of New York and James G. Birney for president of the United States. Both men were defeated in the 1840 elections. See Dumas Malone, ed., *Dictionary of American Biography* (New York: Charles Scribner's Sons, 1936), 18:5; Luther R. Marsh, ed., *Writings and Speeches of Alvan Stewart, on Slavery* (1860; reprint, New York: Negro Universities Press, 1969), 10-11, 22; Gerald Sorin, *The New York Abolitionists: A Case Study of Political Radicalism* (Westport, Conn.: Greenwood, 1971), 47-52.

20. Blassingame, ed., *Douglass Papers, Series One*, 1:xci, does not include this meeting in its itinerary of Douglass' speaking activities.

21. *Herkimer Journal* quoted in the *Liberator*, 25 August 1843, 134.

22. Douglass, *Life and Times*, 227-28; Frederick Douglass to Maria Weston Chapman, 10 September 1843, Weston Family Papers, Boston Public Library; Frederick Douglass, "Reminiscences of the Anti-Slavery Struggle," in *The Papers of Frederick Douglass* (Washington, D.C.: Library of Congress Photoduplication Service, 1974), reel 18, frame 257; McFeely, *Frederick Douglass*, 104-5; *Liberator*, 21 July 1843, 115; Charles W. Chesnutt, *Frederick Douglass* (1899; reprint, New York: Johnson Reprint Company, 1971), 41.

23. Eunice Collins, wife of John A. Collins, reported to Maria Weston Chapman that her husband was suffering from "inflammation and pain in his side." His pain had become so intense that he was "obliged to keep perfectly quiet" and, therefore, could not speak in public (Eunice Collins to Maria Weston Chapman, 15 August 1843, Weston Family Papers, Boston Public Library).

24. Frederick Douglass to Maria Weston Chapman, 10 September 1843, Weston Family Papers, Boston Public Library.

25. Ibid.

26. Ibid.

27. Ibid.; Abby Kelley to Maria Weston Chapman, 2 August 1843, Weston Family Papers, Boston Public Library; Abby Kelley to Maria Weston Chapman, 28 August 1843, Weston Family Papers, Boston Public Library.

28. John A. Collins to Maria Weston Chapman, 23 August 1843, Weston Family Papers, Boston Public Library.

29. Maria Weston Chapman to Abby Kelley, 3 September 1843, Kelley-Foster Papers, American Antiquarian Society; Douglass, *Life and Times*, 228; Frederick Douglass to Maria Weston Chapman, 10 September 1843, Weston Family Papers, Boston Public Library; McFeely, *Frederick Douglass*, 104, 107-8; William H. Pease and Jane H. Pease, "Boston Garrisonians and the Problem of Frederick Douglass," *Canadian Journal of History* 2 (September 1967): 47-48.

30. Blassingame, ed., *Douglass Papers, Series One*, 1:xci, erroneously states that the Rochester meeting of 3-6 August met 3-5 August.

31. *Liberator*, 25 August 1843, 133, 135; *Liberator*, 1 September 1843, 139; Douglass, *Life and Times*, 227.

32. Douglass, *Life and Times*, 229; Bradburn to Francis Jackson, 14 August 1843, American Anti-Slavery Collection, Boston Public Library.

33. *Liberator*, 21 July 1843, 115; Douglass, *Life and Times*, 229.

34. Frederic May Holland, *Frederick Douglass: The Colored Orator* (New York: Funk and Wagnalls, 1891), 93-94. In early September 1846, Douglass shared the story of Sam with an English audience. See "A Simple Tale of American Slavery: An Address Delivered in Sheffield, England, on 11 September 1846," in Blassingame, ed., *Douglass Papers, Series One*, 1:405-6.

35. Douglass, *Life and Times*, 229; *Herald of Freedom*, 8 September 1843, 115; *Liberator*, 22 September 1843, 151; Raymond W. Logan and Michael R. Winston, eds., *Dictionary of American Negro Biography* (New York: Norton, 1982), 71; *William Edward Farrison, William Wells Brown, Author and Reformer* (Chicago: University of Chicago Press, 1969), 75-76, 78-79; Fulkerson, "Frederick Douglass," pt. 1, 64; Robert L. Heath, "William Wells Brown (c. 1814-1884), abolitionist, author," in *African-American Orators: A Biocritical Sourcebook*, ed., Richard W. Leeman (Westport, Conn.: Greenwood, 1996), 10-12.

36. *Liberator*, 1 September 1843, 139; *National Anti-Slavery Standard*, 10 August 1843, 38; Fulkerson, "Frederick Douglass," pt. 1, 64.

37. *Liberator*, 21 July 1843, 115; Howard H. Bell, *A Survey of the Negro Convention Movement, 1830-1860* (1953; reprint, New York: Arno Press, 1969), 71-72; "Minutes of the National Convention of Colored Citizens: Held at

Buffalo, on the 15th, 16th, 17th, 18th, and 19th of August, 1843," in *Minutes of the Proceedings of the National Conventions 1830-1864*, ed. Howard H. Bell (New York: Arno Press, 1964), 10; Carleton Mabee, *Black Freedom: The Non-Violent Abolitionists from 1830 Through the Civil War* (New York: Macmillan, 1970), 57-59. Boston's black citizens met in the Belknap Church on 20 July 1843. Before electing Douglass and Remond as delegates to the national convention, the meeting resolved that although they thought the convention was an "important movement," they "considered that such a convention should be a convention of the people, and not exclusively of any particular class." The time had come, they declared, "when all distinction, except that of a common humanity, should be abolished, especially among those who are uniting their energies in a warfare against oppression and injustice." In the end, they decided to participate in the convention "as a medium through which we may deliberately devise ways and means to operate and co-operate with our white friends, against two of the greatest evils ever inflicted upon an innocent and inoffensive people—slavery and prejudice" (*Liberator*, 4 August 1843, 122). Blacks in New Bedford met on 11 August 1843 at the Third Christian Church. After considerable debate they resolved not to send delegates to the convention, which they condemned as "a useless waste of time and money" because it "does not propose any measure to reach the cause of the evil; because it is exclusive in its character," and because "measures are now urged by the friends of freedom, which, if properly encouraged by the colored people, in common with the white people, will ultimately do away the necessity of calling conventions." They also expressed their unwillingness to be part of a convention that was organized by men who "went over to the new organization"—that is, men who seceded from the American Anti-Slavery Society in 1840 and formed the American and Foreign Anti-Slavery Society and endorsed the formation of the Liberty Party (*Liberator*, 25 August 1843, 135).

38. Blassingame, ed., *Douglass Papers, Series One*, 1:xci, incorrectly states that Douglass attended the Liberty Party Convention in Buffalo from 19-29 August. According to the *Liberator*, 15 September 1843, 147, Abby Kelley and Stephen S. Foster attended the Liberty Party meeting; there is no mention of Douglass attending.

39. For more on the Liberty Party and its roots in New York state, see Dwight Dumond, *Antislavery: The Crusade for Freedom in America* (New York: Norton, 1961), 286-87; Dwight Dumond, *Antislavery Origins of the Civil War* (Ann Arbor: University of Michigan Press, 1959), 87-88; William Goodell, *Slavery and Anti-Slavery; A History of the Great Struggle in Both Hemispheres; With a View of the Anti-Slavery Question in the United States* (New York, W. Goodell, 1853), 468-75; Theodore Clarke Smith, *The Liberty and Free Soil Parties in the Northwest* (New York: Russell and Russell, 1897), 27-68; Vernon L. Volpe, *Forlorn Hope of Freedom: The Liberty Party in the Old Northwest, 1838-1848* (Kent, Ohio: Kent State University Press, 1990), 34-35; Margaret L. Plunkett, "A History of the Liberty Party With Emphasis Upon its Activities in the Northwestern States" (Ph.D. diss., Cornell University, 1930), 56-93; Alan M. Kraut, "The Liberty Party Men of New York: Political

Abolitionism in New York State, 1840-1848" (Ph.D. diss., Cornell University, 1975); Reinhard O. Johnson, "The Liberty Party in New England, 1840-1848: The Forgotten Abolitionists" (Ph.D. diss., Syracuse University, 1976), 13-55.

40. Bell, *Minutes*, 4, 7-10; Bell, *Survey of the Negro Convention Movement*, 72-73.

41. Bell, *Minutes*, 11-12; Bell, *Survey of the Negro Convention Movement*, 76; Allen Johnson and Dumas Malone, eds., *Dictionary of American Biography* (New York: Charles Scribner's Sons, 1931), 7:154; Logan and Winston, eds., *Dictionary of American Negro Biography*, 252; Benjamin Quarles, *Black Abolitionists* (New York: Oxford University Press, 1969), 68, 184, 226; Joel Schor, *Henry Highland Garnet: A Voice of Black Radicalism in the Nineteenth Century* (Westport, Conn.: Greenwood, 1977), 4-16; Cynthia P. King, "Henry Highland Garnet (1815-1882), minister, abolitionist, U.S. ambassador," in Leeman, ed., *African-American Orators*, 143-44. Besides Garnet, the other seven black men among the founders of the American and Foreign Anti-Slavery Society were Rev. Jehiel Beman; his son Amos G. Beman, then on the verge of a successful career as a pastor of the Temple Street African Church in New Haven; Christopher Rush, second bishop of the African Methodist Episcopal Zion Church; and four Presbyterian ministers—Samuel E. Cornish, Theodore Wright, Stephen Gloucester, and Andrew Harris (Quarles, *Black Abolitionists*, 68).

42. *Walker's Appeal in Four Articles, David Walker. An Address to the Slaves of the United States of America, Henry Highland Garnet* (1848; reprint, New York: Arno Press, 1969), 94; Bell, *Survey of the Negro Convention Movement*, 76; Mabee, *Black Freedom*, 60.

43. *Walker's Appeal*, 96.

44. Bell, *Minutes*, 12-13; *Emancipator and Free American*, 12 October 1843, 96.

45. Bell, *Minutes*, 13-14, 18-19; Quarles, *Black Abolitionists*, 226. Toward the end of the convention, a resolution was passed calling for a reconsideration of the vote. Douglass once again spoke forcefully against Garnet's address, which was rejected by a vote of 14-9 (Bell, *Minutes*, 23-24). Maria Weston Chapman applauded the convention's action which, she wrote in the *Liberator*, was a sign of "love, forgiveness, and magnanimity." The person "who imagines that a civil and servile war would ultimately promote freedom knows nothing of nature, human or divine, of character, good or evil" (*Liberator*, 22 September 1843, 151).

46. Douglass, *Life and Times*, 226; Leslie Friedman Goldstein, "Morality and Prudence in the Statesmanship of Frederick Douglass: Radical as Reformer," *Polity* 16 (summer 1984): 608.

47. Bell, *Minutes*, 15-16; Bell, *Survey of the Negro Convention Movement*, 74-75; *Liberator*, 8 September 1843, 142. Later in the convention, the issue was raised again and, despite objections from Douglass, Remond, and Brown, the delegates once more endorsed the Liberty Party, which stood for allowing the vote to all free men regardless of color (Bell, *Minutes*, 21-22). The convention's endorsement of the Liberty Party and its rejection of Garnet's address reflected sharply diverging views as to the best means to end slavery in the United

States. For thoughtful analysis of these views, see Joel Schor, "The Rivalry Between Frederick Douglass and Henry Highland Garnet," *Journal of Negro History* 64 (winter 1979): 30-32.

48. Bell, *Minutes*, 15-16, 19-22, 25, 27.

49. *National Anti-Slavery Standard*, 7 September 1843, 55; *Buffalo Daily Gazette*, 18 August 1843, 3. Maria Weston Chapman wrote in the *Liberator*: "Much as Messrs. Douglass and Remond have been missed by the friends of Ohio, it seems hardly to be regretted that they yielded to their desire of attending" the National Negro Convention, "where they did so much good" (*Liberator*, 22 September 1843, 151).

50. *Liberator*, 22 September 1843, 151; *National Anti-Slavery Standard*, 10 August 1843, 38. Blassingame, ed., *Douglass Papers, Series One*, 1:xci, incorrectly states that Douglass spoke in Green Plain, Ohio, on 30-31 August. Because Douglass did not leave Buffalo until 1 September, he could not have been in Green Plain on 30 August.

51. Blassingame, ed., *Douglass Papers, Series One*, 1:xci, erroneously locates Douglass in Oakland on 4 September in its itinerary of Douglass' speaking activities.

52. *Liberator*, 22 September 1843, 151.

53. *Clinton Republican* quoted in the *Liberator*, 13 October 1843, 162.

54. Douglass, "Reminiscences of the Anti-Slavery Struggle," reel 18, frame 257.

55. Although there are no surviving minutes from the proceedings in Cambridge, the stop was scheduled well in advance and there is every reason to believe that Douglass had rejoined his companions by this time.

56. Blassingame, ed., *Douglass Papers, Series One*, 1:xci, inaccurately dates the Richmond meeting of 13 September as taking place on 28-29 September in its itinerary of Douglass' speaking activities. By the end of September, Douglass had returned to Ohio to lecture in Clinton County.

57. *Liberator*, 22 September 1843, 151; Douglass, *Life and Times*, 230; *Liberator*, 13 October 1843, 163.

58. Douglass, *Life and Times*, 230; Fulkerson, "Frederick Douglass," pt. 1, 66; *Liberator*, 22 September 1843, 151; *Liberator*, 13 October 1843, 163; *National Anti-Slavery Standard*, 19 October 1843, 78.

59. *Liberator*, 13 October 1843, 163; *National Anti-Slavery Standard*, 19 October 1843, 78; Douglass, *Life and Times*, 230; Lloyd Lewis, "Quaker Memories of Frederick Douglass," *Negro Digest* 5 (September 1947): 38.

60. *Liberator*, 13 October 1843, 163; *National Anti-Slavery Standard*, 19 October 1843, 78.

61. Ibid.

62. *Liberator*, 13 October 1843, 163; *Herald of Freedom*, 20 October 1843, 138; *National Anti-Slavery Standard*, 19 October 1843, 78.

63. *National Anti-Slavery Standard*, 19 October 1843, 78; Douglass, *Life and Times*, 231; John L. Forkner and Bryon H. Dyson, eds., *Historical Sketches and Reminiscences of Madison County* (Logansport, Ind.: Press of Wilson, Humphreys and Co., 1897), 751; Robert C. Smedley, *History of the Underground Railroad in Chester and the Neighboring Counties of Pennsylvania* (1883; reprint, New York: Negro Universities Press, 1968), 187. For other accounts of this incident, see *History of Madison County Indiana: A Narrative Account of its Historical Progress, Its People and Its Principal Interests, Volume 1*, comp. John L. Forkner, (Chicago: Lewis Publishing Company, 1914), 1:71-72; J. J. Netterville, *Centennial History of Madison Co., Indiana, Volume 1* (Anderson, Ind.: Historians' Association, 1925), 1:321-22; *History of Madison County, Indiana from 1820 to 1874*, comp. Samuel J. Harden (Markleville, Ind.: n.p., 1874), 203-5.

64. Frederick Douglass to William A. White, Edinburgh, Scotland, 30 July 1846, in *The Papers of Frederick Douglass*, reel 1, frame 622.

65. Joseph Borome, ed., "Two Letters of Frederick Douglass," *Journal of Negro History* 33 (October 1848): 470-71.

66. Blassingame, ed., *Douglass Papers, Series One*, 1:xcii, states that the meeting in Noblesville occurred on 18 September. While this is plausible, William White's report on the Pendleton meeting stated that Douglass was able to lecture the day after he was assaulted. If White is correct, his account would date the Noblesville meeting as being on 17 September, the day after the incident at Pendleton. See the *Herald of Freedom*, 20 October 1843, 138.

67. *Liberator*, 20 October 1843, 168; Abraham Brooke to Maria Weston Chapman, 5 October 1843, Weston Family Papers, Boston Public Library.

68. In Douglass' version of the incident, as reported by Brooke to Chapman, Remond "neither called the chair a jackass nor the people monkies" (Abraham Brooke to Maria Weston Chapman, 10 October 1843, Weston Family Papers, Boston Public Library).

69. *Liberator*, 20 October 1843, 168; Abraham Brooke to Maria Weston Chapman, 5 October 1843, Weston Family Papers, Boston Public Library; Abraham Brooke to Maria Weston Chapman, 10 October 1843, Weston Family Papers, Boston Public Library; Fulkerson, "Frederick Douglass," pt. 1, 67.

70. Abraham Brooke to Maria Weston Chapman, 5 October 1843, Weston Family Papers, Boston Public Library; Fulkerson, "Frederick Douglass," pt. 1, 67-68; McFeely, *Frederick Douglass*, 112-13.

71. Blassingame, ed., *Douglass Papers, Series One*, 1:xci, identifies Douglass as attending a convention at Richmond, Indiana, on 28 September in its itinerary of Douglass' activities. As we saw earlier, however, the Richmond convention took place on 13 September.

72. Abraham Brooke to Maria Weston Chapman, 5 October 1843, Weston Family Papers, Boston Public Library; Fulkerson, "Frederick Douglass," pt. 1, 67. McFeely, *Frederick Douglass*, 113, incorrectly asserts that Douglass and Remond broke away from the Hundred Conventions tour after the Jonesboro

incident. Douglass temporarily left the tour to lecture in Clinton County, Ohio, while Remond remained with it and traveled with Gay and Monroe on their scheduled stops in Indiana. See Sydney Howard Gay to William Lloyd Garrison, 5 October 1843, in the *Liberator*, 20 October 1843, 168.

73. Abraham Brooke to Maria Weston Chapman, 10 October 1843, Weston Family Papers, Boston Public Library.

74. The final convention of the Indiana leg of the Hundred Conventions tour was held at Liberty on 2-3 October (*Liberator*, 22 September 1843, 151).

75. Blassingame, ed., *Douglass Papers, Series One*, 1:xci, does not include this meeting in its itinerary of Douglass' speaking activities.

76. *Cincinnati Philanthropist* in the *Liberator*, 8 December 1843, 196.

77. *New Lisbon Advocate* in the *Liberator*, 17 November 1843, 182.

78. George Bradburn to John A. Collins, 22 November 1843, quoted in Benjamin Quarles, *Frederick Douglass* (1948; reprint, New York: Atheneum, 1968), 33.

79. For the complete itinerary of conventions scheduled in Pennsylvania, see the *National Anti-Slavery Standard*, 26 October 1843, 83.

80. Blassingame, ed., *Douglass Papers, Series One*, 1:xci, includes the New Brighton meeting of 3-4 November in its itinerary of Douglass' activities, but does not identify its date.

81. *National Anti-Slavery Standard*, 26 October 1843, 83; *Liberator*, 8 December 1843, 194.

82. *Liberator*, 8 December 1843, 194.

83. Ibid. In the evening, Douglass delivered a lecture on "prejudice against color," which, according to Townsend, "was a masterly effort" (Ibid.).

84. *Pittsburgh Spirit of Liberty* in the *Liberator*, 24 November 1843, 186. Blassingame, ed., *Douglass Papers, Series One*, 1:xci, includes the Pittsburgh meetings in its itinerary of Douglass' activities, but he does not identify their dates.

85. *Pittsburgh Spirit of Liberty* in the *Liberator*, 24 November 1843, 186.

86. At the time of Douglass' speech, Webster was demanding restitution from the British government for the slaves that had been freed after their rebellion on board the *Creole*. See the *National Era* (Washington, D.C.), 28 July 1853.

87. *National Era*, 28 July 1853.

88. George Bradburn to John A. Collins, 21 November 1843, American Anti-Slavery Collection, Boston Public Library; *New Lisbon Aurora* in the *Liberator*, 8 December 1843, 196. Blassingame, ed., *Douglass Papers, Series One*, 1:xci, does not include the Fallston meeting in its itinerary of Douglass' speaking activities.

89. Bradburn complained about Douglass traveling independently from the Hundred Conventions tour and not keeping his scheduled appointments: "All along this State [Pennsylvania], as elsewhere, our friends complain of being

made to lie to the people, in announcing Douglass for our meeting. The truth is, neither Douglass nor Remond seems to have given himself any more concern about the appointments made for him, than as if none had been made" (George Bradburn to John A. Collins, 21 November 1843, American Anti-Slavery Collection, Boston Public Library).

90. *National Anti-Slavery Standard*, 14 December 1843, 110.

91. *National Anti-Slavery Standard*, 16 November 1843, 94-95; *Liberator*, 1 December 1843, 191; McFeely, *Frederick Douglass*, 113; Quarles, *Black Abolitionists*, 23-24, 145, 148, 155.

92. *National Anti-Slavery Standard*, 14 December 1843, 110.

93. *Philadelphia Weekly Cultivator* in the *Liberator*, 22 December 1843, 202.

94. *Twelfth Annual Report*, 34, 37; *Liberator*, 22 December 1843, 203; *Liberator*, 19 January 1844, 11.

𝒞𝒽𝒶𝓅𝓉𝑒𝓇 𝒮𝑒𝓋𝑒𝓃

The Hundred Conventions Tour of Massachusetts: Torrents of Eloquence, January-May 1844

THE HUNDRED CONVENTIONS tour of the West was so successful that in January 1844 the Massachusetts Anti-Slavery Society decided a similar campaign should be organized to canvass the central counties of Massachusetts. The leadership of the society planned to carry out approximately 100 conventions by sending five teams of lecturers to tour the state simultaneously. Frederick Douglass was among the lecturers hired to conduct the tour, which began in mid-February.[1] In the interim, he undertook a brief series of abolitionist lectures in New Hampshire. Although Douglass did not mention either his brief lecture tour of New Hampshire or the Hundred Conventions tour of Massachusetts in any of his autobiographies, it is possible to reconstruct his itinerary and activities from newspaper reports, journal accounts, and letters written to the *Liberator*. These sources capture vividly the details of Douglass' rhetorical efforts during the first five months of 1844. As we shall see, these sources document clearly the rhetorical artistry and eloquence of his message and the profound impact it had on audiences during this period, a period that has been largely ignored by students of Douglass and his oratory.[2]

I

After the December 1843 anniversary meeting of the American Anti-Slavery Society in Philadelphia, Douglass returned home to Lynn, Massachusetts, to rest and enjoy some time with his family. In late January 1844 he attended the twelfth annual meeting of the Massachusetts Anti-Slavery Society in Boston. The "superbly attended" three-day convention began in Faneuil Hall on Wednesday, 24 January.[3] Douglass, perhaps still fatigued from the Hundred Conventions tour of the West, spoke only once during the first day's sessions, commenting briefly on a resolution presented by William Lloyd Garrison on behalf of the business committee condemning the proslavery character of the American church. The following morning Douglass addressed the meeting in support of a group of resolutions calling on the board of managers of the society to "make immediate provision for a series of ONE HUNDRED CONVENTIONS" to be held within the State of Massachusetts "during the present winter and ensuing spring." The resolutions were discussed and adopted by the convention. This act, the *Liberator* reported, "constituted the great practical measure of the occasion. It was heard with joy, and responded to in a manner that evinced but 'one heart and one mind' on the part of the delegates, and a determination to carry it but to the letter, in revolutionary style." Throughout the remainder of the convention, Douglass sat silently as resolutions denouncing political action, proclaiming the proslavery nature of the Constitution, and advocating the dissolution of the Union were debated.[4]

Immediately following the meeting, the board of managers set to work organizing the Hundred Conventions tour of Massachusetts. Its plan was "to unite economy and despatch with thorough and energetic action" by arranging to have five series of conventions occurring simultaneously, with each series being conducted by at least three lecturers. Each group of lecturers was expected to hold three two-day conventions per week. Their mission was to "awaken the old, and create a new anti-slavery zeal throughout the commonwealth." The board "secured the services of the ablest and most devoted agents they could procure, and sent them into the field with the least possible loss of time." Among those invited to participate in the tour were Douglass, Abby Kelley, Charles Lenox Remond, Stephen S. Foster, Parker Pillsbury, Erasmus D. Hudson, William A. White, John M. Spear, Sydney Howard Gay, George W. Stacy, and James N. Buffum.[5]

Douglass received his formal invitation early in February, in a letter from Wendell Phillips, the new general agent of the Massachusetts Anti-Slavery Society.[6] Before responding in the affirmative to Phillips' invitation, however, Douglass wished "to say a word" about two points in the letter. The first related "to the principle upon which compensation" was to be "rendered to agents." Douglass insisted that the sum to be paid to each agent be made definite. "If I am to have 7—or 8 Dolls. per week," he stated, "I should have that and no more. If 7 Dolls. is sufficient for an agent—more is superfluous—and ought not to be given." Douglass also insisted that the Massachusetts Anti-Slavery Society pay each agent equally. "I would not consent to work side by side" with another agent "paying the same for the necessaries [of] life—laboring as hard as myself," he wrote, "and yet for his labor getting less than myself. Nor could I on the other hand be satisfied with a reversed arrangement by which I should have less than an equal fellow laborer."[7]

Douglass' second concern related to Phillips' expectation that "due prominence . . . be given to the subject of [the] liberty party." Douglass responded strongly to this demand:

> Now if by this it is meant that we are to make the liberty party as such a special object of attack, candor compels me to confess I am not a suitable person to be engaged in your service carrying on the one hundred conventions. But if it means that I must as freely and faithfully expose the corruption of the 3d party and its leaders—as I would expose the same in either of the great political parties—I most heartily agree with yourself and the committee.[8]

Douglass' letter to Phillips is significant because it reveals that Douglass was now in a position within abolitionist ranks to call into question the terms of his employment as a lecturer. Equally important, the letter discloses both Douglass' belief in equal pay for equal work and his rhetorical approach to the Liberty Party and its leaders.

Having communicated his concerns, Douglass concluded his letter by accepting Phillips' invitation to join the tour. I "will gladly serve the cause under your direction," he wrote, "if it shall be your pleasure to employ me."[9] In turn, Phillips assigned Douglass to team with Pillsbury and White. They would begin their four-month campaign in Middlesex and Norfolk Counties in mid-February.[10]

Before leaving on the Massachusetts tour, however, Douglass traveled to New Hampshire to deliver a series of antislavery lectures. On Sunday, 11 February, he presented two speeches at Concord. Nathaniel P. Rogers, editor of the *Herald of Freedom*, attended both and reported on the proceedings. Rogers' descriptive accounts of Douglass' speeches give us a richer, more distinct view of his oratory during this time period than we have had before. In his report, published in the *Herald of Freedom* of 16 February, Rogers presented a detailed description of Douglass' platform presence, his antislavery message, his manner of delivery, and his power over listeners.[11]

Before Douglass' arrival in Concord, Rogers wrote, every meetinghouse "shut up their clean and comfortable synagogues" against the abolitionists. Consequently, the meeting was forced to convene in the "cold and noisy" Court House, where Douglass was forced to speak "in an inconvenient, uncomfortable room." As cold and unfriendly as the churches of the city were toward Douglass' visit, however, his reception by the people of Concord was warm and friendly and, according to Rogers, "there was great curiosity to see him, and hear his eloquence."[12]

On Sunday afternoon, Rogers reported, "Douglass spoke excellently . . . to a pretty numerous audience" on the proslavery church. In Rogers' report of this meeting, he paraphrased Douglass' message and, at times, quoted his words directly. According to Rogers, Douglass began by asserting that he had been advertised as a "fugitive *from* slavery." Unhappy with the wording of the advertisement, Douglass declared "he was not a fugitive *from* slavery—but a fugitive *slave*. He was a fugitive, he said, not *from* slavery—but *in* slavery. To get from it—he must go beyond the limits of the American Union."[13] Douglass then asked his auditors "why it was that he—such as they saw him before them, must wander about in their midst, a *fugitive* and a *slave*. He *demanded* the reason." In providing a reply, Douglass launched a stinging attack on the audience: "It is because of your Religion . . . which sanctifies the system under which I suffer, and dooms me to it, and the millions of my brethren now in bondage." He continued by aligning his listeners with southern slaveholders:

> Your religion justifies our tyrants, and you are yourselves our enslavers. I see my enslavers here in Concord, and before my eyes—if any are here who countenance the church and the religion of your country. Other influences helped sustain the system of slavery . . . but this is its sanctioner and main support.[14]

From Douglass' perspective, organized religion as practiced by whites throughout the country—North and South—constituted the bulwark of American slavery. Accordingly, he accused the members of his audience who supported the church as being the sustainers of slavery. He branded them as slaveholders and made them morally responsible for his enslavement and for the enslavement of his brethren in bonds. In so doing, he made the slaveholder visible and the system of slavery immediate for his auditors in Concord.

In the evening, Douglass returned to the Court House and delivered, according to Rogers, "a masterly and most impressive speech" to a crowded house. He began with "a calm, deliberate and very simple narrative of his life. He did not detail personal sufferings—though he said he might—if inclined to." Rogers recounted Douglass' remarks as follows:

> He, to be sure, had to go naked, pretty much during the earlier years of childhood, and feed at a trough like a pig, under the care of his old grandmother [Betsy Bailey], who, past her labor, was turned out, charged to dig her own subsistence, and that of a few little ones, out of a patch of ground allotted her. These little ones were separated from their mothers, that they might early be without ties of kindred. He did not remember his mother, I think he said, and never knew who was his father. He never knew in his first six years anything about a bed—any more than the pigs did. He remembered stealing an old salt bag, into which he used to creep,

and sleep, on the earth floor of the negro hut, at his old grandmother's. She, by the way, had reared twelve children of her own,
for the market—all sold and gone from her—and she now blind
and alone, if she is alive, and none left with her to bring her a cup
of cold water. His own back he said was scarred with the whip—
but still he had been a favored slave. He was sent to a slave-break-
er, when some 16 or 17 years old—his master not being able to
manage him. An attempt at breaking him once brought on a struggle between him and the Jockey [Edward Covey]. The result of it
was such that the Jockey did not care to repeat it, while his care
for his reputation, as a successful breaker, kept him from getting
help to manage a slave boy—and Frederick escaped farther whipping from him afterwards. After narrating his early life briefly—his
schooling—the beginning of the wife of his master's relative to
teach him letters, and the stern forbidding of it, by her husband—
which Frederick overheard—how he caught a little teaching here
and there from the children in the streets . . . after getting through
this, in a somewhat suppressed and hesitating way—interesting all
the while for its facts, but dullish in manner . . . he closed his slave
narrative.[15]

   Here, in capsule form, are many of the key incidents of Douglass' early
life that, in 1845, would find their way into his first autobiography,
*Narrative of the Life of Frederick Douglass, An American Slave, Written
By Himself*. Although Douglass did not provide names, places, and dates
from his slave past during his speech at Concord, he did present the most
disclosive and descriptive account of his slave experience available in his
speeches up to this time. Rogers' report provides evidence that Douglass'
message began to undergo a significant transformation in 1844.
Throughout 1844 Douglass gradually increased the length and descriptive-
ness of his slave narrative. Indeed, he may have been forced to. As his message became increasingly polished and eloquent, he needed to provide
more information about his slave past to quiet doubts that he had ever
been a slave. In Concord, he was most likely responding to his audience's
demand for specifics about his slave experience—specifics he had previously withheld to protect himself from being returned to his slave master.
   As Douglass concluded the narrative of his slave experience, Rogers
"discerned, at times, symptoms of a brewing storm" as Douglass "gradually let out the outraged humanity that was laboring in him, in indignant and
terrible speech." The closing section of Douglass' lecture, Rogers declared,
"was unrivalled." Indeed, he could offer his readers "no adequate description of it." He had "heard the leading anti-slavery speakers, as well as the
pro-slavery orators, and the great advocates at the bar," Rogers explained,

but he had "never seen a man leave the platform, or close a speech, with more real dignity and eloquent majesty." Calling up all his linguistic resources, Rogers tried to capture in words Douglass' rhetorical power:

It was not what you could describe as oratory or eloquence. It was sterner—darker—deeper than these. It was the volcanic outbreak of human nature long pent up in slavery and at last bursting its imprisonment. It was the storm of insurrection—and I could not but think, as he stalked to and fro on the platform, roused up like the Numidian Lion—how that terrible voice of his would ring through the pine glades of the South, in the day of her visitation—calling the insurgents to battle and striking terror to the hearts of the dismayed and despairing mastery. . . .

There was great oratory in his speech—but more of dignity and earnestness than what we call eloquence. He was not up as a speaker—performing. He was an insurgent slave taking hold on the right of speech, and charging on his tyrants the bondage of his race.[16]

Stephen S. Foster followed Douglass to the stand, but Rogers declared that he "was sorry he did," for Douglass "ought not to have been followed at all. That speech ought to have been the last, for the time. It could not well be surpassed, and if it could be equalled, it was not needed." Deeply affected by Douglass' address, Rogers wanted others to experience his eloquence. "I want the people of New-Hampshire to know him, and to hear him," Rogers wrote, "for their sakes, and for the cause. He is one of the most impressive and majestic speakers I have ever heard."[17]

After the Concord meetings, Douglass joined Parker Pillsbury for a brief lecture tour of New Hampshire. Their itinerary included Bradford, New London, Henniker, Milford, Nashua, New-Market, Dover, and Great Falls.[18] Unfortunately, the tour went largely unreported. The only information we have about these meetings comes from the town of Bradford, where Douglass and Pillsbury reportedly had "crowded meetings."[19] On Tuesday evening, 20 February, Douglass returned alone to Concord to deliver a lecture at the Court Room. His last meeting in New Hampshire before returning to Massachusetts did not go well. "Unusual influences were exerted and unusual inducements felt," a correspondent reported to the *Herald of Freedom*, "to keep from the meeting, and prevent the people from attending." As a result, a small audience attended the lecture.[20]

II

On Thursday, 22 February, Douglass joined the Hundred Conventions tour of Massachusetts at Lowell, where the two-day event "was attended by crowded audiences, and excited a very lively sensation throughout the town—especially in consequence of a resolution being offered . . . reflecting in severe terms on the Rev. Messrs. Naylor and Hanks, for refusing to read a notice of the Convention from their pulpits."[21] The first day's meetings were held in the "grand, airy and spacious" City Hall. During the morning session, Nathaniel P. Rogers presented a resolution denouncing the two ministers who withheld announcing the convention. Douglass was among the speakers who participated in the debate over the resolution. In the evening, White, Garrison, Douglass, Collins, and Pillsbury "made capital speeches" to a crowded house. During the evening session there was "considerable hissing," Rogers reported in the *Herald of Freedom*, "but when it was distinctly admitted they had the right of hissing, they forbore the exercise and listened kindly to the speakers."[22]

Friday's meetings were held in the Colburn Street Chapel, where the "character of political action was largely discussed during the day." Rogers reported that Garrison "showed strongly and conclusively the illiberal character of the 3d Party movement in Massachusetts" and its "unprincipled origin" in the American and Foreign Anti-Slavery Society. Douglass followed Garrison to the platform. On this issue, at least, he and Garrison disagreed. From his travels in the West, Douglass had learned that not all supporters of the Liberty Party were affiliated with the American and Foreign Anti-Slavery Society. He realized that Liberty Party supporters could still be strong abolitionists, and he made an "able" effort to defend the Liberty Party. During his speech, Rogers reported, he "endeavored strenuously to distinguish Western 3d Party, from that of Massachusetts, and with some degree of success." In New England, Douglass argued, political abolition's main purpose was to put down women and Garrisonism, whereas in the West, its overriding purpose was to end slavery through balloting and legislation. Douglass' willingness to debate Garrison, the leader of the antislavery movement in New England, on this issue demonstrated his confidence and independence of mind. At this stage of his career, he was unwilling to eliminate any means that could lead to the abolition of slavery—even if those means did not conform strictly with Garrisonian principles. Although he would change his position on the Liberty Party by the end of 1844, at the beginning of the year, he was reluctant to dismiss out of hand all Liberty Party supporters.[23]

In the evening, the abolitionists met in the new Universalist Church. "It was a magnificent temple and very honorably and magnanimously opened," Rogers observed. The meeting was "thronged to overflowing" and remained in session until almost midnight. Pillsbury spoke first and "made a very able speech on the nature of the anti-slavery movement." Garrison then took the pulpit and "read the sentence of death just passed by a Carolina Judge on a young man named Brown, for slave stealing." His remarks, Rogers wrote, "made a deep and hushing impression on the vast audience." Lunsford Lane, the former slave, next addressed the meeting. He was followed by Douglass, who "poured forth a tide of outraged feeling at the slave system and the cruel and barbarous indifference of the people of the North."[24] According to Rogers, Douglass declared that he, unlike Lane, was still a slave and a fugitive liable at any moment to be captured and returned to the South. Because Douglass' remarks at Lowell are not included in any historical record of his oratory, they deserve to be presented here in their entirety:

> Lunsford Lane, he [Douglass] said, had spoken of his escape from slavery and the rescue of his wife and children. He, he cried, was still a *slave*. He stood before them, a SLAVE. And while he was speaking, liable, without the possibility of protection—every moment, to be taken and bound there before their eyes, and carried back to the mercy of his enraged master—to be scourged, and consigned to the sugar service of the far South. And it would not be in the power of all Lowell to protect him from being carried off from their midst. Yes, yes it would, they cried from various parts of the house. No, no, my friends, said Douglass, gravely and calmly—your constitution and your army are stronger than you.[25]

The following morning, Douglass, White, Pillsbury, and Lane conducted an antislavery meeting in Groton.[26] Their reception was less than enthusiastic. A disappointed Douglass wrote to Garrison that "Groton abolitionism is not where it once was" and had virtually abandoned "all moral and religious reform." White reported to the *Liberator* that many of Groton's "best abolitionists" had become Millerites and had "lost their interest in the cause." "It was truly chilling, on the morning of our meeting," Douglass wrote, "to look around on the empty seats in that hall, once thronged with warm hearts and cheerful faces." Douglass informed Garrison that during the opening session of the convention he "made a few remarks on the state of our cause in that place" and the meeting adjourned until 2 o'clock in the afternoon. During the afternoon session, White addressed a "considerably larger" gathering for an hour and a half, after which Douglass offered "a few words." The evening session, Douglass observed, "was quite well attended and was somewhat interesting." On Sunday evening, Douglass was invited to lecture at the Baptist Church which, White reported, "was crowded full" to hear him "hold up the sins of the church of this country with regard to the slave."[27]

On Monday afternoon, 26 February, Douglass, White, and Lunsford Lane began a two-day convention at the Christian Baptist Church in Townsend.[28] (Pillsbury, too sick to travel, had left the tour at Groton to return home to Concord, New Hampshire.) From all accounts, the Townsend meeting went quite well and, in Douglass' words, "did much to set our cause right in that place." White reported to the *Liberator* that on the first day of the meeting, "a party of friends from New Hampshire" joined the proceedings. On the morning of the second day, a group of approximately thirty to forty people attended from nearby Fitchburgh and, according to White, "gave quite an interest to our meeting." All in all, the proceedings were well attended "and a good spirit pervaded the meeting."[29]

On Tuesday evening, as Douglass, White, and Lane prepared to leave Townsend for a one-day meeting that was scheduled to begin at Action the following morning, a "blocking snow-storm" closed the roads and prevented the lecturers from traveling. They finally started their journey to Action on Wednesday morning, but with the "roads being next to impassable," they did not reach their destination until between 8 and 9 p.m. and were forced to cancel their meetings. Nevertheless, White wrote positively about the progress of the tour. "The meetings, so far, have been most encouraging," he reported to the *Liberator*, "as we have been in one of the hardest parts of the State. We have got people out, who never heard an anti-slavery lecture before. Wherever we have been, we have been kindly received."[30]

On Friday, 1 March, Douglass, Lane, and George Latimer traveled east to Bedford to hold a two-day meeting.[31] A letter written by an abolitionist in Bedford and published in the *Liberator* testifies to the impression made by Douglass and his colleagues. "They came to enlighten us upon the great subject of slavery," the correspondent wrote, "and their visit was very much needed; for the people here seemed to be grossly ignorant of the awful injustice we are constantly practising upon our colored countrymen." Of all the lecturers, the correspondent reported, Douglass made far and away the greatest impression as he inspired the audience with "mingled feelings of awe and delight." According to the correspondent, Douglass

arose and addressed us with a voice, the slightest tone of which is sufficient to command the attention of any one capable of appreciating this truly noble man. He spoke calmly and deliberately at first; but as he went on, his soul kindling as the subject opened before him, his voice grew louder, clearer, and deeper—his whole frame seemed to expand, while he poured forth the feeling of his 'mighty heart,' in a torrent of eloquence, loftier and more powerful than I have ever before listened to. . . . I can only say, God be thanked, that he has raised up such a powerful champion for the distressed. Coming as he does from that deeply injured and downtrodden portion of the human family, it is astonishing to see how he has risen superior to all surrounding circumstances, and stands before the world to teach us all that is noble, generous, and good.[32]

Douglass' belief that if the American people could "know slavery as I knew it, they would hasten to the work of its extinction" was, at least in this instance, being realized. Indeed, a resident of Bedford informed Garrison in late April that the "breath of antislavery life" Douglass had inspired in Bedford during the March convention had "not died out" and was "still at work."[33]

After lecturing "to a good audience" in Concord, New Hampshire, on Sunday evening, 3 March, Douglass rejoined Latimer and Lane on 4 March for a scheduled two-day meeting at Sudbury.[34] "Of all the dark places in Massachusetts," Douglass wrote to Garrison, "this is the darkest." The traveling lecturers found it impossible to organize a meeting. "The clergy here," Douglass complained, bear "almost entire sway. They decide for the people what they shall hear, and what they shall not hear." The ministers in Sudbury, Douglass continued, "devoted a good part of the last Sabbath in warning their congregations against attending our meeting!" As a result, Douglass and his companions were threatened with mob violence if they attempted to convene a meeting. "We should not . . . be intimidated by that," Douglass declared, "if we could get the people out. But this we cannot do, and must, therefore, pass this place by, at least for the present."[35]

Douglass and Lane next carried the Hundred Conventions campaign to Framingham, where they were joined by Garrison and James N. Buffum for a two-day convention on 6-7 March.[36] Framingham, too, would prove a difficult town for the abolitionists. Prior to the lecturers' arrival, the Reverend David Brigham had warned the people to stay away from their meetings. As a result, "scarcely any of the inhabitants of the place attended," a correspondent reported to the *Liberator*, except "a gang of profligate rowdies, who appeared in defense of the said Brigham in particular, and of the churches generally." The mob did their best to disrupt the convention. Determined not to be intimidated, however, the abolitionists met both days and passed resolutions condemning the conduct of Reverend Brigham and denouncing the mobocratic spirit of those who sought to disrupt their meeting. The convention also passed resolutions proclaiming that the American clergy were the most formidable adversaries of the antislavery movement and declaring that the main goal of the Massachusetts Anti-Slavery Society was to end slavery and was not, as Brigham had charged, to "overthrow Christian institutions."[37]

From Framingham, Douglass and Lane traveled east to Needham, where they held a one-day convention on 8 March.[38] On 11 March the two men journeyed to Medford, where Wendell Phillips and Parker Pillsbury joined them for a one-day convention that, unlike the meetings at Sudbury and Framingham, attracted a large audience and was warmly received. "The resolutions introduced were most uncompromising," Pillsbury reported to Garrison, "and the discussions were mainly by Phillips, Douglass, and

Lunsford Lane, which is sufficient assurance that they were of the highest order." During the evening session, Pillsbury noted, Phillips and Douglass spoke "with surprising force and power of reasoning" and the audience "listened with almost breathless attention, until between 10 and 11 at night."[39]

After holding meetings at Waltham on 13-14 March and at Dorchester on 15-16 March, Douglass and his colleagues traveled to Dedham, where they held a two-day convention at the Town Hall on Monday and Tuesday, 18 and 19 March.[40] Although attendance at the first session was so small, reported the *Dedham American*, that "the spirit of the abolitionists sank within them," Douglass, Pillsbury, White, Garrison, and others poured out "their vials of wrath" upon "the pro-slavery character of Dedham" and specifically upon "the position of the clergy and the politicians." Douglass and his companions must have spoken forcefully, for the correspondent to the local newspaper noted that "a stranger of this place would have supposed, to hear these fellows talk, that Dedham was indeed a second Sodom, and her inhabitants deserving of a second storm of fire and brimstone." During the morning and afternoon sessions of the second day, the convention turned to "a spirited discussion respecting the whig and democratic parties, Henry Clay and Martin Van Buren, . . . and the annexation of Texas." Upon reconvening for the evening session, however, a correspondent reported to the *Liberator*, the meeting "was almost constantly interrupted, in an indecent, profane and mobocratic manner, by a considerable number of rowdies, who piously came to rescue the clergy and the church." The mob "swore that they would not 'stand such damned nonsense,' nor allow such 'rascally charges' to be brought against the divine order." Doing their best to disrupt the meeting, the mob "hissed, stamped, yelled, threatened, raved, and gloried in their shame." Unlike some antiabolitionist groups, however, this one remained nonviolent, and Douglass and his colleagues carried on with their scheduled agenda, discussing and passing resolutions condemning the church and clergy.[41]

Following the convention in Dedham, the band of itinerant lecturers traveled to Braintree on 20-21 March and Foxboro on 22-23 March for a series of meetings.[42] On Sunday evening, 24 March, Douglass addressed the people of Walpole in the vestry of the Unitarian Church. Although he was "worn down by previous exertions" and had to shorten his lecture, a correspondent reported to the *Liberator*, he still "contrived to compress a good deal of truth into a short space." The audience listened attentively, the correspondent observed, "and manifested a willingness to hear more."[43]

The next day, Douglass, Pillsbury, and White traveled to Medway for a two-day meeting and then journeyed southeast to Wrentham to conduct a two-day convention.[44] On Friday, 29 March, Douglass traveled alone to

Pawtucket, where he led a three-day meeting that "was conducted throughout with spirit and interest."[45] The proceedings of this convention were recorded by Daniel Mitchell, chair of the meeting, whose account gives us a revealing portrait of Douglass' rhetorical artistry at this juncture of his career. During the opening session, Douglass reportedly gave a "thrilling speech of some length, showing that through the coldness and apathy of the people on the subject of slavery, he had grown almost desperate." Although Mitchell characterized Douglass' speech as "beyond description powerful and convincing," he did his best to summarize it. According to Mitchell, Douglass argued that slavery continued to exist, in part, because it brought prosperity to the slaveholder and to the nation, prosperity that made the slaves' lives more difficult and demanding:

> He took the position, that the prosperity of the nation is dangerous to the cause of the slave, and most nobly sustained it by a formidable amount of evidence. He stated that prosperity to the slaveholder brought adversity and additional toil to the slave. Henry Clay had said, that fifty years ago the question was asked, could slavery be abolished? and it had been answered by fifty years of prosperity to this nation in sustaining the institution. He showed, in part, the present condition of the slave, though he knew things of which he could not, dared not speak; if he should do so, the blood of the audience would boil; yea, they would moan in deepest agony. When the imagination had conceived the most diabolical system in its power or capacity to devise, it could not be more horrible than slavery as it is.[46]

Following Douglass' speech, four resolutions were offered, the third of which dominated the convention. This resolution declared that those gathered at the meeting could not recognize "as Christian bodies, any of those religious sects of our country which have fellowship with slaveholders and their abettors." Douglass, Stephen S. Foster, and Cyrus Burleigh actively participated in the debate over this resolution. During Saturday's proceedings, Foster and Burleigh were constantly interrupted by a Mr. Chace, "who, with pious indignation, denounced Foster and Burleigh as infidels, with no sense of propriety." Douglass joined Foster, Burleigh, and J.M. Spear in responding to the charge and, according to Mitchell, "plainly showed that to the church and clergy belonged the sin of which they were accused."[47]

On Sunday evening a large crowd gathered to listen to the speakers again debate the third resolution. After Mr. Stone, "a young exhorter attached to the Wesleyan Church," was repeatedly interrupted, Burleigh "spoke earnestly in favor of the right of speech" and protested strongly against the interrupting of Stone. But it was Douglass who seized the moment and delivered a brief speech of singular "power and eloquence" in support of freedom of speech. Drawing from his slave experience, Douglass showed how slavery was perpetuated in the South through the denial of free speech and how slavery could not be abolished if freedom of expression were not protected. According to Mitchell's account of the meeting, Douglass said:

> Destroy the right of speech, and slavery would be perpetual. The slaveholders' efforts and energies are all directed to this point. They know the power of language; they dread the attacks made on their favorite institution by those who boldly and fearlessly advocate this right. They claim the privilege which they deny to others. The slave must be dumb while the master speaks, and not the slave only, but everyone who speaks in his behalf. This is necessary to perpetuate the system; without this prop, it would fall—fall never to rise again.[48]

Douglass continued his remarks by referring to his 10 August 1841 speech at Nantucket, "when he was ignorant and unlearned, barely capable of making himself understood." Douglass, of course, was exaggerating the state of his intellect at the genesis of his career three years earlier as a lecturer for the Massachusetts Anti-Slavery Society—just as he would in his autobiographies. Here his purpose appears to have been to use his Nantucket experience to make a larger point. If his audience at Nantucket, he reportedly said, "had not borne with his imperfections and hesitancy, he should not at this time have been more capable of addressing them than he then was." If as a slave "he had the right of speech at the South," he claimed, "he would speak to them in such thundertones of this great abomination, as would destroy it, root and branch." For Douglass, oratory was the most powerful weapon available for overcoming the evils of slavery. To him, the right of free speech was essential to bringing down the wickedness of slavery, and his address on this topic at Pawtucket was, according to Mitchell, "grand beyond description." The audience listened "with deep and earnest attention, although it was nearly 11 o'clock when the meeting closed." So great was the impact of Douglass' speech that, even with the lateness of the hour, the audience was "unwilling to separate."[49]

On Thursday, 4 April, Douglass rode to Essex to attend a quarterly meeting of the Essex County Anti-Slavery Society.[50] According to a report of the meeting published in the *Liberator*, the abolitionists gathered for the one-day meeting in the Christian meetinghouse. During the course of the proceedings, Douglass joined Foster and others in advocating a resolution that pronounced American slavery "a sin, with which there can be no innocent compromise," and that declared it the duty of every true abolitionist "to come out from every institution which in any wise supports it."

The meeting attracted so much interest that the evening session convened at the more spacious Universalist Church, where it listened to Douglass, Foster, and others speak in favor of the resolutions presented in the afternoon.[51]

During the remainder of April, Douglass joined Erasmus D. Hudson, Sydney Howard Gay, and Abby Kelley in conducting conventions in the towns of Fitchburg, Ashburnham, Gardner, Hubbardston, Petersham, and Athol, all of which were in Worcester County.[52] Following the Athol meeting, Douglass returned to Lynn to attend the last of a series of conventions in Essex County. Also in attendance were Garrison, Foster, Buffum, and Charles Lenox Remond. The meeting began in Lyceum Hall on Thursday morning, 25 April, and ended Sunday evening, 28 April.[53] During the first day, Douglass was called upon to chair the proceedings. On Friday, he stepped down from the chair and delivered a speech "of surpassing pathos and tenderness" commemorating "the case of the unfortunate John L. Brown, who was on that day publicly scourged for the mercy he showed to a poor female slave in South Carolina." A correspondent reported to the *Liberator* that it "was a meeting of great solemnity and feeling."[54]

Douglass left the Lynn meeting before it was over to return to western Massachusetts to attend an antislavery convocation at Northampton in Hampshire County. On Saturday afternoon, 27 April, he arrived at Northampton's Association of Education and Industry, a community established as an experiment in communal living.[55] The following morning, he "preached" before residents of the community. The lecture, delivered in the community's dining room, was well attended. According to Asa Hutchinson, a member of the Hutchinson Family Singers, Douglass spoke with great power as he "told the tale of John L. Brown who was to have been whipped . . . which made many of his hearers shed tears of real grief, tears for suffering humanity."[56]

In the evening, Douglass conducted an antislavery meeting in Northampton's Town Hall. The meeting was well publicized. According to the *Hampshire Gazette*, "glaring handbills" were posted throughout the streets of the town announcing "that Frederick Douglass, a fugitive slave, would deliver an anti-slavery address at the Town Hall in the evening."[57] As a result, said a letter published in the *Liberator*, the hall was "densely crowded by men, women and children, and of all *colors*." The correspondent estimated that Douglass' lecture attracted more than 600 people, "a large number for the pro-slavery, sectarian town of Northampton."[58] Reporting on the meeting, a correspondent to the *Liberator* provided a summary of Douglass' speech. Because the summary gives us a rare view of Douglass' message during the Massachusetts Hundred Conventions tour, it is worth reprinting here:

> Friend Douglass spoke, with great earnestness, of the enormity of slavery. "Consider it as you may, the fact of your being a slave

is enough to sicken the heart, and curdle the blood in your veins."
He then went on to prove that the American churches and clergy
are the mighty bulwarks of American slavery; and not a proposition
did he state, that was not proved by unanswerable demonstration.

He next attacked the citadel of the Whig party, which being
upon a *Clay*-ey foundation, was soon razed to the ground. Some of
the Whig devotees, who were present, commenced a hissing noise,
indicating that their indignation was aroused by such an exposure
of the villainies of their patriotic leader, Henry Clay.

The Democrats of America were next assailed—those professional friends of equality—and were faithfully scourged for their
recreancy.

Reference was then made by him to the case of John L. Brown,
of Bath, Me., who was sentenced, as every abolitionist is aware, to
be hung in South Carolina, for rendering assistance to a poor slave
sister. This was alluded to by the speaker in a very pathetic, vehement and powerful manner; it seeming as though the truth that he
expressed must carry conviction to every mind.

He then gave us part of his experience while in slavery; a sad
tale, truly, but intermingled with humorous hits at the fallacy of
the slaveholders' reasoning, if it can be so called. Also his inimitable sermon of the southern priest, from the favorite text,
'Servants, obey your masters,' &c.

In conclusion, he ended with a most eloquent appeal to all present to become coadjutors in the cause of freedom; to discard all
associations that bind them to the enslavement of their brethren
now in bonds; to come out, be free and independent.[59]

From all accounts, Douglass' remarks angered some members of the audience. The correspondent to the *Northampton Courier* reported that
Douglass was "disturbed and often times insulted by lawless boys and over-
grown and bearded striplings." The *Hampshire Gazette* indicated that
some members of the audience "were inclined to make disturbance."
Nevertheless, Douglass must have performed admirably. "He was the most
fluent speaker we have ever heard from the colored race," the *Courier's*
correspondent reported, "and his command of language evinced a rare
intellect."[60]

From Northampton, Douglass traveled west to Pittsfield, where he
rejoined Hudson, Gay, and Kelley on 29 April for a two-day convention.
The group next moved to Lenox for a two-day meeting and concluded the
Hundred Conventions tour of Massachusetts in Stockbridge on 3-4 May.[61]
The leadership of the Massachusetts Anti-Slavery Society immediately
declared the tour a triumph. "One of the most encouraging results of this

movement," the society's annual report of 1844 observed, "was the awakening of a warm interest in the cause in towns where but little Anti-Slavery labor had been bestowed." Douglass and his companions had done their work "thoroughly and well" as they traveled from town to town preaching the "Anti-Slavery Gospel."[62] Despite his grueling schedule and the sometimes virulent opposition of anti-abolitionists, Douglass' speeches often inspired and, at times, overwhelmed his listeners. His eloquent message, strong voice, and powerful delivery moved audiences from tears to laughter and further strengthened his standing as one of the foremost abolitionist orators in Massachusetts. In the months ahead, he would continue to speak out strongly against slavery and the nation that seemed determined to keep him a fugitive in bondage. As a result, the demand for his services would persist and his stature among abolitionists would continue to grow.

Notes

1. *Liberator*, 9 February 1844, 22; *Liberator*, 16 February 1844, 27; *National Anti-Slavery Standard*, 7 March 1844, 155; *Thirteenth Annual Report, Presented to the Massachusetts Anti-Slavery Society, By Its board of managers, January 22, 1845* (1845; reprint, Westport, Conn.: Negro Universities Press, 1970), 25.

2. Of Douglass' biographers, only Holland, Quarles, Foner, and Fulkerson give attention to his activities during this five-month period. Blassingame includes this period in his itinerary of Douglass' speaking activities, but he leaves out places and dates and often misdates meetings. See Frederic May Holland, *Frederick Douglass: The Colored Orator* (New York: Funk and Wagnalls Company, 1891), 98-100; Benjamin Quarles, *Frederick Douglass* (1948; reprint, New York: Atheneum, 1968), 33-34; Philip S. Foner, ed., *The Life and Writings of Frederick Douglass, Volume 1* (New York: International Publishers, 1950), 1:58-59; Raymond Gerald Fulkerson, "Frederick Douglass and the Anti-Slavery Crusade: His Career and Speeches, 1817-1861," pt. 1 (Ph.D. diss., University of Illinois, 1971), 70-71; John W. Blassingame, ed., *The Frederick Douglass Papers, Series One: Speeches Debates, and Interviews, Volume 1* (New Haven, Conn.: Yale University Press, 1979), 1:xcii-xciii.

3. Blassingame, ed., *Douglass Papers, Series One*, 1:xcii, incorrectly states that this convention met on 24 January only.

4. *Liberator*, 2 February 1844, 18-19; *Herald of Freedom*, 9 February 1844, 204.

5. *Liberator*, 9 February 1844, 22; *National Anti-Slavery Standard*, 7 March 1844, 159; *Thirteenth Annual Report*, 25.

6. In early January 1844, the board of managers of the Massachusetts Anti-Slavery Society had accepted John A. Collins' resignation as general agent and chose Phillips to take his place (*Liberator*, 5 January 1844, 3).

7. Frederick Douglass to Wendell Phillips, 10 February 1844, Crawford Blagdon Papers, Harvard College Library, Harvard University.

8. Ibid.

9. Ibid.

10. *Liberator*, 16 February 1844, 27.

11. *Herald of Freedom*, 16 February 1844, 208. An incomplete account of Douglass' Concord lectures may be found in Blassingame, ed., *Douglass Papers, Series One*, 1:23-27 and the *Liberator*, 23 February 1844, 29. A segment of the lecture was reprinted by Fulkerson, "Frederick Douglass," pt. 1:70.

12. *Herald of Freedom*, 16 February 1844, 208.

13. To the best of my knowledge, this is the first published instance of Douglass suggesting that he would have to leave the United States in order to escape his status as a fugitive slave.

14. *Herald of Freedom*, 16 February 1844, 208.

15. Ibid.

16. Ibid.

17. Ibid.

18. Most of Douglass' activities in New Hampshire during February 1843 have been overlooked by his biographers. Stating erroneously that Douglass was in Concord from 11-18 February, Blassingame fails to include the subsequent New Hampshire meetings in his itinerary of Douglass' speaking activities. Fulkerson discusses the Concord meeting of 11 February, but does not identify any of Douglass' other activities in New Hampshire. The same is true of Quarles and Foner, who make the further mistake of suggesting that the address of 11 February was part of the Hundred Conventions tour of Massachusetts. See Blassingame, ed., *Douglass Papers, Series One*, 1:xcii; Fulkerson, "Frederick Douglass," pt. 1, 69-70; Quarles, *Frederick Douglass*, 33-34; Foner, *Life and Writings*, 1:58-59.

19. *Herald of Freedom*, 9 February 1844, 205; *Herald of Freedom*, 16 February 1844, 209.

20. *Herald of Freedom*, 1 March 1844, 7.

21. Blassingame, ed., *Douglass Papers, Series One*, 1:xcii, does not identify the date of the Lowell convention in its itinerary of Douglass' activities.

22. *Liberator*, 1 March 1844, 35; *Herald of Freedom*, 1 March 1844, 6-7; *Herald of Freedom*, 8 March 1844, 10.

23. *Liberator*, 1 March 1844, 35; *Herald of Freedom*, 1 March 1844, 6-7; *Herald of Freedom*, 8 March 1844, 10. During a heated confrontation with George Bradburn at a Liberty Party convention in New Bedford on 23 October, Douglass attacked the character of the Liberty Party and argued the superiority of moral suasion over political action. From October 1844 until August 1845, when he left the United States for a lecture tour of the British Isles, Douglass repeatedly attacked the character and leadership of the Liberty Party.

24. *Herald of Freedom*, 1 March 1844, 6-7; *Herald of Freedom*, 8 March 1844, 10.

25. *Herald of Freedom*, 8 March 1844, 10.

26. Blassingame, ed., *Douglass Papers, Series One*, 1:xcii, does not identify the date of the Groton convention in its itinerary of Douglass' speaking activities.

27. *Liberator*, 8 March 1844, 39; *Liberator*, 15 March 1844, 42.

28. Blassingame, ed., *Douglass Papers, Series One*, 1:xcii, does not identify the dates of the Townsend convention in its itinerary of Douglass' speaking activities. In addition, he erroneously identifies Pillsbury as being present at Townsend.

29. *Liberator*, 8 March 1844, 39; *Liberator*, 15 March 1844, 42.

30. Ibid.

31. Blassingame, ed., *Douglass Papers, Series One*, 1:xcii, incorrectly identifies this meeting as being held in New Bedford, Massachusetts.

32. *Liberator*, 15 March 1844, 42.

33. Ibid.; Frederick Douglass, *Life and Times of Frederick Douglass, Written by Himself* (1892; reprint, New York: Macmillan, 1962), 226; *Liberator*, 21 June 1844, 99.

34. Blassingame, ed., *Douglass Papers, Series One*, 1:xcii, does not include the Concord meeting of 3 March in its itinerary of Douglass' speaking itinerary. In addition, it misdates the Sudbury convention of 4-5 March as meeting circa 6 March.

35. *Liberator*, 15 March 1844, 42.

36. Blassingame, ed., *Douglass Papers, Series One*, 1:xcii, does not identify the date of the Framingham convention in its itinerary of Douglass' speaking activities.

37. *Liberator*, 22 March 1844, 47.

38. Blassingame, ed., *Douglass Papers, Series One*, 1:xcii, does not include this convention in its itinerary of Douglass' speaking activities.

39. *Liberator*, 16 February 1844, 27; *Liberator*, 15 March 1844, 42.

40. *Liberator*, 16 February 1844, 27; *Liberator*, 15 March 1844, 43. I am assuming that Douglass and his companions kept their lecture date at Waltham. Although no record exists to confirm that they traveled there, they had met all their scheduled appointments up to this time, and it seems safe to conclude that they held a convention in Waltham as planned. However, Blassingame, ed., *Douglass Papers, Series One*, 1:xcii, does not include the Waltham convention in its itinerary of Douglass' speaking activities. It does include the Dorchester meeting, but does not identify its date.

41. *Liberator*, 22 March 1844, 47; *Dedham American* in the *Liberator*, 5 April 1844, 53.

42. *Liberator*, 15 March 1844, 43. Blassingame, ed., *Douglass Papers, Series One*, 1:xcii, does not identify the dates of the Braintree and Foxboro conventions in

its itinerary of Douglass' speaking activities. Unfortunately, there are no surviving accounts of the meetings.

43. *Liberator*, 19 April 1844, 62.

44. *Liberator*, 15 March 1844, 43. Blassingame, ed., *Douglass Papers, Series One*, 1:xcii, does not identify the dates of the Medway and Wrentham conventions in its itinerary of Douglass' speaking activities.

45. *Liberator*, 26 April 1844, 67. According to the itinerary published in the *National Anti-Slavery Standard*, 28 March 1844, Douglass and his colleagues were scheduled to speak at Rutland on 28-29 March and at Princeton on 30-31 March, but because Douglass was attending the meetings at Pawtucket, he missed the stops at Rutland and Princeton. Blassingame, ed., *Douglass Papers, Series One*, 1:xciii, incorrectly dates the Pawtucket convention of 29-31 March as meeting on 29-30 March.

46. *Liberator*, 26 April 1844, 67.

47. Ibid.

48. Ibid.

49. Ibid.

50. According to the itinerary published in the *National Anti-Slavery Standard*, 28 March 1844, 171, conventions were scheduled at Westminster on 1-2 April and at Leominster on 3-4 April. Because Douglass had traveled alone to Pawtucket and then to Essex, it is unlikely that he attended any of the sessions at Westminster or Leominster. There are no published proceedings from these meetings to verify whether or not Douglass was in attendance.

51. *Liberator*, 12 April 1844, 59.

52. According to the published schedule, Douglass and his colleagues were to appear at Fitchburg on 5-6 April, at Ashburnham on 8-9 April, at Gardner on 10-11 April, at Hubbardston on 12-13 April, at Petersham on 15-16 April, and at Athol on 17-18 April (*National Anti-Slavery Standard*, 28 March 1844, 171; *Liberator*, 12 April 1844, 59). Blassingame, ed., *Douglass Papers, Series One*, 1:xciii, does not include any of the Worcester County stops in its itinerary of Douglass' speaking activities.

53. Blassingame, ed., *Douglass Papers, Series One*, 1:xciii, incorrectly dates the Lynn meeting as occurring on 25 April only.

54. *Liberator*, 10 May 1844, 75. John L. Brown, a white man from South Carolina, was tried and convicted in 1843 of assisting in the escape of a young female slave. He was initially sentenced to hang, but his sentence was later reduced to thirty-nine lashes and then commuted altogether. See Dale Cockrell, ed., *Excelsior: Journals of the Hutchinson Family Singers, 1842-1846* (Stuyvesant, N.Y.: Pendragon Press, 1989), 268.

55. Cockrell, ed., *Excelsior*, 265, 267.

56. Ibid., 268.

57. *Hampshire Gazette*, 30 April 1844, reprinted in Cockrell, ed., *Excelsior*, 269.

58. *Liberator*, 10 May 1844, 75.

59. Ibid.

60. *Northampton Courier* in the *Liberator*, 28 June 1844, 101; *Hampshire Gazette*, 30 April 1844, reprinted in Cockrell, ed., *Excelsior*, 269.

61. *Liberator*, 12 April 1844, 59; Sydney Howard Gay to E. D. Hudson, 20 April 1844, Special Collections and Archives, University Library, University of Massachusetts at Amherst. Unfortunately, these conventions went unreported. Blassingame, ed., *Douglass Papers, Series One*, 1:xciii, does not include the Pittsfield, Lenox, or Stockbridge conventions in its itinerary of Douglass' speaking activities.

62. *Thirteenth Annual Report*, 25-26.

Chapter Eight

No Union With Slaveholders: The Proslavery Character of the United States Constitution, May-August 1844

IN EARLY MAY 1844, Frederick Douglass returned home to Lynn from western Massachusetts. Now that the Hundred Conventions tour of Massachusetts had come to an end, Douglass would enter into another important period of antislavery agitation. Although overlooked by most Douglass scholars, the time from May through August 1844 marked a critical stage in his development as an abolitionist and as an orator.[1] His growing significance to the movement can be seen in his being invited by the board of managers of the American Anti-Slavery Society to be the guest of the society at their annual May meeting with all expenses paid. In early August, during the opening session of the Eastern Pennsylvania Anti-Slavery Society, he was invited to speak on the status of the antislavery movement in New England and its prospects for the future. Later in the same month he was the featured speaker at an antislavery meeting in the State House yard at Philadelphia, after which he undertook a lecture tour in eastern Pennsylvania with Charles Lenox Remond. In all of these activities, he continued to speak impressively and eloquently on behalf of African Americans.

This period, moreover, includes two complete texts of speeches by Douglass never before documented or studied. The first is from a 28 May 1844 meeting of the New England Anti-Slavery Society in Boston, the other is from a 12 August 1844 meeting of the Eastern Pennsylvania Anti-Slavery Society at Norristown. Both these speech texts, previously undiscovered by scholars, will be closely examined in this chapter.

I

Following the final meeting of the Hundred Conventions tour of Massachusetts at Stockbridge in early May, Douglass headed home to Lynn, Massachusetts. He then traveled to New York to attend the tenth annual convention of the American Anti-Slavery Society, held in New York City's Apollo Hall from 7-10 May.[2] In recognition of Douglass' importance to the campaign to end slavery, the board of managers of the American society had invited him as one of its honored guests with all expenses paid.[3] The chief issue under discussion during the convention was the immediate peaceful dissolution of the Union. After "grave deliberation" and "a long and earnest discussion," the society went on record, "by a vote of nearly three to one of the members present," in support of William Lloyd Garrison's call for the immediate peaceful dissolution of the Union and the repeal of the U. S. Constitution. The subject of disunion had long been a topic of discussion among abolitionists at antislavery meetings.[4] By officially endorsing the dissolution of the Union resolves, abolitionists took the revolutionary step of proclaiming that "as long as the existing Union endures or the present Constitution lasts, they plainly perceived that there was no course left for them either by duty to the Slaves or a due regard for their own rights, but to renounce and repudiate them both, and to demand the immediate dissolution of the one and abrogation of the other." Although Douglass was appointed as one of twenty-five members of the business committee, he was uncharacteristically quiet throughout the four-day meeting, and there is no record of him speaking on Garrison's resolution.[5] Indeed, he did not even vote when the question was called during the final session of the convention.[6]

At the end of May, Douglass attended the annual meeting of the New England Anti-Slavery Society in Boston. The deliberations began on Tuesday, 28 May, in the Marlboro Chapel and continued for three days. The sessions, a correspondent reported to the *Practical Christian*, were conducted before "immense audiences. . . . The gathering of the anti-slavery friends, and the interest in the meeting were unprecedented. Never before were such multitudes assembled at any anniversary of the kind in this country." Those who spoke, the reporter wrote, "discoursed powerfully from the platform." A correspondent to the *Liberator* reported that the meetings "have been attended by a great concourse of people, all deeply interested in the eloquent and stirring discussions on the resolutions for the dissolution of the Union."[7]

The New England Anti-Slavery Society's convention was virtually a repetition of the American Anti-Slavery Society's meeting in early May. For two out of the three days of the meeting, the major issue under discussion was the question of the dissolution of the Union. Douglass, however, did not remain silent at this convention. In fact, he was active throughout the three-day meeting. During the opening session, while the business committee was preparing resolutions for the meeting to consider, he reportedly "spoke with excellent effect." More important, on Tuesday evening, he was one of four speakers who spoke in support of resolutions calling for the dissolution of the Union.[8] Fortunately, a correspondent for the *National Anti-Slavery Standard* transcribed the speech Douglass made that evening. The text, previously undiscovered by scholars, is the first published instance of Douglass' position on the proslavery nature of the Constitution and the dissolution of the Union. He had spoken numerous times in support of resolutions characterizing the Constitution as a proslavery document and demanding the dissolution of the Union, but, none of those speeches was published.[9]

Douglass' chief rhetorical strategy in this speech was to discredit the Constitution by describing it as a document hostile to human liberty and then to demand the immediate dissolution of the political union between North and South. He first focused his attention on the U. S. Constitution, a document he believed was proslavery in character and intent. He began his attack on the Constitution by calling into question the integrity of the document and its framers. "I confess, that had it descended to me from the clouds," Douglass stated, "I might not have questioned its merits, in consequence of what appears upon the face of it." However, after carefully studying "its origin, and the character of its framers," and discovering "how it was written, as it were, in the blood of thousands and thousands of slaves," he concluded that it was "*not* an Anti-Slavery document."[10]

To prove that the Constitution was intended as a proslavery document, Douglass first pointed to the clause that required the return of fugitive slaves to the South, a clause that troubled him deeply. To prove further that the framers of the Constitution had deliberately drafted a document that was intended to sustain slavery, he noted that "the laws passed immediately after its adoption, and by the very men who framed and accepted it, were laws upholding Slavery. That shows that they knew they might maintain Slavery under it." Douglass made this point more vivid and forceful by emphasizing that he was a slave under the very Constitution and laws that the framers had advanced. "Wherever the stars and stripes wave," he noted, "I am a slave!"[11]

Douglass' solution to overcoming the proslavery character of the Constitution was the immediate dissolution of the Union. To continue the alliance between North and South, he argued, meant the continuation of slavery: "That's the reason that we have Slavery now—(and the *slaveholder* knows it, however gentlemen here may fail to perceive it)—that the North strengthens him with all her own strength. It is because this whole nation have sworn by the God who made them, that the slave should be a slave or die!" According to the transcript of the speech, Douglass' words, "be a slave or die," were followed by a *"Stillness of strong sensation."* Sensing that he had deeply affected his auditors, Douglass addressed the members of the audience in personal terms. The slave, he stated, "knows that you are pledged and bound to each other to crush him down. It is this bloody Union that I wish should cease." Then, pleading with his auditors on behalf of all the slaves, he made a request: "I only ask you, that you will no longer crush and slay us. Tell the slaveholder that if he will still hold slaves, it must be on his own responsibility; by his own unaided strength."[12]

Having called into question the character of the Constitution and its framers, and having demanded that the Union be immediately dissolved, Douglass made clear the nature of the political Union which bound slave and free together. In so doing, he revealed a broadening of his disunionist philosophy. In previous speeches, he had condemned the religious alliance between northern and southern churches. In this section of the speech, however, he focused on the political union between North and South, a union sustained by a commitment to a proslavery Constitution. "The South," he charged, "brings forward for your President, Henry Clay, and the North stands ready with the Vice-President—the Rev. Mr. Frelinghuysen!" Douglass believed that the nomination of these candidates symbolized the political union of the "piety of the North" and "the Slavery of the South." Using a combination of humor and metaphor to make his point, Douglass stated, "They have married Henry to Frelinghuysen, (tremendous applause), and it's a type of . . . National Union; but I am astonished that Freemen do not forbid the banns."[13]

Douglass then explained why his audience should oppose a close, dependent union with the slaveholding South. Focusing on the savage instruments used by the slaveholder to oppress the slave and to sustain slavery, he pressed his auditors: "Why should you love such association with the whip, and with the pistol, and with the bowie-knife?" Even in Congress, he said, slaveholders bullied northern politicians with the same savagery as they bullied slaves in the South. Instead of using the whip, pistol, and knife, they used their voices to badger and intimidate northern representatives. Douglass illustrated this claim by referring to a recent incident in Congress. "There are your great men in Congress—look at them! Your Choate, and your Bates! Do they rise to say a word about your business that they're sent there to do—they're bullied down, and obliged to sit there and hear Massachusetts scoffed at and insulted!"[14] Then Douglass generalized from the experience of Massachusetts senators to the entire North. "They had to sit and listen," he insisted, "and so are all the North bullied down" by southern slaveholders. Yet despite being "bullied down," the North still agreed to support the South—"to be their kidnappers!

their putters down of insurrections!" To Douglass, it was clear that south-erners "do not care about the Union, except as it supports Slavery."[15]

In the next section of the speech, Douglass responded to the arguments of those opposed to dissolution. First, he addressed the concern that if dis-solution occurred, the influence of the North over the South would decrease. Initially, he used humor to respond to his opponents' position. "My friends . . . seem to think that there is some geographical change to take place in consequence" of disunion, he asserted. "They seem to think that the North is to go to the North pole, and the South to fly away out of sight to the South pole." In fact, though, no such geographical shift would take place. What dissolving the Union would produce was a moral shift in the North, a shift, Douglass proclaimed, that would "be all-sufficient." Indeed, only after the dissolution of the Union could the slaveholder's true identity be seen by the people of the North. To advance his claim, Douglass used a combination of questions, sarcasm, harsh language, repetition, and parallelism to call into question the integrity of the venerable men from the South:

> Who can fix the brand of murderer—thief—adulterer, on the brow of the man that you associate with, and salute as *honorable*? The *Honorable* Henry Clay! the *Honorable* John C. Calhoun! And those ministers who come to the North with the price of blood in their hands—how shall moral principle be diffused among the people on the subject of slavery, while they are hailed as *Reverend!* Withdraw from them the Sanction of the men who do not hold slaves, and how quickly would the character of Slavery be seen as it is.[16]

Having responded to one concern over disunion, Douglass took issue with a comparison Amasa Walker, a previous speaker, had made between British and American oppression. Douglass began by summarizing Walker's argument: "The Briton says to his victim, Work for me or you shall starve; and the American says to the slave, Work, or you shall be whipped. This was defined by Mr. Walker to be the difference." Then, utilizing his expe-rience as a slave, Douglass drew striking contrasts between British acts of oppression and American slavery. By so doing, he linked the evils and per-petuation of slavery to the union between North and South. The "hungry Englishman," Douglass asserted, "is a *freeman*; while the slave is not only hungry, but a slave." The Briton's manhood remained intact, while the slave was "entirely unmanned." The master, unlike the noble Briton, held God-like dominion over the slave, a dominion made possible by the alliance between North and South:

> The master is at once his conscience, his owner, body and spirit, his all. The master decides when and where, and with whom he shall go—when and where, and how, and by whom he shall be

punished. None of these may be decided, as I am informed, by a nobleman of England, be he ever so noble. But here the master lays his foul clutch upon the throat—he makes his iron grasp felt in the soul. He says to the immortal spirit, thou shalt not aspire! he says to the intellect, thou shalt not expand! to the body, thou shalt not go at large! *Could* he say all this were it not for the Union! I say, then, the Union does it (Great applause).[17]

But Douglass was not yet through showing how the union between the North and South helped to maintain slavery. In the next section of the speech, he presented an allegory through which he imaginatively illustrated how the North worked in concert with the South to keep slaves in bondage. Within the allegory, Douglass becomes the slaveholder, while the audience becomes the slaveholder's northern allies who, in the end, give slavery their blessing:

> The Union may be illustrated in this way. I have ten men in a bight of rope. Now, it is plain that one man can't hold ten, and I call to you, and you, and you, gentlemen, and beg your aid. But you say to me, Douglas[s], we've decided objections to holding men in that way. We've conscientious scruples. We're not friendly to holding men. We will surround you, however, and take an interest in the matter as far as to hinder their getting away from you. Just so the circle of Northern opinion and political union unites with that of the South around the slave.[18]

As long as there was a union between North and South, Douglass argued, the circle of cooperation would remain unbroken and the slave would remain in bondage. Through the allegory, moreover, Douglass demonstrated convincingly how dependent the southern slaveholder was on northern opinion in keeping slaves in bondage. The solution, he proposed, was to act on Garrison's motto of "No Union With Slaveholders."[19]

Next, Douglass took issue with the position expressed by William White, who had spoken prior to Douglass, "that Slavery existed before the Union, and not in consequence of the Union." Directing his response to White, Douglass exclaimed: "Sir, I *lived* before I drew the present air I draw; but I live now, *by* the air I draw. Had Slavery been deprived of the benefit it formed the Union to obtain, it could not have lived." In fact, Douglass insisted, were it not for this Union, slavery would have long ago "ceased by public opinion or insurrection." Through pledging allegiance to the Union, the North was obligated to meet any slave rebellion with force. The Union, Douglass declared, had sustained slavery, thereby "blunting our moral sense, till we have lost our moral discrimination." From Douglass' perspective, the North, by its union with the South, had become desensitized to the slaves' humanity. To demonstrate how slavery had blunted the moral sensibilities of the North, Douglass contrasted the way white people responded to a white man's suffering with how they responded to a black man's suffering. "When a white man suffers," he asserted, "we are full of sympathy," but "when a slave shrieks out in his agony—when McIntosh calls out of the flames to the whole assembled people round the stake—'shoot me! shoot me!'" whites respond by saying "'who cares! he's a negro! he's a slave! what right had he to defend his wife or daughter against a white man! he shall die in a slow fire.'"[20]

The North's commitment to a Union that supported the institution of slavery not only had blunted the region's moral sensibilities, Douglass charged, but had induced slaves to take extreme measures to escape from bondage. To illustrate the desperation felt by slaves on account of the Union's commitment to slavery, he related a story told to him by Seth M. Gates, a former U.S. congressman from New York. In the story, an escaped slave woman in Washington, D.C., chooses death over being returned to bondage. According to Douglass' account, Gates saw

> a woman start out of a half-opened slave-prison gate; and before she had run far, three men who witnessed it also started at a distance, started to head her off before she should be able to cross the bridge, which would give her a chance of escape. True to their Virginia instincts, they succeeded in reaching the bridge immediately after her. A moment more, and she would have been in their grasp. But her resolution was taken. She leaped from the bridge into the river, and sunk to rise no more. She preferred death to the protection of the Union.[21]

It was the North's "fearful union with slaveholders," Douglass declared, "that makes the weight and strength—the power and perpetuity of that system which we have met to abolish." He urged the audience "to yield" to slaveholders' demands "no longer."[22]

In the final moments of the speech, Douglass sought to emphasize further the helplessness of the slave within a Union pledged to support slaveholders. He began by discussing his experience as a slave. Revealing how the memories of the cruelties of slavery fueled his desire to see the Union dissolved, Douglass disclosed, "I have had the sound of the lash to impel me on in my labors for its termination." Had he "invoked the Union" during any of his sufferings as a slave, he observed, he would have summoned it "in vain." Not only did the Union help suppress individual slaves, Douglass argued, but it also lent its support to slaveowners in times of general slave uprisings.[23] To support his argument, Douglass turned to the rebellions led by Nat Turner and Madison Washington and showed how the North came to the aid of the South in each instance. To some extent, it is surprising that Douglass chose to use two militant slaves who relied on armed force to free themselves from the bonds of slavery to support his argument. At this point in his career, Douglass was an adherent to Garrison's policies of nonresistance and nonviolence, and both Turner and Washington had used violence against white people to aid their escape attempts. Douglass, however, did not use these two men to advance an argument for violent slave insurrection. Rather, he employed them to demonstrate the inconsistency between a nation founded to preserve liberty on the one hand and pledged to uphold the institution of slavery on the other.

Douglass first invoked the name of Nat Turner. From 21-23 August 1831, Turner directed an unsuccessful slave insurrection in Southampton County, Virginia. A fiery slave preacher, Turner led approximately seventy slaves in a revolt that killed more than fifty white people, including eighteen women and twenty-four children, before being stopped by the local authorities.[24] Nat Turner could not "appeal to this Union, formed to preserve Liberty" for assistance, Douglass declared. Rather, it was the slaveholders who could summon "the Union for help, and obtained it."[25] For Douglass the irony was clear. Turner and his band of slaves had struck out for liberty by organizing a slave rebellion against slaveholders. Yet under the Constitution, the North was obligated to come to the aid of the South and help them crush the slaves' rebellion.[26]

Continuing in the same vein, Douglass next drew upon the example of Madison Washington, who had led a slave mutiny on board the brig *Creole* on 7 November 1841. The *Creole* was carrying 135 slaves from Hampton Roads, Virginia, to New Orleans. During the voyage, nineteen slaves participated in a mutiny. They seized control of the brig, wounding the captain and the ship's mate and killing one white passenger. Two blacks were seriously wounded in the incident, and one of them later died. After being convinced by the crew that the ship did not have enough provisions to travel to Liberia, the mutineers decided to sail for Nassau. Two days later, the *Creole* arrived in Nassau, where Washington and his fellow mutineers placed themselves at the mercy of the British authorities.[27] "Why could not Madison Washington strike for Liberty on the soil of Virginia," Douglass asked. "The *Union* overawed him! he must wait till he is at the mercy of the waves, with less odds against him than a whole nation to brand him as mutineer and a murderer." Daniel Webster, the secretary of state, Douglass charged, demanded that Washington and his fellow slaves be returned to the South, "not in the name of the South alone, but of this whole country." In Douglass' view, Webster's demand on behalf of the U.S. government for the return of the mutineers proved that the Union was "pledged to keep down the slaves."[28]

In his concluding comments, Douglass appealed directly to the audience. Repeating his central theme, he alleged that northerners who stood pledged to the Union were, consciously or not, acting in sympathy with the South. The "two millions . . . ignorant suffering slaves," he charged, were being suppressed by the "fourteen millions of 'free and enlightened people'" of the North pledged against them. He then ended the speech with a comparison to illustrate the overwhelming power of the Union over the slave. Trying to shame his audience into voting in support of the resolution calling for the dissolution of the Union, he declared: "You see it plainly when a great lubber-headed fellow gets hold of a little one in the street. Just so the whole world sees your American Union for the holding of slaves." Douglass left little doubt that the world realized the Union was responsible for sustaining slavery, and therefore, the political Union between North and South had to be dissolved.[29]

Douglass returned to his seat to the sounds of enthusiastic applause. His "eloquent and stirring" speech had been heard and well received. He had skillfully blended logical demonstration, humor, emotional appeals, and examples to produce a compelling address. More important, in this speech, Douglass moved from denouncing the church to denouncing the Union. He departed from his usual attack on the alliance between northern and southern churches as the major obstacle to the abolition of slavery and argued that the Constitution and the political union it established were the main obstructions to abolition. In doing so, he aligned himself with Garrison and the disunionists, a position he would faithfully maintain and defend in the months ahead. Yet, contrary to what some scholars have intimated, Douglass was not blindly following Garrisonian doctrine. He had conscientiously studied the origins of the Constitution and the character of its framers and had come to the conclusion that the Constitution was not an antislavery document. Douglass' speech at Boston illuminates his careful approach toward accepting or rejecting Garrisonian doctrine and his independence of mind when it came to engaging new principles and positions advanced by Garrison to his followers. Douglass had not simply accepted Garrison's disunionist stance. He had considered the issue carefully and arrived at a conclusion on his own.[30]

On the final day of the New England convention, Douglass continued to participate actively in the proceedings. During the morning session, he joined those voting in favor of the dissolution of the Union resolutions. In the afternoon, resolutions denouncing the American church were again introduced for discussion, during which Douglass engaged a Reverend Goodenow in a debate over the proslavery character of the American church and clergy. The exchange, not discussed by any of Douglass' biographers, is worth examining here. From it, we gain a sense of the power of Douglass' reasoning and its impact on those who disagreed with him. According to a report published in the *Liberator*, Goodenow declared that "nearly all churches and clergy of this land are honestly and earnestly devoted to the cause of the slave." Douglass, the correspondent observed, responded with "such blows of truth, and such blasts of eloquence," as to leave the minister defenseless. Douglass began by noting "the Union of the ministers and churches of the North with those of the South who held slaves." In response, reported the *Liberator*, Goodenow conceded that "he and his brethren received the aid of slaveholders in circulating the Bible, [and] carrying on the missionary cause," but he defended these actions by asserting, "we would receive aid from the Devil in hell, if he chose to send it to us for the promotion of a good cause!" To this Douglass scathingly replied, "Nay, . . . but you go to the Devil, and solicit his aid. Besides, you elect him into the Executive Committees of your great societies, and give him the place of honor in your solemn assemblies. You recognize slaveholders as good Christian brethren, and admit them into your pulpits. Is this your anti-slavery?" So forceful was Douglass' speech that Goodenow was compelled to agree with most of his claims.[31]

II

After the New England Anti-Slavery Society Convention, Douglass resumed his antislavery activities as an agent for the Massachusetts Anti-Slavery Society. In early June, he traveled to Hallowell, Maine, to deliver a lecture on American slavery.[32] It was his first venture into Maine, and it proved to be a success. He attracted a large audience to Hallowell's Town Hall, where he attributed "the existence and perpetuation of slavery to the church" and "denounced the whole church, north and south." A correspondent to the *Hallowell Cultivator* reported that Douglass was "one of the best speakers we ever heard" and marveled that "a *man* only six years out of slavery" had "presented the best specimen of true and graceful native eloquence, ever heard in a town blessed with as good a system of schools as any place in New England."[33]

Douglass returned from Maine in time to attend the Middlesex County Anti-Slavery Society meeting in Concord, Massachusetts, on 12-13 June.[34] The meeting convened in the Universalist Church, and Douglass actively participated throughout the proceedings. On the first day, during the afternoon session, Douglass offered a resolution which supported in principle the recent action taken at the New England Anti-Slavery Society meeting to agitate for the peaceful dissolution of the Union. The resolution closely resembled the main ideas he had expressed during his speech at the New England society's annual meeting two weeks earlier. "This Convention do most fully concur in opinion with the New-England Convention," Douglass' resolution read, that "liberty and slavery are antagonisms—that freemen can have no union with slaveholders—that the Constitution of the United States is a slaveholding instrument; and that no abolitionist can take office or swear to support it without gross and palpable violation of the abolition principle." After William A. White proposed a substitute motion holding that the Constitution was not a proslavery document and calling for a repudiation of the position taken by the American and New England Anti-Slavery Societies, Douglass spoke in support of his original resolution "until time for adjournment." Douglass' resolution and White's amendment were the subjects of debate during the evening session, with White speaking in support of his amendment and Douglass and Charles Lenox Remond defending the original motion.[35]

The following morning, Thursday, 13 June, a motion was made to lay the disunion resolutions on the table. A resolution was then introduced condemning the ministers and churches "who do not bear testimony against slavery at all times." These churches and those who support them, the resolution continued, should be "branded as infidels and deniers of the supremacy of God." To this resolution, Douglass added two of his own, which he, White, and others discussed. Douglass' first resolution praised the recent decision of the Methodist Episcopal Church not to elect any person to the office of bishop who was a slaveholder. "We rejoice to learn," the resolution stated, "that the Methodist Episcopal Church, by its General Conference now in session in the city of New-York, have decided that it is incompatible with the office of Bishop, for its occupant to be a mansteal-er." Douglass' second resolution, however, called into question the motive behind the church's decision. "While we hail this movement of the Methodist Episcopal Church as an indication of the progress of our cause," the second resolution announced, "we cannot, in the light of facts, accord to the Conference . . . any higher motive than that of expediency." Then, listing the sins of the union between the Methodist Churches of the North and those of the South, Douglass declared "that while northern churches remain in fellowship with the southern, by meeting with slaveholders, in the General Conference, and by allowing their Bishops to ordain as ministers of the gospel, manstealers and their guilty abettors, we must continue to brand that body as a slaveholding church." Discussion of these resolutions dominated the rest of the afternoon, with Douglass speaking at length in their defense. At the end of the session, however, the resolutions were "laid on the table," where they remained for the rest of the convention. In the evening, Douglass' disunion resolution was discussed, with Douglass, Remond, and White emerging as the principal speakers. Unfortunately, there is no published account of what they said, and Douglass' resolution was tabled when the convention came to a close.[36]

During the Concord meeting, Douglass not only spoke numerous times, but also offered resolutions for discussion. Before this time, he had usually commented on the resolutions of others, and it was rare for him to present even one resolution at a meeting. His introduction of three resolutions at Concord reflects his growing self-confidence and his command of the issues facing the abolitionist movement. Offering resolutions allowed him to guide the proceedings, to influence the course of the discussion, and to have abolitionists address concerns of special interest to him. He would continue to introduce resolutions at subsequent abolitionist meetings.

On Thursday, 1 August,[37] Douglass returned to Concord to participate in the commemoration of the anniversary of the emancipation of 800,000 slaves in the British West Indies.[38] Despite a rain storm and troubles with securing a meeting place, reported a correspondent to the *Liberator*, the occasion was one "of deep and thrilling interest." The meeting, initially scheduled for out-of-doors, convened at eleven o'clock in the Court House. Ralph Waldo Emerson, the featured speaker of the celebration, addressed the "large and spirited meeting" for more than two and a half hours, during which time "the whole audience gave the most undivided attention." In the afternoon, Douglass was one of five speakers to appear before the meeting.[39] Although there is no full text of Douglass' speech, we do have a sketch of it by Laura Hosmer, a member of the committee of arrangements for the celebration. Because this is the sole account of Douglass' address, it is worth printing in full. From it, we gain a sense both of Douglass' message and the power of his delivery. According to Hosmer, Douglass

> had spoken with the deep feeling which a man of his strong mind, who had felt all the dread horrors of Slavery, must have on such an occasion; he rejoiced with a joy that was truly unspeakable, over the resurrection of so many thousands from that living grave in which they had lain buried for so many long, dreary years; he told of the unutterable joy which must have been felt by those poor bondmen, when they received the boon of liberty—a joy which, he said, could only be conceived of by those who had, like himself, suffered as they had suffered—a joy which might be felt, but never could be told; and, said he, "I *rejoice* with them, I rejoice with them, I REJOICE with them." As he uttered these words, his every look and gesture showed how utterly inadequate language was to express the intensity of his feeling; his whole frame quivered with emotion, as he stood silent for a moment. "But," said he, "while I rejoice with them, my thoughts *will* revert to my own country, and to the millions who are here suffering miseries from which *they* are now delivered." He then depicted the state of things in our country, in language which I cannot remember to repeat, and with a power which I cannot imitate. When he had done speaking, the house was silent as if there were not a living being in it.[40]

As Hosmer's account testifies, Douglass' address made a powerful impression on the audience. The correspondent to the *Liberator* may have had

Douglass' speech in mind when he wrote, "We have been strengthened, we have been refreshed, and all I doubt not who participated with us on that day, will look back upon it as one of the bright spots on their anti-slavery course." Certainly, Douglass' masterful address had been one of the day's "bright spots."[41]

During the second week of August, Douglass traveled to Pennsylvania, where he remained until early September. It would be a busy three weeks. He attended the annual meeting of the Eastern Pennsylvania Anti-Slavery Society at Norristown, was the featured speaker at an antislavery meeting in the State House yard in Philadelphia and, with Remond, spent two weeks lecturing in Chester County and in and around Philadelphia under the auspices of the American and Eastern Pennsylvania antislavery societies. As we shall see, Douglass dominated most of the meetings he attended during the tour.

He began his efforts in Pennsylvania by attending the annual meeting of the Eastern Pennsylvania Anti-Slavery Society at Norristown, where he was joined by Garrison, Remond, and James N. Buffum. The four-day meeting began on 12 August in the Baptist Church.[42] "The attendance was large throughout the whole four days," a correspondent to the *Pennsylvania Freeman* reported, "at times, indeed, filling the spacious Baptist meetinghouse to overflowing, crowding the seats and thronging the aisles with those who, for want of room to sit, were obliged to stand." Garrison reported in the *Liberator* that he "never saw a more respectful, dignified and substantial body of men and women assembled together."[43]

The meeting was important for Douglass, who played a major role throughout. On the first day of the convention, during the morning session, he and Buffum were called upon to address the meeting "in reference to the removal of prejudice against color, and the progress of the general cause in New England." Buffum, embarrassed at being called upon to address the convention, immediately deferred to Douglass. Douglass, eager to speak on the cause he was proud to be a part of, seized the moment and began his speech by declaring that he was "always ready to speak on slavery." Fortunately, a correspondent for the *Pennsylvania Freeman* provided a text of Douglass' remarks. Because Douglass' speech on this occasion has been overlooked by previous scholars, it is important to examine it carefully here.[44]

After proclaiming his willingness to speak, Douglass defined his role at the convention and his purpose for addressing the audience. He reportedly said he "was there as an abolitionist, and as a slave, for whose redemption abolitionists were toiling, and he felt it to be a duty and a privilege to testify in behalf of anti-slavery, and to strive to warm the hearts of all who were laboring to promote the spread of its principles." It is revealing that Douglass identified his role as an abolitionist first and a slave second. His role in this speech was not to tell of his slave experiences, but to provide testimony as an abolitionist. His audience looked to him to provide guidance and insight into the progress of antislavery in New England.[45]

After defining his role and purpose, Douglass provided testimony as to the progress of the antislavery cause in eastern Pennsylvania. Adapting his remarks to his immediate audience, he shared how he "had listened with deep interest to the soul-stirring report" of the executive committee of the Eastern Pennsylvania Anti-Slavery Society "and rejoiced in the evidences it presented of the progress of anti-slavery in this quarter." Douglass then compared the advances of the antislavery cause in New England with the advances in eastern Pennsylvania. Although he had been in Pennsylvania "but a short time," Douglass averred, "he had seen a great improvement" in the growth of abolitionism "since he was last among us, and he felt cheered and encouraged by it."[46]

Having congratulated the abolitionists in his audience for their efforts on behalf of the slave, Douglass focused his comments on the tangible gains made by the cause in overcoming northern prejudice toward black people. This is the issue the convention had called him to the platform to address, and he consciously fashioned his remarks to meet their expectations. In sharing his knowledge and insights on the progress of the cause, his message was optimistic and encouraging. He wished to bolster the faith of the abolitionists and to inspire them to move forward. "Colored people in New England," he asserted, "are much better treated than they were a short time since." He then contrasted the way black people had been treated in the past with how they were treated in the present and explained how the change in treatment was achieved:

> It had been but two or three years since they were every where repulsed. They were treated with indignity in meeting houses, subjected to insult upon highways and by-ways, in the stage, the steamboat, and railroad car. Everywhere were they met by a prejudice which crushed them to earth. This existed yet to some extent, but had very much dwindled away. On all the railroads in New England, except one of some thirty or forty miles, all distinctions on account of color were done away with. A great advance had been made. Two years since, a colored man who would have ventured into any other than the Jim Crow car would have been kicked and cuffed and dragged out, and it was useless for him to appeal to law for redress, for courts and railroads were both prejudiced. How was this change effected? By preaching the truth—by showing the absurdity of this prejudice—that the black man was no less a man because of his color.[47]

To demonstrate further that antislavery was making significant progress in New England, Douglass pointed to a recent "heart-cheering" event that had occurred in Massachusetts on the first of August. "The celebration of West India Emancipation, in Hingham," he proclaimed, "was one of the most brilliant and glorious gatherings of abolitionists which had ever taken place in this country—there were not less than seven thousand persons there, and the spirit which prevailed, as well as the number, was cheering." The abolitionists throughout New England, Douglass declared, "were amply compensated by it for all the afflictions and trials they had endured since the commencement of the warfare" against prejudice and slavery. Although major battles had yet to be fought, Douglass declared, abolitionists saw at Hingham "in miniature" what they would eventually see "in full reality." Once again, Douglass reminded his audience how all this had been accomplished. Implying that the crusade to end slavery was a Christian and a moral one, he boldly declared:

> . . . and this was done, sir, by "scattering the living coals of truth" upon the nation's naked heart. Abolitionists have used no other means than preaching the truth—they have been scoffed at and persecuted, but the result of their labors as seen that day—the number and spirit of that gathering will exert an influence which shall be felt not only in Boston but from one end of Massachusetts to the other. We should feel encouraged to go forward.[48]

Douglass' speech abounded with hope. Addressing the Eastern Pennsylvania society as the representative voice of Massachusetts abolitionism, he provided an optimistic outlook for the future and encouraged the Pennsylvania abolitionists to continue to speak out against slavery and prejudice. Armed with only the truth and the freedom of speech, he argued, abolitionists were making tangible gains against racial prejudice in the North. Douglass' speech also provides evidence of his growing stature in the abolitionist movement. He had become a figure of sufficient consequence and he had been invited by the Pennsylvania abolitionists, not to discuss his slave experiences, but to comment on the progress of abolitionism in New England and its prospects for the future. He responded to their request with a spirited message urging the faithful in Pennsylvania to go forward with the struggle to end prejudice and slavery.

Douglass spoke twice more during the Eastern Pennsylvania society convention. On Tuesday morning, he participated in a lively debate over resolutions calling for the dissolution of the Union.[49] On the final day of the convention, he spoke on the subject of finances and called upon the abolitionists present to contribute to the cause of abolitionism in Pennsylvania. Approximately $600 in much-needed donations and subscriptions were collected. After the meeting, abolitionist J. Miller McKim wrote a letter to Garrison stating, we are "infinitely indebted" to you and our "dear friends from Massachusetts, for the timely aid your long-to-be-remembered visit has afforded us." Douglass and the delegation from Massachusetts, McKim continued, had given the abolitionists of Pennsylvania a "new impulse . . . and a mountain load of prejudice [was] removed from the minds of the people, which but for your coming, would have stood as a strong barrier to much of the effort we hope to make in [the] future, conjointly with you, for the promotion of the cause."[50]

With the conclusion of the Norristown meeting, Douglass rode to Philadelphia, where on Sunday, 17 August, he was the featured speaker at an antislavery meeting in the State House yard. Well publicized by the local newspapers and on placards posted throughout the city, the meeting was attended by some 1,000 persons and was especially noteworthy given Philadelphia's history of antiblack, anti-abolitionist sentiments.[51] Throughout the 1820s, white citizens in Philadelphia regularly drove blacks away from Independence Square on the Fourth of July because they were thought not to have had any part in the struggle to establish the nation. In August 1834 a white mob marched through the black section of Philadelphia and beat and stoned its inhabitants, destroyed homes, churches, and meeting halls, forced many to flee the city, and left others homeless. The mob activity lasted three days before police put an end to it. Philadelphia's antislavery movement had also prompted numerous outbreaks of unrest among proslavery supporters who feared that the city and communities to its south would be overrun by a migration of blacks from Maryland and beyond if they were no longer restrained by slavery. Proslavery mobs often disturbed antislavery meetings, ridiculing and harassing speakers and threatening violence. In May 1838 a proslavery mob burned Philadelphia Hall, the abolitionists' meeting place, to the ground. Only two years before Douglass' speech, white mobs had attacked a parade of blacks commemorating the abolition of slavery in the British West Indies. The attack triggered a disturbance that ended only after whites had beaten many blacks, destroyed several homes, and burned down the African Hall and the Colored Presbyterian Church. State troops had to be called upon to assist local police in calming the city.[52]

At six o'clock in the evening, Douglass ascended the steps of Independence Hall and addressed the massive audience. Although there is no surviving text of his speech, it is possible to reconstruct some of what he said from the *Pennsylvania Freeman*'s account of the meeting. "At first he seemed embarrassed and spoke with some hesitancy," the *Freeman* observed, "but soon his embarrassment disappeared; his heart began to play, and he poured forth a stream of glowing thought and thrilling eloquence." Standing under the eaves of the old hall in which the Declaration of Independence was adopted, Douglass reportedly "made one or two allusions to this circumstance with thrilling effect." He also preached his slaveholder's sermon and, "full of cutting sarcasm as it was, it was received with enthusiastic applause."[53]

Although "some symptoms of disapprobation were apparent" in the audience, reported a correspondent to the *Philadelphia Ledger*, the speech was "interesting, and of an excellent style of composition, delivered in an easy, fluent manner" and "the applause of the majority drowned the dissenting voices." Only one hour into the speech, however, it came to an abrupt end when police officers, as a precaution against a riot, intervened and dispersed the crowd. Indeed, the correspondent to the *Pittsburgh Mystery* was astounded that an antislavery meeting was held in the State House yard "without receiving the usual mobbing!" The only mobbing Douglass experienced was a friendly one. Almost everyone present, McKim wrote to Garrison, "seemed to be deeply impressed by his address, and quite a number pressed forward [at the end of his speech] to give him a hearty and approving shake of the hand." McKim also reflected on the greater significance of successfully holding an outdoor antislavery meeting in Philadelphia. "After all the riots and bloodshed we have had," he wrote to Garrison, "to hold an anti-slavery meeting in the State House yard, where such a thing was never before successfully attempted, and to have for our speaker on the occasion a colored man and a slave, is something on which, both as friends of abolition and good order, I think we may congratulate ourselves." In light of the heritage of violent anti-black, anti-abolitionist sentiment, Douglass' performance in the State House yard on the steps of Independence Hall was all the more significant and impressive.[54]

After delivering an antislavery address at Gardiner's Church in Philadelphia on 19 August,[55] Douglass joined Charles Lenox Remond for a seven-day speaking tour of Chester County under the auspices of the American and Pennsylvania antislavery societies. While there are no surviving speech texts from the tour, we can get a good view of it from personal correspondence, from reports published in the *Liberator*, and from Douglass' summaries of the meetings published in the *Pennsylvania Freeman*. In addition to informing us about Douglass' activities on the tour, these accounts tell us much about the details of life as an abolitionist agent during the 1840s.

Douglass and Remond held their first meeting of the tour on Thursday, 22 August, at West Chester.[56] After unsuccessfully seeking a place to hold their meetings, they planned to speak, according to Douglass' account, "in a beautiful grove, less than a mile distant from the village." The weather, however, turned stormy and the meeting was forced to gather in the markethouse, which, "fortunately for us and the slave," Douglass reported, "was doorless, and could not be shut." According to Douglass, the "extremely damp and uncomfortably cool" weather, "coupled with the disgraceful fact that the people of the town have sunken inextricably into the mire and *Clay*, which in this county, and at the present time everywhere besets the feet of the unsuspecting," resulted in "a very small meeting."

Although Douglass believed that many of the people who did attend "came with no higher motive than to gratify an idle curiosity," the audience gave the speakers "very good attention." Douglass was especially inspired by the few women abolitionists in attendance who, "almost alone in the community of thousands," asserted truths and lived out principles "at once hated and feared by almost the entire community." They carried forward their antislavery beliefs, Douglass continued, "with a composure and serenity of soul which would well compare with the most experienced champion and standard bearer of our cause, Friend Garrison himself."[57]

Douglass and Remond next traveled southwest to Oxford, where on Saturday, 24 August, they attended a meeting of the Clarkson Anti-Slavery Society in the Friend's Meetinghouse.[58] After his negative experience at West Chester, Douglass was delighted with the Clarkson society, which he found to be "one of the most venerable and impressive anti-slavery bodies with which it has been my fortune to meet." Unlike the gathering at West Chester, the Clarkson convention attracted a very large audience and "many had to stand outside, not being able to gain admission into the house." As Douglass reported, he and Remond "were listened to both within and without the house, with a deep stillness, that indicated an absorbing interest in the subjects we were but feebly attempting to set forth." The positive response cheered and energized Douglass greatly. "Whatever of gloom was cast over my spirits by our meeting at West Chester," he wrote, "was completely dispelled by our meeting at Oxford."[59]

The next day, Sunday, 25 August, Douglass and Remond held an afternoon antislavery meeting on the steps of the London Grove Meetinghouse.[60] The outdoor meeting, Douglass wrote exuberantly, "was a most splendid demonstration. The day was fine, the heavens clear, the sun bright, the air salubrious, and the scenery by which we were surrounded extremely grand; all nature seemed redolent with anti-slavery truth." People came from as far as fifteen miles away to attend the meeting. "It was truly delightful, a short time before the commencement of the meeting," Douglass reflected, "to look down the long roads in various directions, and see them almost literally alive with the gathering multitude. The old and young, the men and women on foot, on horseback and in wagons, were all pressing their way amid dust and din, towards the great Quaker meeting house, under the eaves of which, we had to hold our meeting, as it . . . stood locked and bolted against us." Remond addressed the meeting first. "He stood upon a large horse block," Douglass reported, "and spoke for more than an hour, in a strain of stern rebuke." When Remond had finished, Douglass addressed the audience for an hour and a half. Because Remond "had left but little for me to do in the way of rebuke," Douglass noted, "of consequence I pursued a somewhat different course, and I think reached another class of minds present, as necessary to the cause as any other." Unfortunately, Douglass did not disclose what subject he pursued in his speech.[61]

From London Grove, Douglass and Remond traveled to Marlboro to attend a two-day meeting of the Chester County Anti-Slavery Society.[62] Douglass characterized the 27-28 August annual meeting as "interesting to the last." On the first day, the convention gathered in the Friend's Meetinghouse. At times, reported a correspondent to the *Pennsylvania Freeman*, there "were probably about eight hundred people in attendance." After the minutes from the previous meeting of the society and the report of the board of managers were read, Remond and Douglass "made some remarks upon the prejudice on account of color, &c." In the afternoon, resolutions were introduced which denounced American churches as being proslavery and called on abolitionists to vote only for candidates "as will support the abrogation of all constitutional and legal provisions which sustain slavery." Another resolution called the annexation of Texas "a great evil" and demanded that abolitionists not vote for Henry Clay or James Polk for president of the United States. The discussion of these resolutions lasted most of the day and the following morning.[63]

According to the minutes from the meeting, during the afternoon session, Douglass made a stirring speech against voting for Clay for president. The recording secretary wrote in the minutes that Douglass "expressed such sentiments as 'rail-roads to emancipation, cannot rest on *Clay* foundation,' in such *musical* tones as have but seldom been heard in the gallery of Friend's meeting house." Douglass most likely quoted these "musical tones" from a song written by Jesse Hutchinson and performed by the Hutchinson Family Singers, an abolitionist singing group from New Hampshire. The lines Douglass quoted came from the sixth stanza of "Get Off the Track":

Rail Roads to Emancipation

Cannot *rest* on *Clay* Foundation,

And the *tracks* of *"the Magician"*

Are but Railroads to perdition.

Pull up the Rails! Emancipation

Cannot rest on such foundation.[64]

The following day, the Chester County meeting gathered in a grove near the Friend's Meetinghouse. During the morning session, Douglass reportedly joined in a discussion over a resolution condemning the church as a "den of thieves" who should "be cast out as evil by all who love pure and undefiled religion." Douglass and Remond, the correspondent to the *Pennsylvania Freeman* reported, "those tried and true friends of the cause," with the "words of ready eloquence, and deep and thrilling tones, attuned to the anti-slavery of heart," had done much to "'help the cause along.'" in Marlboro.[65]

From Marlboro, Douglass and Remond returned to Philadelphia for a week of intensive antislavery activity. On Friday evening, 30 August, they addressed a meeting at Wilbur Fisk Hall, and on Saturday, 31 August, they conducted a meeting at Clarkson Hall. On Sunday morning, 1 September, they spoke to an audience gathered in Gardiner's Church, and on that afternoon they traveled to nearby Byberry, where they were scheduled to hold an antislavery meeting at a small schoolhouse called the Academy.[66] According to McKim, who was in attendance, quite a few people made the short journey from Philadelphia to Byberry to attend the meeting. At the last minute, fearing the Academy would not be large enough to hold those wishing to hear Douglass and Remond, the doors of the spacious Friend's Meetinghouse were opened, "and at the time appointed, quite a large audience was assembled." Douglass spoke first, McKim reported, and "related some passages in his experience as a slave, and particularly the manner in which he learned to read and write." Eight months later, he most likely provided a similar account of how he learned to read and write for his readers in the pages of his autobiography, *Narrative of the Life of Frederick Douglass, An American Slave, Written By Himself*.[67] Remond followed with "a very able discourse on the general subject of slavery." Both orators, McKim observed, "were listened to with deep attention, and the people went away apparently satisfied with the meeting."[68]

Before leaving Philadelphia to return to Massachusetts, Douglass reflected on his Pennsylvania tour. "I have formed a decidedly favorable opinion of Pennsylvania Anti-Slavery people by recent contact with them," he wrote to McKim. "They have not yet quite rid themselves of what seems to me to be prejudice against color; but they are advancing and I trust will soon free themselves from its last vestige." He looked forward to the time when he, McKim, "and the anti-slavery friends of Pennsylvania" would meet again.[69]

Douglass' impressive and eloquent performances during the summer of 1844—especially his dramatic address from the steps of Philadelphia's Independence Hall—added fuel to the doubts that he had ever been a slave. Four years on the public platform had matured Douglass. As his oratory had become more sophisticated and his power over audiences more masterful, he found it increasingly necessary to reveal details of his slave past. After all, Douglass later recalled, he "did not talk like a slave, look like a slave, nor act like a slave," and he had been warned by the leaders of the movement that he should not "seem too learned" because people would not believe he had been brought up in slavery. In discussing his life as a slave, though, he faced a formidable rhetorical challenge. The more he revealed about his past, the greater was the danger of his being recaptured and returned to slavery. Yet if he withheld too many of the facts about his years in bondage, his credibility as an authentic voice from slavery would be diminished and he might be perceived as an imposter. By the end of August 1844, those fears were being realized as doubts over his slave past were published in abolitionist journals and rumors spread through New England that he was an educated free black acting as an uneducated fugitive slave. Dealing with this issue was to pose a major problem for Douglass and would have a profound impact not only on his activities as an abolitionist but also on the full course of his public career.[70]

Notes

1. Of Douglass' biographers, only Fulkerson and McFeely investigate briefly this four-month term. See Raymond Gerald Fulkerson, "Frederick Douglass and the Anti-Slavery Crusade: His Career and Speeches, 1817-1861," pt. 1 (Ph.D. diss., University of Illinois, 1971), 71-73; William S. McFeely, *Frederick Douglass* (New York: Norton, 1991), 114.

2. Blassingame misdates this meeting as taking place on 6-11 May. See John W. Blassingame, ed., *The Frederick Douglass Papers, Series One: Speeches, Debates, and Interviews, Volume 1* (New Haven, Conn.: Yale University Press, 1979), 1:xciii.

3. Other honored guests included Abby Kelley, Stephen S. Foster, Erasmus D. Hudson, Charles Lenox Remond, and Sydney Howard Gay (Sydney Howard Gay to Erasmus D. Hudson, 20 April 1844, Special Collections and Archives, University Library, University of Massachusetts, Amherst).

4. Garrison's notion of disunion had been evolving since 1842 and was translated into official action during the eleventh annual meeting of the Massachusetts Anti-Slavery Society in January 1843. On the third day of that convention Garrison resolved, "That the compact which exists between the North and the South is 'a covenant with death, and an agreement with hell'-involving both pt.ies in atrocious criminality; and should be immediately annulled." The resolution was adopted by the convention. See the *Liberator*, 3 February 1843: 18.

5. Wendell Phillips, Charles Lenox Remond, Stephen S. Foster, and Edmund Quincy were among those who spoke in support of Garrison's resolution (*National Anti-Slavery Standard*, 16 May 1844, 198-99).

6. *National Anti-Slavery Standard*, 16 May 1844, 198-99; *Thirteenth Annual Report, Presented to the Massachusetts Anti-Slavery Society, By Its Board of Managers, January 22, 1845* (1845; reprint, Westport, Conn.: Negro Universities Press, 1970), 27-30; *National Anti-Slavery Standard*, 23 May 1844, 203; *National Anti-Slavery Standard*, 30 May 1844, 206.

7. *Liberator*, 21 June 1844, 97; *Practical Christian* in the *Liberator*, 7 June 1844, 91; *Liberator*, 31 May 1844, 87.

8. *Liberator*, 7 June 1844, 91; *National Anti-Slavery Standard*, 13 June 1844, 6.

9. The text of his speech at the New England Anti-Slavery Society meeting was published in the *National Anti-Slavery Standard*, 25 July 1844, 301, and is reproduced in appendix C of this work. It is not included in any published collection of Douglass' speeches or writings.

10. *National Anti-Slavery Standard*, 25 July 1844, 30.

11. Ibid.

12. Ibid.

13. Ibid.

14. Rufus Choate (1799-1859), was a member of the Massachusetts House of Representatives in 1825 and served in the state senate in 1826. In 1830 he was elected as a Whig to the U.S. Congress, where he served from 1831 through 1834. In 1840 he was elected to the Senate and served until March 1845, when he retired from public life to devote his time to practicing law. Isaac Chapman Bates (1779-1845), was a member of the Massachusetts House of Representatives in 1808 and 1809. In 1826 he was elected to the U.S. Congress and remained a congressman until 1835. Six years later, he was elected to the U.S. Senate, where he served until his death in 1845. For information on both men, see *Biographical Directory of the American Congress, 1774-1971* (Washington, D.C.: U.S. Government Printing Office, 1971), 563, 735.

The incident Douglass referred to occurred in the Senate in January 1844. Senator Bates presented resolutions from the Massachusetts legislature against the annexation of Texas and in favor of an amendment to the U.S. Constitution to apportion representation and direct taxation among the states, thereby avoiding the slave population in each. Senators King and Bagby of Alabama responded to the Massachusetts resolves in a manner that, according to the *New York Express*, was "most personal and disrespectful towards the Commonwealth of Massachusetts." King and Bagby, wrote the editor of the *Lowell Journal*, "abused the State, and the Legislature, of Massachusetts-talked of incendiarism and fanaticism in the usual style of Southern bravado." Throughout the "insulting treatment and opprobrious abuse of the State they represented," the Thirteenth Annual Report of the Massachusetts Antislavery Society declared, Bates and Choate "sat tamely by and had not a word of indignant remonstrance to utter in her behalf." See the *New York Express* in the *Liberator*, 16 February 1844, 27; *Lowell Journal* in the *Liberator*, 1 March 1844, 34; *Thirteenth Annual Report*, 4-5.

15. *National Anti-Slavery Standard*, 25 July 1844, 30.

16. Ibid.

17. Ibid.

18. Ibid.

19. Ibid.

20. Ibid. Douglass may have been referring to Frank McIntosh, a free black steam-boat porter and cook who was burned at the stake by an angry St. Louis mob of white people on 28 April 1836 for having killed a white police officer while resisting arrest. A short time after killing the police officer, McIntosh was arrested and was followed to jail by a mob of approximately five thousand people. Yielding to the mob's demand for a swift execution, the sheriff gave up McIntosh, who was immediately strung to a tree and burned to death. A witness to the scene reported McIntosh lived only ten minutes and "died singing at the top of his voice, 'O, when shall I see Jesus, and reign with him above?'" About one month later, the case came to trial. In deciding the case, Judge Luke E. Lawless blamed the killing of the police officer on "abolitionist fanatics." No members of the mob were punished for the lynching of McIntosh. See John Gill, *Tide Without Turning: Elijah P. Lovejoy and Freedom of the Press* (Boston: Starr King Press, 1959), 60-75.

21. *National Anti-Slavery Standard*, 25 July 1844, 30. Gates was elected as an antislavery Whig representative from New York to the U.S. House of Representatives in 1839 and again in 1841. After unsuccessfully campaigning for re-election in 1843, he returned to his law practice in Le Roy, New York. For a detailed account of the incident Douglass described, see Seth M. Gates, "The Long Bridge—the Escape," on the front page of the *Herald of Freedom*, 25 July 1845. For more about Gates, see *Biographical Directory of the American Congress, 1774-1971*, 990.

22. *National Anti-Slavery Standard*, 25 July 1844, 30.

23. Ibid.

24. Approximately sixteen of Turner's followers were executed, and other members of the rebellion were transported to sundry parts of the South. Turner remained hidden for over six weeks. After being captured, he was quickly brought to trial, convicted, and hanged. See Dumas Malone, ed., *Dictionary of American Biography* (New York: Charles Scribner's Sons, 1936), 19:69-70; Herbert Aptheker, *Nat Turner's Slave Rebellion* (New York: Humanities Press, 1966); Alfred Celestine, *Confessions of Nat Turner* (London: Many Press, 1978); Stephen B. Oates, *The Fires of Jubilee: Nat Turner's Fierce Rebellion* (New York: Harper and Row, 1975); William Styron, *The Confessions of Nat Turner* (New York: New American Library, 1967).

25. *National Anti-Slavery Standard*, 25 July 1844, 30.

26. To the best of my knowledge, this is the first published instance of Douglass mentioning Nat Turner's rebellion during a speech. Four years later, he evoked Turner's name to advance a similar argument during a 30 May 1848 speech at Boston's Faneuil Hall. See "The Slaves' Right to Revolt: An Address Delivered in Boston, Massachusetts, on 30 May 1848" in *The Frederick Douglass Papers, Series One: Speeches, Debates, and Interviews, Volume 2*, ed. John W. Blassingame (New Haven, Conn.: Yale University Press, 1982), 2:130-31.

27. On 12 November 1841, the British government, ignoring the requests of the American consul to return the slaves and the nineteen mutineers to the United States, freed all the slaves not involved in the mutiny and jailed the mutineers. Southern congressmen demanded the return of the mutineers and insisted on compensation for the freed slaves. Daniel Webster, secretary of state under President John Tyler, intervened on behalf of the U.S. government and called for reparations. In 1842 the Nassau attorney general freed the nineteen mutineers. The conflict between the United States and Great Britain over the *Creole* incident remained unresolved until 1855, when an Anglo-American claims commission awarded $110,330 to the owners of the freed slaves. See Howard Jones, "The Peculiar Institution and National Honor: The Case of the *Creole* Slave Revolt," *Civil War History* 21 (March 1975): 28-50; *Liberator*, 10 June 1842: 89; Blassingame, ed., *Douglass Papers, Series One*, 1:68n. The story of Madison Washington's role in the mutiny aboard the *Creole* later inspired Douglass' novella, "The Heroic Slave," in *Autographs For Freedom*, ed. Julia W. Griffiths (Boston, Mass.: John P. Jewitt, 1853), 174-239.

28. *National Anti-Slavery Standard*, 25 July 1844, 30. According to my research, this was the first published instance of Douglass mentioning Madison Washington during a speech. One year later, Douglass invoked Washington's name during an address he delivered in Cork, Ireland. See "American Prejudice Against Color: An Address Delivered in Cork, Ireland, 23 October 1845" in Blassingame, ed., *Douglass Papers, Series One*, 1:67-69.

29. *National Anti-Slavery Standard*, 25 July 1844, 30.

30. When the vote was taken on the dissolution of the Union resolutions, they passed by a vote of 247 to 23. *Liberator*, 31 May 1844, 87; *National Anti-Slavery Standard*, 13 June 1844, 6.

31. *National Anti-Slavery Standard*, 13 June 1844, 6; *Liberator*, 14 June 1844, 95; *Liberator*, 21 June 1844, 97. According to the report in the *Liberator*, Goodenow admitted that church bodies "composed chiefly of what he called good anti-slavery people, sent delegates to ecclesiastical bodies which were in full fellowship with slaveholders, and received delegates from those bodies." He also conceded "that those slaveholding ministers when sent as delegates, were taken to the communion table, conducted into the pulpit, and otherwise treated as Christian ministers of exceptionable character" (*Liberator*, 21 June 1844, 97).

32. Blassingame, ed., *Douglass Papers, Series One*, 1:xciii, does not include this meeting in its itinerary of Douglass' speaking activities. Fulkerson, "Frederick Douglass," pt. 1, 72, misstates that Hallowell is located in Massachusetts.

33. *Hallowell Cultivator* in the *Liberator*, 14 June 1844, 93.

34. Blassingame, ed., *Douglass Papers, Series One*, 1:xciii, misdates this meeting as taking place on 12 June only.

35. *Liberator*, 21 June 1844, 99.

36. Ibid.

37. Douglass' activities from mid-June to the end of July are difficult to determine. Neither the *Liberator* nor the *National Anti-Slavery Standard* advertised any of his lectures or documented his participation in any antislavery meetings during this period. According Blassingame, ed., *Douglass Papers, Series One*, 1:xciii, on 28 June Douglass attended the Essex County Anti-Slavery Society meeting in Methuen, Massachusetts. However, Douglass' name does not appear in the minutes of the meeting, published in the *Liberator*, 12 July 1844, 111, and it is probable that he was not in attendance. Douglass was invited to attend an antislavery meeting in Nashua, New Hampshire, from 26 to 29 July, but there is no indication of his presence in the accounts of the proceedings published in the *Liberator*, 27 September 1844, 153.

38. Douglass had also been invited to be the chief speaker at the 1 August celebration in Providence, Rhode Island, but he did not attend, an outcome that greatly disappointed the organizers and left many of Providence's blacks "much grieved" (*Liberator*, 16 August 1844, 131). On 17 August, Douglass wrote to the *Liberator* that he "deeply regretted" missing the meeting at Providence and explained his absence (*Liberator*, 31 August 1844, 138).

39. *Liberator*, 12 July 1844, 111; *National Anti-Slavery Standard*, 18 July 1844, 27; *Liberator*, 9 August 1844, 127; *National Anti-Slavery Standard*, 15 August 1844, 41. The other speakers were William A. White, Samuel J. May, Moses Grundy, and Cyrus Pierce (*National Anti-Slavery Standard*, 15 August 1844, 42).

40. *National Anti-Slavery Standard*, 15 August 1844, 42.

41. Ibid.; *Liberator*, 9 August 1844, 127; *Liberator*, 23 August 1844, 135.

42. Blassingame, ed., *Douglass Papers, Series One*, 1:xciii, erroneously states that this meeting occurred on 12 August only.

43. *Liberator*, 9 August 1844, 127; *Pennsylvania Freeman*, 22 August 1844, 2; *Liberator*, 23 August 1844, 135.

44. The text of the speech was published in the *Pennsylvania Freeman*, 22 August 1844, 3, and is reproduced in appendix D of this work.

45. *Pennsylvania Freeman*, 22 August 1844, 1-3.

46. Ibid., 3.

47. Ibid.

48. Ibid.

49. Although the minutes from the proceedings do not identify the subject of his remarks or account for what he said, according to Garrison's account of the meeting, Douglass was among the speakers who spoke in favor of disunion (*Liberator*, 23 August 1844, 135).

50. *Pennsylvania Freeman*, 22 August 1844, 2; *Liberator*, 23 August 1844, 135; *Liberator*, 31 August 1844, 138.

51. The estimate of the crowd is from the *Pittsburgh Mystery* in the *Liberator*, 13 September 1844, 46. The *Philadelphia Ledger* sought to downplay the meeting

by claiming that it was attended by no more than two hundred persons, "about one-third of whom were colored" (*Philadelphia Ledger* in the *National Anti-Slavery Standard*, 29 August 1844, 51). Abolitionist J. Miller McKim reported to Garrison that the "audience was a very good one both in point of numbers and in character, embracing persons of almost every class, and some of both sexes" (*Liberator*, 31 August 1844, 138).

52. See Leon F. Litwack, *North of Slavery: The Negro in the Free States, 1790-1860* (Chicago: University of Chicago Press, 1961), 100-2; John Hope Franklin, *From Slavery to Freedom: A History of Negro Americans*, 3d ed. (New York: Knopf, 1967), 234-35; McFeely, *Frederick Douglass*, 113; Edward T. James, ed., *Notable American Women, 1607-1950: A Biographical Dictionary* (Cambridge, Mass.: Harvard University Press, 1971), 2:98.

53. *Pennsylvania Freeman*, 22 August 1844, 3.

54. *Philadelphia Ledger*, 26 August 1844, in the *National Anti-Slavery Standard*, 29 August 1844, 51; *Pittsburgh Mystery* in the *Liberator*, 13 September 1844, 146; *Pennsylvania Freeman*, 22 August 1844, 3; *Liberator*, 31 August 1844, 138.

55. Blassingame, ed., *Douglass Papers, Series One*, 1:xciii, does not include this address in its itinerary of Douglass' speaking activities. According to the *Pennsylvania Freeman*, 22 August 1844, 3, the Monday evening gathering in Gardiner's Church was well attended despite the "notice of the meeting being very short" and the outbreak of a thunderstorm just before the meeting.

56. Blassingame, ed., *Douglass Papers, Series One*, 1:xciii, does not include this meeting in its itinerary of Douglass' speaking activities, McFeely, *Frederick Douglass*, 114, misdates the meeting as taking place in September 1844.

57. *Pennsylvania Freeman*, 22 August 1844, 3; *Pennsylvania Freeman*, 5 September 1844, 2.

58. Blassingame, ed., *Douglass Papers, Series One*, 1:xciii, does not include this meeting in its itinerary of Douglass' speaking activities.

59. *Pennsylvania Freeman*, 22 August 1844, 3; *Pennsylvania Freeman*, 5 September 1844, 2.

60. Blassingame, ed., *Douglass Papers, Series One*, 1:xciii, does not include this meeting in its itinerary of Douglass' speaking activities. McFeely, *Frederick Douglass*, 114, misspells the location of the meeting as "Landon Grove."

61. *Pennsylvania Freeman*, 22 August 1844, 3; *Pennsylvania Freeman*, 5 September 1844, 2.

62. Blassingame, ed., *Douglass Papers, Series One*, 1:xciii, does not include this meeting in its itinerary of Douglass' speaking activities.

63. *Pennsylvania Freeman*, 10 October 1844, 4.

64. First performed during an antislavery meeting in Lowell, Massachusetts, 22 February 1844, the song proved to be one of the Hutchinsons' most famous productions. See Dale Cockrell, ed., *Excelsior: Journals of the Hutchinson Family Singers, 1842-1846* (Stuyvesant, N.Y.: Pendragon Press, 1989), 252-58.

65. *Pennsylvania Freeman*, 10 October 1844, 4.

66. Blassingame, ed., *Douglass Papers, Series One*, 1:xciii, misdates Douglass' and Remond's speeches on 1 September at Gardiner's Church and at Byberry as occurring on 21 September. Unfortunately, there are no records of what Douglass and Remond said in their speeches of 30 August, 31 August, and 1 September except for the meeting at Byberry.

67. *Pennsylvania Freeman*, 5 September 1844, 3. See Frederick Douglass, *Narrative of the Life of Frederick Douglass, An American Slave, Written By Himself* (1845; reprint, New York: Signet, 1968), 49-50, 53-54, 57-58.

68. *Pennsylvania Freeman*, 5 September 1844, 3. For another account of the Byberry meeting, see Lucretia Mott to Nathaniel and Eliza Barney, 17 September 1844, Foulger Library, Nantucket Historical Association.

69. *Pennsylvania Freeman*, 5 September 1844, 2.

70. Frederick Douglass, *My Bondage and My Freedom* (1855; reprint, New York: Dover, 1969), 362; "The Cambria Riot, My Slave Experience, and My Irish Mission: An Address Delivered in Belfast, Ireland, on 5 December 1845," in Blassingame, ed., *Douglass Papers, Series One*, 1:89.

Chapter Nine

Douglass the Imposter: I Am a Slave, September 1844-August 1845

SINCE THE GENESIS of his career as a lecturer for the Massachusetts Anti-Slavery Society in 1841, Frederick Douglass' fame as an eloquent fugitive slave had steadily increased and his oratory had constantly advanced in sophistication and power. It is no surprise, then, that people began to question whether Douglass had ever been a slave. How, they wondered, could anyone who had been a slave and deprived of a formal education speak so eloquently and conduct himself with so much dignity and grace on the platform? Growing public skepticism about his past compelled him to devote a large portion of his time from October 1844 through April 1845 to committing his slave experiences to paper. His literary efforts culminated in May 1845 with the publication of his autobiographical *Narrative of the Life of Frederick Douglass, An American Slave, Written By Himself.*

Because the *Narrative* has become such an important historical and literary document, most scholars have overlooked Douglass' oratorical activities from September 1844 through August 1845.[1] Although Douglass reduced his speaking schedule while he was writing the *Narrative*, he continued to participate in local, county, and regional abolitionist meetings, delivered numerous antislavery lectures, and participated in two out-of-state lecture tours. After his autobiography was published in May 1845, he traveled alone through Massachusetts and New York lecturing at antislavery meetings, promoting the *Narrative*, and raising funds for his trip to Great Britain. He remained on tour through the first week of August. On 16 August 1845, he and James N. Buffum boarded the steamer *Cambria* in Boston harbor bound for Liverpool, England, thereby closing the curtain on the early stage of Douglass' career as an orator and an abolitionist.

I

After spending two weeks promoting the cause of antislavery in eastern Pennsylvania, Douglass and Charles Lenox Remond left Philadelphia for New England on 4 September 1844.[2] When Douglass arrived in Lynn, he found "one of his children dangerously ill with the measles." In a brief letter to William Lloyd Garrison that was published in the *Liberator*, Douglass informed his antislavery friends in Dover, New Hampshire, that he would not be able to join them on a scheduled lecture tour of that state until his child was well.[3] It was also during this period that newspaper accounts were published in the *Liberator* and the *Pennsylvania Freeman* reporting on Douglass' speech of 17 August at the State House yard in Philadelphia. What Douglass read in these reports must have troubled him deeply. In both accounts his background as a slave was called into question. J. Miller McKim recounted to Garrison and the readers of the *Liberator*:

> Many persons in the audience seemed unable to credit the statements which he gave of himself, and could not believe that he was actually a slave. How a man, only six years out of bondage, and who had never gone to school a day in his life, could speak with such eloquence—with such precision of language and power of thought—they were utterly at a loss to devise.[4]

McKim published a similar account in the *Pennsylvania Freeman*. After a slow start, McKim reported to his readers, Douglass

> poured forth a stream of glowing thought and thrilling eloquence, which, coming from an unlettered colored man, seemed to many of the audience utterly amazing. They could scarcely believe him when he said that he was still a slave, and liable at any moment, under the constitution and laws of the country, to be sent back to hopeless bondage. How a man not six years freed from the yoke, and never having been, as he said, a single day to school in his life, should exhibit such a command of language and force of thought, they were utterly at a loss to imagine.[5]

These two accounts, published in two widely circulated abolitionist newspapers, marked the first time that Douglass' slave past had been called into question in the abolitionist press. Douglass recalled in 1855, as he wrote his second autobiography, that by 1844 many of his audiences had come to doubt if he had ever been a slave. He recalled "going down the aisles of the churches" where he spoke "and hearing the free Yankees saying, repeatedly, '*He's never been a slave, I'll warrant ye*'":

They said I did not talk like a slave, look like a slave, nor act like a slave, and that they believed I had never been south of Mason and Dixon's line. "He don't tell us where he came from—what his master's name was—how he got away—nor the story of his experience. Besides he is educated, and is, in this, a contradiction of all the facts we have concerning the ignorance of the slaves." Thus, I was in a pretty fair way to be denounced as an imposter.[6]

During antislavery meetings he could respond immediately to questions about his background. Rebutting the doubts published in abolitionist journals required a different kind of answer. Douglass resolved, therefore, "to dispel all doubt, at no distant day, by such a revelation of facts as could not be made by any other than a genuine fugitive."[7]

In the meantime, however, he had a sick child to attend to and was committed to a lecture tour of New Hampshire with Remond, Abby Kelley, Stephen S. Foster, Parker Pillsbury, and J. M. Spear. He joined his fellow agents near the middle of September. Although there are no detailed accounts of their efforts, the tour appears to have been highly successful.[8] In October the *Liberator* reported that the speakers had thus far "met with good success" and called on the people of the Granite State to continue to attend the conventions. In November the *National Anti-Slavery Standard* informed its readers that "a full corps of the agents of the American Anti-Slavery Society, in cooperation with the New Hampshire Anti-Slavery Society, have been engaged in lectures and conventions in various parts of the State, with the best results." The editors of the *Standard* estimated that more than 100 meetings and conventions had been held.[9]

Douglass returned to Lynn from New Hampshire in early October. The time had arrived to begin writing his autobiography.[10] Over the next seven months, he would spend most of his time at home. He reduced his speaking schedule and confined the majority of his lecturing and convention appearances to eastern New England. In the middle of October, he took time off from writing to attend the Bristol County Anti-Slavery Society convention in New Bedford. The meeting began Saturday, 19 October, at the spacious Liberty Hall. Due to a "violent storm," Edmund Quincy reported to the *National Anti-Slavery Standard*, the attendance at the opening session was small. Still, there were enough people present to organize the meeting. During the opening session, Douglass was appointed to the business committee. In the afternoon, a series of resolutions were introduced by Quincy on behalf of the business committee. Douglass was one of four speakers to support the first resolution, which declared that "slavery is the greatest wrong man can do to a man." The next day, during the afternoon session, resolutions calling for the immediate dissolution of the Union were debated, and Douglass reportedly "gave his views on the subject in a clear and able manner." During the final session of the convention, Douglass addressed the audience on the proslavery character of the Whig, Democratic, and Liberty Parties. During his speech, Quincy reported, Douglass "interwove with his argument an account of his arrival in New Bedford, and his early experiences there, and concluded with his slaveholder's sermon." The story of Douglass' arrival in New Bedford and his early experiences there would soon be available to readers in his *Narrative*. Not everyone in attendance at the meeting found Douglass' "slaveholder's sermon" a proper conclusion. One observer was distressed at Douglass' "somewhat mirthful and comic" manner. "There is too much of dredful [sic] injustice and wrong," he wrote, "to be treated otherwise than by sober argument or solemn denunciation."[11]

Following the Bristol County convention, Douglass and Remond remained in New Bedford to attend a two-day Liberty Party meeting scheduled for 22-23 October.[12] This important meeting has been overlooked by all of Douglass' biographers. In a letter to Garrison, Douglass explained that he and Remond decided to attend the Liberty Party convention because they had learned their "old and esteemed friend," George Bradburn, would be present and would "state his reasons for joining the Liberty party." Desiring to learn what these reasons might be, Douglass and Remond were "induced to stay and attend the convention." The first day's sessions went smoothly. Approximately 100 people, including Douglass and Remond, listened to a speech by S. P. Andrews of Boston in which he gave, according to Douglass, "a fair exposé of the pro-slavery character of the Whig party, saying but little against the Democratic party." At the close of Andrews' speech, the chair announced that Bradburn would be present the next day.[13]

On the next day, the morning session was poorly attended and no one who was there at the start seemed inclined to speak. Bradburn had not yet arrived and there was a lull in the proceedings. The silence was broken when the president of the meeting invited Remond and Douglass to address the gathering. The two Garrisonians did not comply with the request for, according to Douglass, three "very good reasons":

> First—we had no sympathy with the convention, as such. Second—we know the convention had no sympathy with us. Third—calling upon us to speak at that time, and under the circumstances, satisfied us, that they merely wished to make tools of us. We were therefore impelled, by a sense of self-respect, as well as a high regard for our noble enterprise, to refuse co-operation with the convention, and let them do their own speaking, with their own speakers, in their own way.[14]

Bradburn finally arrived toward the end of the morning session. Douglass reported that he greeted his old friend warmly. "I was glad to take him by the hand," Douglass informed Garrison, "and as I did so, looking him in the face, our mutual hardships, trials and conflicts, in attending the never-to-be forgotten One Hundred Anti-Slavery Conventions, held in the western States in 1843, . . . came full into view." Still, Douglass felt there was a "chasm" between Bradburn and himself and that both men were aware of it.[15]

The chasm Douglass sensed was a portent of things to come in the afternoon session, when Bradburn finally spoke and, according to Douglass, "eulogized the ballot-box and Liberty party as the only hope of the slave." He also denounced the American Anti-Slavery Society's position on not voting and questioned the efficacy of moral suasion over political action. "His whole speech was mere assertion, abounding in denunciation," Douglass observed, "and betraying the most wilful hyperbole, and distortion of facts." After Bradburn had finished, he extended an invitation to Douglass and Remond to respond. Douglass accepted because, in his words, he "now felt it his duty to speak." In his speech, Douglass defended the American Anti-Slavery Society's position in regard to voting and the Constitution. He also worked to expose "the absurd heresy, that moral suasion, as applied to slavery, is ineffectual." However, what was "the most trying and painful to Mr. Bradburn, and most offensive to the convention," Douglass reported, was his attack on the "character of the Liberty party, and exposing the corruption of its leaders." Douglass also told the convention that Bradburn, "their honored speaker, had branded these same leaders of the Liberty party as a set of '*unmitigated rogues*' less than one year since."[16]

Not surprisingly, Bradburn responded to Douglass "in the harshest possible manner." In addition, he attacked the executive committee of the American society and denied ever having said anything against the Liberty Party. Douglass stood to reply, but the meeting adjourned and, according to one eyewitness, "left him standing." In the evening, Douglass returned to the convention hoping that the leaders "would have the magnanimity" to allow him to explain his remarks, as he "had been directly charged with misrepresentation." But despite the audience's chanting of "DOUGLASS, DOUGLASS," his request was refused "and the convention broke up in confusion." Not to be denied the opportunity to express their side of the argument, Douglass and Remond then announced their intent to hold a meeting the following evening in Liberty Hall, where they would "expose the machinery of Third party, its commencement and tactics." When the time arrived, Douglass opened the meeting by attacking the Liberty Party and the character of James G. Birney, its nominee for president of the United States. Remond followed Douglass to the stand and continued the attack. Both men, a correspondent reported to the *Liberator*, nobly sustained "old school abolitionism."[17]

Following the meeting, Douglass returned to Lynn. For most of November, he confined his antislavery activities to places close to home.

On Sunday, 3 November, he presented an evening lecture before the Salem Female Anti-Slavery Society. His was the third in a series of lectures delivered in Mechanics' Hall that featured such esteemed abolitionists as Garrison, Remond, Wendell Phillips, John Pierpont, and William A. White.[18] The following day, he traveled the short distance to Marblehead to attend the quarterly meeting of the Essex County Anti-Slavery Society. The two-day meeting, a correspondent reported to the *Liberator*, "was highly interesting." Resolutions were introduced "of a stringent character" denouncing the three political parties. Douglass joined Remond, James N. Buffum, Addison Davis, and others in the discussions. "The meeting passed off with the greatest enthusiasm and tremendous cheering," a correspondent observed, "and will undoubtedly produce a lasting effect."[19]

Toward the end of November, Douglass traveled to Providence to attend the annual meeting of the Rhode Island Anti-Slavery Society.[20] During the three-day meeting that began in Mechanics' Hall on 20 November, he created a storm of controversy for his stand against voting for Henry Clay for president of the United States. The incident occurred during the evening session on the opening day of the convention. After resolutions were introduced by the business committee criticizing those free black men of the city "who cast their ballots for a slaveholder at the recent presidential elections," Douglass took the platform and spoke in support of the resolutions. According to one observer, he rebuked "in the most kind and considerate, but plain and uncompromising manner" the black voters of Rhode Island who voted for Clay. The following evening, Abraham M. Peterson, a Rhode Island Whig and an abolitionist, reportedly "replied with great spirit . . . to Douglass for his abuse of the colored voters of the State, for supporting 'Law and Order, and Henry Clay.'" Peterson, the secretary of the minutes noted, "attempted to justify the colored people in voting for Henry Clay and offered a series of resolutions censuring F. Douglass." The resolutions had been drafted the evening before by a committee representing Rhode Island's Whig black population.[21] Douglass, however, maintained his composure throughout Peterson's invective and, according to the *Liberator*, responded in such a manner as to satisfy "every candid person, if not of the justness of his views, certainly of the purity of his motives." After Douglass' speech, the resolutions of censure were laid on the table. They came before the convention again the following day, but no action was taken. [22]

Shortly after returning from Rhode Island, Douglass traveled from his home in Lynn to Cambridgeport's Town Hall to attend the 26 November meeting of the Middlesex County Anti-Slavery Society. Despite the small attendance, during the opening session Douglass, White, Garrison, Remond, and others spoke on the state of the antislavery cause. Douglass remained quiet for the remainder of the day.[23] Following the meeting at

Cambridgeport, Douglass returned home, where he remained throughout most of December 1844 and January 1845. His only speaking engagement for December occurred toward the end of the month, when he traveled to Portsmouth, New Hampshire, to deliver antislavery lectures on Saturday and Sunday, 21 and 22 December, in response to an invitation from the Ladies' Anti-Slavery Society.[24] In early January, he traveled to New Hampshire with Stephen S. Foster for a brief antislavery lecture tour.[25]

After returning to Massachusetts later that month, Douglass attended the thirteenth annual convention of the Massachusetts Anti-Slavery Society in Boston on 24-26 January. According to a correspondent for the *National Anti-Slavery Standard*, the meeting in Marlboro Chapel "was thronged day after day, and night after night, through storm and sunshine, with the advocates of the cause." Douglass' most noteworthy contribution to the proceedings came during the final session, which was convened in the hall of the House of Representatives at the State House. After speeches by Phillips and Remond, Douglass took the stand. Although the correspondent to the *Liberator* published only a segment of the speech, the section he quoted demonstrated Douglass' desire to proclaim his slave status before his listeners. According to the correspondent, Douglass "was peculiarly impressive" as he uttered, "with a subdued manner and a tremulous tone of voice," the following words:

> I have no country to love or cherish—*I am a slave*; I have African and European blood running in my veins, but no home, no abiding-place—*I am a slave*; it is not for the fire of patriotism to glow in my bosom as an American—*I am a slave*; there is no mountain so high, there is no valley so deep, there is no plain so wide, in this land, as to insure me perfect security and freedom—*I am a slave*; should I flee, in case of pursuit, to Bunker Hill, and ascend the summit of its mighty shaft of granite, even from thence I might be taken and reduced again to bondage, for—*I am a slave*.[26]

From Douglass' perspective, he was an outcast—a man without a home, without citizenship rights, without security and freedom. By repeating the phrase "I am a slave," he reinforced his slave status and played on his listeners' sympathies. At the conclusion of this section of Douglass' address, the entire audience "exhibited a feeling of intense sympathy for the speaker, and of shame and indignation in view of the recreancy of this country to the principles embodied in its Declaration of Independence."[27]

New England abolitionists saw little of Douglass in February and March. He joined Remond, Foster, and Charles C. Burleigh in New Hampshire for antislavery conventions in Cornish on 14-16 February and in Claremont 17-18 February.[28] Back in Massachusetts, he traveled to New Bedford in early March to attend a two-day antislavery convention. The meeting began on Saturday, 8 March, at Liberty Hall. "Though the weather was quite unpropitious," a correspondent reported to the *Liberator*, "the attendance in the day time was numerous." According to Edmund Quincy, all six sessions of the meeting were "uniformly well attended, the interest and numbers increasing with every session." The convention addressed such issues as the foreign and domestic slave trade, the annexation of Texas to the Union, the admission of Florida into the Union as a slave state, the Democratic, Whig, and Liberty Parties, and the immediate dissolution of the Union. These issues, the secretary recorded in the minutes, "were discussed with great spirit, and in strains of thrilling eloquence." Douglass, a correspondent wrote in the *Liberator*, "was uncommonly powerful."[29] Indeed, after listening to Douglass' "masterly eloquence," a correspondent to the *National Anti-Slavery Standard* exclaimed: "If a fugitive slave, only five or six years from his master's plantation, can stand beside the first orators of our land, and even . . . rival Patrick Henry in his eloquence, what may we not expect, when that mighty company of three millions of the same race shall have their chains broken, and receive the advantages that we have so long enjoyed?"[30] Although there is no surviving text of Douglass' speech, Wendell Phillips, who was in attendance, noted a few days later that Douglass had told the New Bedford audience that he was writing an account of his life, including his name, "the name of his master, and the place he ran from."[31] This is the first recorded public disclosure about the composition of Douglass' *Narrative*—a sign, perhaps, that the work was nearly complete.

Later in March, Douglass attended the quarterly meeting of the Worcester county South Division Anti-Slavery Society at Worcester's Brinley Hall.[32] The 18 March meeting, a correspondent reported to the *Liberator*, was "of deep interest to all who were present." The morning session was occupied by delegates from throughout Worcester county reporting on the progress of the antislavery cause in their towns. In the afternoon, Garrison presented a series of resolutions urging abolitionists "to summon all their manhood for a final conflict with the Slave Power," demanding that abolitionists boycott any goods produced by slave labor, calling for the immediate dissolution of the Union, denouncing the Whig, Democratic, and Liberty Parties as proslavery, and branding the American church as "a synagogue of Satan" and the clergy as "a brotherhood of thieves." These resolutions, the *Liberator*'s correspondent observed, "were discussed with an earnestness and seriousness becoming of the present solemn crisis." Garrison spoke in support of his resolutions and was followed to the platform by Douglass, Samuel J. May, and others. After considerable discussion, the resolutions were unanimously adopted. During the evening session, Douglass addressed a crowded hall and reportedly "acquitted himself like a MAN, though he is *Constitutionally* nothing but 'a fugitive SLAVE,' and produced a powerful impression on the audience."[33]

During the first part of April, Douglass worked on completing his auto-biography. Consequently, he did not attend any antislavery meetings or deliver any antislavery lectures. By the middle of April, he had completed the story of his slave past and was ready to resume his antislavery speaking activities.[34] On 19-20 April he attended the quarterly meeting of the Essex County Anti-Slavery Society in Manchester. "The Convention was well attended," a correspondent reported to the *Liberator*, "not only by many of the people of Manchester . . . but also by large delegations of abolitionists from various towns." At no time during the two-day meeting at Dodge's Hall were resolutions discussed or debated. Instead, each abolitionist was encouraged to "speak upon such points on the anti-slavery question as suggested itself to his mind." Douglass, Buffum, Henry Clapp, Jr., and others participated in the discussion. The correspondent reported that the "Sunday afternoon session was particularly impressive," as Douglass' "fervent appeals" to the meeting "touched a chord in many a heart, that will not soon cease to vibrate in compassion for the slave."[35]

Four days later, Douglass attended the Norfolk County Anti-Slavery Society meeting at the Town Hall in Dedham. The 24 April meeting focused on a series of resolutions calling on abolitionists to conquer the South's "foul system of slavery," condemning efforts to annex Texas to the Union, denouncing the Constitution as a proslavery document, and urging abolitionists to attend the anniversary meeting of the American Anti-Slavery Society in May. Garrison, Quincy, Douglass, and others discussed the resolutions "with much spirit and ability." In the evening, "a large audience" returned to the Town Hall to listen to "eloquent expositions" from Garrison and Douglass on "the nature of slavery, and of the guilt and the duties of the North, especially as to ceasing from all union with slaveholders."[36]

In early May, Douglass traveled to New York City to attend the eleventh anniversary meeting of the American Anti-Slavery Society. The three-day meeting, which convened on Tuesday morning, 6 May, in the Broadway Tabernacle, proved to be an important one for Douglass.[37] "It was the largest Anti-Slavery meeting that has been held in this city for several years," reported a correspondent to the *National Anti-Slavery Standard*, with abolitionists from New England, New York, and Pennsylvania in attendance. The *Liberator* reported that the "clergy were pretty numerously represented on the occasion, curious to see and hear what might be said and done, especially in regard to their position." Also in attendance were Robert Owen, the English socialist, Ralph Randolph Gurley, the former secretary of the American Colonization Society, and Alvan Stewart, a leader of the Liberty Party in New York state.[38]

Garrison, the president of the society, called the meeting to order at 10 a.m. After the opening prayer and presentation of the Treasurer's Report and the Annual Report of the Executive Committee, the speeches began.

Douglass was scheduled as the final speaker of the morning session. On this day, there were five speakers ahead of him. Jeremiah B. Sanderson, a black acquaintance of Douglass' from New Bedford, spoke first. He was followed to the platform by Wendell Phillips. Jane Elizabeth Hitchcock, who during the past year had been lecturing with Abby Kelley in New Hampshire and Pennsylvania, followed Phillips to the stand. William C. Bell of Kentucky, who was working with Cassius M. Clay to establish an antislavery newspaper in that state, spoke next. Rev. Henry Grew followed Bell to the platform. Douglass, after a wait of nearly three and a half hours, spoke next and addressed the audience for thirty minutes.[39]

Garrison introduced Douglass to the audience by "observing that he was one who, by the laws of the South, had been *a chattel* but who was now, by his own intrepid spirit and the laws of God, *a man.*" With the publication of his autobiography only days away, Douglass then disclosed publicly for the first time the name of one of his former masters and other specific facts relating to his background as a slave. After a few familiar introductory comments, he briefly reviewed the facts of his recent history. He began by stating that he had escaped from the South seven years ago. He then told of how he had lived three years in New Bedford before becoming "publicly known to the anti-slavery people." Since then, Douglass stated, "I have been engaged for three years in telling the people what I know" of slavery and the South. His purpose in addressing the convention, he stated, was "to say a word about the sunny South" and the realities of slavery. Reminding his audience that he was an authentic voice from bondage, he declared: "I can tell you what I have seen with my own eyes, felt on my own person, and know to have occurred in my own neighborhood." Although he was from Maryland, "where Slavery is said to exist in its mildest form," rather than "any of those States where the slaves are said to be in their most degraded condition," he would reveal "atrocities" that would make their "blood to boil at the statement of them."[40]

In discussing these atrocities, Douglass began by revealing the name of the man who owned the plantation where he lived and its location in Maryland. Again, this marked the first time he had revealed such information in a speech. "I lived on the plantation of Col. Lloyd, on the eastern shore of Maryland," he stated, "and belonged to that gentleman's clerk [Aaron Anthony]." Douglass then interrupted the flow of his narrative to explain the risk he was taking by mentioning the names of his master and of the persons who had perpetrated the deeds he was about to relate. "I am . . . running the risk," he told his listeners, "of being hurled back into interminable bondage—for I am yet a slave."[41] Douglass explained his motive for taking such a risk:

> For the sake of the cause—for the sake of humanity, I will mention the names, and glory in running the risk. I have the gratification to know that if I fall by the utterance of truth in this matter, that

if I shall be hurled back into bondage to gratify the slaveholder—
to be killed by inches—that every drop of blood which I shall shed,
every groan which I shall utter, every pain which shall rack my
frame, every sob in which I shall indulge, shall be the instrument,
under God, of tearing down the bloody pillar of Slavery, and of has-
tening the day of deliverance for three millions of my brethren in
bondage.[42]

By this explanation Douglass created a heroic image for himself. Like the
men and women within the Christian tradition who were persecuted and
killed for acting on their beliefs, Douglass was willing to stand up for his
ideals and, if necessary, sacrifice his life to deliver his people from
bondage.

Having discussed his motive for revealing the facts about his slave background, Douglass told of several of the atrocities committed against slaves
by Austin Gore, a "highly respected" overseer on the Lloyd plantation.
Douglass' account of the horrors of slavery in this portion of the address
closely resemble the style and content of sections of chapter four in his
forthcoming *Narrative*. Douglass began his tale by trying to capture the
gruesome nature of Gore's character. "He never spoke but to command,
nor commanded but to be obeyed," Douglass stated. "He was lavish with
the whip, sparing with his word." Next, he described several of the cruel
acts committed by Gore: "I have seen that man tie up men by the two
hands, and for two hours, at intervals, ply the lash." To make Gore's acts
of cruelty even more despicable, Douglass described how Gore would also
beat female slaves: "I have seen women stretched up on the limbs of trees,
and their bare backs made bloody with the lash."[43]

Not all slaves, however, would readily submit to Gore's cruel treatment.
Douglass told the story of a slave named Derby who, having committed
"some trifling offence . . . refused to be whipped, and ran." But before going
into the details of Derby's situation, Douglass compared Derby's running
away to the stand he took as a slave against his inhumane overseer. Derby
"did not stand to and fight his master as I did once, and might do again,"
Douglass declared. Instead, "he ran and stood in a creek, and refused to
come out."[44] The contrast between Douglass standing his ground against
an evil overseer and Derby running away and seeking refuge in a creek was
striking. By alluding to this incident, Douglass may have been trying to sustain the heroic image he had fashioned earlier in the speech. In any event,
he next recounted for his audience what happened to Derby:

At length his master told him he would shoot him if he did not
come out. Three calls were to be given him. The first, second, and
third, were given, at each of which the slave stood his ground.
Gore, equally determined and firm, raised his musket, and in an

instant poor Derby was no more. He sank beneath the waves, and naught but the crimsoned waters marked the spot.[45]

Gore, Douglass revealed, was never arrested for this offense. Instead, "He remained on the plantation, and his fame went abroad. He still lives in St. Michaels, Talbot county, Maryland, and is now, I presume, as much respected, as though his guilty soul had never been stained with his brother's blood."[46]

Before leaving this section of the speech, Douglass mentioned two additional instances of deadly, vulgar crimes committed against slaves by slaveholders. In both instances, the slaveholders were never arrested for their crimes against humanity—a fact that greatly troubled Douglass. In the first instance, he pointed to his wife's cousin, "who was terribly mangled in her sleep, while nursing the child of a Mrs. Hicks." Upon discovering the girl asleep, Douglass declared, Mrs. Hicks beat the slave to death "with a billet of wood, and the woman has never been brought to justice." In the second instance, Douglass told of a man he once knew "who boasted he had killed two slaves, and with an oath would say, 'I'm the only benefactor in the country.'"[47]

Having recounted the horrors of slavery, Douglass linked the atrocities to the proslavery nature of the Constitution and the union between North and South. In so doing, he voiced many of the themes he had articulated in speeches during the preceding year. He began by ridiculing the people of the North for what he believed to be their unreasonable expectation that slaves should rise on their own and escape from bondage:

> The people at the North say—"Why don't you rise? If we were thus treated we would rise and throw off the yoke. We would wade knee deep in blood before we would endure the bondage." You'd rise up! Who are these that are asking for manhood in the slave, and who say that he has it not, because he does not rise? The very men who are ready by the Constitution to bring the strength of the nation to put us down![48]

To make the point more concrete and immediate, Douglass directly confronted his audience. "You, the people of New-York, the people of Massachusetts, of New England, of the whole Northern States," he charged, "have sworn under God that we shall be slaves or die!" Speaking now on behalf of all the slaves, Douglass asked, "And shall three millions be taunted with a want of the love of freedom, by the very men who stand upon us and say, submit, or be crushed?"[49]

Continuing to speak on behalf of the slaves, Douglass clarified what he wanted his auditors to do. "We don't ask you to engage in any physical warfare against the slaveholder," he stated. "We only ask that in

Massachusetts, and the several non-slaveholding States which maintain a union with the slaveholder—who stand with your heavy heels on the quivering heart-strings of the slave, that you will stand off." He was not calling for a violent civil war between North and South, but for nonviolent resistance to the Constitution. If this should happen, he explained, the slaves would be left alone "to take care" of their masters. He did not explain what he meant by this statement. Rather, he left it to his auditors' imaginations to decide what deeds might follow if the North stood by while slaves attended to their masters.[50]

Douglass next endeavored to prove that the Union and, by extension, the U.S. Constitution, supported slavery. To make this point more concrete, he presented a stirring contrast between the message sent to the slaveholder and the message sent to the slave by the people of the North in their union with the South. The North, Douglass explained, tells slaveholders "that they ought to shoot us—to take away our wives and our little ones—to sell our mothers into interminable bondage, and sever the tenderest ties." Conversely, the North said to the slave, "if you dare to carry out the principles of our fathers, we'll shoot you down." The slaves dared not become revolutionaries and strike against their oppressors, for if they did, the North was pledged to defeat them. But not even the power of the Union could crush Douglass' spirit. Once again advancing the heroic image he had introduced earlier in the speech, he declared: "Others may tamely submit; not I. You may put the chains upon me and fetter me, but I am not a slave, for my master who puts the chains upon me, shall stand in as much dread of me as I do of him."[51]

At this point, Douglass appealed directly to the audience "in the name of my three millions of brethren at the South" to undo what they had done. Appealing to their consciences, patriotism, and sense of personal responsibility, he stated, "I am your brother, white as you are. I'm your bloodkin." Yet within "this land of liberty," Douglass reminded them, "I'm a slave":

> The twenty-six States that blaze forth on your flag, proclaim a compact to return me to bondage if I run away, and keep me in bondage if I submit. Wherever I go, under the aegis of your liberty, there I'm a slave. If I go to Lexington or Bunker Hill, there I'm a slave, chained in perpetual servitude. I may go to your deepest valley, to your highest mountain, I'm still a slave, and the bloodhound may chase me down.[52]

From Douglass' point of view, the irony was clear. A nation founded upon the principle of liberty supported slavery. Even in the North, where slavery had been outlawed, he could not find safe refuge. Playing on the emotions of the audience, he portrayed himself as the victim of an unjust Union that was pledged to keep him "chained in perpetual servitude."

Douglass concluded by aligning the American Anti-Slavery Society with sacred law and God, and the Constitution with secular law and man. "God says thou shalt not oppress: the Constitution says oppress: which will you serve, God or man? The American Anti-Slavery Society says God, and I am thankful for it."[53]

Douglass, the *New York Journal of Commerce* reported, spoke "with much warmth and manly energy." Divulging the facts that he would use in his forthcoming *Narrative*, he boldly revealed the name of his former master and the place he was from, thereby inviting arrest as a fugitive from slavery. In so doing, he fashioned a heroic image for himself. Regardless of the consequences, he was willing to risk being captured and returned to slavery for the glory of the cause. Beyond offering a stirring eyewitness account of slavery, Douglass linked the horrors of slavery to the proslavery character of the U.S. Constitution and the union between North and South. Speaking on behalf of all the slaves, he made an eloquent and earnest appeal for his auditors to withdraw from the Union. Only then, he argued, could slaves take care of their masters and be free. Only then, could Douglass himself cease being a fugitive slave and live free.[54]

II

At the conclusion of the anniversary meeting, Douglass returned home to Lynn, Massachusetts. Shortly thereafter, his autobiography was published. The 9 May 1845 issue of the *Liberator* announced that Douglass' *Narrative* was "in press, and will be published in a few days." On the same page, the *Liberator* published Garrison's preface to Douglass' book. Immediately, other abolitionist newspapers spread the news. On 22 May the *Pennsylvania Freeman* announced that Douglass' "narrative of his own life" was "in the hands of the binder." His autobiography, the *Freeman* opined, "will of course be a most interesting volume, and one that will have a wide and useful circulation." The editors were expecting copies of the work at their office, "where they will be sold." The next day, the *Liberator* announced that the 125-page *Narrative* was available for fifty cents at its office at 25 Cornhill Street. "It was written entirely by Mr. Douglass," observed the *Liberator*, "and reveals all the facts in regard to his birthplace—the names of his mother, master, overseer, &c." The editors of the *Liberator* presented extracts from Douglass' work to "excite a lively desire in all quarters to possess a copy of this extraordinary volume." During the first week of June, copies of Douglass' autobiography also arrived in Philadelphia and New York City, where they were sold in the offices of the *Pennsylvania Freeman* and the *National Anti-Slavery Standard*.[55]

Reviews of Douglass' work appeared promptly in newspapers throughout the North and were reprinted in the antislavery journals.[56] As

Benjamin Quarles has noted, the *Narrative* became Douglass' "passport to prominence."[57] Prior to the publication of the autobiography, Douglass' life had been spent in relative obscurity. He had become known among abolitionists but had remained virtually unknown to most other Americans. By putting Douglass' slave experiences into print, the *Narrative* reached a broader audience than was possible for Douglass in his capacity as a lecturer. The first edition of 5,000 copies was sold within four months, and within a year four more editions of 2,000 copies each were printed to meet demand. By 1850, Douglass' *Narrative* had become an international bestseller and had sold more than 30,000 copies. The book was much more widely read than Henry Thoreau's *Walden* or the first edition of Walt Whitman's *Leaves of Grass*.[58]

Douglass' literary success may be attributed, in part, to the oratorical style of his autobiography. The *Narrative* contained a number of passages that strongly resembled the content and style he had used on the antislavery platform over the past four years.[59] At this stage of his life, Douglass was predominantly an orator. That he read the manuscript of the *Narrative* aloud to Phillips, Garrison, and Maria Weston Chapman attests to his preference for the spoken word over the written word.[60] Those who had not heard Douglass speak from the platform received in the *Narrative* both a lesson on the realities of the slave experience and a discourse denouncing the inherent evils of the peculiar institution. Readers, moreover, were at once brought into contact with Douglass' rhetorical brilliance. To compose the *Narrative*, Douglass drew from the form, function, and processes of oratory he had mastered over the years as a lay preacher and an abolitionist lecturer. Readers experienced his masterful use of logical argument, withering sarcasm, anecdotes, allegories, Biblical illusions, and such rhetorical techniques as repetition, parallelism, antithesis, metaphor, simile, vivid imagery, and alliteration. In addition, Douglass used contractions to add to the *Narrative*'s oral quality and employed commas and dashes to indicate pauses between phrases and to give a strong rhythmic pattern to his written prose. As in his antislavery speeches, his autobiography went beyond simply narrating his slave experiences and exhorted his audience to act against the slaveholder's vile corruption, his lust for power and dominion, his cowardice, and his unprincipled religion. It is no wonder that Phillips declared that reading Douglass' story was the equivalent of hearing an antislavery lecture.[61]

III

After publication of the *Narrative*, Douglass remained at home for most of May. From late May through the end of June, he delivered formal lectures and attended antislavery meetings in Massachusetts, New Hampshire, and

New York. Toward the end of the month, he traveled to New Bedford, where he and Remond addressed antislavery meetings in Liberty Hall on Sunday, 25 May.[62] Two days later, Douglass traveled north to Boston to attend the annual meeting of the New England Anti-Slavery Society in Marlboro Chapel. The meeting, a correspondent reported to the *Lowell Journal*, "attracted great interest and was crowded day and night."[63] From all accounts, Douglass played a major role in the proceedings. Not only did he participate in debates over resolutions that came before the meeting, but he also engaged George Bradburn in a heated exchange over the need for abolitionists to give more liberally of their time, talents, and money to the antislavery campaign. On Tuesday, 27 May, during the opening session of the meeting, Wendell Phillips, chair of the business committee, presented the following resolution proclaiming the publication of Douglass' autobiography:

> Resolved, That we joyfully welcome to our ranks the new Anti-Slavery lecturer—The Narrative of the Life of Frederick Douglass, written by himself; and that we commend it with confidence to the attention of all those who believe the slaves of the South to be either well-treated, or happy, or ignorant of their right to freedom, or in need of preparation to make them fit for freedom; and that we urge upon the friends of the cause the duty of circulating it among all classes.[64]

Phillips also offered resolutions declaring proslavery to be anti-Christian and denouncing the American church as the bulwark of American slavery. Douglass spoke in support of the latter two resolutions, as did Foster, Garrison, and Buffum. On Wednesday afternoon, Douglass was one of two speakers to speak in support of two additional resolutions offered by the business committee. The first resolution declared that it was the "duty of abolitionists, to counsel and aid the slaves, by all peaceful and moral means, to make their escape from the house of their bondage." A second resolution saluted David Ruggles as "one of the most devoted, self-sacrificing and efficient friends of the slave" and called on abolitionists to assist him now that he had lost his eyesight. After Douglass and a Mr. Parker had concluded their remarks, the resolutions were adopted by the meeting.[65]

Douglass' most important performance at the convention occurred on Thursday afternoon, when he became embroiled in a debate with Bradburn over Phillips' resolution calling for abolitionists to give more liberally of their time, talents, and funds to the antislavery cause. After Phillips had read his resolution to the convention, Bradburn took the stand, defended the Liberty party, and closed his speech by stating "that if he had the wealth of John Jacob Astor, he would not give a cent" to the New England Anti-Slavery Society. Remond responded to Bradburn "in a very able and eloquent speech, in which he defended the society and attacked the Liberty Party." He concluded his remarks by branding Bradburn as a "mercenary." Douglass next took the stand, but graciously yielded it to Bradburn who, according to an account in the *Liberator*, "made one of his vehement and fiery speeches denouncing the old society with great severity." At the conclusion of Bradburn's remarks, Douglass returned to the platform and charged Bradburn with being a "deserter, who had left the old society from selfish and unprincipled motives, and joined those whom he once denounced as corrupt and unprincipled." According to a correspondent for the *Boston Daily Times*, Douglass' "torrent of declamation and invective . . . made even Bradburn wince." The reporter quoted Douglass as saying, "never was there a more abusive and scurrilous party than the Liberty party, and *never was there a more fit representative of its abuse and scurrility than George Bradburn.*"[66]

At this point, according to the *Liberator*, Bradburn attempted to interrupt Douglass, "and for some minutes a scene of great interest and excitement ensued" until Douglass allowed Bradburn to explain his position. After Bradburn denied that he had ever denounced the Liberty party, Douglass seized the moment and took Bradburn to task. The "gentleman denies that he ever denounced the Liberty party," Douglass began. "Is James G. Birney a Liberty man? Is Joshua Leavitt a Liberty man? Are the men who transferred the *Emancipator* Liberty men? If they are, then did George Bradburn less than two years ago in Pittsburgh, denounce them as '*a set of unmitigated scoundrels,*' and I heard him." Some members of the audience reportedly came to Douglass' support and shouted, "So did I."[67] The exchange, a correspondent wrote to the *Liberator*, "was one of the most exciting personal contests I ever witnessed." Douglass continued with a speech of such "great force and power" that when it was over, the correspondent confessed, "I hated slavery worse than ever."[68]

In early June, Douglass traveled to Concord, New Hampshire, to attend the annual meeting of the New Hampshire Anti-Slavery Society scheduled to begin Wednesday, 4 June. The chaotic meeting lasted three days.[69] The first day's sessions, reported a correspondent to the *Liberator*, were "disorderly and disgraceful in the extreme," and the second day's were unprofitable as well. At the center of debate was the question of whether the convention should proceed in an orderly manner or whether the meeting should be free of rules so members could speak on any subject they desired. Parker Pillsbury, Garrison, Phillips, Foster, Remond, Buffum, and Douglass supported efforts to organize the meeting, while Nathaniel P. Rogers, John B. Chandler, and John R. French led the opposition. As a result, no business was carried out and almost all the sessions ended in chaos. "It is not worthwhile to describe every session," a correspondent to the *National Anti-Slavery Standard* reported. "They were all alike, except that each succeeding session was more disorderly and more mobocratic in its character than that which preceded it."[70]

During one of the sessions, Douglass and John B. Chandler, a local abolitionist, became involved in a bitter debate. Their exchange captures the chaotic nature of the meeting. In an account of the incident published in the *Herald of Freedom*, Rogers, an opponent of organized meetings, criticized Douglass' actions:

> Douglass made some charge which Chandler deemed false, and he appealed to him to correct it. Douglass spurned his appeal with contempt. Chandler there upon renewed it. Douglass turned his back upon him, and raising his voice higher, continued his offensive charges against the friends of free meeting, charging them with forming a plan to mob down the right of speech. Chandler reiterated his appeal. Douglass became more vehement in his contempt. Chandler called him familiarly and good humoredly by name, not after the grave manner, to be sure, of a public meeting, and not in a way to raise the self-esteem of Douglass, or flatter the self-complacency of any of us, there, as we were, in public assembly. It was quite trying to witness it, but Chandler was evidently to me, not intending to insult Douglass, but to overcome his haughty persistence, by good natured importunity. Douglass at length made mouths at him—mocked him, and fiercely demanded that he should be taken out of the house! . . . Douglass continued his harangue in the most offensive and abusive style, and Chandler his *quiet, good humored*, annoying appeals to him until he finished.[71]

Douglass' speech, Rogers stated, was "of a most aggravating and offensive character, and intended to brow-beat and put down the friends of freedom. It was very much, I thought at the time, in what I suppose the vein of a plantation slave with the overseers whip put into his hands. The slave made master." Continuing his account of the meeting, Rogers noted that he was "prodigiously *tried* by Chandler's boyish importunity of Douglass" but was "indignant at the *insolent tyranny* of Frederick Douglass. . . . His having been a slave—or now being one—does not entitle him to play the master—though it undoubtedly had a tendency to make him want to."[72]

By Thursday afternoon, those supporting an organized public meeting decided they had had enough. "It having become evident that no friend of organization could speak without the most unpleasant interruption and disturbance," the secretary of the meeting recorded in the minutes, "it was voted to leave the Town Hall . . . to the friends of no-organization, and procure some other place of meeting." In the evening, those wishing to hold an organized meeting convened in the vestry of the Unitarian Church. A correspondent to the *Herald of Freedom* reported that Douglass, Remond, and Buffum addressed the audience "in a deeply interesting manner." On Friday morning, the meeting convened in the old North Church, where the business of the society continued without interruption.[73]

The afternoon session was held in the State House yard and, reported Pillsbury in the *Herald of Freedom*, "exceeded in interest almost any thing that occurred during the week." Both houses of the state legislature were present, as were members of the executive branch and a "very large number of the people of Concord, and elsewhere." Douglass was the featured speaker. Although there is no text of his speech, according to Pillsbury, he commenced "with some account of the slave system as revealed in his own sad experience, and ended with showing in a masterly manner the connexion of the North, particularly New-Hampshire, and more particularly her Legislature, with her slave system." Pillsbury declared that the "logic was irrefutable, the facts unquestionable, the satire flamed like blazing steel, and the manner of delivery was worthy [of] the Roman forum."[74]

From Concord, Douglass traveled southwest toward Albany, New York. On his way, he stopped at Springfield, Massachusetts, where he held a spontaneous antislavery meeting on Saturday, 7 June.[75] "We succeeded in getting a Hall for him," a local abolitionist wrote to the *Liberator*, and he "gave us three fine lectures." The audience "had a blessed time. Some converts were made and much interest felt."[76] Two days later, Douglass arrived in Albany, where he presented an evening lecture entitled "Human Freedom" in the County Court Room at the City Hall. In the advertisement for the lecture in the *New York Tribune*, observed a correspondent to the *Pennsylvania Freeman*, the letters "F.S. (Fugitive Slave)" were appended to Douglass' name. "Those who read his Narrative will agree," wrote the correspondent, "that his title has at least been well earned."[77] On the day of Douglass' lecture, the editors of the *Albany Evening Journal* acknowledged receiving a copy of Douglass' autobiography from "a benevolent lady." Douglass' story, reported the editors, "presents a view of Slavery, as it exists in Maryland which cannot be contemplated without shuddering and remorse." The editors then reprinted excerpts from the book and announced that Douglass would be speaking that evening. The following day, the *Evening Journal* reviewed Douglass' speech. "Frederick Douglass, the fugitive slave whose book we noticed yesterday," the Journal observed, "delivered a lecture here last evening, which is spoken of as very eloquent and effective. He evinces extraordinary mental powers, the development of which in defiance of all obstacles, is still more extraordinary." Should Douglass return to Albany, the *Journal* concluded, "we hope the citizens will not fail to hear him."[78]

In the middle of June, the *Liberator* announced that "our friends Douglass and Buffum are going to England."[79] The trip apparently had been contemplated since early in the year. "Douglass who is now writing

out his story," Wendell Phillips wrote to Elizabeth Pease, a British abolitionist, in February 1845, "thinks of relaxing by arranging a voyage."[80] In
the ensuing months, Douglass had consulted with the leaders of the anti-
slavery movement and come to the conclusion that he should indeed travel abroad.[81]

In the 1846 Dublin edition of the *Narrative*, Douglass disclosed his reasons for traveling to the British Isles. "I wished to be out of the way during
the excitement consequent on the publication of my book," he wrote, "lest
the information I had there given as to my identity, and place of abode,
should induce my *owner* to take measures for my restoration to his 'patri-
archal care.'" Another reason for going to England, he wrote, "was a desire
to increase my stock of information, [and] my opportunities for self-
improvement." He also hoped to induce cooperation between the "thousands and tens of thousands of the intelligent and philanthropic" and "the
noble band of American abolitionists, for the overthrow of the meanest,
hugest, and most dastardly system of iniquity that ever disgraced any
country laying claim to the benefits of religion and civilization." As
Douglass explained his motives, however, the most important reason for
his trip was to lecture against slavery and to denounce the sins of America
before an international audience:

> My . . . chief object was, by the public exposition of the contami-
> nating and degrading influences of Slavery upon the slaveholder
> and his abettors, as well as the slave, to excite such an intelligent
> interest on the subject of American Slavery, as may react upon my
> own country, and may tend to shame her out of her adhesion to a
> system so abhorrent to Christianity and to her republican institu-
> tions.[82]

Contrary to the standard view, then, avoiding recapture and return to slavery was only one—and perhaps not the most important—reason for
Douglass' trip to Great Britain. Of at least equal importance was his desire
to continue his career as an abolitionist orator and to advance his "position of public usefulness."[83]

Buffum shared this view of the trip. In a letter of 21 June 1845 to Gerrit
Smith, Buffum described the potential impact of Douglass' message on
English audiences. Douglass will tour England, he wrote, "as a representa-
tive from the prison-house of bondage. . . . He will stand up before that peo-
ple as one who has experienced the withering and blighting influence of
Slavery upon his own Soul." Buffum believed Douglass' message would
excite "a deeper hatred in the breasts of the English people of American
Slavery" and create "a warmer Sympathy" for abolitionism:

> When they shall see before them a man so noble and elegant as
> Frederick, and learn from his own lips, that he is only seven years

out of bondage; that he has now the marks of the whip upon his back, which he will carry with him until the day of his death; that he has near and dear relatives that are now pining in bondage; they will realize to a considerable extent, the horrors of the American Slave trade; the effect cannot be otherwise than good.[84]

For the remainder of June, Douglass appeared at antislavery meetings in Massachusetts. On 14-15 June he attended the eleventh annual meeting of the Essex County Anti-Slavery Society in Georgetown.[85] The meeting began in Savory Hall on Saturday afternoon. During the first session, Douglass was appointed to the committee to nominate officers for the society for the coming year. During the evening session, he spoke in support of Stephen S. Foster's resolution declaring that the political union between North and South and the "religious sects of the country" were the "main bulwarks of the slave system." Following the discussion of this resolution, Buffum presented a resolution praising Douglass' *Narrative* "as a powerful auxiliary" in the crusade against slavery and recommending "to all who would know the horrid nature of slavery to purchase and read this book." On motion, the resolution was adopted. On Sunday morning, Douglass joined in the discussion over "free and unorganized meetings." No doubt, given his terrible experience in Concord, New Hampshire, two weeks earlier, he spoke against such meetings. In the afternoon, the meeting discussed and voted to accept the report of the nomination committee, a report that nominated Douglass to serve on the society's executive committee.[86]

Ten days later, Douglass attended a two-day meeting of the Worcester County South Division Anti-Slavery Society in the Unitarian meetinghouse at Uxbridge. "A beautiful June sun shone upon us," wrote a correspondent to the *Practical Christian*. "All was harmony and pleasure, curtailed only by the thought of the sighing captive, whose chains were brought before us." Douglass addressed the meeting on Wednesday afternoon, 25 June, in a speech that the *Practical Christian's* correspondent characterized as "touching beyond description." "He spoke as no one can," the correspondent wrote, "who has not felt the cold steel of oppression piercing the soul." Douglass presented "himself as an outcast, without protection, living in the midst of monuments reared to *liberty*, and steeples towering to heaven, and yet a *slave*." The correspondent also quoted Douglass directly, "'Ay,' said Frederick, 'if I go bleeding and panting, fugitive as I am, to yonder Orthodox church, I am bolted out by your Rev. Mr. Orcutt!' 'Shame,' said the voice of Father Henry, and we all felt to echo with becoming indignation—SHAME."[87]

IV

Toward the end of June, the *Liberator* announced that Douglass would soon be launching an extensive lecture tour of Massachusetts and New York. The tour was scheduled to begin on 1 July and end in early August. Douglass planned to travel to at least twenty-three places in thirty-five days. "He intends going as far West as Buffalo," the *Liberator* announced, "and returning will hold a series of meetings in such towns as he may find convenient."[88]

As Douglass traveled alone through Massachusetts and New York, he must have lived with the constant fear of being recaptured and returned to bondage. Shortly after the *Narrative* was published, he received information that his former master was intent on carrying him back to slavery.[89] In addition, mainstream and abolitionist newspapers alike announced his meetings well in advance and used his autobiography and his status as a fugitive slave as drawing cards. Early in his career, abolitionist newspapers had capitalized upon his being a runaway slave to draw audiences, but that was before publication of the *Narrative*. Now that his true identity was known, slave hunters, using the newspapers, could easily track him down. As Douglass explained in his 1855 autobiography, "It was felt that I had committed the double offense of running away, and exposing the secrets and crimes of slavery and slaveholders." Hence, there was a "double motive for seeking my reenslavement—avarice and vengeance." By traveling alone from place to place, he recalled, "I was constantly in danger of being spirited away, at a moment when my friends could render me no assistance."[90]

Yet despite the risk, Douglass continued to lecture and to maintain a high profile. There are a number of possible explanations. One is that the danger was not as great as subsequent generations of scholars have supposed. "It is not probable that any open attempt to secure me as a slave could have succeeded," Douglass wrote in 1855, "further than the obtainment, by my master, of the money value of my bones and sinews." Douglass also may have felt safe because during his four years of antislavery labor he had gained many friends who, he stated, "would have suffered themselves to be taxed to almost any extent to save me from slavery."[91] He may have also risked re-enslavement, in his words, for the "sake of the cause—for the sake of humanity" and gloried in "running the risk."[92] Beyond these motivations, surely he realized that by going on tour he could promote in person the sale of his book, proceeds of which could be used to finance his trip to the British Isles and to support his family while he was away. As we shall see, promoting his autobiography was one of Douglass' major activities during his lecture tour. Indeed, he carried copies of the *Narrative* with him and sold them at the end of his lectures.

Although there are no surviving speeches from the tour, there are a number of published accounts of Douglass' activities that provide information as to what he was saying and doing.[93] On Monday, 14 July, for example, he addressed a large audience in West Winfield, New York, at the Baptist Church. Two abolitionists in New York reported to Sydney Howard Gay, editor of the *National Anti-Slavery Standard*, that Douglass was "logical, eloquent, and gifted." In his address, Douglass exposed the proslavery character of the Constitution in a "clear, candid, powerful, and masterly manner," stripping it "of the sophistry, which the ingenuity of the Liberty party has thrown around it." Douglass must have spoken eloquently. "We have truly had a feast," the correspondents concluded. "Our souls have been fed with knowledge and truth, our hearts warmed by principles of eternal justice, and our energies pledged anew in the cause of bleeding humanity."[94]

The following evening, Douglass delivered a ninety-minute lecture in Utica, New York, during which he reportedly denounced "the Union, the Constitution, and the Liberty Party." Sometime prior to delivering his lecture, Douglass visited the office of the Utica *Liberty Press* to give the editors a copy of his book, which they reviewed in the next issue of the paper. "This is a neatly printed volume of 125 pages," they wrote, "and we find it quite interesting as to its contents, from the few chapters we have had time to peruse. Thanks to the author for the copy." Douglass probably repeated the practice of distributing copies of his autobiography to editors of local newspapers throughout the lecture tour in hopes that they would favorably review it, promote its sale and, at the same time, publicize his lectures.[95]

Two days later, on Thursday, 17 July, Douglass presented an evening lecture "to a fair audience" at the Congregational Church in Syracuse. "His subject was 'Prejudice against Color,'" reported a correspondent to the *Religious Recorder*, "taking the ground that it was the *condition* not the *complexion* which degraded man." Douglass, the correspondent concluded, "reasons well and is truly an eloquent man."[96] Nearly a week after the Syracuse lecture, during a trip between Palmyra and Rochester aboard the packet *St. Louis*, Douglass ran into trouble. After being accommodated with a bed for the evening "like the rest of the passengers," he reportedly sat down at the breakfast table with his fellow travelers. After only a few minutes, he was requested to leave the table. "Our friend Douglass," a correspondent wrote to the *Liberator*, "fatigued with great previous exertion in speaking, and loss of sleep, felt little or no disposition to resent the outrage," and calmly left his seat. Those in charge reportedly told Douglass that if he wanted "he might eat with 'the hands,'" an invitation Douglass refused. After a brief confrontation with a white passenger over his right to eat wherever he wished, Douglass, apparently too tired to argue, left the scene.[97]

Douglass reached Buffalo at the end of July. He presented lectures at Talman Hall on Wednesday, 30 July, and Thursday, 31 July.[98] He then journeyed eastward and made his way back to Massachusetts, holding meetings in places he found hospitable. By 11 August he was in Lynn preparing for his trip to England and had purchased his ticket for the voyage aboard the steamship *Cambria*.[99] Before leaving for the British Isles, Douglass made two final appearances at antislavery meetings. On Wednesday, 13 August, he attended a "large gathering" in New Bedford's Town Hall where, a correspondent reported to the *Liberator*, he delivered "one of the grandest speeches I ever heard him make."[100] Two days later, he took part in "a crowded and most enthusiastic meeting" at Lynn's Lyceum Hall. Douglass, Buffum, and others addressed the meeting, and the Hutchinsons, who joined Douglass and Buffum on their trip to England, "sang in their inimitable strains." After the speeches and music, resolutions were offered wishing Douglass and Buffum the "heartiest good wishes" for a successful journey. One of the resolutions saluted Douglass:

> Resolved, That we are especially desirous that Frederick Douglass, who came to this town a fugitive from slavery, should bear with him to the shores of the Old World, our unanimous testimony to the fidelity with which he has sustained the various relations of life, and to the deep respect with which his is now regarded by every friend of liberty throughout our borders.[101]

The next day, Saturday, 16 August, Douglass, Buffum, and the Hutchinsons traveled to Boston and boarded the *Cambria*, bound for Liverpool. As the ship left port, Douglass stood on the deck waving his hat at those gathered to see him off.[102] After nearly seven years of antislavery agitation as a fugitive slave, he was leaving his family, his friends, and his country to seek refuge and to further the cause of freedom by continuing his oratorical career on another platform.

Notes

1. See, for instance, William S. McFeely, *Frederick Douglass* (New York: Norton, 1991), 114-18; Waldo E. Martin, Jr., *The Mind of Frederick Douglass* (Chapel Hill: University of North Carolina Press, 1984), 23-25; Nathan Irvin Huggins, *Slave and Citizen: The Life of Frederick Douglass* (Boston: Little, Brown and Company, 1980), 19-20; Philip S. Foner, ed., *The Life and Writings of Frederick Douglass, Volume 1* (New York: International Publishers, 1950), 59-62; Gerald Raymond Fulkerson, "Frederick Douglass and the Anti-Slavery Crusade: His Career and Speeches, 1817-1861," pt. 1 (Ph.D. diss., University of Illinois, 1971), 73-75; Benjamin Quarles, *Frederick Douglass* (1948; reprint, New York: Atheneum, 1968), 34-36; James Gregory, *Frederick Douglass: The Orator* (1893; reprint, Chicago: Afro-Am Press, 1971), 30.

2. *Pennsylvania Freeman*, 5 September 1844, 2.

3. *Liberator*, 13 September 1844, 147.

4. *Liberator*, 31 August 1844, 138.

5. *Pennsylvania Freeman*, 22 August 1844, 3.

6. Frederick Douglass, *My Bondage and My Freedom* (1855; reprint, New York: Dover, 1969), 362-63.

7. Douglass, *Bondage and Freedom*, 363.

8. *The National Anti-Slavery Standard*, 14 November 1844, 95, explained that the lack of correspondence reporting the progress of the lecturers across New Hampshire was due in part to their "being overwhelmed with the heavy duties of each day."

9. *Liberator*, 4 October 1844, 158, 159; *National Anti-Slavery Standard*, 14 November 1844, 95. Toward the end of September, Douglass and several other agents crossed into Maine to hold a series of conventions, "but for want of sufficient concert of action on the part of the friends of that State," their efforts were "not so generally successful" (*Thirteenth Annual Report Presented to the Massachusetts Anti-Slavery Society by its Board of Managers, January 22, 1845* [1845; reprint, Westport, Conn.: Negro Universities Press, 1970], 36).

10. Sometime between October and December, Douglass also wrote, at the invitation of Maria Weston Chapman, a short essay entitled "The Folly of Our Opponents" for the 1845 edition of the *Liberty Bell*, a collection of reformist and abolitionist literature published each year and sold at the Massachusetts Anti-Slavery Fair in Boston. At the beginning of the essay Douglass wrote: "It was intended for a place in the *Liberty Bell*, but my literary advantages have been so limited, that I am ill prepared to decide what is, and what is not, appropriate for such a collection. I looked exceedingly strange in my own eyes, as I sat writing. The thought of writing for a book—and only six years since a fugitive from a Southern cornfield—caused a singular jingle in my mind." From this statement, it is safe to assume that Douglass wrote the piece for the *Liberty Bell* prior to writing his autobiography. See Maria Weston Chapman, ed., *Liberty Bell* (Boston: Andrew, Prentiss, and Studley, 1845), 166-72. The essay is reprinted in Foner, ed., *Life and Writings*, 1:113-15.

11. *Liberator*, 25 October 1844, 171; *National Anti-Slavery Standard*, 14 November 1844, 95; Samuel Rodman, *Diary of Samuel Rodman*, ed. Zephaniah W. Pease (New Bedford, Mass.: Reynolds Printing Company, 1927), 263.

12. Douglass' third son, Charles Remond Douglass, was born 21 October 1844 (McFeely, *Frederick Douglass*, 103). Blassingame does not include the meeting of 22-23 October in Douglass' itinerary. See John W. Blassingame, ed., *The Frederick Douglass Papers, Series One: Speeches, Debates, and Interviews, Volume 1* (New Haven, Conn.: Yale University Press, 1979), 1:xciii.

13. *Liberator*, 1 November 1844, 174.

14. Ibid., 174, 175.

15. Ibid., 174.

16. Ibid.

17. Ibid., 174, 175.

18. *Liberator*, 25 October 1844, 171.

19. *Liberator*, 29 November 1844, 190.

20. According to Blassingame, ed., *Douglass Papers, Series One*, 1:xciv, Douglass spoke at Salem, Massachusetts, on or around 11 November 1844. I have been unable to locate any record of this meeting.

21. The resolutions censuring Douglass were reprinted in *The National Anti-Slavery Standard*, 9 January 1845, 125.

22. *Liberator*, 6 December 1844, 195; Liberator, 13 December 1844, 199; *National Anti-Slavery Standard*, 9 January 1845, 125.

23. *Liberator*, 6 December 1844, 195. According to the minutes of the meeting, at the beginning of the afternoon session Garrison offered a series of resolutions condemning the annexation of Texas and asserting that if Texas were annexed to the United States, Massachusetts should "dissolve her connexion with the Union, and proclaim her freedom and independence." Garrison reportedly made a few remarks in support of his resolves and Douglass joined those gathered in unanimously adopting the resolutions.

24. *Liberator*, 13 December 1844, 199.

25. In a 10 January 1845 letter to John Bailey, Garrison mentioned that Douglass and Foster were touring in New Hampshire (Walter M. Merrill, ed., *The Letters of William Lloyd Garrison, Volume III* [Cambridge, Mass.: Harvard University Press, 1973], 3:275). Although details about the tour are not available in either the abolitionist or the non-abolitionist press, the yearly report of the American Anti-Slavery Society in 1845 included a brief note that Foster and Douglass had toured New Hampshire under the auspices of the American and New Hampshire antislavery societies and that their campaign had met with "the best results" (in *The National Anti-Slavery Standard*, 10 July 1845, 22). Blassingame, ed., *Douglass Papers, Series One*, 1:xciv, does not include the New Hampshire tour in its itinerary of Douglass' speaking activities.

26. *Liberator*, 31 January 1845, 19.

27. Ibid. In addition to this speech, Douglass spoke on at least two other occasions. On Wednesday, the first day of the convention, during the evening session, he supported Stephen S. Foster's resolution "concerning the future conduct of Massachusetts in the case of the expulsion of her officer, the Hon. Samuel Hoar, from the port of Charleston, South Carolina." During the Thursday afternoon session, he spoke in support of a resolution that condemned "the conduct of Capt. Gilbert Ricketson, of New Bedford, in returning to Virginia to surrender his steward and the poor fugitive that had taken refuge on board his ship, to hunters and sellers of men."

28. *National Anti-Slavery Standard*, 13 February 1845, 147; Garrison to John Bailey, 13 February 1845, in Merrill, ed., *Letters of William Lloyd Garrison*, 3:281.

29. *Liberator*, 14 March 1845, 43; *National Anti-Slavery Standard*, 20 March 1845, 166; *National Anti-Slavery Standard*, 27 March 1845, 170.

30. *National Anti-Slavery Standard*, 20 March 1845, 166.

31. *Liberator*, 28 March 1845, 51.

32. Although Blassingame, ed., *Douglass Papers, Series One*, 1:xciv, indicates that Douglass spoke in Worcester on 11 March, I have been unable to locate any record of a meeting there on that date.

33. *Liberator*, 21 March 1845, 47.

34. Sometime during the week of 13-18 April, Douglass read his *Narrative* to Wendell Phillips. A few days later, Phillips wrote a letter to Douglass in which he described his response to the autobiography. The letter, dated 22 April 1845, was printed immediately after Garrison's preface in the first edition of the *Narrative*. At roughly the same time, Douglass read his autobiography to Garrison and to Maria Weston Chapman (*Boston Journal*, 13 September 1886). Soon after, Garrison penned a preface to Douglass' autobiography dated 1 May 1845. See Frederick Douglass, *Narrative of the Life of Frederick Douglass, An American Slave, Written By Himself* (1845; reprint, New York: Signet, 1968), v-xviii.

35. *Liberator*, 13 June 1845, 95.

36. *Liberator*, 2 May 1845, 71.

37. Blassingame, ed., *Douglass Papers, Series One*, 1:xciv, incorrectly dates this meeting as occurring on 6 May only.

38. *National Anti-Slavery Standard*, 8 May 1845, 195; *Liberator*, 16 May 1845, 78.

39. *National Anti-Slavery Standard*, 15 May 1845, 197-98; *National Anti-Slavery Standard*, 22 May 1845, 202; *Pennsylvania Freeman*, 8 May 1845, 3; *Liberator*, 16 May 1845, 79; Raymond Gerald Fulkerson, "Frederick Douglass and the Anti-Slavery Crusade: His Career and Speeches, 1817-1861," pt. 2 (Ph.D. diss., University of Illinois, 1971), 463; Dorothy Sterling, *Ahead of Her Time: Abby Kelley and the Politics of Antislavery* (New York: Norton, 1991), 189, 193, 196, 210-12. The text of the speech was printed in *The National Anti-Slavery Standard*, 22 May 1845, 202. It is reproduced in Blassingame, ed., *Douglass Papers, Series One*, 1:27-34, and in Fulkerson, "Frederick Douglass," pt. 2, 461-66.

40. Blassingame, ed., *Douglass Papers, Series One*, 1:29.

41. Ibid., 1:29-30.

42. Ibid., 1:30.

43. Ibid., 1:31.

44. For Douglass' account of his battle with his overseer, Edward Covey, see Douglass, *Narrative*, 77-83.

45. Blassingame, ed., *Douglass Papers, Series One*, 1:31-32.

46. Ibid., 1:32.

47. Ibid.

48. Ibid.

49. Ibid.

50. Ibid., 1:33.

51. Ibid.

52. Ibid. Douglass had made a similar statement during an address at the State House in the hall of the House of Representatives at the thirteenth annual meeting of Massachusetts Anti-Slavery Society in Boston, Massachusetts, on 26 January 1845.

53. Ibid.

54. *New York Journal of Commerce*, 6 May 1845, quoted in Fulkerson, "Frederick Douglass," pt. 2, 463. During the afternoon session of the convention, Douglass was appointed to the business committee and to the committee to nominate officers for the society. Although the minutes indicate that Douglass did not take part in the proceedings for the remainder of the convention, Sydney Howard Gay, the recording secretary for the meeting, admitted to losing his notes "and other documents" from the convention. Gay had to rely "almost entirely" on memory to produce the minutes which, he granted, provided an "imperfect record of the proceedings" (*National Anti-Slavery Standard*, 15 May 1845, 197).

55. *Liberator*, 9 May 1845, 75; *Pennsylvania Freeman*, 22 May 1845, 3; *Liberator*, 23 May 1845, 82; *Pennsylvania Freeman*, 5 June 1845, 3; *National Anti-Slavery Standard*, 12 June 1845, 7; *National Anti-Slavery Standard*, 19 June 1845, 11.

56. See, for example, *Liberator*, 30 May 1845, 86; *Liberator*, 6 June 1845, 89, 90; *Liberator*, 15 August 1845, 129; *New York Tribune*, 10 June 1845, 2; *National Anti-Slavery Standard*, 12 June 1845, 7; *National Anti-Slavery Standard,* 7 August 1845, 39; *Pennsylvania Freeman*, 19 June 1845, 2; *Pennsylvania Freeman*, 31 July 1845, 3.

57. Editor's introduction to Frederick Douglass, *Narrative of the Life of Frederick Douglass, An American Slave, Written By Himself*, ed. Benjamin Quarles (Cambridge, Mass.: Harvard University Press, 1960), vii.

58. Ibid., xiii; William L. Andrews, "Introduction," in *Critical Essays on Frederick Douglass*, ed. William L. Andrews (Boston, Mass.: G.K. Hall and Company, 1991), 2.

59. Compare, for instance, the following: Douglass' description of overseer Austin Gore in the *Narrative* (38-41) with his description of Gore during a speech to the American Anti-Slavery Society on 6 May 1845 (in Blassingame, ed., *Douglass Papers, Series One*, 1:31); Douglass' account of the Demby incident in the *Narrative* (39-40) with his account of the same incident during a speech to the American Anti-Slavery Society on 6 May 1845 (in Blassingame, ed., *Douglass Papers, Series One*, 1:31-32); Douglass' story of Mrs. Hicks in the *Narrative* (41) with the story he told during a speech to the American Anti-Slavery Society on 6 May 1845 (in Blassingame, ed., *Douglass Papers, Series*

One, 1:32); and Douglass' disclosures about his personal sufferings as a slave in the *Narrative* (43-44) with the statements he made during an antislavery lecture at Concord, New Hampshire, on 11 February 1844 (in *Herald of Freedom*, 16 February 1844, 208). Striking similarities also appear between Douglass' descriptions of his master, Thomas Auld, beating his lame cousin Henny in the *Narrative* (68) and his speeches at Lynn in October 1841 and at Hingham, Massachusetts on 4 November 1841 (in Blassingame, ed., *Douglass Papers, Series One*, 1:3, 13).

60. *Boston Journal*, 13 September 1886.

61. *Liberator*, 6 June 1845, 91. On the oratorical style of the *Narrative*, also see Robert G. O'Meally, "Frederick Douglass' 1845 Narrative: The Text Was Meant to be Preached," in *Afro-American Literature: The Reconstruction of Instruction*, ed. Dexter Fisher and Robert B. Stepto (New York: Modern Language Association of America, 1979), 197, 200-1, 210.

62. *Liberator*, 23 May 1845, 83.

63. *Lowell Journal* in the *Liberator*, 13 June 1845, 94.

64. *Liberator*, 6 June 1845, 91.

65. Ibid.

66. *Boston Daily Times* in the *Liberator*, 6 June 1845, 90.

67. On 23 October 1844, during a Liberty Party convention in New Bedford, Massachusetts, Douglass had used a similar argument against Bradburn. See Douglass to William Lloyd Garrison, 27 October 1844, in the *Liberator*, 1 November 1844, 174.

68. *Liberator*, 13 June 1845, 94.

69. Blassingame, ed., *Douglass Papers, Series One*, 1:xciv, mistakenly dates this meeting as beginning 31 May and ending 4 June.

70. *Liberator*, 13 June 1845, 94; *National Anti-Slavery Standard*, 12 June 1845, 6.

71. *Herald of Freedom* in the *Liberator*, 20 June 1845, 98.

72. Ibid. Rogers took offense at any efforts made at "speechifying." He did not believe "anybody had a right—so incompatible with the right of free speech, as that of speechifying." By "speechifying," he meant "a long, uninterrupted and uninterruptible harangue" (*Liberator*, 20 June 1845, 98).

73. *National Anti-Slavery Standard*, 12 June 1845, 6-7; *Herald of Freedom* in *The National Anti-Slavery Standard*, 26 June 1845, 14. For other accounts of the New Hampshire meeting, see *Liberator*, 13 June 1845, 94; *National Anti-Slavery Standard*, 12 June 1845, 6.

74. *Liberator*, 13 June 1845, 94; *Herald of Freedom* in the *Liberator*, 20 June 1845, 98. Blassingame, ed., *Douglass Papers, Series One*, 1:xciv, does not include this speech in its itinerary of Douglass' speaking activities.

75. Blassingame, ed., *Douglass Papers, Series One*, 1:xciv, incorrectly places Douglass in Springfield on 8 June.

76. *Liberator*, 18 July 1845, 115.

77. *Pennsylvania Freeman*, 19 June 1845, 4.

78. *Albany Evening Journal*, 9 June 1845, 2; *Albany Evening Journal*, 10 June 1845, 2.

79. *Liberator*, 13 June 1845, 95.

80. Wendell Phillips to Elizabeth Pease, 24 February 1845, American Anti-Slavery Collection, Boston Public Library. As soon as Phillips learned of Douglass' plans to travel to Great Britain, he began preparing British abolitionists for Douglass' visit. See, for example, Wendell Phillips to Richard D. Webb, May 1845, American Anti-Slavery Collection, Boston Public Library; Ann and Wendell Phillips to Elizabeth Pease, 5 July 1845, Norcross Collection, Massachusetts Historical Society.

81. Douglass, *Bondage and Freedom*, 364.

82. Frederick Douglass, *Narrative of the Life of Frederick Douglass, An American Slave, Written By Himself*, 2d Dublin ed. (Dublin, Ireland: Webb and Chapman, 1846), III-IV.

83. Douglass, *Bondage and Freedom*, 364

84. James N. Buffum to Gerrit Smith, 21 June 1845, Special Collections, Syracuse University Library. Buffum also informed Smith that he and Douglass were "to visit Europe this season" and that he hoped Smith and his friends would support the trip financially.

85. Blassingame, ed., *Douglass Papers, Series One*, 1:xcv, misdates this meeting as convening on 14 June only.

86. Douglass, *Bondage and Freedom*, 364; *Liberator*, 4 July 1845, 107.

87. *Practical Christian* in the *Liberator*, 4 July 1845, 106. According to the minutes from the meeting, Reverend Orcutt, the pastor of the Orthodox church in Uxbridge, had, on the Sunday previous to the scheduled antislavery meeting, urged his congregation not to attend the convention.

88. *Liberator*, 20 June 1845, 99.

89. *Boston Journal*, 13 September 1886.

90. Douglass, *Bondage and Freedom*, 363-64.

91. Ibid., 363.

92. "My Slave Experience in Maryland: An Address Delivered in New York, New York, on 6 May 1845," in Blassingame, ed., *Douglass Papers, Series One,* 1:30.

93. According to the itinerary published in the *Liberator*, 20 June 1845, 99, Douglass was scheduled to lecture at the following places in Massachusetts during July: Worcester (1 July), Holden (2 July), Westminster (3 July), Athol (4-5 July), Hubardstown (6 July), Princeton (7 July), Barre (8 July), West Brookfield (10 July), South Wilbraham (11 July). The same issue of the *Liberator* published Douglass' New York schedule, as follows: Albany (12 July), Troy (13 July), Winfield (14 July), Utica (15 July), Rome (16 July), Syracuse (17 July),

Skaneateles (18 July), Waterloo (19-20 July), Palmyra (21-22 July), Rochester (23-24 July). According to the *Liberator*, 18 July 1845, 115, Douglass was scheduled to speak at the following places in Massachusetts in August: Weymouth (7 August), Hingham (8 August), Kingston (9 August), Dukesbury (10 August).

94. *National Anti-Slavery Standard*, 14 August 1845, 42.

95. *Liberty Press*, 19 July 1845, 146, 147.

96. *Religious Recorder* (Syracuse, N.Y.), 24 July 1845.

97. *Liberator*, 20 June 1845, 99; *Liberator*, 15 August 1845, 131.

98. *Liberator*, 5 September 1845, 141.

99. *Liberator*, 18 July 1845, 115; John W. Hutchinson, *Story of the Hutchinsons, Volume 1*, ed. Charles E. Mann (Boston: Lee and Shepard, 1896), 1:142.

100. *Liberator*, 22 August 1845, 135. Douglass' remarks probably dealt with the case of Jonathon Walker, an abolitionist from Barnstable, Massachusetts, who was imprisoned in Pensacola, Florida, for assisting seven slaves to escape from bondage in June 1844. In Pensacola on a business trip, Walker took the slaves on board his boat and sailed for Nassau. The party was intercepted by a sloop off the Florida gulf coast. Walker was transported to Pensacola where, in November 1844, he was tried and convicted of slave stealing, fined $150, required to pay court fees of approximately $450, set in the pillory for one hour, and branded with the letters S.S. (slave stealer) in the palm of his right hand. He spent eleven months in jail before abolitionists could raise enough money to secure his release. After being set free in July 1845, Walker returned to Massachusetts, where he was honored by northern abolitionists. See *Liberator*, 22 August 1845, 135; *National Anti-Slavery Standard*, 12 December 1844, 111; *National Anti-Slavery Standard*, 26 June 1845, 13-14; *National Anti-Slavery Standard*, 17 July 1845, 26; Blassingame, ed., *Douglass Papers, Series One*, 1:116n.

101. *Liberator*, 22 August 1845, 135.

102. *National Anti-Slavery Standard*, 21 August 1845, 47; *Liberator*, 22 August 1845, 135.

✤ Epilogue

IN BRINGING HIS 1892 *Life and Times of Frederick Douglass* to a close, Frederick Douglass admitted to having lived "several lives in one: first, the life of slavery; secondly, the life of a fugitive from slavery; thirdly, the life of comparative freedom; fourthly, the life of conflict and battle; and fifthly, the life of victory, if not complete, at least assured." The first two stages of Douglass' life have been the focus of this study. As we have seen, his experiences as a slave and a fugitive contributed profoundly to his understanding of rhetoric and to his development as an orator and an abolitionist.

Douglass' long and arduous journey from slavery to freedom, from obscurity to prominence, began during his boyhood days in bondage. At an early age he was enticed by the power of language. In the slave quarters, he was immersed in the African oral traditions of secular storytelling and religious preaching. On the fields of the plantation he listened to and sang slave songs and spirituals. His understanding of the power of the spoken word was further advanced with the purchase of Caleb Bingham's *The Columbian Orator*. This collection of orations, poems, playlets, and dialogues gave him the words to meet proslavery arguments, provided him with detailed instructions on how to deliver a speech, inspired him to master the art of oratory as a means to end slavery, and fueled his desire to be free. He was most deeply affected by a "Dialogue Between a Master and Slave," which demonstrated a slave's ability to use rational argument to convince his master to release him from the bonds of slavery.

Soon after acquiring Bingham's book, Douglass underwent a religious awakening, which roused within him a sense of mission and purpose and fixed him on a course to become a preacher. Around the same time, he discovered that there were abolitionists in the North working to end slavery, and he immediately declared himself an abolitionist as well. For the rest of his days in bondage, Douglass pursued his interests in oratory, religion, and abolitionism. In meetings of the East Baltimore Mental Improvement

Society, he delivered speeches and engaged in debates and discussions over black elevation, theology, and abolitionism. In the streets and churches of Baltimore and in the fields and plantations of the Eastern Shore, he preached to his fellow slaves from the Bible and from the *Columbian Orator*, and he actively sought out occasions to advance his understanding of public speaking, religion, and abolitionism.

Within weeks of his escape from slavery in 1838, Douglass joined the African Methodist Episcopal (A.M.E.) Zion Church in New Bedford, Massachusetts. He quickly distinguished himself as one of the congregation's leading members. Within two years, he became a licensed lay preacher, in which capacity he received formal training as an orator and advanced his public speaking skills by preaching to the congregation on a regular basis. While in New Bedford, Douglass also became involved with the city's black abolitionists. He attended, and often spoke at, their meetings. Contrary to the standard view of Douglass, he did not emerge miraculously as an abolitionist orator at the 10-12 August 1841 Nantucket meeting of the Massachusetts Anti-Slavery Society. Steeped in the oral traditions of the African American community, trained as a preacher in the A.M.E. Zion Church, committed to abolitionism for at least a decade, and active in New Bedford's black antislavery movement for three years, he was well prepared to take on the duties of a lecturer for the Massachusetts Anti-Slavery Society.

It is important to recognize as well the extent to which Douglass' preparation was grounded in the African American experience. Although clearly captivated in New Bedford by the rhetoric, personality, and ideology of William Lloyd Garrison, he did not come to abolitionism primarily through his contact with Garrison or the *Liberator*. Nor did he acquire his rhetorical proclivities from Garrison. Outspoken in his condemnation of southern slavery and northern racial prejudice, often harsh and abrasive in his language, consistently vivid and dramatic in his imagery, Douglass was a perfect match for Garrison's brand of antislavery discourse. But these traits of Douglass' oratory had developed across the years out of the oral traditions of the slave community, his internalization of Bingham's *Columbian Orator*, his speaking activities while a slave in Maryland, and his training in the rhetorical practices of the A.M.E. Zion Church. As important as his exposure to Garrison doubtless was, it came late in his life compared to his experiences within the African American community, both slave and free. It was those experiences above all that shaped his oratory and his commitment to abolitionism.

Once Douglass began his work for the Massachusetts Anti-Slavery Society in August 1841, his only occupation was that of traveling antislavery lecturer. While other abolitionists had careers outside of the antislavery enterprise, at this stage of Douglass' life his livelihood depended solely on his success as an abolitionist orator. For four years he traveled almost daily through the North preaching the antislavery gospel. In doing so, he spoke with a power and eloquence that contributed mightily to the growth of antislavery sentiment. As he lectured across Massachusetts, Maine, New Hampshire, Vermont, and Rhode Island, down into Connecticut, New York, and Pennsylvania, and over to the western states of Ohio and Indiana, listeners repeatedly commented on his powerful physical presence, his captivating delivery, his forceful, melodic voice, and his use of logical demonstration, wit, satire, irony, invective, sarcasm, and vivid descriptions to capture the brutality of slavery and the injustice of northern prejudice. From the outset, he astounded his white audiences with his intellectual capacity and rhetorical genius. He told the story of his slave past and fugitive present with such force that it enabled him to speak with an authenticity unequaled by even the most talented white orators. While white abolitionists could only imagine the horrors of bondage and the hardships of being a fugitive slave, Douglass drew from his own experience to produce vivid illustrations of slavery and freedom as he had experienced them. In so doing, he confirmed his manhood and demonstrated his humanity.

Douglass, however, did more than recount the horrors of his life as a slave. From the beginning of his probationary period as a lecturer for the Massachusetts Anti-Slavery Society, he acted independently by refusing to conform to the limitations imposed on him by the leaders of the antislavery movement. Instead of merely reciting a narrative of his slave experiences, he spoke out on such issues as the supremacy of moral suasion over political action, the oppressive force of racial prejudice in the North, the racism of northern churches, and the peaceful dissolution of the Union as a means of combating slavery. Equally important, although Douglass adhered strictly to the dictates of Garrisonian abolitionism, he at times disagreed with white abolitionists in his speeches. Some of those disagreements were over the role of political action in the campaign to abolish slavery, while others revolved around introducing subjects foreign to the cause into antislavery meetings. But whatever the issue, Douglass was not prepared to assume a subsidiary role in the abolitionist crusade on account of his skin color. He not only argued for the rights of the slave, but in his speeches and his actions he also fought for the right of blacks to equal status with whites in the abolitionist movement and in northern society in general.

Although Douglass' independent spirit dismayed some abolitionists—especially those with whom he clashed on the platform—his stature in the movement grew steadily from 1841 to 1845. Whereas in 1841 he was unknown to most abolitionists, by 1844 he had achieved such stature that he was being publicized as a featured speaker at the annual meeting of the American Anti-Slavery Society. As early as 1842, abolitionists recognized

Douglass' potential as a drawing card and hired him as one of eight agents to lecture through western and central New York. His overwhelming success on that assignment led to his being recruited for other important campaigns, including a four-month visit to Rhode Island during the winter of 1842, the Hundred Conventions tour of the West in the last six months of 1843, the Hundred Conventions tour of Massachusetts in the spring of 1844, and a three-week circuit through eastern Pennsylvania in the summer of 1844. By the time he left for England in 1845, he was regarded as one of the premier orators of American abolitionism.

Douglass earned this distinction by forging a dynamic antislavery message. From the outset of his career as a lecturer, he used moral suasion to convince his auditors that they ought to work to abolish slavery. Early on, his favorite strategy from the stand was to expose and shame the acts of slaveholders and northern and southern ministers. Over time, he also came to shame other segments of the nation. He rebuked the Liberty Party and its founders for working against the moral crusade to end slavery, charged the Whig and Democratic Parties with being proslavery, denounced the U.S. Constitution and its framers for legalizing slavery, and criticized Henry Clay, John C. Calhoun, and Daniel Webster for their positions on slavery. Douglass' charges were often harsh, uncompromising, and graphic, for he firmly believed that public observation of the shameful acts associated with slavery and its minions would move the nation to abolish the slave system. To make the acts of individuals more vivid and concrete for his auditors, he used mimicry to bring to light their words and behaviors. He transformed himself into the southern minister preaching to the slaves, he imitated the northern minister speaking to African American congregants, and he mimicked Henry Clay addressing the U.S. Senate.

Douglass' message, however, went far beyond using moral suasion and mimicry to persuade his listeners of the sinful nature of slavery. He used irony to reveal the inconsistencies between the nation's professions and practices where the slaves were concerned. He created striking imagery to capture the horror and ruthlessness of slavery. He employed allegory to display the racial prejudice of northern churches when administering the sacraments of baptism and Communion to African Americans. He developed a critique of religion wherein he linked the religious practices of the churches of the North with the churches of the South, and then demonstrated how those practices helped sustain the South's peculiar institution. He also developed a social critique that connected the material wealth enjoyed by white people of the North and South to the continuance of slavery. As his antislavery message became more sophisticated and polished, his fame as an eloquent fugitive from slavery spread, and people gathered from near and far to experience his rhetorical brilliance.

From the moment Douglass accepted the offer to become an agent for the Massachusetts Anti-Slavery Society, he devoted his life to the crusade to free his brothers and sisters from bondage. In the process, he distinguished himself as among the most eloquent orators of the day—a man deeply committed to stirring the hearts and minds of the American people against slavery and racial prejudice. Day and night he used his mighty voice to demand freedom for the slaves. Never doubting the power of the spoken word to reach the hearts and minds of his listeners, he truly believed that if people could know slavery as he knew it and feel it as he had felt it, they would recognize its immorality and work toward its extinction. This was the belief he carried with him through the North—a conviction that fueled his unwavering commitment to the crusade to end slavery and that helped make him one of the most enduring and consequential public voices in American history.

Appendix A

Douglass' Speaking Itinerary: 1839-1845

1839

12 March:	New Bedford, Massachusetts: Third Christian Church: Anti-Colonization Meeting of Black Citizens.

1841

30 June:	New Bedford, Massachusetts: Third Christian Church: Meeting of Black Citizens.
9 August:	New Bedford, Massachusetts: Liberty Hall: Annual Meeting of the Bristol County Anti-Slavery Society.
10-12 August:	Nantucket, Massachusetts: Atheneum Hall: Nantucket Anti-Slavery Society Convention.
17-18 August:	Millbury, Massachusetts: Quarterly Meeting of the Massachusetts Anti-Slavery Society.
31 August-1 September:	Groton, Massachusetts: Liberty Hall: Middlesex County Anti-Slavery Society Meeting.
3 September:	Abington, Massachusetts: Reverend Alden's Meetinghouse: Anti-Slavery Lecture.
4 September:	Abington, Massachusetts: Town House: Quarterly Meeting of the Abington Anti-Slavery Society.
8-10 September:	Dover, New Hampshire: Court House, Congre-gational Meetinghouse: Annual Meeting of the Strafford County Anti-Slavery Society.

October:	Lynn, Massachusetts: Anti-Slavery Speech.
5 October:	West Brookfield, Massachusetts: Congrega-tional Meetinghouse: Quarterly Meeting of the Worcester County South Division Anti-Slavery Society.
6 October:	Holden, Massachusetts: Town Hall: Worcester County North Division Anti-Slavery Society.
12 October:	Concord, Massachusetts: Universalist Meeting-house: Middlesex Anti-Slavery Society.
13 October:	Boston, Massachusetts: Annual Meeting of the Boston Female Anti-Slavery Society.
20 October:	Wrentham, Massachusetts: Centre Meeting-house: Quarterly Meeting of the Norfolk County Anti-Slavery Society.
4 November:	Hingham, Massachusetts: Baptist Church: Quarterly Meeting of the Plymouth County Anti-Slavery Society.
11-13 November:	Providence, Rhode Island: Franklin Hall: Rhode Island Anti-Slavery Society.
18-20 November:	Providence, Rhode Island: Dorrite "People's Convention."
23 November:	Fall River, Massachusetts: Columbia Hall: Quarterly Meeting of the Bristol County Anti-Slavery Society.
2-3 December:	Woonsocket Falls, Rhode Island: Regional Anti-Slavery Convention to protest Dorr constitution.
7 December:	North Scituate, Rhode Island: Freewill Baptist Church: Regional Anti-Slavery Convention to protest Dorr constitution.
14 December:	Phenix and Fiskville, Rhode Island: Regional Anti-Slavery Conventions to protest Dorr constitution.
15 December:	East Greenwich, Rhode Island: Regional Anti-Slavery Convention to protest Dorr constitution.
21-22 December:	Kingston, Rhode Island: Regional Anti-Slavery Convention to protest Dorr constitution.
24-25 December:	Newport, Rhode Island: Regional Anti-Slavery Convention to protest Dorr constitution.
27-28 December:	Providence, Rhode Island: Regional Anti-Slavery Convention to protest Dorr constitution.

1842

5-6 January:	Worcester, Massachusetts: Annual Meeting of the Worcester County South Division Anti-Slavery Society.
7 January:	Barre, Massachusetts: Town Hall: Worcester County North Division Anti-Slavery Society.
26-28 January:	Boston, Massachusetts: Melodeon: Annual Meeting of the Massachusetts Anti-Slavery Society.
28 January:	Boston, Massachusetts: Faneuil Hall.
8-9 February:	Andover, Massachusetts: Methodist Meeting-house: Essex County Anti-Slavery Society.
16 February:	Hubbardston, Massachusetts: Worcester County North Division Anti-Slavery Society.
25 March:	South Scituate, Massachusetts: Quarterly Meeting of the Plymouth County Anti-Slavery Society.
31 March:	Groton, Massachusetts.
1 April:	Harvard, Massachusetts: Harvard Anti-Slavery Society.
2 April:	Dedham, Massachusetts.
3 April:	Bolton, Massachusetts.
4-5 April:	Lanesborough, Massachusetts.
6 April:	Westborough, Massachusetts.
7 April:	Upton, Massachusetts: Upton Female Anti-Slavery Society.
8 April:	Milford, Massachusetts.
9 April:	Medway, Massachusetts.
10 April:	Bellingham, Massachusetts.
11 April:	Franklin, Massachusetts.
12 April:	Wrentham, Massachusetts.
13 April:	Foxboro, Massachusetts.
14 April:	Sharon, Massachusetts.
15 April:	Canton, Massachusetts.

23 April:	Canton, Massachusetts.
23 April:	Medfield, Massachusetts (evening lecture).
24 April:	Dedham, Massachusetts.
24 April:	Medway, Massachusetts (evening lecture).
25 April:	Dover, Massachusetts.
25 April:	Medfield, Massachusetts (evening lecture).
26 April:	Needham, Massachusetts.
26 April:	Lexington, Massachusetts: Baptist Meeting-house: Middlesex County Anti-Slavery Society.
27 April:	Natick, Massachusetts.
27 April:	Malden, Massachusetts (evening lecture).
28 April:	Sherburne, Massachusetts.
28 April:	Medford, Massachusetts (evening lecture).
29 April:	Hopkinton, Massachusetts.
29 April:	Woburn, Massachusetts (evening lecture).
30 April:	Grafton, Massachusetts.
30 April:	Stoneham, Massachusetts (evening lecture).

Locations also Visited in April (From the "Treasurer's Account" in *Liberator*, 13 May 1842: 75):

	Weymouth, Massachusetts.
	Fairhaven, Massachusetts.
	Mattapoisett, Massachusetts.
	Westport, Massachusetts.
	Assonett, Massachusetts.
	North Rochester, Massachusetts.
1 May:	Millbury, Massachusetts.
1 May:	Stoneham, Massachusetts (evening lecture).
2 May:	Auburn, Massachusetts.
2 May:	South Reading, Massachusetts (evening lecture).
3 May:	Oxford, Massachusetts.

4 May: Charlton, Massachusetts.

5 May: Sturbridge, Massachusetts.

6 May: Southbridge, Massachusetts.

7 May: Dudley, Massachusetts.

8 May: Webster, Massachusetts.

10-13 May: New York, New York: Broadway Tabernacle: Annual Meeting of the American Anti-Slavery Society.

24-27 May: Boston, Massachusetts: Chardon Street Chap-el: Annual Meeting of the New England Anti-Slavery Society.

3 June: Northbridge, Massachusetts: Congregational Church.

5 June: Millville, Massachusetts: Rev. Stacy's Church.

6 June: Northbridge, Massachusetts.

9 June: Northbridge, Massachusetts.

16 June: Barnstable, Massachusetts: Non-Resistance Meeting: With Garrison.

17 June: Yarmouth Port, Massachusetts: Anti-Slavery Meeting: With Garrison and George Bradburn.

18 June: Centreville, Massachusetts: Anti-Slavery Meeting: With Garrison and Bradburn.

19 June: Osterville, Massachusetts: Non-Resistance Meeting: With Garrison and Bradburn.

20 June: Hyannis, Massachusetts: Anti-Slavery Meeting: With Garrison, Bradburn, and Henry C. Wright.

21 June: North Dennis, Massachusetts: Non-Resistance Meeting: With Garrison, Bradburn, and Wright.

22 June: Brewster, Massachusetts: Anti-Slavery Meeting: With Garrison, Bradburn, and Wright.

1-3 August: Norristown, Pennsylvania: Annual Meeting of the Eastern Pennsylvania Anti-Slavery Society.

8-9 August: New Bedford, Massachusetts: Bristol County Anti-Slavery Society.

10-15 August: Nantucket, Massachusetts: The Great Hall, Atheneum: Anti-Slavery Convention.

c. 16-17 August:	Sutton and Grafton, Massachusetts: Anti-Slavery Lectures.
21 August:	Lynn, Massachusetts: Lyceum Hall: Non-resistance Meeting.
26-27 August:	Rochester, New York: With Abby Kelley, Erasmus D. Hudson, and John A. Collins.
30 August:	Genesee, New York: With Kelley and Collins.
2-3 September:	Victor, New York: With Kelley, Collins, and Hudson.
6 September:	Pen Yan, New York: With Kelley and Collins.
9-10 September:	Palmyra, New York: With Kelley, Collins, and Hudson.
13-14 September:	Ithaca, New York: With Kelley, Collins, and Hudson.
16 September:	Waterloo, New York: With Kelley and Hudson.
20 September:	Millport, New York: With Kelley.
23 September:	Ledyard, New York: With Kelley.
26-27 September:	Port Byron, New York: With Kelley.
29-30 September:	Cato Four Corners, New York: With Kelley and Hudson.
4-5 October:	Cortland, New York: With Kelley and Collins.
5-6 October:	Syracuse, New York: Liberty Party Convention: With Hudson, Collins, and J.N.T. Tucker.
7-8 October:	Syracuse, New York: With Kelley, Collins, Tucker, and Hudson.
11 October:	Oxford, New York.
14 October:	Pulaski, New York.
18 October:	Cazenovia, New York.
21 October:	Rome, New York.
25 October:	Cooperstown, New York.
30 October:	Boston, Massachusetts: Faneuil Hall: Latimer Meeting.
1-8 November:	New Bedford, Massachusetts: Latimer Meet-ings: With Charles Lenox Remond.
4 November:	New Bedford, Massachusetts: Universalist Society Meetinghouse: Latimer Meeting.

6 November:	New Bedford, Massachusetts: Town Hall: Latimer Meeting.
6-18 November:	Providence, Rhode Island: Town Hall: Annual Meeting of the Rhode Island Anti-Slavery Society.
21 November:	Salem, Massachusetts: Mechanics' Hall: Latimer Meeting: With Remond and George Latimer.
26-27 November:	Essex, Massachusetts: Universalist Meeting-house: Essex County Anti-Slavery Society.
December:	Douglass lecturing in Rhode Island.

1843

25-27 January:	Boston, Massachusetts: Faneuil Hall: Annual Meeting to the Massachusetts Anti-Slavery Society.
28-31 January:	Lynn, Massachusetts: Society of Universal Inquiry and Reform (Met through 2 February).
1-2 February:	Princeton, Massachusetts: Annual Meeting of the Worcester County North Division Anti-Slavery Society.
19 February:	Providence, Rhode Island: Franklin Hall: Lecture on Slavery under auspices of the Rhode Island Anti-Slavery Society.
26 February:	Providence, Rhode Island: Westminster Hall: Lecture on Slavery under the auspices of the Rhode Island Anti-Slavery Society.
5 March:	Providence, Rhode Island: Franklin Hall: Lecture on Slavery under the auspices of the Rhode Island Anti-Slavery Society.
6 March:	Boston, Massachusetts: Armory Hall: Boston Female Anti-Slavery Society: Lecture: "Slavery, as actually existing at the South."
9-11 March:	Lynn, Massachusetts: Silsbee Street Chapel: Quarterly Meeting of the Essex County Anti-Slavery Society.
18 March:	Providence, Rhode Island: Rhode Island Anti-Slavery Society: Executive Committee Meeting.

19 March:	Providence, Rhode Island: Franklin Hall: Lecture on Slavery under the auspices of the Rhode Island Anti-Slavery Society.
26 March:	Providence, Rhode Island: Lecture: "Colonization and its connexion with slavery, and the degradation of the colored people of the United States" under the auspices of the Rhode Island Anti-Slavery Society.
2 April:	Providence, Rhode Island: Lecture: "The Progress of the Cause" under the auspices of the Rhode Island Anti-Slavery Society.
12-13 April:	East Greenwich, Rhode Island: Rhode Island Anti-Slavery Society.
20 April:	Dedham, Massachusetts: Town Hall: Annual Meeting of the Norfolk County Anti-Slavery Society.
24-25 April:	Lowell, Massachusetts: Appleton Street Church: Anti-Slavery Lectures with Remond and Latimer.
9-11 May:	New York, New York: Apollo Saloon: Annual Meeting of the American Anti-Slavery Society.
14 May:	Hartford, Connecticut: Gilman's Hall: Anti-Slavery Lecture.
15-16 May:	Hartford, Connecticut: Connecticut Anti-Slavery Society.
30 May-1 June:	Boston, Massachusetts: Faneuil Hall, Miller Tabernacle: Annual Meeting of the New England Anti-Slavery Society.
7-9 June:	Concord, New Hampshire: Annual Meeting of the New Hampshire Anti-Slavery Society.
14 June:	Lunenburg, Massachusetts: Worcester County North Division Anti-Slavery Society: With Remond and Cyrus M. Burleigh.
19 June:	Fall River, Massachusetts: Anti-Slavery Lecture.
20-21 June:	New Bedford, Massachusetts: Town Hall: Bristol County Anti-Slavery Convention.
23-25 June:	Nantucket, Massachusetts: Atheneum Hall: Anti-Slavery Convention.
27 June:	Fall River, Massachusetts: Columbian Hall: Anti-Slavery Convention: With Remond and Burleigh.

4 July:	Kingston, Massachusetts: Town Hall: Annual Meeting of the Plymouth County Anti-Slavery Society: With Remond and Sydney Howard Gay.
13-14 July:	Middlebury, Vermont: With Bradburn and Collins.
17-18 July:	Ferrisburg, Vermont: With Bradburn and Collins.
27 July:	Utica, New York: With Bradburn and Collins.
30 July-2 August:	Syracuse, New York: With Collins, Remond, and Kelley.
3-6 August:	Rochester, New York: Bethel Church: Annual Meeting of the American Anti-Slavery Society of Western New York: With Bradburn, Collins, and Jacob Ferris.
7 August:	Buffalo, New York: With Bradburn.
8-9 August:	Buffalo, New York: Douglass Conducting Anti-Slavery Meetings.
10-14 August:	Buffalo, New York: Conducting Anti-Slavery Meetings: With Remond.
15-19 August:	Buffalo, New York: National Convention of Colored Citizens of the United States: With Remond.
20 August-September 1:	Buffalo-Rochester, New York, Area: Conducting Anti-Slavery Meetings with Remond.
7 September:	Oakland, Ohio: With Remond.
11-12 September:	Cambridge, Indiana: With Bradburn and White.
c. 13 September:	Richmond, Indiana: With Bradburn and White.
15-16 September:	Pendleton, Indiana: With Bradburn and White.
17 September:	Noblesville, Indiana: With Bradburn and White.
21-23 September:	Jonesboro, Indiana: Annual Meeting of the Indiana Anti-Slavery Society: With James Monroe, Gay, Bradburn, Remond, and White.
24 September-End of October:	Clinton County, Ohio.
30-31 October:	Lloydsville, Ohio: With Remond, Gay, and Monroe.
c. 1 November:	New Lisbon, Ohio: With Remond, Gay, and Monroe.
3-4 November:	New Brighton, Pennsylvania.

c. 6-13 November:	Pittsburgh, Pennsylvania: With Remond, Gay, Monroe, White, and Bradburn.
c. 16 November:	Fallston, Pennsylvania.
25 November:j	West Chester, Pennsylvania: With White and Bradburn.
4-7 December:	Philadelphia, Pennsylvania: Second Independent Universalist Church: Tenth Anniversary of the American Anti-Slavery Society.

1844

24-26 January:	Boston, Massachusetts: Faneuil Hall: Annual Meeting of the Massachusetts Anti-Slavery Society.
11 February:	Concord, New Hampshire: Court House: Douglass Presented Afternoon and Evening Anti-Slavery Lectures.
12-19 February:	Bradford, New London, Henniker, Milford, Nashua, New-Market, Dover, and Great Falls: With Pillsbury.
20 February:	Concord, New Hampshire: Court Room: Anti-Slavery Lecture.
22-23 February:	Lowell, Massachusetts: With Pillsbury, Collins, William Lloyd Garrison, William A. White, Nathaniel P. Rogers, and Lunsford Lane.
24 February:	Groton, Massachusetts: With White, Pillsbury, and Lane.
26-27 February:	Townsend, Massachusetts: With White and Lane.
1-2 March:	Bedford, Massachusetts: With Lane and Latimer.
3 March:	Concord, New Hampshire: Anti-Slavery Lecture
4 March:	Sudbury, Massachusetts: With Latimer and Lane.
6-7 March:	Framingham, Massachusetts: With Lane, Garrison, and James N. Buffum.
8 March:	Needham, Massachusetts: With Lane.
11 March:	Medford, Massachusetts: With Lane, Pillsbury, and Wendell Phillips.
13-14 March:	Waltham, Massachusetts: With Pillsbury and White.
15-16 March:	Dorchester, Massachusetts: With Pillsbury and White.

18-19 March: Dedham, Massachusetts: With Pillsbury, White, Garrison.

20-21 March: Braintree, Massachusetts: With Pillsbury and White.

22-23 March: Foxboro, Massachusetts: With Pillsbury and White.

24 March: Walpole, Massachusetts: With Pillsbury.

25-26 March: Medway, Massachusetts: With Pillsbury and White.

27-28 March: Wrentham, Massachusetts: With Pillsbury and White.

29-31 March: Pawtucket, Massachusetts: With Stephen S. Foster and Burleigh.

1-2 April: Westminster, Massachusetts: With Pillsbury and White.

3 April: Leominster, Massachusetts: 3 April With Pillsbury and White.

4 April: Essex, Massachusetts: Quarterly Meeting of the Essex County Anti-Slavery Society: With Remond and Foster.

5-6 April: Fitchburg, Massachusetts: With Hudson, Gay, and Kelley.

8-9 April: Ashburnham, Massachusetts: With Hudson, Gay, and Kelley.

10-11 April: Gardner, Massachusetts: With Hudson, Gay, and Kelley.

12-13 April: Hubbardston, Massachusetts: With Hudson, Gay, and Kelley.

15-16 April: Petersham, Massachusetts: With Hudson, Gay, and Kelley.

17-18 April: Athol, Massachusetts: With Hudson, Gay, and Kelley.

25-27 April: Lynn, Massachusetts: With Buffum, Foster, Garrison, and Remond.

28 April: Northampton, Massachusetts: Dining Room at the Association of Education and Industry: Sunday Morning Anti-Slavery Lecture.

28 April: Northampton, Massachusetts: Town Hall: Sunday Evening Anti-Slavery Lecture.

29-30 April:	Pittsfield, Massachusetts: With Hudson, Gay, and Kelley.
1-2 May:	Lenox, Massachusetts: With Hudson, Gay, and Kelley.
3-4 May:	Stockbridge, Massachusetts: With Hudson, Gay, and Kelley.
7-10 May:	New York, New York: Apollo Hall, Concert Hall: Annual Meeting of the American Anti-Slavery Society.
28, 29, 31 May:	Boston, Massachusetts: Marlboro Chapel: Annual Meeting of the New England Anti-Slavery Society.
June:	Hallowell, Maine: Town Hall: Anti-Slavery Lecture.
12-13 June:	Concord, Massachusetts: Universalist Church: Middlesex County Anti-Slavery Society.
26-28 July:	Nashua, New Hampshire: Anti-Slavery Meeting.
1 August:	Concord, Massachusetts: Court House: 1st of August Celebration.
12-16 August:	Norristown, Pennsylvania: Baptist Church: Annual Meeting of the Eastern Pennsylvania Anti-Slavery Society: With Garrison, Remond, and Buffum.
17 August:	Philadelphia, Pennsylvania: State House Yard: Anti-Slavery Meeting.
19 August:	Philadelphia, Pennsylvania: Gardiner's Church: With Remond.
22 August:	West Chester, Pennsylvania: Market House: Anti-Slavery Meeting: With Remond.
24 August:	Oxford, Pennsylvania: Friend's Meetinghouse: Clarkson Anti-Slavery Society: With Remond.
25 August:	London Grove, Pennsylvania: Outside Friend's Meetinghouse: Anti-Slavery Meeting: With Remond.
27-28 August:	Marlboro, Pennsylvania: Friend's Meeting-house: Annual Meeting of the Chester County Anti-Slavery Society: With Remond.
30 August:	Philadelphia, Pennsylvania: Wilbur Fisk Hall: Anti-Slavery Meeting: With Remond.
31 August:	Philadelphia, Pennsylvania: Clarkson Hall: Anti-Slavery Meeting: With Remond.

1 September:	Philadelphia, Pennsylvania: Gardiner's Church: Anti-Slavery Meeting: With Remond.
1 September:	Byberry, Pennsylvania: Friend's Meetinghouse: Anti-Slavery Meeting: With Remond.
15-30 September:	New Hampshire and Maine: With Kelley, Foster, Pillsbury, Remond, and J.M. Spear.
19-20 October:	New Bedford, Massachusetts: Liberty Hall: Bristol County Anti-Slavery Society.
22-23 October:	New Bedford, Massachusetts: Liberty Party Meeting: With Remond.
24 October:	New Bedford, Massachusetts: Liberty Hall: With Remond.
3 November:	Salem, Massachusetts: Mechanics' Hall: Salem Female Anti-Slavery Society.
4-5 November:	Marblehead, Massachusetts: Quarterly Meeting of the Essex County Anti-Slavery Society.
20-23 November:	Providence, Rhode Island: Mechanics' Hall: Annual Meeting of the Rhode Island Anti-Slavery Society.
26 November:	Cambridgeport, Massachusetts: Town Hall: Middlesex County Anti-Slavery Society.
21-22 December:	Portsmouth, New Hampshire: Ladies Anti-Slavery Society: Anti-Slavery Lectures.

1845

January:	New Hampshire Lecture Tour: With Foster.
24-26 January:	Boston, Massachusetts: Marlboro Chapel, Hall of the House of Representatives: Annual Meeting of the Massachusetts Anti-Slavery Society.
14-16 February:	Cornish, New Hampshire: Anti-Slavery Meetings: With Remond, Foster, and Charles C. Burleigh.
17-18 February:	Claremont, New Hampshire: Anti-Slavery Meetings: With Remond, Foster, and Burleigh.
8-9 March:	New Bedford, Massachusetts: Liberty Hall: Anti-Slavery Meetings.
18 March:	Worcester, Massachusetts: Brinley Hall: Quarterly Meeting of the Worcester County South Division Anti-Slavery Society.

19-20 April:	Manchester, Massachusetts: Dodge's Hall: Annual Meeting of the Essex County Anti-Slavery Society.
24 April:	Dedham, Massachusetts: Town Hall: Annual Meeting of the Norfolk County Anti-Slavery Society.
6-8 May:	New York, New York: Broadway Tabernacle, Minerva Rooms: Annual Meeting of the American Anti-Slavery Society.
25 May:	New Bedford, Massachusetts: Liberty Hall: Anti-Slavery Meeting: With Remond.
27-29 May:	Boston, Massachusetts: Marlboro Chapel: Annual Meeting of the New England Anti-Slavery Society.
4-6 June:	Concord, New Hampshire: Town Hall, Unitarian Church, North Church, State House Yard: Annual Meeting of the New Hampshire Anti-Slavery Society.
7 June:	Springfield, Massachusetts: Anti-Slavery Lec-tures.
9 June:	Albany, New York: City Hall: Anti-Slavery Lecture.
14-15 June:	Georgetown, Massachusetts: Savory Hall: Annual Meeting of the Essex County Anti-Slavery Society.
25-26 June:	Uxbridge, Massachusetts: Unitarian Meeting-house: Quarterly Meeting of the Worcester County South Division Anti-Slavery Society.
1 July:	Worcester, Massachusetts.
2 July:	Holden, Massachusetts.
3 July:	Westminster, Massachusetts.
4-5 July:	Athol, Massachusetts.
6 July:	Hubardstown, Massachusetts.
7 July:	Princeton, Massachusetts.
8 July:	Barre, Massachusetts.
10 July:	West Brookfield, Massachusetts.
11 July:	South Wilbraham, Massachusetts.
12 July:	Albany, New York.
13 July:	Troy, New York.
14 July:	West Winfield, New York: Baptist Church.

15 July:	Utica, New York.
16 July:	Rome, New York.
17 July:	Syracuse, New York.
18 July:	Skaneateles, New York.
19-20 July:	Waterloo, New York.
21-22 July:	Palmyra, New York.
23-24 July:	Rochester, New York.
30-31 July:	Buffalo, New York: Talman Hall.
7 August:	Weymouth, Massachusetts.
8 August:	Hingham, Massachusetts.
9 August:	Kingston, Massachusetts.
10 August:	Dukesbury, Massachusetts.
13 August:	New Bedford, Massachusetts: Town Hall: Jonathan Walker Meeting.
15 August:	Lynn, Massachusetts: Lyceum Hall: Farewell Meeting for Buffum and Douglass.
16 August:	Sails from Boston aboard *Cambria* bound for Liverpool, England: With Buffum.

✤ *Appendix B*

Frederick Douglass in behalf of Geo. Latimer.
Lynn, Massachusetts: November 8th, 1842.

DEAR FRIEND GARRISON:

The date of this letter finds me quite unwell. I have for a week past been laboring, in company with bro. Charles Remond, in New-Bedford, with special reference to the case of our outraged brother, George Latimer, and speaking almost day and night, in public and in private; and for the reward of our labor, I have the best evidence that a great good has been done. It is said by many residents, that New-Bedford has never been so favorably aroused to her anti-slavery responsibility as at present. Our meetings were characterized by that deep and solemn feeling which the importance of the cause, when properly set forth, is always calculated to awaken. On Sunday, we held three meetings in the new town hall, at the usual meeting hours, morning, afternoon, and evening. In the morning, we had quite a large meeting, at the opening of which, I occupied about an hour, on the question as to whether a man is better than a sheep. Mr. Dean then made a few remarks, and after him, Mr. Clapp, of Nantucket, arose and gave his testimony to the truth, as it is in anti-slavery. The meeting then adjourned, to meet again in the afternoon. I said that we held our meetings at the regular meeting hours. Truth requires me to make our afternoon meeting an exception to this remark. For long before the drawling, lazy church bells commenced sounding their deathly notes, mighty crowds were making their way to the town hall. They needed no bells to remind them of their duty to bleeding humanity. They were not going to meeting to hear as to the best mode of performing water baptism; they were not going to meeting to have their prayers handsomely said for them, or to say them, merely, themselves; but to pray, not in word, but in deed and in truth; they were not going thither to be worshipped, but to worship, in spirit and in truth; they were not going to sacrifice, but to have mercy; they did not go there to find God; they had found him already. Such I think I may safely say of a large portion of the vast assembly that met in the afternoon. As I gazed upon them, my soul leaped for joy; and, but for the thought that the time might be better employed, I could have shouted aloud.—After a short space, allotted to secret or public prayer, bro. J.B. Sanderson arose and requested the attention of the audience to the reading of a few passages of scripture, selected by yourself in the editorial of last week. They did give their attention, and as he read the solemn and soul-stirring denunciations of Jehovah, by the mouth of his prophets and apostles, against oppressors, the deep stillness that pervaded that magnificent hall was a brilliant demonstration, that the audience felt that what was read was but the reiteration of words which had fallen from the great Judge of the universe. After reading, he proceeded to make some remarks on the general question of human rights. These, too, seemed to sink deep into the hearts of the gathered multitude. Not a word was lost; it was good seed, sown in good ground, by a careful hand; it must, it will bring forth fruit.

After him, rose bro. Remond, who addressed the meeting in his usual happy and deeply affecting style. When he had concluded his remarks, the meeting adjourned to meet again at an early hour in the evening. During the interval, our old friends and the slaves' friends, John Butler, Thomas Jones, Noah White, and others, were engaged in carrying benches from liberty hall to the town hall, that all who came might be accommodated with seats. They were determined to do something for humanity, though by so doing, they should be ranked with sabbath-breakers. Christianity prays for more of just such sabbath-breakers as these, and may God grant by an overwhelming revival of anti-slavery truth, to convert and send forth more just such.

The meeting met according to adjournment, at an early hour. The splendid hall was brilliantly lighted, and crowded with an earnest, listening audience, and notwithstanding the efforts of our friends before named to have them seated, a large number had to stand during the meeting, which lasted about three hours; where the standing part of the audience were, at the commencement of the meeting, there they were at the conclusion of it; no moving about with them; any place was good enough, so they could but hear. From the eminence which I occupied, I could see the entire audience; and from its appearance, I should conclude that prejudice against color was not there, at any rate, it was not to be seen by me; we were all on a level, every one took a seat just where they chose; there were neither men's side, nor women's side; white pew, nor black pew; but all seats were free, and all sides free. When the meeting was fully gathered, I had something to say, and was followed by bro. Sanderson and Remond. When they

had concluded their remarks, I again took the stand, and called the attention of the meeting to the case of bro. George Latimer, which proved the
finishing stroke of my present public speaking. On taking my seat, I was
seized with a violent pain in my breast, which continued till morning, and
with occasional raising of blood; this past off in about two hours, after
which, weakness of breast, a cough, and shortness of breath ensued, so
that now such is the state of my lungs, that I am unfit for public speaking,
for the present. My condition goes harder with me, much harder than it
would at ordinary times. These are certainly extraordinary times; times
that demand the efforts of the humblest of our most humble advocates of
our perishing and dying fellow-countrymen. Those that can but whisper
freedom, should be doing even that, though they can only be heard from
one side of their short fire place to the other. It is a struggle of life and
death with us just now. No sword that can be used, be it never so rusty,
should lay idle in it scabbard. Slavery, our enemy, has landed in our very
midst, and commenced its bloody work. Just look at it; here is George
Latimer a man—a brother—a husband—a father, stamped with the like-
ness of the eternal God, and redeemed by the blood of Jesus Christ, outlawed, hunted down like a wild beast, and ferociously dragged through the
streets of Boston, and incarcerated within the walls of Leverett-st. jail. And
all this is done in Boston—liberty-loving, slavery-hating Boston—intellectual, moral, and religious Boston. And why was this—what crime had
George Latimer committed? He had committed the crime of availing himself of his natural rights, in defence of which the founders of this very
Boston enveloped her in midnight darkness, with the smoke proceeding
from their thundering artillery. What a horrible state of things is here presented. Boston has become the hunting-ground of merciless men-hunters,
and man-stealers. Henceforth we need not portray to the imagination of
northern people, the flying slave making his way through thick and dark
woods of the South, with white fanged blood-hounds yelping on his blood-
stained track; but refer to the streets of Boston, made dark and dense by
crowds of professed christians. Take a look at James B. Gray's new pack,
turned loose on the track of poor Latimer. I see the blood-thirsty animals,
smelling at every corner, part with each other, and meet again; they seem
to be consulting as to the best mode of coming upon their victim. Now they
look sad, discouraged;—tired, they drag along, as if they were ashamed of
their business, and about to give up the chase; but presently they get a
sight of their prey; their eyes brighten, they become more courageous,
they approach their victim unlike the common hound. They come upon
him softly, wagging their tails, pretending friendship, and do not pounce
upon him, until they have secured him beyond possible escape. Such is the
character of James B. Gray's new pack of two-legged blood-hounds that
hunted down George Latimer, and dragged him away to the Leverett-street

slave prison but a few days since. We need not point to the sugar fields of Louisiana, or to the rice swamps of Alabama, for the bloody deeds of this soul-crushing system, but to the city of the pilgrims. In future, we need not uncap the bloody cells of the horrible slave prisons of Norfolk, Richmond, Mobile, and New-Orleans, and depict the wretched and forlorn condition of their miserable inmates, whose groans rend the ear, pierce heaven, and disturb the Almighty; listen no longer at the snappings of the bloody slave-driver's lash. Withdraw your attention, for a moment, from the agonizing cries coming from hearts bursting with the keenest anguish at the South, gaze no longer upon the base, cold-blooded, heartless slave-dealer of the South, who lays his iron clutch upon the hearts of husband and wife, and, with one mighty effort, tears the bleeding ligaments apart which before constituted the twain one flesh. I say, turn your attention from all this cruelty abroad, look now at home—follow me to your courts of justice—mark him who sits upon the bench. He may, or he may not—God grant he may not—tear George Latimer from a beloved wife and tender infant. But let us take a walk to the prison in which George Latimer is confined, inquire for the turn-key; let him open the large iron-barred door that leads you to the inner prison. You need go no further. Hark! listen! hear the groans and cries of George Latimer, mingling with which may be heard the cry—my wife, my child—and all is still again.

A moment of reflection ensues—I am to be taken back to Norfolk—must be torn from a wife and tender babe, with the threat from Mr. Gray that I am to be murdered, though not in the ordinary way—not to have my head severed from my shoulders, not to be hanged—not to have my heart pierced through with a dagger—not to have my brains blown out. No, no, all these are too good for me. No: I am to be killed by inches. I know not how; perhaps by cat-hauling until my back is torn all to pieces, my flesh is to be cut with the rugged lash, and I faint; warm brine must now be poured into my bleeding wounds, and through this process I must pass, until death shall end my sufferings. Good God! save me from a fate so horrible. Hark! hear him roll in his chains; "I can die, I had rather, than go back. O, my wife. O my child!" You have heard enough. What man, what Christian can look upon this bloody state of things without his soul swelling big with indignation on the guilty perpetrators of it, and without resolving to cast in his influence with those who are collecting the elements which are to come down in ten-fold thunder, and dash this state of things into atoms?

Men, husbands, and fathers of Massachusetts—put yourselves in the place of George Latimer; feel his pain and anxiety of mind; give vent to the groans that are breaking through his fever-parched lips, from a heart emersed in the deepest agony and suffering; rattle his chains; let his prospects be yours, for the space of a few moments. Remember George Latimer in bonds as bound with him; keep in view the golden rule—"All lings whatsoever ye would that men should do unto you, do ye even so to hem." "In as much as ye did it unto the least of these my brethren ye have lone it unto me."

Now make up your minds to what your duty is to George Latimer, and when you have made your minds up, prepare to do it and take the consequences, and I have no fears of George Latimer going back. I can sympathize with George Latimer, having myself been cast into a miserable jail, on suspicion of my intending to do what he is said to have done, viz. appropriating my own body to my use.

My heart is full, and had I my voice, I should be doing all that I am capable of, for Latimer's redemption. I can do but little in any department; but if one department is more the place for me than another, that one is before the people.

I can't write to much advantage, having never had a day's schooling in my life, nor have I ever ventured to give publicity to any of my scribbling before; nor would I now, but for my peculiar circumstances.

Your grateful friend,
FREDERICK DOUGLASS.

Liberator, 18 November 1842, 182.

✿ *Appendix C*

No Union With Slaveholders:
An Address Delivered in Boston, Massachusetts:
28 May 1844

MR. DOUGLAS[S].—I do not know, Sir, that I shall be able to throw any new light upon this subject. I am here more to bear testimony, than to argue the question. I rejoice, however, to see so large a portion of the people here to discuss it, and may the discussion only cease when Slavery shall be no more.

I have heard many things said as to the utility of dissolving the Union. We are told by the opponents of that measure, that the Constitution depends on the people, and we are told also, on the same side, that it needs no alteration. I confess, that had it descended to me from the clouds, I might not have questioned its merits, in consequence of what appears upon the face of it. But, knowing as I do its origin, and the character of its framers, and seeing as I do, how it was written, as it were, in the blood of thousands and thousands of slaves, I think it *not* an Anti-Slavery document. Even had it come to me from above, I do not think it could have stood the test of impartial examination. I should have been compelled, when I came to the clause respecting the return of persons held to service or labor, to think that something else than freedom was meant, if not to acknowledge that Slavery stared me in the face. But without going into a minute examination of every clause, I should conceive its intent respecting Slavery to be proved by this fact, if there were no other; that the laws passed immediately after its adoption, and by the very men who framed and accepted it, were laws upholding Slavery. That shows that they knew they might maintain Slavery under it.

Mr. President, it is sufficient for me at least to prove its character, that I am a slave under the Constitution. Wherever the stars and stripes wave,

I am a slave! It's cold—it's dead—it falls twice dead on my ear—all this talk about the Anti-Slavery Constitution, and the glorious Union. There is not law enough, or strength enough in any State of the Union, to hinder me from being dragged away for being a slave—not even here in Massachusetts. If you resist what the men appointed to decide upon the meaning of the Constitution declare to be the law, you are a mobocrat—an insurrectionist.

But when I heard this sound of disunion with slaveholders, it fell like angelic melody on my heart. That's good for the slave, I said: that will free the slave! That's the reason that we have Slavery now—(and the *slaveholder* knows it, however gentlemen here may fail to perceive it,)—that the North strengthens him with all her own strength. It is because this whole nation have sworn by the God who made them, that the slave should be a slave or die! (*Stillness of strong sensation.*) The Slave knows this. He knows that you are pledged and bound to each other to crush him down. It is *this* bloody Union that I wish should cease. I only ask you, that you will no longer crush and slay us. Tell the slaveholder that if he will still hold slaves, it must be on his own responsibility; by his own unaided strength.

I am astonished at the existence of any desire on the part of pious and religious men, to be in union with slaveholders. What is their character? Are they so very pious and religious? Oh, yes! they're *very pious*; and the North knows how to suit them, when there's to be a nomination, with a style of piety that will unite perfectly with their own. The South brings forward for your President, Henry Clay, and the North stands ready with the vice-President—the Rev. Mr. Frelinghuysen!

[Great and long-continued applause mingled with hissing.]

Mr. President, of course I did not mean any harm to Mr. Frelinghuysen; I was only illustrating the nature and the character of the Union, by this match that they have made between the piety of the North, and the Slavery of the South. I meant no harm to Henry Clay. They have married Henry to Frelinghuysen, (tremendous applause,) and it's a type of the National Union; but I am astonished that Freemen do not forbid the banns. Why, what have they about them at the South, that you should endure this political Union? Why should you love such association with the whip, and with the pistol, and with the bowie-knife? There are your great men in Congress—look at them! Your Choate, and your Bates! Do they rise to say a word about your business that they're sent there to do—they're bullied down, and obliged to sit there and hear Massachusetts scoffed at and insulted! They had to sit and listen; and so are all the North bullied down by them. And you consent to be their kidnappers! their putters down of insurrections!

I admit, with friend White, that they do not care about the Union, except as it supports Slavery. [*Mr. Douglas[s] here read the testimony of Mr. Arnold, of Tennessee, and of the Editor of the Maysville Intelligencer, to show the reliance of the Slaveholder upon the Union for the support of the system.*]

My friends have spoken of the decrease of our influence, which they think will be the consequence of dissolution. They seem to think that there is some geographical change to take place in consequence. They seem to think that the North is to go to the North pole, and the South to fly away out of sight to the South pole. They overlook the fact, that no such change can take place, and that a moral change is the only one to follow. But this moral change will be all-sufficient. Until it takes place, the slaveholder cannot be seen and known as he is by the people. Who can fix the brand of murderer—thief—adulterer, on the brow of the man that you associate with, and salute as *honorable?* The *Honorable* Henry Clay! the *Honorable* John C. Calhoun! And those ministers who come to the North with the price of blood in their hands—how shall moral principle be diffused among the people on the subject of slavery, while they are hailed as *Reverend!* Withdraw from them the Sanction of the men who do not hold slaves, and how quickly would the character of Slavery be seen as it is. The people would then as soon think of seeking a union with Algerine pirates themselves. We acknowledge, now, in words, that Slavery is a crime; but still, we have been so long in association with it, that we think a man may commit it, and yet be honorable.

I heard something said of British and American oppression. But, Sir, the hungry Englishman is a *freeman;* while the slave is not only hungry, but a slave. The Briton says to his victim, Work for me or you shall starve; and the American says to the slave, Work, or you shall be whipped. This was defined by Mr. Walker to be the difference. But *I* know something of this matter at home, and I have found that we say, "whip!" and "starve!" too. The slave is entirely unmanned. The master is at once his conscience, his owner, body and spirit, his all. The master decides when and where, and with whom he shall go—when and where, and how, and by whom he shall be punished. None of these may be decided, as I am informed, by a nobleman of England, be he ever so noble. But here the master lays his foul clutch upon the throat—he makes his iron grasp felt in the soul. He says to the immortal spirit, thou shalt not aspire! he says to the intellect, thou shalt not expand! to the body, thou shalt not go at large! *Could* he say all this were it not for the Union! I say, then, the Union does it. (Great applause.)

The Union may be illustrated in this way. I have ten men in a bight of rope. Now, it is plain that one man can't hold ten, and I call to you, and you, and you, gentlemen, and beg your aid. But you say to me, Douglas[s], we've decided objections to holding men in that way. We've conscientious scruples. We're not friendly to holding men. We will surround you, however, and take an interest in the matter as far as to hinder their getting away from you. Just so the circle of Northern opinion and political union unites with that of the South around the slave.

I take for my watch-word, "No Union with Slaveholders," not because I have any hatred to the Slaveholder. I love him as truly as I do the slave. But I do it because I see that there is, comparatively, no efficacy in all that you can say or do against his crime, as long as he can taunt you with your co-operation. True, he says, I run my fist in my slave's pocket, but you say you'll strike him down if he resists me; you are as bad as I am.

My friend White said, that Slavery existed before the Union, and not in consequence of the Union. Sir, I *lived* before I drew the present air I draw; but I live now, *by* the air I draw. Had Slavery been deprived of the benefit it formed the Union to obtain, it could not have lived. It would, long ere this, have ceased by public opinion or insurrection. But through the means of the Union, it has gone on, blunting our moral sense, till we have lost our moral discrimination. When a white man suffers we are full of sympathy. A nation was in tears at the bursting of the Paixhan gun. But when a slave shrieks out in his agony—when McIntosh calls out of the flames to the whole assembled people round the stake—"shoot me! shoot me!"—who cares! he's a negro! he's a slave! what right had *he* to defend his wife or daughter against a white man! he shall die in a slow fire. This was in one of the slave States of our *Union*. Look now at the District of Columbia, the seat of our United Government. The Hon. Seth M. Gates told me that he saw there a woman start out of a half-opened slave-prison gate; and before she had run far, three men who witnessed it, also started at a distance, started to head her off, before she should be able to cross the bridge, which would give her a chance of escape. True to their Virginia instincts, they succeeded in reaching the bridge immediately after her. A moment more, and she would have been in their grasp. But her resolution was taken. She leaped from the bridge into the river, and sunk to rise no more. *She* preferred death to the protection of the Union. The slaves flee as from a pestilence, away from the Union. It is this fearful union with slaveholders, that makes the weight and strength—the power and perpetuity of that system which we have met to abolish; and I ask the good people here to-night, to yield to its demands no longer.

I have been, Mr. President, all my life, in a situation to see and feel the practical bearings of the Union. I have had the sound of the lash to impel me on in my labors for its termination. Had I invoked the Union in any of my sufferings under it, I had done it in vain. Who is it that *can* do so, in case of need! Could Nat Turner do so? (A nobler name is not to be found in the annals of revolutions!) It was not *he* who could appeal to this Union, formed to preserve Liberty.

But the Slaveholders—(he gave them enough to do, to watch their own cradles and their own hearths;) and *they* flew to the Union for help, and obtained it. I have been informed that one hundred men from Maine, were immediately ordered to their assistance, commanded by a Colonel White, of Manchester, Massachusetts. Why could not Madison Washington strike for Liberty on the soil of Virginia? The *Union* overawed him! he must wait till he is at the mercy of the waves, with less odds against him than a whole nation to brand him as mutineer and a murderer. Yes, Sir, Daniel Webster demanded him as such, and not in the name of the South alone, but of this whole country. One such fact on the side of dissolution would show *me* that I ought to go for it.

I have not much intellect, but nobody need pretend to me that by being a party to the Union he is not pledged to keep down the slaves. Why are you pledged to what you agree to? and how ineffably mean do you look— how cowardly, standing with fourteen millions of "free and enlightened people!" to keep down two millions of ignorant suffering slaves in the dust! You see it plainly when a great lubber-headed fellow gets hold of a little one in the street. Just so the whole world sees your American Union for the holding of slaves. [*Continued applause.*]

National Anti-Slavery Standard, 25 July 1844, 30.

✿ *Appendix D*

The Progress of the Cause: An Address Delivered in Norristown, Pennsylvania: 12 August 1844

FREDERICK DOUGLASS SAID he was always ready to speak on slavery, and added, in reply to some one who desired to have his name and that of the preceding speaker [James N. Buffum] announced, that he was afraid we cared too much to know *who* it is that speaks, instead of weighing well *what* was said. He was accustomed to meetings where it was not decided who should speak, but where any one might speak on any proposition, either in favor or against it, and bear his testimony by voting or in any other way. He did not find fault with the proceedings of the Society in declaring who should and who should not be members, but he did not feel so much at home in such meetings. This, however, should not prevent his speaking. He was there as an abolitionist, and as a slave, for whose redemption abolitionists were toiling, and he felt it to be a duty and a privilege to testify in behalf of anti-slavery, and to strive to warm the hearts of all who were laboring to promote the spread of its principles.

To him, there was no more deeply interesting time in the history of the anti-slavery cause than the present. We were receiving intelligence from all parts of the growth of the cause, and he had listened to the soul-stirring report [of the Executive Committee of the Eastern Pennsylvania Antislavery Society] we had just heard read, and rejoiced in the evidences it presented of the progress of anti-slavery in this quarter. It has advanced rapidly in Massachusetts, and, in fact, throughout New England, but abolitionists here have as much reason to congratulate themselves, as we have there. Although he had been here but a short time, he had seen a great improvement since he was last among us, and he felt cheered and encouraged by it. Colored people in New England are much better treated than they were a short time since. It had been but two or three years since they were every where repulsed. They were treated with indignity in meeting houses, subjected to insult upon highways and by-ways, in the stage, the steamboat, and railroad car. Everywhere were they met by a prejudice which crushed them to earth. This existed yet to some extent, but had very much dwindled away. On all the railroads in New England, except one of some thirty or forty miles, all distinctions on account of color were done away with. A great advance had been made. Two years since, a colored man who would have ventured into any other than the Jim Crow car would have been kicked and cuffed and dragged out, and it was useless for him to appeal to law for redress, for courts and railroads were both prejudiced. How was this change effected? By preaching the truth—by showing the absurdity of this prejudice—that the black man was no less a man because of his color.

On the first of August they had a heart-cheering demonstration of the progress which anti-slavery had made in New England. The celebration of West India Emancipation, in Hingham, was one of the most brilliant and glorious gatherings of abolitionists which had ever taken place in this country—there were not less than seven thousand persons there, and the spirit which prevailed, as well as the number, was cheering. They evinced a feeling which cannot be conceived by those who were not present, and the abolitionists of New England were amply compensated by it for all the afflictions and trials they had endured since the commencement of the warfare. They there saw in miniature what they will see in full reality, and this was done, sir, by "scattering the living coals of truth" upon the nation's naked heart. Abolitionists have used no other means than preaching the truth—they have been scoffed at and persecuted, but the result of their labors as seen that day—the number and spirit of that gathering will exert an influence which shall be felt not only in Boston but from one end of Massachusetts to the other. We should feel encouraged to go forward.

We are great sticklers for individualism in Massachusetts—we express our own thoughts in our own way—speak out our own ideas in independence, and that is what we want.

Pennsylvania Freeman, 22 August 1844, 3.

✽ Bibliography

I. Archives and Collections

American Anti-Slavery Collection. Boston Public Library. Boston.

Blagdon, Crawford. Papers. Harvard College Library. Harvard University. Cambridge, Mass.

Brown University Library. Brown University. Providence, R.I.

Chapman Family Papers. Boston Public Library. Boston.

Douglass, Frederick. Collection. Moorland-Spingarn Research Center. Howard University. Washington, D.C.

Douglass, Frederick. National Historic Site. Cedar Hill, Anacostia, Washington, D.C.

Douglass, Frederick. Papers. Library of Congress. Washington, D.C.

Foulger Library, Nantucket Historical Association. Nantucket, Mass.

Garrison, William Lloyd. Papers. Boston Public Library. Boston.

Gay, Sydney Howard. Papers. Columbia University. New York.

Hudson, Erasmus D. Papers. University Library. University of Massachusetts. Amherst, Mass.

Kelley Foster, Abigail. Papers. American Antiquarian Society. Worcester, Mass.

Library of Congress. Frederick Douglass Collection. Washington, D.C.

Lynn Historical Society. Lynn, Mass.

Massachusetts State Historical Society. Boston.

May, Samuel J. Jr. Papers. Boston Public Library. Boston.

New Bedford Public Library. New Bedford, Mass.

Old Dartmouth Historical Society, Whaling Museum. New Bedford, Mass.

Rhode Island State Historical Society. Providence, R.I.

Rochester Public Library. Rochester, N.Y.

Smith, Gerrit. Papers. Syracuse University Library. Syracuse, N.Y.

University of Rochester Library. Rochester, N.Y.

Weston Family Papers. Boston Public Library. Boston.

Wisconsin State Historical Society Library. Madison, Wis.

Worcester Historical Museum. Worcester, Mass.

II.   Newspapers and Journals

Albany Evening Journal (Albany, N.Y.).

Boston Journal (Boston)

Buffalo Daily Gazette (Buffalo, N.Y.).

Christian Freeman (Hartford, Conn.).

Cincinnati Philanthropist (Cincinnati, Ohio).

The Colored American (New York).

Commercial Advertiser and Journal (Buffalo, N.Y.).

The Daily Bee (Boston).

The Daily Evening Bulletin (New Bedford, Mass.).

Daily Evening Chronicle (Providence, R.I.).

Emancipator and Free American (Boston).

Herald of Freedom (Concord, N.H.).

Hingham Patriot (Hingham, Mass.).

The Ithaca Chronicle (Ithaca, N.Y.).

Ithaca Journal and General Advertiser (Ithaca, N.Y.).

The Liberator (Boston).

The Liberty Press (Utica, N.Y.).

Narragansett Chief (Providence, R.I.).

National Anti-Slavery Standard (New York).

New Age and Constitutional Advocate (Providence, R.I.).

New Bedford Daily Mercury (New Bedford, Mass.).

New Bedford Daily Register (New Bedford, Mass.).

New Bedford Morning Register (New Bedford, Mass.).

New National Era (Washington, D.C.).

New York Daily Tribune (New York).

New York Herald (New York).

New York Morning Express (New York).

Pennsylvania Freeman (Philadelphia, Pa.).

Providence Daily Journal (Providence, R.I.).

Religious Recorder (Syracuse, N.Y.).

Rochester Daily Democrat (Rochester, N.Y.).

Suffrage Examiner (Providence, R.I.).

Tompkins Volunteer (Ithaca, N.Y.).

Yates County Whig (Penn Yan, N.Y.).

III.   Books, Articles, and Dissertations

Adams, Alice D. *The Neglected Period of Anti-Slavery in America, 1808-1831.* Boston: Gun and Company, 1908.

Adams, Virginia M., ed. *On the Altar of Freedom: A Black Soldier's Civil War Letters from the Front/James Henry Gooding.* Boston: University of Massachusetts Press, 1991.

Alexander, William T. *History of the Colored Race In America.* New York: Palmetto, 1888.

Andrews, William L. "Frederick Douglass, Preacher." *American Literature* 54 (December 1982): 592-97.

———. *To Tell A Free Story: The First Century of Afro-American Autobiography, 1760-1865.* Urbana: University of Illinois Press, 1986.

———, ed. *Critical Essays on Frederick Douglass.* Boston: G.K. Hall, 1991.

Aptheker, Herbert. *Nat Turner's Slave Rebellion.* New York: Humanities Press, 1966.

———. *The Negro in the Abolitionist Movement.* New York: International Publishers, 1941.

Austin, George Lowell. *The Life and Times of Wendell Phillips.* 1884. Reprint, Chicago: Afro-Am Press, 1969.

Bacon, Thomas. *Sermons Addressed to Masters and Servants, and Published in the Year 1743, by the Rev. Thomas Bacon, Minister of the Protestant Episcopal Church in Maryland, Now Republished with Other Tracts and Dialogues On the Same Subject, and Recommended to All Masters and Mistresses to be used in their Families.* Edited by William Meade. Winchester, Va.: John Heiskell, 1813.

Baker, Houston A., Jr. *The Journey Back: Issues in Black Literature and Criticism.* Chicago: University of Chicago Press, 1980.

———. *The Long Black Song: Essays in Black American Literature and Culture.* Charlottesville: University Press of Virginia, 1972.

Barnes, Gilbert H. *The Antislavery Impulse, 1830-1844.* New York: Harcourt, Brace and World, 1963.

Barnes, Joseph W., ed. "The Autobiography of Reverend Thomas James." *Rochester History* 37 (October 1975): 1-32.

Bartlett, David W. *Modern Agitators: or Pen Portraits of Living Reformers*. New York: Miller, Orton, and Mulligan, 1855.

Bartlett, Irving H. Wendell, and Ann Phillips: *The Community of Reform, 1840-1880*. New York: Norton, 1981.

Barton, Rebecca Chalmers. *Witnesses for Freedom: Negro Americans in Autobiography*. New York: Harper and Brothers, 1948.

Baskerville, Barnet. *The People's Voice: The Orator in American Society*. Lexington: University Press of Kentucky, 1979.

Bell, Howard H. "Expressions of Negro Militancy in the North, 1840-1860." *Journal of Negro History* 45 (January 1960): 11-20.

———. "National Negro Conventions in the Middle 1840's: Moral Suasion vs. Political Action." *Journal of Negro History* 42 (October 1957): 247-60.

———. "Survey of the Negro Convention Movement, 1830-1861." Ph.D. diss., Northwestern University, 1953.

———, ed. *Minutes of the Proceedings of the National Conventions 1830-1864*. New York: Arno Press, 1964.

Bennett, Lerone, Jr. *Before the Mayflower: A History of the Negro in America, 1619-1966*. 3d ed. Chicago: Johnson Publishing Company, 1966.

Benson, Thomas W., ed. *Rhetoric and Political Culture in Nineteenth-Century America*. East Lansing: Michigan State University Press, 1997.

Bilhartz, Terry D. *Urban Religion and the Second Great Awakening: Church and Society in Early National Baltimore*. Cranbury, N.J.: Associated University Presses, 1986.

Bingham, Caleb, ed., *The Columbian Orator*. Boston: Manning and Loring, 1797.

Blackwell, Rev. G.L., ed. *The Doctrines and Discipline of the African Methodist Episcopal Zion Church*. Charlotte, N.C.: A.M.E. Zion Publication House, 1901.

Blassingame, John W. "Black Autobiographies as History and Literature." *Black Scholar* 5 (December 1973-January 1974): 2-9.

———. *The Clarion Voice*. Washington, D.C.: The National Park Service Division of Publications, 1976.

———. *The Slave Community: Plantation Life in the Antebellum South*. New York: Oxford University Press, 1979.

——— et al., eds. *The Frederick Douglass Papers, Series One: Speeches, Debates, and Interviews*. 5 vols. New Haven, Conn.: Yale University Press, 1979-1992.

Blight, David W. *Frederick Douglass' Civil War: Keeping Faith in Jubilee*. Baton Rouge: Louisiana State University Press, 1989.

Bloom, Harold, ed. *Modern Critical Interpretations: Frederick Douglass's Narrative of the Life of Frederick Douglass*. New York: Chelsea House Publishers, 1988.

Bontemps, Arna. *Free At Last: The Life of Frederick Douglass*. New York: Dodd, Mead, 1971.

Bormann, Earnest G., ed. *Forerunners of Black Power: The Rhetoric of Abolition*. Englewood Cliffs, N.J.: Prentice-Hall, 1971.

Borome, Joseph A. "Two Letters of Frederick Douglass." *Journal of Negro History* 33 (October 1948): 469-71.

Boss, Judith A., and Joseph D. Thomas. *New Bedford: A Pictorial History*. Norfolk, Va.: Donning Publishers, 1983.

Brackett, Jeffrey R. *The Negro in Maryland: A Study of the Institution of Slavery*. Baltimore, Md.: John Murphy and Company, 1889.

Bradley, David Henry, Sr. *A History of the A.M.E. Zion Church, Part 1: 1796-1872*. Nashville, Tenn.: Parthenon Press, 1956.

Brewer, J. Mason. *American Negro Folklore*. Chicago: Quadrangle Books, 1968.

Brown, William Wells. *The Rising Son: The Antecedents and Advancement of the Colored Race*. Boston: A.G. Brown, 1874.

Butcher, Margaret Just. *The Negro in American Culture*. New York: Alfred A. Knopf, 1956.

Butterfield, Stephen. *Black Autobiography in America*. Amherst: University of Massachusetts Press, 1974.

Celestine, Alfred. *Confessions of Nat Turner*. London: Many Press, 1978.

Chapman, Maria Weston, ed. *The Liberty Bell*. Boston: Andrew, Prentiss and Studley, 1845.

Chesnutt, Charles W. *Frederick Douglass*. 1899. Reprint, New York: Johnson Reprint Corporation, 1970.

Child, Lydia Marie. *The Freedmen's Book*. 1865. Reprint, New York: Arno, 1968.

Clasby, Nancy T. "Frederick Douglass's *Narrative*: A Content Analysis." *College Language Association Journal* 14 (March 1971): 242-50.

Clayton, Barbara, and Kathleen Whitley. *Guide to New Bedford*. Montpelier, Vt.: Capital City Press, 1979.

Cockrell, Dale, ed. *Excelsior: Journals of the Hutchinson Family Singers, 1842-1846*. Stuyvesant, N.Y.: Pendragon, 1989.

Coles, Howard W. *The Cradle of Freedom: A History of the Negro in Rochester, Western New York and Canada*. Rochester, N.Y.: Oxford Press, 1942.

Condit, Celeste Michelle, and John Louis Lucaites. *Crafting Equality: America's Anglo-African Word*. Chicago: University of Chicago Press, 1993.

Cook, J.W. "Freedom in the Thoughts of Frederick Douglass, 1845-1860." *Negro History Bulletin* 32 (February 1969): 6-10.

Crapo, Henry C., comp. *The New-Bedford Directory*. New Bedford, Mass.: 1838, 1839, 1841.

Curry, Richard O., ed. *The Abolitionists, Reformers or Fanatics?* New York: Holt, Rinehart, and Winston, 1965.

Cushing, Elizabeth Hope. *The Lynn Album: A Pictorial History*. Virginia Beach, Va.: Donning Co., 1990.

Daniel, Jack L., and Geneva Smitherman. "How I Got Over: Communication Dynamics in the Black Community." *Quarterly Journal of Speech* 62 (1976): 26-39.

Daniels, John. *In Freedom's Birthplace: A Study of Boston Negroes.* Boston: Houghton Mifflin, 1914.

Davis, Allison. *Leadership, Love, and Aggression.* New York: Harcourt, Brace, Jovanovich, 1983.

Davis, Charles T., and Henry Lewis Gates, Jr., eds. *The Slave's Narrative.* New York: Oxford University Press, 1985.

Davis, Lenwood G. "Documents: Frederick Douglass As A Preacher, and One of his Last Most Significant Letters." *Journal of Negro History* 66 (summer 1981): 140-43.

DePietro, Thomas. "Vision and Revision in the Autobiographies of Frederick Douglass." *College Language Association Journal* 26 (June 1983): 384-96.

Dick, Robert C. *Black Protest: Issues and Tactics.* Westport, Conn.: Greenwood Press, 1974.

Dorson, Richard M., ed. *American Negro Folktales.* Greenwich, Conn.: Fawcett Publications, 1967.

Douglass, Frederick. *Life and Times of Frederick Douglass, Written by Himself.* 1892. Reprint, New York: Macmillan, 1962.

———. *My Bondage and My Freedom.* 1855. Reprint, New York: Dover, 1969.

———. *Narrative of the Life of Frederick Douglass, An American Slave, Written By Himself.* 1845. Reprint, New York: Signet, 1962.

———. *Narrative of the Life of Frederick Douglass, An American Slave, Written By Himself.* 2d Dublin Ed. Dublin, Ireland: Webb and Chapman, 1846.

———. "Reminiscences." *The Cosmopolitan* 7 (August 1889): 376-82.

Douglass, Helen Pitts, ed. *In Memoriam: Frederick Douglass.* Philadelphia, Pa.: John C. Yorston and Co., 1897.

Duberman, Martin, ed. *The Antislavery Vanguard.* Princeton, N.J.: Princeton University Press, 1965.

DuBois, W.E.B. *The Souls of Black Folk.* 1903. Reprint, New York: Signet, 1982.

Dudley, David L. *My Father's Shadow: Intergenerational Conflict in African American Men's Autobiography.* Philadelphia: University of Pennsylvania Press, 1991.

Duffy, Bernard K., and Halford R. Ryan, eds. *American Orators Before 1900: Critical Studies and Sources.* New York: Greenwood Press, 1987.

Dumond, Dwight L. *Antislavery: The Crusade for Freedom in America.* Ann Arbor: University of Michigan Press, 1961.

Ellis, Leonard Bolles. *History of New Bedford and its Vicinity: 1602-1892.* Syracuse, N.Y.: D. Mason and Company, 1892.

Epstein, Dena J. *Sinful Tunes and Spirituals: Black Music to the Civil War.* Urbana: University of Illinois Press, 1977.

Farrison, William Edward. *William Wells Brown: Author and Reformer.* Chicago: University of Chicago Press, 1969.

Felgar, Robert. "The Rediscovery of Frederick Douglass." *Mississippi Quarterly* 35 (fall 1982): 427-38.

Filler, Louis. *The Crusade Against Slavery, 1830-1860.* New York: Harper and Brothers, 1960.

————. *Crusade Against Slavery: Friends, Foes, and Reforms, 1820-1860.* Algonac, Mich.: Reference Publications, 1986.

————, ed. *Abolition and Social Justice in the Era of Reform.* New York: Harper and Row, 1972.

Fisher, Dexter, and Robert B. Stepto, eds. *Afro-American Literature, The Reconstruction of Instruction.* New York: Modern Language Association, 1978.

Foner, Philip S.. *Frederick Douglass.* New York: Citadel Press, 1964.

————. *Frederick Douglass on Women's Rights.* Westport, Conn.: Greenwood Press, 1976.

————, ed. *The Life and Writings of Frederick Douglass.* 5 vols. New York: International Publishers, 1950-1975.

Forkner, John L., and Bryon H. Dyson, eds. *Historical Sketches and Reminiscences of Madison County.* Logansport, Ind.: Press of Wilson, Humphreys and Co., 1897.

Forkner, John L., comp. *History of Madison County Indiana: A Narrative Account of its Historical Progress, Its People and Its Principal Interests, Volume 1.* Chicago: Lewis Publishing Company, 1914.

Foster, Frances. *Witnessing Slavery: The Development of Ante-bellum Slave Narratives.* Westport, Conn.: Greenwood Press, 1979.

Franklin, John Hope. *From Slavery to Freedom: A History of Negro Americans.* 3d ed. New York: Alfred A. Knopf, 1967.

Fredrickson, George M. *The Black Image in the White Mind: The Debate on Afro-American Character and Destiny, 1817-1914.* New York: Harper and Row, 1971.

Fulkerson, Raymond Gerald. "Frederick Douglass and the Anti-Slavery Crusade: His Career and Speeches, 1817-1861." Ph.D. diss., University of Illinois, 1971.

Fulkerson, Richard P. "The Public Letter as a Rhetorical Form: Structure, Logic, and Style in King's 'Letter from Birmingham Jail.'" *Quarterly Journal of Speech* 65 (April 1979): 121-36.

Gara, Larry. "The Professional Fugitive in the Abolition Movement." *Wisconsin Magazine of History* 48 (spring 1965): 196-204.

Gardner, Bettye. "Ante-bellum Black Education in Baltimore." *Maryland Historical Magazine* 71 (fall 1976): 360-66.

Garrison, Wendell Phillips, and Francis Jackson Garrison. *William Lloyd Garrison, 1805-1879: The Story of His Life Told by His Children.* 4 vols. 1885-1889. Reprint, New York: Arno Press, 1969.

Garrison, William Lloyd. *The Letters of William Lloyd Garrsion.* 6 vols. Edited by Walter M.Merrill and Louis Ruchames. Cambridge, Mass.: Harvard University Press, 1971-1981.

Gates, Henry Lewis, Jr. "Frederick Douglass and Language of the Self." *Yale Review* 70 (summer 1981): 592-611.

————. *The Signifying Monkey: A Theory of African American Literary Criticism.* New York: Oxford University Press, 1988.

————, ed. *Figures in Black: Words, Signs, and the "Racial" Self.* New York: Oxford University Press, 1987.

Genovese, Eugene D. *Roll Jordan Roll: The World the Slaves Made.* New York: Random House, 1976.

Gibson, Donald B. "Reconciling Public and Private in Frederick Douglass' *Narrative.*" *American Literature* 57 (December 1985): 549-69.

Gill, John. *Tide Without Turning: Elijah P. Lovejoy and Freedom of the Press.* Boston: Starr King Press, 1959.

Goerler, Raimund E. "Family, Self and Anti-Slavery: Sydney Howard Gay and the Abolitionist Commitment." Ph.D. diss., Case Western Reserve University, 1975.

Golden, James L., and Richard D. Rieke. *The Rhetoric of Black Americans.* Columbus, Ohio: Merrill, 1971.

Goldstein, Leslie Friedman. "Morality and Prudence in the Statesmanship of Frederick Douglass: Radical as Reformer." *Polity* 16 (summer 1984): 606-23.

————. "The Political Thought of Frederick Douglass." Ph.D. diss., Cornell University, 1974.

————. "Violence As An Instrument of Social Change: The Views of Frederick Douglass (1817-1895)." *Journal of Negro History* 61 (January 1976): 61-72.

Goodell, William. *Slavery and Anti-Slavery; A History of the Great Struggle in Both Hemispheres; With a View of the Anti-Slavery Question in the United States.* New York: W. Goodell, 1853.

Grayson, John T. "Frederick Douglass' Intellectual Development: His Concept of God, Man, and Nature in Light of American and European Influences." Ph.D. diss., Columbia University, 1981.

Gregory, James M. *Frederick Douglass, the Orator.* 1893. Reprint, Chicago: Afro-Am Press, 1971.

Griffiths, Julia W., ed. *Autographs For Freedom.* Boston: John P. Jewitt, 1853.

Grimke, Archibald H. *William Lloyd Garrison, the Abolitionist.* New York: Funk and Wagnalls, 1891.

Bibliography • 331

Gutman, Herbert G. *The Black Family in Slavery and Freedom: 1750-1925*. New York: Vantage, 1967.

Harden, Samuel J., comp. *History of Madison County, Indiana from 1820 to 1874*. Markleville, Ind.: n.p., 1874.

Harris, Arthaniel Edgar, Sr. "Worship in the A.M.E. Zion Church." *A.M.E. Zion Quarterly Review* 97 (July 1986): 33-36.

Haynes, Robert V. *Blacks in White America Before 1865: Issues and Interpretations*. New York: David Mckay Company, 1972.

Hedin, Raymond. "Muffled Voices: The American Slave Narrative." *CLIO* 10 (winter 1981): 129-42.

Hill, Samuel S., ed. *Varieties of Southern Religious Experience*. Baton Rouge: Louisiana State University Press, 1988.

Hinshaw, George Asher. "A Rhetorical Analysis of the Speeches of Frederick Douglass During and After the Civil War." Ph.D. diss., University of Nebraska, 1972.

Hodges, Danforth Comstock. "'Formerly a Slave': Frederick Douglass Comes to Lanesborough." Edited by Terry Alford. *New England Quarterly* 60 (March 1987): 86-88.

Holland, Frederic May. *Frederick Douglass: The Colored Orator*. New York: Funk and Wagnalls, 1891.

Hood, James W. *One Hundred Years of the African Methodist Episcopal Zion Church*. New York: A.M.E. Zion Book Concern, 1895.

Howard-Pitney, David. "The Jeremiads of Frederick Douglass, Booker T. Washington, and W.E.B. DuBois and Changing Patterns of Black Messianic Rhetoric, 1841-1920." *Journal of American Ethnic History* 6 (fall 1986): 47-61.

Huggins, Nathan Irvin. *Slave and Citizen: The Life of Frederick Douglass*. Boston: Little, Brown, and Company, 1980.

Hughes, Langston. *Famous American Negroes*. New York: Mead and Company, 1954.

Hughes, Langston, and Arna Bontemps, eds. *The Book of Negro Folklore*. New York: Dodd, Mead and Company, 1958.

Hutchinson, John W. *Story of the Hutchinsons*. Edited by Charles E. Mann. Boston: Lee and Shephard, 1896.

Hyman, Harold R., and Leonard W. Levy, eds. *Freedom and Reform: Essays in Honor of Henry Steele Commager*. New York: Harper and Row, 1967.

Inge, M. Thomas, Maurice Duke, and Jackson R. Bryer, eds. *Black American Writers: Bibliographical Essays*. 2 vols. New York: St. Martin's Press, 1978.

Jacobs, Donald M., ed. *Courage and Conscience: Black and White Abolitionists in Boston*. Bloomington: Indiana University Press, 1993.

James, Edward T., ed. *Notable American Women, 1607-1950: A Biographical Dictionary*. 3 vols. Cambridge Mass.: Harvard University Press, 1971.

Johannesen, Richard L. "Caleb Bingham's *American Preceptor* and *Columbian Orator*." *The Speech Teacher* 18 (March 1969): 139-43.

Johnson, Allen et al., eds. *Dictionary of American Biography*. 20 vols. New York: Scribner's, 1928-1936.

Johnson, Clifton. *Old-Time Schools and School-Books*. 1904. Reprint, Gloucester, Mass.: Peter Smith, 1963.

Johnson, David N. *Sketches of Lynn*. 1880. Reprint, Westport, Conn.: Greenwood Press, Publishers, 1970.

Johnson, Oliver. *W. L. Garrison and His Times*. 1881. Reprint, Miami, Fla.: Mnemosyne Publishing Company, 1969.

Johnson, Reinhard O. "The Liberty Party in New England, 1840-1848: The Forgotten Abolitionists." Ph.D. diss., Syracuse University, 1976.

Joint Committee on Printing, Congress of the United States, comp. *Biographical Directory of the American Congress, 1774-1971*. Washington, D.C.: U.S. Government Printing Office, 1971.

Jones, Howard. "The Peculiar Institution and National Honor: The Case of the Creole Slave Revolt." *Civil War History* 21 (March 1975): 28-50.

Kennicott, Patrick Curtis. "Negro Antislavery Speakers in America." Ph.D. diss., Florida State University, 1967.

Kibbey, Ann. "Language in Slavery: Frederick Douglass's Narrative." *Prospects: The Annual of American Cultural Studies* (Cambridge, England) 8 (1983): 163-82.

Kingston, Steve. *Frederick Douglass: Abolitionist, Liberator, Statesman*. New York: National Negro Congress, 1945.

Kinney, Lois Belton. "A Rhetorical Study of the Practice of Frederick Douglass on the Issue of Human Rights, 1840-1860." Ph.D. diss., Ohio State University, 1974.

Kiven, Arline Ruth. *Then Why the Negroes: The Nature and Course of the Anti-Slavery Movement in Rhode Island: 1637-1861*. Providence, R.I.: Urban League of Rhode Island, 1973.

Kraditor, Aileen S. *Means and Ends in American Abolitionism; Garrison and His Critics on Strategy and Tactics, 1834-1850*. New York: Pantheon Books, 1969.

Kraut, Alan M. "The Liberty Party Men of New York: Political Abolitionism in New York State, 1840-1848." Ph.D. diss., Cornell University, 1975.

Lemons, J. Stanley, and Michael A. McKenna. "Re-enfranchisement of Rhode Island Negroes." *Rhode Island History* 30 (winter 1971): 2-13.

Lerner, Gerda. *The Grimke' Sisters from South Carolina; Pioneers for Woman's Rights and Abolition*. New York: Schocken Books, 1971.

———. *The Grimke' Sisters from South Carolina; Rebels Against Slavery*. Boston: Houghton-Mifflin, 1967.

Levine, Lawrence W. *Black Culture and Black Consciousness: Afro-American Folk Thought from Slavery to Freedom*. New York: Oxford University Press, 1977.

Lewis, Lloyd. "Quaker Memories of Frederick Douglass." *Negro Digest* 5 (September 1947): 37-41.

Lincoln, C. Eric, and Lawrence H. Mamiya. *The Black Church in the African American Experience.* Durham, N.C.: Duke University Press, 1990.

Litwack, Leon. *North of Slavery: The Negro in the Free States, 1790-1860.* Chicago: University of Chicago Press, 1961.

Litwack, Leon, and August Meier, eds. *Black Leaders of the Nineteenth Century.* Chicago: University of Illinois Press, 1988.

Logan, Raymond W., and Michael R. Winston, eds. *Dictionary of American Negro Biography.* New York: Norton, 1982.

Loggins, Vernon. *The Negro Author: His Development in America to 1900.* Port Washington, N.Y.: Kennikat, 1931.

Lovell, John. *Black Song: the Forge and the Flame; the Story of How the Afro-American Spiritual was Hammered Out.* New York: Macmillan, 1972.

McFeely, William S. *Frederick Douglass.* New York: Norton, 1991.

Mabee, Carlton. *Black Freedom: The Nonviolent Abolitionists from 1830 throughout the Civil War.* New York: Macmillan, 1970.

Marsh, Luther R., ed. *Writings and Speeches of Alvan Stewart, on Slavery.* 1860. Reprint, New York: Negro Universities Press, 1969.

Martin, Waldo E., Jr. *The Mind of Frederick Douglass.* Chapel Hill: University of North Carolina Press, 1984.

Marty, Martin E. *Pilgrims in their own Land: 500 Years of Religion in America.* New York: Viking Press, 1984.

Massachusetts Anti-Slavery Society. *Annual Reports of the Massachusetts Anti-Slavery Society.* 1838-1845.

Matlack, James. "The Autobiographies of Frederick Douglass." *Phylon* 40 (March 1979): 15-28.

May, Samuel J. *Some Recollections of our Antislavery Conflict.* Boston: Fields, Osgood, and Company, 1869.

Mays, Benjamin E., and Joseph W. Nicholson. *The Negro's Church.* New York: Institute of Social and Religious Research, 1933.

Medhurst, Martin J., and Thomas W. Benson, eds. *Rhetorical Dimensions in Media: A Critical Casebook.* Dubuque, Iowa: Kendall Hunt, 1984.

Meier, August. *Negro Thought in America: 1880-1915.* Ann Arbor: University of Michigan Press, 1983.

Miller, Kelly. *Radicals and Conservatives, and Other Essays on the Negro in America.* New York: Schocken Books, 1968.

Mitchell, Henry H. *Black Preaching.* Philadelphia, Pa.: Lippincott, 1970.

Monroe, James. *Oberlin Thursday Lectures Addresses and Essays.* Oberlin, Ohio: Edward J. Goodrich, 1897.

Moore, John J. *History of the A.M.E. Zion Church in America*. York, Pa.: Teachers' Journal Office, 1884.

Mowry, Arthur May. *The Dorr War: The Constitutional Struggle in Rhode Island*. Providence, R.I.: Preston and Rounds Co., 1901.

Netterville, J. J. *Centennial History of Madison Co., Indiana, Volume 1*. Anderson, Ind.: Historians' Association, 1925.

Nichols, Charles H. *Many Thousand Gone: The Ex-Slaves' Account of Their Bondage and Freedom*. Leiden, Holland: E.J. Brill, 1963.

———. "Who Read the Slave Narratives?" *Phylon* 20 (summer 1959): 149-62.

Nichols, William W. "Individualism and Autobiographical Art: Frederick Douglass and Henry Thoreau." *CLA Journal* 16 (December 1972): 145-58.

Nye, Russel B. *William Lloyd Garrison and the Humanitarian Reformers*. Boston: Little, Brown, 1955.

Oates, Stephen E. *The Fires of Jubilee: Nat Turner's Fierce Rebellion*. New York: Harper and Row, 1975.

Oliver, Robert T. *History of Public Speaking in America*. Boston: Allyn and Bacon, 1965.

Payne, Daniel A. *History of the African Methodist Episcopal Church*. 1891. Reprint, New York: Johnson Reprint Corporation, 1968.

Pease, Jane H., and William H. Pease. "Antislavery Ambivalence: Immediatism, Expediency, and Race." *American Quarterly* 17 (winter 1965): 682-95.

———. "Boston Garrisonians and the Problem of Frederick Douglass." *Canadian Journal of History* 2 (September 1967): 29-48.

———. "Ends, Means, and Attitudes: Black-White Conflict in the Antislavery Movement." *Civil War History* 18 (June 1972): 117-28.

———. "Negro Conventions and the Problem of Black Leadership." *Journal of Black Studies* 2 (September 1971): 29-44.

Penn, I. Garland. *The Afro-American Press, and its Editors*. 1891. Reprint, New York: Arno Press, 1969.

Perry, Lewis. *Radical Abolitionism: Anarchy and the Government of God in Anti-Slavery Thought*. Ithaca, N.Y.: Cornell University Press, 1973.

Perry, Lewis, and Michael Fellman, eds. *Antislavery Reconsidered: New Perspectives on the Abolitionists*. Baton Rouge: Louisiana State University Press, 1979.

Pillsbury, Parker. *Acts of the Anti-Slavery Apostles*. Concord, N.H.: Clague, Wegman, Schlicht, 1883.

Piper, Henry Dan. "The Place of Frederick Douglass's Narrative of an American Slave in the Development of a Native American Prose Style." *The Journal of Afro-American Issues* 5 (1977): 183-91.

Pitre, Meline. "Frederick Douglass: the Politician vs. the Social Reformer." *Phylon* 40 (September 1979): 270-77.

Plunkett, Margaret L. "A History of the Liberty Party With Emphasis Upon its Activities in the Northwestern States." Ph.D. diss., Cornell University, 1930.

Porter, Dorothy B. "David Ruggles, An Apostle of Human Rights." *Journal of Negro History* 28 (January 1943): 23-50.

Preston, Dickson. *Young Frederick Douglass*. Baltimore, Md.: Johns Hopkins University Press, 1980.

Quarles, Benjamin. *Black Abolitionists*. New York: Oxford University Press, 1969.

————. "The Breach Between Douglass and Garrison." *Journal of Negro History* 23 (April 1938): 144-54.

————. "Douglass' Mind in the Making." *Phylon* 6 (spring 1945): 5-11.

————. *Frederick Douglass*. 1948. Reprint, New York: Atheneum, 1968.

————. "Frederick Douglass and the Women's Rights Movement." *Journal of Negro History* 25 (January 1940): 35-44.

————. "Frederick Douglass: Black Imperishable." *Quarterly Journal of the Library of Congress* 29 (July 1972): 159-62.

————. "Frederick Douglass: Bridge Builder in Human Relations." *Negro History Bulletin* 29 (February 1966): 99-100, 112.

————, ed. *Frederick Douglass: Great Lives Observed*. Englewood Cliffs, N.J.: Prentice Hall, 1968.

————, ed. Frederick Douglass. *Narrative of the Life of Frederick Douglass, An American Slave, Written By Himself*. Cambridge, Mass.: Harvard University Press, 1960.

Reed, Harry. *Platform for Change: The Foundations of the Northern Free Black Community, 1775-1865*. East Lansing: Michigan State University Press, 1994.

Render, Sylvia Lyons. "Freedom." *Quarterly Journal of the Library of Congress* 31 (July 1974): 161-65.

Richardson, Harry V. *Dark Salvation: The Story of Methodism as it Developed Among Blacks in America*. Garden City, N.Y.: Anchor Press, 1976.

Ricketson, Daniel. *The History of New Bedford, Bristol County, Massachusetts*. New Bedford, Mass.: Ricketson Publishers, 1858.

Ripley, C. Peter, "The Autobiographical Writings of Frederick Douglass." *Southern Studies* 24 (spring 1985): 5-29.

————, ed. *Witness for Freedom: "African American Voices," Volume 5*. Chapel Hill: University of North Carolina Press, 1993.

Rodman, Samuel. *The Diary of Samuel Rodman*. Edited by Zephaniah W. Pease. New Bedford, Mass.: Reynolds Printing Co., 1927.

Rogers, William B. "The Prophetic Tradition in Nineteenth Century America, William Lloyd Garrison and Frederick Douglass." Ph.D. diss., Drew University, 1992.

Rosenblatt, Roger. "Black Autobiography: Life as the Death Weapon." *The Yale Review* 65 (June 1976): 515-27.

Rountree, Louise M., ed. *An Index to Biographical Sketches and Publications of the Bishops of the A.M.E. Zion Church.* Salisbury, N.C.: Louise M. Rountree, 1963.

Rush, Christopher. *A Short Account of the Rise and Progress of the African Methodist Episcopal Zion Church in America.* New York: Christopher Rush, 1843.

Rush, Christopher, and George Collins, eds. *The Doctrines and Discipline of the African Methodist Episcopal [Zion] Church in America, Established in the City of New York, October 25, 1820.* New York: Christopher Rush and George Collins, 1820.

Schor, Joel. *Henry Highland Garnet: A Voice of Black Radicalism in the Nineteenth Century.* Westport, Conn.: Greenwood, 1977.

———. "The Rivalry Between Frederick Douglass and Henry Highland Garnet." *Journal of Negro History* 64 (winter 1979): 30-38.

Sekora, John. "Comprehending Slavery: Language and Personal History in Douglass' *Narrative* of 1845." *College Language Association Journal* 29 (December 1985): 157-70.

———. "The Legacy of Frederick Douglass." *African American Review* 28 (fall 1994): 473-79.

Sekora, John, and Darwin T. Turner, eds. *The Art of the Slave Narrative: Original Essays in Criticism and Theory.* Macomb: Western Illinois Press, 1982.

Shaw, James Beverly F. *The Negro in the History of Methodism.* Nashville, Tenn.: Parthenon Press, 1954.

Sheffeld, Charles A., ed. *The History of Florence, Massachusetts.* Florence, Mass.: Charles A. Sheffeld, 1895.

Shepherd, Henry E., ed. *History of Baltimore, Maryland: From Its Founding as a Town to the Current Year: 1729-1898.* Baltimore, Md.: S.B. Nelson, 1898.

Sherwin, Oscar. *Prophet of Liberty: The Life and Times of Wendell Phillips.* New York: Bookman Associates, 1958.

Singleton, George A. *The Romance of African Methodism: A Study of the African Methodist Episcopal Church.* New York: Exposition Press, 1952.

Small, Bishop John B. *Code on the Discipline of the African Methodist Episcopal Zion Church.* York, Pa.: York Dispatch Print, 1898.

Smedley, Robert C. *History of the Underground Railroad in Chester and the Neighboring Counties of Pennsylvania.* 1883. Reprint, New York: Negro Universities Press, 1968.

Smith, Edward D. *Climbing Jacob's Ladder: The Rise of Black Churches in Eastern American Cities, 1740-1877.* Washington, D.C.: Smithsonian Institution Press, 1988.

Smith, Theodore Clark. *The Liberty and Free Soil Parties in the Northwest.* New York: Russell and Russell, 1897.

Smitherman-Donaldson, Geneva. *Discourse and Discrimination.* Detroit: Wayne State University Press, 1988.

———. *Talkin' and Testifyin': The Language of Black America*. Boston: Houghton-Mifflin, 1977.

Snow, Malinda. "Martin Luther King's 'Letter from Birmingham Jail' as Pauline Epistle." *Quarterly Journal of Speech* 71 (August 1985): 318-34.

Sorin, Gerald. *The New York Abolitionists, A Case Study of Political Radicalism*. Westport, Conn.: Greenwood Publishers, 1971.

Sprague, Rosetta Douglass. "Anna Murray-Douglass—My Mother As I Recall Her." *Journal of Negro History* 8 (January 1923): 93-101.

Starling, Marion Wilson. *The Slave Narrative*. 2d ed. Washington, D.C.: Howard University Press, 1988.

Staudenraus, P.J. *The African Colonization Movement, 1816-1865*. New York: Columbia University Press, 1961.

Stepto, Robert. *From Behind the Veil*. Urbana: University of Illinois Press, 1979.

Stepto, Robert, and Dexter Fisher, eds. *Afro-American Literature: The Reconstruction of Instruction*. New York: Modern Language Association, 1978.

Sterling, Dorothy. *Ahead of Her Time: Abby Kelley and the Politics of Antislavery*. New York: Norton, 1991.

Stewart, James B. "Aims and Impact of Garrisonian Abolitionism." *Civil War History* 15 (September 1969): 197-209.

———. *Wendell Phillips: Liberty's Hero*. Baton Rouge: Louisiana State University Press, 1986.

Stowe, Harriet Beecher. *Men of Our Times, or Leading Patriots of the Day*. Hartford, Conn.: Hartford Publishers, 1868.

Stuckey, Sterling. *Slave Culture: Nationalist Theory and the Foundations of Black America*. New York: Oxford University Press, 1987.

Styron, William. *The Confessions of Nat Turner*. New York: New American Library, 1967.

Sundquist, Eric J., ed. *Frederick Douglass: New Literary and Historical Essays*. New York: Cambridge University Press, 1990.

Thomas, Benjamin P. *Theodore Weld, Crusader for Freedom*. New Brunswick, N.J.: Rutgers University Press, 1950.

Thomas, John L. *The Liberator, William Lloyd Garrison, a Biography*. Boston: Little, Brown, 1963.

———. *Slavery Attacked; the Abolitionist Crusade*. Englewood Cliffs, N.J.: Prentice-Hall, 1965.

Thomas, Lamont D. *Rise To Be A People: A Biography of Paul Cuffe*. Urbana: University of Illinois Press, 1986.

Thorpe, Earl E. "Frederick Douglass, W.E.B. DuBois and Booker T. Washington." *Negro History Bulletin* 20 (November 1956): 39-42.

Tillery, Tyrone. "The Inevitability of the Douglass-Garrison Conflict." *Phylon* 37 (June 1976): 137-49.

Tyler, Alice F. *Freedom's Ferment; Phases of American Social History to 1860.* Minneapolis: University of Minnesota Press, 1944.

Van Deburg, William L. "Frederick Douglass and the Institutional Church." *Journal of the American Academy of Religion* 45 (June 1977): 465-87.

———. "Frederick Douglass: Maryland Slave to Religious Liberal." *Maryland Historical Magazine* 69 (spring 1974): 27-43.

Volpe, Vernon L. *Forlorn Hope of Freedom: The Liberty Party in the Old Northwest, 1838-1848.* Kent, Ohio: Kent State University Press, 1990.

Walker, David. *Walker's Appeal in Four Articles, David Walker. An Address to the Slaves of the United States of America, Henry Highland Garnet.* 1848. Reprint, New York: Arno Press, 1969.

Walker, Peter. *Moral Choices: Memory, Desire, and Imagination in Nineteenth Century American Abolition.* Baton Rouge: Louisiana State University Press, 1978.

Walls, William J. *The African Methodist Episcopal Zion Church: Reality of the Black Church.* Charlotte, N.C.: A.M.E. Zion Publishing House, 1974.

Walters, Ronald G. *American Reformers: 1815-1860.* New York: Hill and Wang, 1978.

Ward, William Edward. "Charles Lenox Remond: Black Abolitionist, 1838-1873." Ph.D. diss., Clark University, 1977.

Washington, Booker T. *Frederick Douglass.* Philadelphia, Pa.: George W. Jacobs and Company, 1906.

Waters, Carver Wendell. "Voice in the Slave Narratives of Olaudah Equiano, Frederick Douglass, and Soloman Northrup." Ph.D. diss., University of Southwestern Louisiana, 1988.

Weld, Theodore. *American Slavery As It Is: Testimony of a Thousand Witnesses.* New York: American Anti-Slavery Society, 1839.

Wheeler, Benjamin F. *The Varick Family.* Mobile, Al.: n.p., 1907.

Williams, George Washington. *History of the Negro Race in America.* New York: Putnam, 1883.

Wilmore, Gayrand S. *Black Religion and Black Radicalism.* Garden City, N.Y.: Doubleday, 1972.

Winsor, Justin, ed. *The Memorial History of Boston.* Boston: J.R. Osgood and Company, 1880-81.

Woodson, Carter G., ed. "Frederick Douglass in Ireland." *Journal of Negro History* 8 (January 1923): 102-7.

———. *The History of the Negro Church.* 2d ed. Washington, D.C.: Associated Publishers, 1921.

————, ed. *The Mind of the Negro as Reflected in Letters Written During the Crisis 1800-1860*. Washington, D.C.: Association for the Study of Negro Life and History, 1926.

————, ed. *Negro Orators and Their Orations*. Washington, D.C.: Associated Publishers, 1925.

Wright, Richard R. *The Bishops of the African Methodist Episcopal Church*. Nashville, Tenn.: A.M.E. Sunday School Union, 1963.

Index